C0-AUV-659

FF COMMUNICATIONS

EDITED FOR THE FOLKLORE FELLOWS

BY

HERMANN BAUSINGER   ALAN DUNDES   LAURI HONKO

MATTI KUUSI   ANNA BIRGITTA ROOTH

VOL. CXI

No. 255

HELSINKI 1995

SUOMALAINEN TIEDEAKATEMIA

ACADEMIA SCIENTIARUM FENNICA

SUOMALAINEN TIEDEAKATEMIA
ACADEMIA SCIENTIARUM FENNICA
Mariankatu 5 · 00170 Helsinki · Suomi – Finland

FF COMMUNICATIONS
Editor: Prof. Dr. LAURI HONKO
Satakielenkatu 8 · 20610 Turku · Suomi – Finland

Editorial Secretary: ANNELI HONKO

FF COMMUNICATIONS No. 255

NARRATIVES IN SOCIETY: A PERFORMER-CENTERED STUDY OF NARRATION

BY

LINDA DÉGH

HELSINKI 1995
SUOMALAINEN TIEDEAKATEMIA
ACADEMIA SCIENTIARUM FENNICA

*Presented at the Finnish Academy of Science and Letters
on April 5, 1994*

Edited by
Linda Kinsey Adams
Distributed in North America by Indiana University Press,
Bloomington, Indiana, USA
ISBN 0-253-31683-9

Copyright © 1995 by
Academia Scientiarum Fennica
and Linda Dégh

ISSN 0014-5815
ISBN 951-41-0748-9

Pieksämäki 1995
Kirjapaino Raamattutalo

CONTENTS

Introduction: What Can Gyula Ortutay and the Budapest School
Offer to Contemporary Students of Narrative? 7

PART ONE: CREATIVITY OF STORYTELLERS
1. The Creative Practices of Storytellers 33
2. Biology of Storytelling 47
3. The Nature of Women's Storytelling 62
4. Manipulation of Personal Experience 70
5. The Legend Teller 79

PART TWO: WORLDVIEW: BETWEEN FANTASY AND
REALITY
6. The World of European Märchen-Tellers 93
7. The Magic Tale and Its Magic 119
8. The Approach to Worldview in Folk Narrative Study 128
9. How Do Storytellers Interpret the Snakeprince Tale? 137
10. The Crack on the Red Goblet, or Truth in Modern Legend
    (with *Andrew Vázsonyi*) 152

PART THREE: CONDUITS OF TRANSMISSION
11. The Hypothesis of Multi-Conduit Transmission in Folklore
    (with *Andrew Vázsonyi*) 173
12. Is There a Difference between the Folklore Of Urban and
    Rural Americans? 213
13. Processes of Legend Formation 226
14. Does the Word 'Dog' Bite? Ostensive Action: A Means of
    Legend-Telling (with *Andrew Vázsonyi*) 236
15. What Did the Grimm Brothers Give to and Take from the
    Folk? 263

PART FOUR: CASE STUDIES FROM THE MODERN
INDUSTRIAL WORLD
16. Symbiosis of Joke and Legend: A Case of Conversational

Folklore 285
17. Two Old World Narrators on the Telephone 306
18. The Jokes of an Irishman in a Multiethnic Urban Environment 325
19. The Legend Conduit 341
20. Satanic Child Abuse in a Blue House 358

Notes 369
Bibliography 381

INTRODUCTION:

WHAT CAN GYULA ORTUTAY AND THE BUDAPEST SCHOOL OFFER TO CONTEMPORARY STUDENTS OF NARRATIVE?

1.

The twenty essays in this book give account of my interest in folktales, in people who tell them, and in communities that pass them on. These writings represent my ideas, theories, and methods of approach as they evolved. The first essay is an extended version of a paper I presented at the first Congress of the International Society for Folk Narrative Research in 1959, and the last two are rewrites of papers I have read at recent meetings of folk narrative specialists. Except for these, all essays were published in conference proceedings, festschrifts, journals, and collections not easily accessible to the reader. While I was placing these writings into a meaningful thematic order, I retouched earlier formulations and added and eliminated some passages. I did not refer to later works by myself or others so as not to confuse the reader's sense of chronology. The first section makes the case for narrator-orientation; the second presents the viewpoint, philosophy, and ideology of narrators as mirrored in their narrated tales or expressed in other ways: their lives, actions, and thinking; the third discusses the intricacies and dynamics of tale transmission; and the fourth contains case studies that illustrate my analytical approach based on intensive field ethnography to substantiate underlying theoretical presumptions.

My approach to folk narrative study has been characterized as "personality study," "study of narrating," "Märchenbiologie," and "sociology of storytelling" by supporters and critics. I prefer to view my work as ethnography: a narrator-centered approach to narrative performance. I see the main advantage of this focus on individual narrators, the people who tell the story, in that the description of the observable ethnographic present can be regarded as a dependable

base and utilized in the study of the folktale in broad temporal and
spatial contexts. This dependable base is the production of a variant,
that is, the emergent, unique performance of a narrator, backed up
by cultural conventions and controlled by an *ad hoc* audience. And
because this performance by a specific narrator is the first step to
make toward a multidimensional folktale study, this telling of a tale
must be recorded and described with the utmost care to validate
further research undertakings. However, the rigorous recording and
micro-analytical description of the mechanics and strategies of verbal
interaction ("conduct of performance") – a practice of discourse analysts, and adapted by the American performance-school (Bauman
1992: 41–49) – in itself is not enough. The performance event, as it is
presented by its proponents, lacks the backup of a thorough and long-
term investigation of the narrator's personality, education, art, and
practice related to society and culture, and allows only impressions,
forcing researchers to speculative interpretations (Bauman 1986).
Without the narrator, the performance cannot be placed into the context of synchronic and diachronic processes to identify its distinctiveness from preceding and subsequent variables. Only continued and
repeated, long-term, problem-oriented ethnographic research can
evaluate the given performance. The second step is determining the
community repertoire composed of the materials of practicing bearers
of tradition in interactional and intergenerational relationship.
Storytellers in the same community constitute an intricate network.
Pursuing the local distribution and variation of stories in a give-and-
take interchange informs the folklorist about processes beyond the
locus and leads the researcher to the third step: the comparative study
of specific and general tendencies of dissemination leading to concerns
of origin and variability: innovation, stabilization, oicotypification,
and so forth.

This field ethnography-based study has a specifically humanistic
character in that it aims at the personal creativity of individuals. The
"sublogical moment of inspiration" – as classicist Károly Marót, the
dedicated researcher of Homeric poetry and underlying "common"
(conventional) poetry described it – is the driving force behind the
nonrepeatable, singular, unique folkloric creation of individuals. The
performance of this single variant of folk poets who take charge and
assume authority to create their own, obscures the communal tradition
sanctioned by history and society (Marót 1956). Marót's poetic idea
comes close to Bogatyrev and Jakobson's elaboration of the distinctive
act of personal creativity on the folklore level, linking the "parole,"
the birth of the individual "folklore fact," to the "preventive censorship" of the community (Bogatyrev and Jakobson 1929). This concept

is opposite to that shared by early professional folklorists who believed that folklore is communal poetry that keeps its individual initiators' identities unknown and unclaimed. Belief in a mythic national poetry that is "made and adjusted by itself," in the words of Wilhelm Grimm (Grimm 1881–1887), manifested by the folk masses as unselfconscious custodians of poetic heritage, was challenged by the publication of Mihály Fedics's tale repertoire by Gyula Ortutay in 1940. The 86-year-old illiterate Fedics not only claimed authorship of his tales but also explained his method of adaptation and internalization of conventional tale elements he had learned from others. He described in great detail how he formulated stories and made sense of meaningless bits and pieces. He took great pride in his art as did other storytellers discovered later.

Researchers following Ortutay's pioneering study of Fedics found similar claims of authorship by storytellers. They discovered that the telling of tales is regarded as a performing art by folk communities, as is the singing of epic songs, playing music, and dancing; carving, painting, and sculpting images; and weaving intricate patterns for the decoration of utensils and objects in everyday use. The traditional folk had defined folktale as fiction, 'a lie' for entertainment and diversion, and made room for occasions when storytellers may perform in public. In my experience, the etiquette of storytelling is a part of cultural learning in traditional rural societies. The folk sets high standards for how tales must be told, developing a code of aesthetics to normalize the use of what Jolles called *Sprachgebärde*, that is, linguistic and semiotic formulas that include polished, structured speech and body language to create witty dialogues, to characterize actors and actions, and to elaborate traditional cadences. Storytellers are judged even more, however, by their degree of imagination, original story development, structuring, and the bridging of everyday reality with fiction in the formulaic introduction and closure of a story. The rules of tale-telling become all the more apparent when compared to legend-telling. Legends are regarded as nonfictional reports of remarkable, often extranormal experiences of the teller or someone else. The legend-teller's rendition is not expected to display narrative refinement but rather accuracy of information. The experience must be framed by reference to circumstances and eyewitnesses submitted to the audience for evaluation and discussion. Many storytellers do not like to tell legends that force them to stay within the facts of environmental reality instead of letting their fantasy soar. Tale tellers often explained to me that they are expected to lie deliberately. The legend teller has to stick to proper information about sober facts without fantasizing.

Storytellers I have known were performing artists and natural entertainers of responsive audiences, unlike tellers of sensitive personal
testimonial narratives such as legends or life experiences. These
storytellers became recognized because it was their personal need to
practice their art. If no one came to their houses, they went to the
pub, the old folk's home, the soup kitchen, the market, wherever
people gathered, to seek an audience. Even an inexperienced, shy
fieldworker has no difficulty finding narrators. On my first student
field assignment, people in the village Bag showed me the house of
Péter Pandur, the old blind narrator. As soon as I entered the gate,
introduced myself, and asked if he knew tales, Uncle Péter started to
narrate his first piece, a risqué chante-fable (AaTh 1360C, Old Hilde-
brand). During two consecutive visits, more than a hundred tales
followed this brief Schwank he tested on me.

Over the years my colleagues have questioned my preoccupation
with "star" performers and their repertoires. How about "untalented"
narrators (Lehtipuro 1979) and "passive tradition-bearers" (Gwyndaf
1976)? Anyone who has read my *Folktales and Society* (Dégh 1969/
1989) knows that my aim was not to focus on outstanding artists and
to disregard others. How could I have done that if I wanted to pursue
the conduits of tale communication and the functions of community
repertoires? I certainly wanted to study all kinds of storytellers –
anyone who knew tales – without discrimination; all the types
described by Sokolov, Chicherov, Asadowskij, Ágnes Kovács and Leza
Uffer; men, women, children, occasional and regular narrators, specialists in certain types of tales, both good and bad performers. I collected
from people who knew one single tale, from others who knew it all
but never told any, and from others who gained respect for their
ten to a hundred-plus pieces readily available upon audience demand.
I do not study creativity in isolation, but symbiotically, as Gyula
Ortutay taught me. My goal was to learn about the distribution of
the total community repertoire (Ortutay 1963b). Kvideland, in his
recent grappling with the concept "repertoire," mentions that I believe
real storytellers must know many tales (Kvideland 1993: 108). Had
he looked further in the quoted book, he would have read my description of the superb artistry of György Andrásfalvi, who had a very small
repertoire – nine Märchen in all (Dégh 1969/1989: 235–254). Of course,
one should keep in mind what August Greguss, the pioneer Hungarian
ballad scholar, wrote in 1863: "Much depends on whether we have
heard a tale from an eminent or an inept narrator. Therefore, collectors
should try to find eminent storytellers." Without them, tale tradition
could not survive. Not only their superior artistry but their impact
justifies our interest in them. Prestigious narrators with large reper-

toires are the custodians of the community's stock and have a tremendous influence on fellow storytellers within the community. As keepers
of ancestral tradition and bold innovators at the same time, they
dominate the network of tale conduits keeping tale-circulation alive.
They are role models for young disciples, the aspiring storytellers of
the next generation. Wisser by 1926 had attributed the existence of
Märchen-rich and Märchen-poor communities to the presence or absence of good storytellers in the lifetime of the last three generations
(Wisser 1926). But beyond the influence of gifted storytellers in the
upkeep of tale tradition, it makes sense to pay special attention to
them because the texts they produce offer more insights into the art
of story construction and stylistic embellishment than the fragmentary
or abstract versions of average or occasional narrators. Comparing
the texts of recognized community reconteurs to that of other, unremarkable local narrators reveals the ways community repertoires are
varied as they go from mouth to mouth. My published (and unpublished) tale collections come from all kinds of narrators within the
same communities, irrespective of the quality or quantity of their tales,
because the exhaustive recording of total repertoires is essential for
the type of empirical study I do.

There is another distinctive feature of narrator-centered, humanistic
empirism. Fieldwork, following intensive preparation in theory and
method, is a long-term enterprise based on a personal involvement
with people, not a series of weekend-visits with questionnaire in
hand. Ortutay hated the word "informant" and hated the concept
"collecting" because of their implied callousness and arrogance. How
can the stranger who intrudes into a totally different world, equipped
with notebook, camera and recording devices, without advance preparation, expect people to be cheerfully cooperative and answer truth-
fully to unexpected personal questions? "How would you feel," Ortutay told us in class, "if someone unknown to you dropped in Sunday
morning and asked you to summarize the contents of the novels you
have recently read, to sing a few songs, to tell about your beliefs,
worldview and occupation; to confess how much money you make,
what you ate yesterday for breakfast, lunch, and dinner, how many
pairs of shoes you own, and what rituals you practice at Easter? Why
do you expect the farmer, the beggar and the fisherman to inform
you about their personal lives?" The collector must realize that his
relationship to the woman who sings a mournful dirge at a funeral
wake cannot be taken for granted, writes Ortutay further. It is not the
collector who does the favor by asking questions but the tired sharecropper, the hungry beggar, the sleepless night watchman who generously give time to answer the questions we ask. Our attitude cannot

be anything else but modest, tactful, concerned, and patient. It is not obvious that we have the right to ask nor the informant the duty to be ready at anytime for an interview (Ortutay 1972a: 3–13).

Over the last decades, much has been written about field etiquette by anthropologists, the par excellence strangers, researching alien, preliterate, preindustrial communities. Much has been also said about ways the fieldworker's natural cultural bias, weakening the validity of collected data, can be reduced – if not totally eliminated. The behavior of the fieldworker on alien grounds, in explosive political situations or in critical periods of social change caused by industrialization and cultural globalization, has been in the firing line for some time and has also become a concern to folklorists. Endless committee meetings of professional associations of anthropologists, ethnologists and folklorists have tried to formulate rules of correct field behavior; project-funding agencies have drafted codes of fieldwork ethics telling researchers how to treat human beings fairly and ethically. Yet, no principles thus far drafted have satisfied everyone. The question is: to whom are we accountable and where should our loyalties go? To the people whom we study or the discipline we represent? Whose side should we take? Our own or the people's subjective sense of truth or an abstract, impersonal scholarly concept of truth? And how can we fulfill our moral obligation if we have to manipulate situations and develop devious strategies to find the truth? Are we to suppress or sugar-coat the truth to please our informants and thus lie to our profession by romanticizing our observations as nineteenth-century pioneers of folkloristics did, rendering their collections pretty much useless for today's scholarly standards? The ethics of fieldwork is still on the agenda, but the problems are so multifarious, and differ almost case by case, that no consensus can be expected. Carolyn Fluehr-Lobban listed several anthropological codes of ethics in the October 1993 issue of the *Anthropology Newsletter* of the American Anthropological Association, complaining about the "lack of a single, unified statement of succinct and readily understandable ethical principles" that would replace the "lengthy and increasingly legalistic statements of professional responsibility," which are "more intimidating than inviting."

Ortutay's students were native ethnographers whose cultural biases were not as great as that of American anthropologists and folklorists on other continents. Still, subcultural differences handicapped the professional considerably in establishing himself/herself in the targeted community. But these researchers made every possible effort to face the difficulties and familiarize themselves with the situation by participating in local activities, making friends with families before beginning to work. It was a rule to be straightforward, sincere, and to tell people about ourselves, our family backgrounds, habits, opinions, likes and dislikes and to explain the nature of our interest in the people. Not in public speeches, not at gatherings arranged for that purpose, not in the local media: newspaper, radio, TV – just informally talking to new friends, potential allies. And since everyone is curious about a newcomer, talk will soon circulate. I often had the feeling that the villagers were studying me as much as I was studying them. If one hung around for some time without becoming a nuisance, people lost interest and the serious work began. To tell the truth about yourself instead of inventing a script for a role to play is the safest because you can't make mistakes and be caught red-handed.

For person-centered monographic field study, passivity is a virtue. Patience, being there, nonaggressive participation in events is the key. I learned never to be pushy, never to "elicit" information. I spent a whole day hanging around the yard of fisherman János Nagy in the village Sára. He saw me but seemed not to notice my presence while he was chopping wood, cleaning the fish, and spanking his grandson for breaking a window with his sling. It was evening when he called me in. The soup was ready. So was he, with a story for me and the neighbors who dropped in. I learned not to ask questions, not to manipulate people to falsify natural behavior; I wanted to see how they behaved without my guidance, how they narrated to each other without interpreting the story for me, how the tale was received by usual listeners.

Folklorists often speak of meanings and stress the need for interpretation. I learned not to interpret from my point of view but to understand specific meanings that individuals create at the time of performance. The meanings I experienced were inconsistent, capricious and multifarious, changing with each person and each telling. Often the meaning of tales seems obvious to all and does not need interpretation. The Märchen of Little Red Riding Hood stands for itself when Mrs. Bónis tells it to her daughters. It is a delightful narrow escape story that makes everyone happy. But this was only a variant telling, the product of a unique occasion from which an overall analytical meaning of the tale type could not be drawn. Actually the "type," that is, the text usually chosen by armchair folklorists from the Grimm collection or other printed literary anthologies, is also only a variant, unfit for interpretation as to the type's general meaning. Ask the folk instead? I experimented with narrators who were close to me and who good-naturedly tolerated my absurd and embarrassing questions. I asked them to elaborate stereotypical formulas and concepts which they repeated in their stories. What does the seven-headed dragon, the iron-nosed witch look like; how could the prince fly on the magic carpet; and how could the wicked sisters of Cinderella put a shoe on their bloody mutilated feet after having had their heels chopped off? These details were integral parts of the stories, never considered separately. The usual, sincere answer was: "This is how the story goes," or, "I have no idea, that's how I heard it." This reaction taught me that it would be impossible to find personal meanings and motivations through direct questioning. It is better to let people use their tales as they wish and to seek explanation of story preferences, variations, and elaborations in other sources such as personal life experiences, momentary mental and physical dispositions, audience reactions, and the cultural climate.

The tape recorder helped my fieldwork significantly because people were fascinated by the prospect of hearing their stories replayed. If some hesitated and shied away at first for fear of their own shortcomings, later they felt hurt and rejected if I did not record everything they said. However, it was my informants who warned me that the machine in the middle of the table distorted the normal flow of narration and that I should conceal it. Otherwise speakers were not performing for those who gathered to hear their story but for the tape recorder that drew their attention like a magnet, representing a more sophisticated, demanding imaginary crowd. To please this fantasy audience, storytellers changed their usual style of performance, adapting unusual mannerisms and affectations. To prevent such artificial, often grotesque distortions, I usually kept the microphone out of sight as I have mentioned in the description of my recording of a conversational legend-exchange (Dégh and Vázsonyi 1976: 103–107). My ethics-sensitive colleagues, unaware of my cordial, almost collegial, or teacher-apprentice relationship with the villagers, criticized me for this routine. Bill Ellis, who collects from his students in the form of class assignments, charged that by "undercover recording" I violated the informant's "right to privacy" and that this "naturally raises questions of ethics" (Ellis 1989a: 38–39). Similarly, Charles Briggs, who succeeded in his book about competence in performance to completely erase the personalities of his performers, was "bothered by the ethics of purposefully misleading" because "hidden microphones violate the right of consultants to choose if and how they will participate in a research project" (Briggs 1988: 54). Why is a researcher who has no regard for individual performers, but upholds the romantic idea of communal creativity (the subtitle of his book is "creativity of tradition") so eager to submit to bureaucratically drafted ethical principles? Briggs calls his informants "consultants" as if they had volunteered to participate in a research project and would not perform for their own pleasure.

But even such hypocrisy would not change the fact that the voice of the narrators is subdued by the interpreter and evaluator of their competence.

Performer-centered folklorists do not need legal documents to regulate their behavior in the field. Asking for signed consents of participation can only raise suspicion of totally harmless natural queries. Fieldworkers' success depends on their capability to establish cordial relationships with the people they study. Without true friendship, respect, and mutual appreciation, their work would be a failure. The ability of caring cannot be learned; the many available fieldwork guides, manuals, and questionnaires can only teach techniques – the tricks of the trade – not human compassion.

My work with the transplanted Bucovina Székely community continued over a span of 11 years. When I returned 18 years later they greeted me with joy: I had published the tales of their great storytellers so that children and grandchildren could learn them and preserve their endangered ethnic pride. When I wrote about the life of Péter Pandur, I did not conceal the fact that his wife was serving a two-year jail term for selling stolen goods. But at that time no clever lawyers made it their business to sue scholars for telling the truth. In a Canadian prairie town, I felt like a rope walker between two religious factions – representatives of each insisted I should not talk to the other. I did without their knowledge, but I never published the two sets of sensitive narratives of religious controversy they entrusted to me. In Gary, Indiana, my informants were surprised that I did not accept a check of gratitude for my visits. "You gave me the gift of wonderful stories," I protested. I was embarrassed by this gesture which had been natural to them. "But you had to buy gasoline to get here, and you spent much time with us," was the answer. A publisher required me to ask for authorization for the publication of miracle legends told to me by members of a Pentecostal assembly in Bloomington. All signed. "I am honored to be in your book," they told me. But when I informed them of the publisher's policy of using only pseudonyms, they were stunned. "Why? We are not ashamed of what we told you." My visits with them since 1985 were a continuing learning experience, changing my concepts of religious legends.

I could go on recalling field projects and the people who gave me the gift of trust and friendship and with whom I maintained contact through occasional visits, telephone calls, and letter exchange. My patience, my curiosity paid off. The more time I spent in a place, the more I learned – in fact, I had the time to see things change and succumb and to see new phenomena emerge at repeated returns. This approach to folklore fieldwork I learned from Gyula Ortutay.

2.

"The Budapest School of Folktale Research" – as its founder, Gyula Ortutay, liked to call it – originated in the specific intellectual atmosphere of Hungary in the 1930s. The ideas and theories behind this school ripened in critical debates. Methodologies evolved and were shaped by actual field projects in the course of half a century.

From the early 1940s, Ortutay's students and followers went to the field to find creative individuals like Mihály Fedics. They found many good storytellers and storytelling communities of great diversity that made them revise theory, modify their orientation and apply new approaches as they encountered new field situations. As one of the closest disciples of Gyula Ortutay, after twenty-five years of detachment and exposure to other schools and trends, I remained faithful to his basic ideas and thought-provoking hypotheses. They still challenge me. He had more ideas than time for patient research in his busy political life. But it was my good fortune to find real storytelling communities and great storytellers, several situations produced by emergent post-peasant conditions, and a new practice of folklorization-traditionalization in industrial society. These conditions enabled me to test his assumptions and to answer some of the questions he had raised.

What was the background of this new approach to the folktale? Since 1908 the Folklore Fellows association had dominated and set the trend for folktale study in Europe and in America. It established its national chapters in the member countries and handed out field-work guides for collectors who provided materials for regional and international historic-geographic text study. Hungarian collectors also contributed to this stock of tales in their own Folklore Archives at the Ethnographic Museum in Budapest, where field studies were accessible for comparative philological analysis. Philology in and outside academia was highly prestigious in Hungary between the two World Wars. Scholars interested in folklore – mostly in epic tradition and mythology – came from a variety of disciplines: Oriental, Indoeuropean, Finno-Ugric, Uralic-Altaic studies, classics, art history, ancient history, prehistory, archaeology, linguistics, literary criticism, and comparative literature. Few scholars could obtain jobs at universities; the lucky few were placed in the National Museum, research libraries, publishing houses, magazines, and the national archives. High school teaching jobs were less attractive to aspiring scholars, although most university educators in arts and sciences began their careers as teachers. Taking advantage of paid summer vacations and doing outstanding research was the way many schoolteachers earned their university appointments. The chair of Hungarian Ethnography at the University of Budapest (named after its founder the theologian Péter Pázmány, 1570–1637) was established in 1934 by István Györffy, the eminent material culture scholar who trained museum-based ethnographers to fill the need of regional museums. Thus, at the time storytellers were discovered, discussions about the folktale and oral folklore in general were being conducted in small intellectual circles outside university instruction. The two leading young scholars who attracted a new generation of students of oral epic poetry were János Honti (1910–1945), librarian at the National Museum, and Gyula Ortutay (1910–1978), program consultant at the Hungarian Radio. Both liked to invite students to their homes, allowing them to browse among their books, the treasured manuals of folklore on shelves that completely covered the walls of their modest apartments. In those days, scholars bought books by saving their lunch allotments. Both Ortutay and Honti were learned comparative philologists whose views and heated discussions we heard with excitement and awe at these extracurricular – so to say illegal – visits, away from formal classroom instruction. But there was a difference between the two. Honti was a library scholar, tracing epic tradition in ancient Egyptian, Hellenic and Celtic relics. At eighteen he had compiled a Hungarian tale-type index for the *Folklore Fellows' Communications* (Honti 1928). Ortutay's philological erudition – he majored in Latin and Greek – was superimposed with his empirical involvement with the rural folk, his exposure to peasant misery on excursions to the villages of former manorial serfs.

During his student years, Ortutay and his friends at the University of Szeged formed a circle, a study group, to orient themselves in a variety of humanistic fields, building on their classroom education by influential teachers. These fields included poetry, literature, theater, fine arts, folklore, sociology, and economics. The members of the circle they called "The College of Arts of Szeged Youths" discussed the books they were reading and essays they were writing. Most importantly, they were also engaged in the empirical exploration of peasant life and made it their goal to assist folk education and enlightenment. Influenced by authors in rural sociology, particularly the works of the Romanian Dmitri Gusti, the emigrant Russian Pitirim Sorokin and the German social anthropologist Richard Thurnwald, these friends visited rural settlements in the vast hinterland of the university town and gave informative lectures to peasant homesteaders and villagers in the area. Coming face to face with the miserable lives of agricultural laborers on the estates of the nobility and the clergy was a traumatic experience for the young intellectuals. But the Szeged friends were

not alone with their concerns. Young Hungarian writers, poets, news-
papermen, economists, and historians raised their voice to advocate
land reform, the parceling of large estates for the benefit of masses
of farmworkers whose labor and living conditions, the result of feuda-
listic-patriarchal rule of lords, had changed little since the abolishment
of serfdom in 1848. The government was not tolerant: the celebrated
authors who wrote best-selling novels, sociographic village studies
and travelogues featuring the pleas of poor peasants were convicted
and sentenced to jail terms in spectacular court trials in front of a
protesting young intellectual audience.

Another contributing factor behind Ortutay's interest in fieldwork
on the creativity of storytellers is historical. It hails back to the legacy
of pioneer folklore collectors János Erdélyi (1814–1868) and János Kriza
(1811–1875) and the specific formation of Hungarian folklorism and
literary populism during the 1930s. Béla Bartók (1881–1945) and Zoltán
Kodály (1882–1967) were the spiritual leaders of a new folklorism and
nationalism. They argued for the collection, application and preservation of archaic forms of folklore as a conscious political and anti-alien,
anti-German movement, to ensure national survival. The idea of the
folk as the purest representative of the nation was particularly inspir-
ing on the eve of World War II, the impending invasion of Hitler's
army.

Ortutay's first fieldtrip to manorial settlements in the Northeast of
the land was revealing. Villagers reacted with suspicion and distrust
upon seeing the approaching "young gentleman," and they closed
the door in his face. Of course, he understood and recorded his feelings
and compassion in his field diary. And then there was old Fedics, the
recluse, ignored by everyone. The visit of the young folklorist made
him happy. Someone wanted to hear his long forgotten tales, and
once again he was the center of attention. "Old Mike will now live
for ever!" he said. In 1936, when Ortutay first listened to the exquisite
poetic language of Fedics's tales, he must have felt the sensation of
nineteenth-century classic poets – Goethe, Heine, Pushkin, and Petöfi
– who had expressed their admiration for folk poetry, a poetry they
deemed superior to their own. For a new generation of intellectuals
at the end of the 1930s, it was impossible not to feel concern for the
landless peasant folk, the creators of magic tales, the most celebrated
folklore genre. This sense of political responsibility accounts for Ortutay's double identity as scholar and cultural politician. This dual
course of life was taken by others among his friends in Szeged and
later in Budapest where I first met him.

I wrote short stories, almost completed a novel, and planned to
become an actress. As a high school student, I had attended poetry

recitals and public lectures at a Literary Club named after the poet János Vajda (1827–1897), a meeting place of avant-garde artists, writers and scholars. I was working for experimental stage director Ferenc Hont, one of the Szeged circle, and through him I met Ortutay, whose lectures at the club attracted my interest to the folktale. I had not been aware of the discipline of folklore, but my childhood attraction to magic tales had been a good beginning. I had spent summer vacations on the estate of my aunt in the same region where Ortutay met Fedics; I had listened to the stories of coachmen in the stables and herdsmen in the pasture. This experience was reactivated when I heard Ortutay lecturing about storytellers at one of the János Vajda Society's gatherings. At the same time, a friend of my brother loaned me the third volume of the "Ethnography of the Hungarian People" (Viski n.d.), containing chapters on folk literature, style, and language. In the Ballad chapter I saw a text with the same content as a Welsh folktale I had read in one of Andrew Lang's Colored Fairy Books. Fascinated by the incongruity I suspected, I wrote to the author, Professor Sándor Solymossy, one of the Szeged teachers of Ortutay. In his reply the 75-year-old scholar addressed me 'Dear Madam' (I was a high school senior) and explained to me the whims of oral transmission. He also included a pamphlet of the Folklore Fellows on collecting folklore. I started collecting the same summer in Piricse, Szabolcs County, and decided to study folklore after I graduated. Retrospectively I wonder, who and what inspired me? Honti's book, *The Tale – its World* (Honti 1937/1975); Ortutay's Fedics, and Marót's review of Fedics's tales (Marót 1940) were my guides to folktale theory. I met Péter Pandur on my first-year student field trip, and four years later his 107 tales became the theme of my doctoral dissertation. Honti and Ortutay were twenty-eight, Marót was fifty-five, Fedics eighty-six, and Pandur fifty-eight. A Folklore Department did not materialize until 1946 when Ortutay chaired the first Folklore Department, sharing the Institute of Ethnography with the other new chair of Material Culture occupied by István Tálasi.

From that time, Gyula Ortutay's career took parallel courses as he committed himself to two causes: cultural politics and the advancement of the discipline of folklore.

During the war years, Ortutay and his friends formed a faction within the Independent Smallholder Party that worked on a new educational system to be realized in a new political order following the defeat of Germany. This system was to end the dominance of the clergy in folk education (all eighth-grade rural schools were parochial), and to replace it with an egalitarian secular schooling system, free to everyone. Ortutay became President of the Hungarian Radio after the war. Later he occupied pivotal positions in cultural-political affairs. He was Minister of Education, Director of the Popular Front, Member of the Parliament and Director of the Council for the Advancement of Culture. But the prominent politician never lost touch with the academic community. Ortutay was chairman of the Council of Museums and later president (rector) of Eötvös University, while also serving as a fulltime folklorist: scholar, educator, and manager. As a university professor and elected member of the Hungarian Academy of Sciences (1959), Ortutay lobbied for the establishment of a Folklore Research Institute at the Academy of Sciences, and it was realized in 1965 under his directorship. He also held the presidency of the Hungarian Ethnographical Society. He taught classes, directed dissertations, and kept lecturing, writing, and publishing.

The publication of the tales of Mihály Fedics in 1940 provoked the conservative folklore establishment. The publisher, the "Institute of Hungarology," itself was controversial. It was a university-based center of area study in the making, supported by Kodály and a few university professors sharing anti-German feelings. Ortutay was appointed editor of the journal *Hungarology* which appeared only once. The book on Fedics was the first volume of the series that indicated its loyalty to the classic *Magyar Népköltési Gyüjtemény* (Collection of Hungarian Folk Literature in 14 volumes, 1882–1924), comprising regional miscellanies of verse, prose and ritual poetry, but it heralded a departure from the old standard by adding the word "Uj" (New) to its title. It certainly appeared new, undermining conservative theories about folklore as communal poetry and its archetypes as self-perpetuating organisms. It also introduced folklore as an ethnographic reportage of the present, with an emphasis on living, creative personalities, in opposition to the ruling quest of survivals from the past.

Two critics expressed their concerns in different ways but for the same reason. Bertalan Korompay, disciple of Kaarle Krohn, felt that "in all seriousness, we cannot imagine a researcher who would agree that all questions of folktale study could be answered by the literary and psychological examination of the storyteller." . . . "These very personal traits do not interest folklorists because they lack the marks of collectivity represented by the folk community," he writes further, "and omits more difficult problems of wandering and dissemination of tales." Korompay expressed his worry that if folklorists focused on current informants, traditional folk culture would have to take a backseat, and the whole discipline would be threatened (Korompay 1941: 176–177).

Honti's main objection against the "personality research method" was that "if folkloristic expressions are evaluated from the individual's viewpoint, the infinite, deep perspective of time and tradition would be lost. The contribution of individuals becomes simplistic and momentary, remains a product of one person, not a community treasure, not the universal expression of total cultures, not folklore but literature" (Honti 1942: 238). "Folklore is distinct from literature," Honti wrote, "because it gains significance only after it passes from the person who was its momentary presenter. Folklore is a historic document that witnesses the past and makes it palpable for the present because the total community, the total and indefinite past, resounds through it." (Honti 1942: 239.)

There were other objections: too much fieldwork involved, why collect more variants when we already have plenty in the archives? Why do we want to encourage talkative informants to expand their stories out of proportion, distorting the Normalform. And so on, and so forth. Ortutay's response to the critics appeared in 1955 (Ortutay 1955: 58–66), concisely summing up his school's opposition to comparative-philological and survivalist approaches with reference to his book on Fedics and that of subsequent authors in the series (Banó 1941; Dégh 1943; and Kovács 1944). Discounting the fact that this defense came as part of a larger survey on Hungarian ethnography during and after the two wars and that it is garnished with the obligatory lip service to Marxist-Leninist ideology and the Soviet model, Ortutay's formulation is accurate and convincing. Prior to 1945 the authors could not have been influenced by Soviet folklorists.

Looking back so many years later, the concerns of the critics seem naive. Focusing on the moment of creation and recording the emergent story – the birth of a new version – does not detract from the broader concern for the cross-cultural, historical flow of tradition of which it is a part. In fact, the penetrating study of storytellers and their complete repertoires allows more feasible conjectures into past and future processes out of the reach of the scholars' limited human life span. It offers deeper insights into the nature of human creativity. The deep study of the relationship between tellers and their tales, of the reinterpretation and internalization of traditional materials, is unlike the ways literary critics approach literary authors. Studying unique, definitive texts is different from studying unfixable texts manifested in personal variables. We are looking for clues to capture rules and tendencies of the nature of narrative tradition; can text philology, pursuing abstract content schemes, ever approximate the meticulousness of field-observation-based study?

What was new in this trend? Ortutay and others were eagerly looking for predecessors, classic names from the past that would excuse and justify new, provocative ideas. They plowed through ethnographic literature for references to authors who spoke about storytellers. But these authors did not inspire Ortutay at all; he found them after the fact, after discovering Fedics. He knew Asadowskij's brief essay, of course, but not his collection from the Siberian Wino-kurowa. Neither did he know Hilferding and Rybnikov's impressive pioneer work with Russian epic singers. Neither he nor his disciples had access to the works of the Russian authors who had studied tale telling; only Juri Sokolov's informative listing of works and narrator types was available in the French translation of his *Russkij folklor* (1941). Ortutay's inspiration came primarily from Marót, one of his Szeged professors already mentioned. Marót enthusiastically endor-sed the Fedics portrait in an extensive book review (Marót 1940) that encouraged Ortutay's followers.

The critics were right in that Fedics was a marginal man at the time Ortutay found him, living isolated from the world in a hut in his daughter's backyard. Tales in his memory had no social relevance at that time, but his personality and repertoire were part of an ongoing regional tradition. Ortutay wanted to demonstrate that routine decon-struction of the tale into constituent motifs, and following up on their international dissemination according to Kaarle Krohn's guidelines, cannot be fruitful without first looking at the performing person, "almost completely ignored by investigators" (Ortutay 1940: 7–8). Ortutay's stated purpose was to observe what happens to the creative individual controlled by the strict order of archaic peasant society: to what extent can he exercise his creative powers through the censorship of tradition, and to what extent can he propose modifications and deviations from its trodden paths – as Cecil Sharp had hypothesized (Sharp 1907: 11, 30). There is a specific tension between personality and community-preserved tradition, suggests Ortutay, that gives us clues toward understanding the nature of folk culture. And because the two are interdependent, we must study both. The introduction of the individual who passes on and modifies tradition is essential because the modification effected by any subsequent individual informs us about the ethnographic present. This variation is the guar-antee for continuation: folktales exist because they can be changed and adjusted to new conditions. The storyteller is an integrating agent whose life history, cultural profile, and total repertoire in terms of content, form, style, and manner of telling must be jointly studied. The example of Fedics shows clearly the significance of personality in the acts of transmission and re-creation of tales preserved by the community; it also shows that the performance of the individual is not a simple "handing down" mechanism but a genuine intuition, a creative act of innovation (Ortutay 1940: 106).

Over the years, Ortutay had studied other narrators. Viewing creative storytellers as integrative agents in the act of telling tales led him to new discoveries. He observed the regularities of story transmission, trends of variation, change, decline and revival, and the formulation of tale-relationships, tale-lineages, and motivic and episodic affinities in emergent texts. In fact, focusing on the interconnectedness of artistic imagination and social conditions, he returned to the question of variability raised by traditional textologists, but from a stronger position, by looking directly at live performance. Developing his theory of oral tradition, he planned to test it cross-culturally in collaboration with an international group of narrative specialists. A "methodology of the philology of oral tradition" was his ambitious last project. His conceptualization of orality in folklore did not target vestiges of the past preindustrial society but was firmly situated in the modern technological world. He never saw oral narration as divorced from professional, literary narration. For Ortutay, the printed, copied and read-aloud stories were dissimilar only insofar as they manifested differently under varying sociocultural conditions.

The accomplishments of the Budapest School of Folklore Study are best represented by the twenty-three volumes of the *New Collection of Folk Literature*, the works of students and followers of Gyula Ortutay. Each contains the corpus of individual storytellers (including tellers of legends) and partial or total communities with detailed analytical notes. Each describes the community, the history, culture, and social and occupational life that frame the ethnographic analysis of storytelling and storytellers. It is unfortunate that language barriers prevented this body of scholarship from reaching potential international followers and remains to this day practically unknown to specialists.

In principle, all authors of these monographic tale studies centered their observations on the personalities of the narrators. But great diversity is shown from case to case. Ortutay evaluated the harvested fruits in 1963 (Ortutay 1963b: 85–95, 109–112), pointing out strengths and weaknesses and setting goals for the future. He felt that much had been learned. Narrator biographies and autobiographies gave account of the education of storytellers from childhood on; and we learned about the crucial "coming out" of new talents, their acceptance in society, the struggle for recognition, acquisition of a profile and a specialized repertoire. The monographs described places and occasions of telling, techniques and styles of performance, and the rhythm of the polyphonic interchange of teller and audience in performance. Diverse social, ethnic, regional, occupational, and gender-specific narrating communities were identified, but Ortutay warned participants that it would be a mistake to believe that the personality-centered approach alone would answer all questions the folktale raises. This complex genre needs a synoptical approach involving interdisciplinary cooperation, he said.

It would not be possible to fully evaluate the contributions of the authors in this introduction, but a brief sketch should inform about the uniqueness and source value of this book series for future researchers.

The second volume after Ortutay's was István Banó's anthology of average narrators from Baranya County (Banó 1941); the next was my collection of Péter Pandur's tales. Pandur was another marginal man and rootless wanderer between urban and rural workplaces, an accomplished liar who also told his life history (Dégh 1943). Ágnes Kovács was the first to present a storytelling community in which women, men, craftsmen, young people and children were characterized as narrators (Kovács 1944). The materials of my Kakasd narrators first appeared in this series (Dégh 1955–1960). On his trip to study corn cultivation, museologist Iván Balassa encountered a village specializing in legends: a remarkable body of 700 texts emerged in natural telling situations (Balassa 1963). Four generations of narrators within a family were presented by Ilona Dobos, showing the transition from agricultural-rural to urban-working class existence (Dobos 1962). A complete repertoire is recaptured by folklorist András Béres, native son of an archaic village (Béres 1967). The largest repertoire of a storyteller is contained in the three volumes of Sándor Erdész (Erdész 1968), recorded from Lajos Ámi, an illiterate Gypsy night watchman, a loner and eccentric in an unresponsive world of cooperative farmers. After Ortutay's death, the continuation of the series was secured by the devoted work and expertise of Ágnes Kovács and Ilona Nagy. It is to their credit that materials of noted tale and legend tellers continued to be published. It is only recently that field recordings have been made by linguists, dialectologists, ethnographers and enthusiastic local lay folklorists: clergymen and teachers whose recorded materials were and are currently being professionally edited, interpreted, organized, structured and annotated by folk narrative specialists. The work continues; the materials are there, awaiting folklorists interested in the humanistic study of oral narration.

Storytelling is not a moribund art and can be studied anywhere in the world. It is only the folklorist who has to modify old approaches and tools to trace its continued existence in the modern world. At one conference Ortutay mentioned a UNESCO report on 700 million illiterate adults in the world (Ortutay 1965). How many natural storytellers! But it is not illiteracy that forces the artificial survival of oral folktales. Telling is the natural way of tale communication: it affects the audience by the sound of the spoken word. Nevertheless, the telling itself is the culmination of a balanced relationship between literary and nonliterary, written and unwritten traditions: it always was and still is. Performer-centered research into storytelling tradition in the future must identify and follow the trail of conduits that cross literary and nonliterary boundaries more aggressively than ever, on the way to manifest narration.

3.

Performer-centered approach to narration, or to any manifestation of culture in the domain of folklore, is not a new proposition. It was there all along since Vico; since scientific interest turned toward expressions of the down-to-earth human being. The concern with what humans tell about themselves and the real world around them and how they project their dreams of the world as it should be was multidisciplinary even in the nineteenth century. In fact, the interest in narratives was to answer queries of a number of humanistic disciplines that emerged simultaneously and interacted with each other: folklore (Volkskunde), anthropology (ethnology), linguistics, history, comparative literature, comparative religion, customary law, and psychology. By the end of the century, each of these disciplines had established their own organizations, methods and theories that best fitted their goals while retaining a common humanistic concern. For example, the first scientific question contemplating the monogenetic or polygenetic origin of humankind resulted in the anthropological doctrine about the dissemination avenues of objects and ideas and the formation of cultural areas (*Kulturkreislehre*), where they showed relative homogeneity. The same concern led folklorists to explore the origin of tales, the most celebrated genre since the Grimm brothers published their *Kinder- und Hausmärchen* (1812–1815). While lay field collectors reported almost mythical storyteller personalities, scholars developed theories of heritage, migration and variation processes to account for dissemination, oicotypification, and localization of tales by the remarkable skills of bearers. The comparative historical-geographical school of folklore developed and refined its ethnographic and philological methods in the course of a long practice: collecting, classifying, analyzing texts, relating them to cultures and living uses (Thompson 1946, 1953); adherents – von Sydow, Christiansen, O'Suilleabhain and their disciples – were actually advocates of the study of narration. Critics – not mentioning those who object to the method because it is too laborsome – raised many questions concerning the value of mono-graphic studies of tale types and the usefulness of type and motif indexes, but proposed modifications and implementations, not total rejection. In fact, narrative specialists routinely utilize the works of the Finnish school in their text analyses and placement in regional and international distribution. In fact, the comparative-philological and the functional-sociological approaches to folk narrative have been fellow travelers for a long time. Folkloristics as a discipline could integrate both as long as it did not lose sight of its main goal: the study of human creativity.

In our day and age, however, there is cause to worry about the survival of the study of folklore as a discipline because of the theo-retical and methodological imperialism of competing disciplines. Folk-lorists study folklore for its own sake, whereas a number of other disciplines in the humanities and the social sciences also study folklore but in very different ways in order to meet their specified commit-ments. Folklorists are intimidated by the concentrated attack of cur-rently fashionable fields: in continental Europe folklorists call them-selves cultural anthropologists or ethnologists, whereas in America there is no such danger. The problem is that more people call them-selves folklorists than is justifiable. Folklore establishments open their doors to non-folklorists who study folklore in non-folkloric ways, bringing in their own theories, methods and terms to replace known folkloristic terms and concepts. This leads to the blurring of the disci-plinary aims of folkloristics. The adapted alien jargon that claims to be new is often simply synonymous with the concepts we are used to, but can endanger the viability of folkloristics. A distinguished anthropologist called attention to the dangers of the attraction of greener pastures of the neighbor:

> Theories seem to be close at hand in the neighboring "sciences of mind," but the borrowing of models and problems from those fields lead to the familiar interdisciplinary problems – the encounter of different languages, different ideologies, and different imperialisms. There is also the temptation to overestimate the accomplishments, the confidence, the superior sophistication of the other field. There is the further danger when one makes use of a neighbor's theoretical and methodological tools and their substantive propositions that one is giving up what the scientist or scholar . . . does, . . . that is, the correction and modification of received theory in the face of data as well as the passive use of theory in ordering data. In the use of borrowed theory there is a danger that the productive read-justment of both data and theory is thrown off. It is difficult to challenge and change borrowed theory; one simply applies it. (Levy 1989: 13.)

As a folklorist on two continents who has committed herself to studying traditional narratives in the complex civilizations of Europe and North America, I have always been open to learning from others. Anthropologists Bronislaw Malinowski, A. R. Radcliffe-Brown, Lucien Lévi-Bruhl, Émile Durkheim, Franz Boas and his disciples Margaret Mead and Ruth Benedict were a part of my early education. I was enthusiastic about Freud and Freudians, Jung and Jungians; and my conceptualization of society and social structure, the contextualization of narration, was influenced by the works of American sociologists W. Lloyd Warner and the Chicago school of sociologists as well as social anthropologists Claude Arensberg, Robert Redfield and Oscar Lewis. There is no point in listing the names I cherish and the trends that influenced me throughout my professional career: none of them made me relinquish the purpose that separate a folklorist from other scholars dealing with folklore. I keep on studying folklore as manifestations of human creativity – an ideological, not a technical transmissional, problem.

My approach is represented by my book *Folktales and Society* that was published in German in 1962, translated into English in 1969, and expanded in 1989. At the time of the first American edition, a new group of folklorists was active in the creative process of forming a new field: American Folklore. The foundations they could depend on were (1) the literary-philological approach imported from Germany and from the Nordic countries by Stith Thompson and Archer Taylor; (2) the products of an anthropological interest in "others": native Americans, southern slaves, French and Latino settlers; and (3) an abiding interest in "us," as manifested in the collections by semi-amateur enthusiasts (Henry Hyatt, John Lomax, Vance Randolph) of regional superstitions, ballads and stories of Anglo extraction. Cultural historian Richard M. Dorson convincingly argued for a historical-sociological frame for the folklore produced by a new multicultural and multiethnic nation that deviated from the European model. Between 1957 and 1981, Dorson trained the first and most prolific generations of American folklorists, who, in critical appraisal of folklore works accessible to them, along with works in related fields, made their original proposals. Through many currents and detours, and out of touch with the mainstream of European folklore scholarship, they were influenced mostly by Russian formalists – linguists, literary, anthropological and folklore structuralists (Propp's *Morphology* was translated 30 years late), and behavioral scientists in psychology, sociology, and anthropology. Dorson's "Young Turks" responded with enthusiasm to appealing intellectual trends as they emerged. In due course, they embraced theoretical proposals of new waves: popular culture, cultural studies, symbolic anthropology, communications study, social history, literary criticism, sociolinguistics, and semiotic study.

In 1971 American folklorists heralded a "new" beginning that was supposed to propose theoretical ideas then allegedly lacking from folklore works. Américo Paredes, editor of the *Journal of American Folklore*, introducing the special issue "Toward New Perspectives in Folklore" (Bauman and Paredes 1972: iii), blamed this lack on the Finnish method which he said bases its works on "assumptions," not theories, and causes confusion and disagreement between scholars because it did not even bother to define basic terms. Bauman, the special issue editor, identified the points of "reorientation" by the authors from what he claims folklorists did in the past: "construction of universal classification systems or functional schemes without due regard for the ethnographic realities of particular cultures or aware-ness of the principle that the cognitive, behavioral, and functional structuring of folklore is not always and everywhere the same" (1972: v). Even if I do not share the charge that classifying was the "predilec-tion" of folklorists, I agree that the authors proposed a crucial change of focus from "item" (text) to "event," "the doing of folklore," empha-sis on performance, commitment to "the integration of form, function and performance" (Bauman 1972: v) by more accurate field observa-tion. No question, there are brilliant papers in the volume which have become canonical in educating new folklorists. (Characteristically, only eight of the thirteen authors are folklorists by training.) The papers of Dan Ben-Amos, Roger D. Abrahams and Bauman in particu-lar have been widely discussed, debated, implemented and even criticized during the decades that have since passed. It is peculiar that the proponents completely ignored the fact that European folklorists were already doing what the Americans proposed. Americans had arrived at their new ideas through the teachings of sociolinguistics and behavioral anthropology and psychology, not through consistent building on disciplinary tradition in folkloristics. One can only agree with the principles the event-oriented performance school demands; unfortunately, however, while these demands are becoming increas-ingly theoretical, distanced from dependable field ethnography-based data, they are burdened by a growing contingent of terms, concepts and goals alien to the foundations of folkloristics. This trend can be seen particularly in a recent critique by Charles Briggs, a linguistic anthropologist, who evaluated 150 years of professional practices of folklorists on the same plane with that of anthropologists, linguists, and other behavioral scientists sharing methods of field inquiry but diverging in research purposes. Ignoring well-known trends of performance and context-centrism in folklore research prior to the 1970s, Briggs concludes that "metadiscursive practices" (Vulgo: "methods used in locating, extracting, editing, and interpreting discourses" [Briggs 1993: 387]) of the last quarter century have "not only adopted, but in some ways, further entrenched, older metadiscursive practices" exemplified by the Grimm brothers (Briggs 1993: 389). How can one ignore the impressive treasury of scholarly publications that oppose everything the Grimms stood for? If folklorists abandon the accumulated disciplinary knowledge, the result is more stagnation than progress, more rhetoric than stimulus. It seems the advancement of folkloristics is not well served by blurring its disciplinary distinctiveness; more productive evaluation would result from a more stringent historical survey of its orientations.

It is my hope that the essays on the following pages, calling attention to the performer in the act of performance, will help toward a reorientation to folklore. I have prepared this book with concern, in defense of folkloristics, the scientific field we are committed to.

Part One

CREATIVITY OF STORYTELLERS

THE CREATIVE PRACTICES OF STORYTELLERS

Even in their seemingly modest, singular endeavors, folktale researchers have been striving toward the solution of essential questions such
as: what is the folktale, what are its salient constituents, what forces
call it into existence, what causes its sustenance and variation, and
what does it mean for its creator, sustainer and audience? Among the
several methods of approach to the folktale, the cultural-historical-
philological direction has a leading role. It is the oldest systematic
approach, most successful in the identification and description of tale
types and their constituent elements. In our day, particularly after
undergoing critical modification and reinterpretation of its originally
stiff theses, the Finnish historical-geographical method has been successful in producing tale monographs to show formation of regional
and ethnic subtypes that allow theorizing about possible archetypes.
Critics (von Sydow 1948: 44–59, 127–145, 189–219), authors of recent
monographic tale studies (Rooth 1951; Swahn 1955) initiated new
theoretical premises, and even respected members of the Finnish
School like Walter Anderson (1955: 118–130; Thompson 1953: 270–
280) lately have shown more flexibility in their work. The result of
industrious evolutionary text study in itself, however, can only indicate broad tendencies and the direction of tale variation and oicotypification; it cannot explain the social role and goal of the tale. Nor can
it reveal how tradition is passed on, how variation is produced from
person to person, how the message of the tale is reinterpreted or how
changing functions influenced the shaping of the tale throughout its
history. Stith Thompson himself has indicated that it would be a futile
attempt to trace the archetype of a tale (1955: 482–488). Results are
necessarily hypothetical because the research material in itself is inauthentic. Researchers have disregarded the social base of tale variants;
indeed, they have used abstracted content outlines, not full texts.
Furthermore, they have depended on accidentally and unevenly
assembled materials from diverse regions and diverse times. For the
study of the mechanisms and the rules of processes as demanded by
the historical-philological method, the body of lifeless texts should

not be regarded as a point of departure. What is needed is the product of the moment when the tale, resulting from the collaboration of creative forces, emerges. The scholar must always observe the formation of a new tale variant with regard to its actual social environment in order to uncover other important processes: internal transformations due to spatial and temporal spread and the integration of new elements that happen as tales cross ethnic borders. Only in recent years has research turned with interest towards the reflection of inter-ethnic contacts in folktales (Dégh and Jech 1957: 567–605; Pop 1958.4: 57–66; Bošković-Stulli 1957: 201–211).

Queries concerning the social function of storytelling and the significance of individual storytellers have opened a new perspective in tale research. Not that this interest has never been indicated before. Recognition of the contribution of exceptionally articulate storytellers was already noted by the Grimm brothers and some of the classic collectors: Rybnikov, Gilferding, Gonzenbach, Bladé, Jahn, Pitré, Bünker and Kálmány provided valuable information about the performance of their narrators. Yet, modern day folklorists working with traditional oral storytellers do not use an agreed system of research. Most of their work was inspired by field experience while doing fieldwork in European countries where storytelling was living practice among villagers prior to industrialization and urbanization and where so-called 'storytelling communities' could be observed. But while comparative philologists have adopted important text study trends and formed interdisciplinary forums concerned with the form, structure, sign and speech behavior in the tales, the empirical study of storytelling did not grow into an interdisciplinary collaboration. Some pioneer storyteller-oriented authors like Asadowskij, Wisser and Henssen were often cited by the so-called Märchenbiologists, while no systematic research method evolved from accumulated experience. Today ideas of social anthropologists Franz Boas and Bronislaw Malinowski, Friedrich Ranke and Julius Schwietering's Märchenbiologie, von Sydow's observations following his visit of the folktale-rich region of Ireland, and the impressive field reports of Sokolov (J. Sokolov 1938/1966) and Pomerantzeva (Bogatyrev 1954: 228–257) constitute the basis for methods of field observation.

Folktale researchers in Hungary, like others interested in the function of storytelling before them, are in an ideal position because they still have access to living and blossoming storytelling communities that give them the opportunity to develop specific approaches. Following their guidelines, my own purpose is to explore and monographically describe living storytelling communities. This means I strive to record and inventorize the total repertoire of the prominent narrators of a village with verbatim accuracy. Verbatim accuracy is crucial; the functional and particularly the personal approach cannot be applied without obtaining accurate texts produced at each telling event, revealing the personal style of individuals. I specify "prominent storytellers" not only because they reveal their personal talent but also because they are the most reliable custodians of tradition and represent public opinion and taste. It is by no means a new discovery that outstanding storytellers are the best representatives of the community corpus of tales. In 1892 Béla Vikár gave account of his experience while recording tales in shorthand:

> The storyteller who shows reluctance is not a real storyteller. The better ones do not make much fuss when asked, and there are some who make their appearance as soon as they hear that someone is looking for stories. It was a good idea to ask each storyteller who were their teachers. This way, we easily can find true storytellers from whom we can obtain the whole material that circulates in the village and in the vicinity among their disciples. Usually these typical storytellers learn tales from their fathers or relatives; older people know more than the young. (Vikár 1892: 120.)

In addition, I strive to record the materials of secondary narrators, occasional tellers and passive bearers of tradition as first featured by Leza Uffer (Uffer 1945: 10–18), in order to reveal their place in the hierarchy of storytelling. At the same time, I try to gain insight into the role and behavior of the community of tale-bearers and the demeanor of the audience while listening to tale performance.

Tale specialists were able to register the subsequent phases of the slow process of devolution of community storytelling. I myself observed how storytelling that still blossomed in 1947 was terminated among the fishermen of Sára in the course of the occupational switch from fishing to farming. Without opportunities to narrate, the stories of once active raconteurs became stabilized. The respected narrator, fisherman János Nagy had not performed since 1951, and when I re-recorded his pieces in 1959, all texts were almost verbatim the same as before and no new story was added to the old stock. Stories living only in memory do not change like those enjoying community appeal. Storytellers like Mihály Fedics (Ortutay 1940) and Péter Pandur (Dégh 1943) were in-migrant aliens in the community where they spent the last years of their lives, and their tales had no community support.

In the course of rigorous investigation of storytelling practices it is sometimes possible to shed light on the immediate provenance and agglomeration of the local community corpus, and in some cases, even to trace the process of transmission, the way a story is "handed down" from person(s) to person(s). By repeated observation, I have had opportunities to discover when, where and how the community tale stock underwent modifications, which latent elements from the past were restored, and in what ways the new storytellers, the apprentices of old masters, applied their learning.

The methods of such problem-oriented research are still experimental and by far not definitive, but I believe my findings already indicate what roles tradition, milieu and teller's personality – the three creative factors – play in the life of the Märchen. My observations have been drawn from my own field experience in the village Kakasd in Southwest Hungary among settlers transplanted from the Bucovina in 1946; in the village Bag, north of Budapest where I recorded and published Péter Pandur's total repertoire in 1942 and where I re-recorded his material 15 years later to check on modifications; and in the aforementioned fishing village Sára, at the banks of the river Bodrog in North Hungary, where I could witness the disintegration of the storytelling community due to occupational change.

At a given time, only a limited part of the traditional Märchen-stock is activated by narrators. The rest remains latent, out of social use, for an indeterminate time. At places where the necessary prerequisites of storytelling cease for a longer time or where no congenial storyteller exists, this passive stock eventually succumbs. Even in such villages, however, the rudiments of the tale live on for long. One might surmise that the wear and devolutionary process of the Märchen mean in certain cases its reduction to a sterile version of the mere plot. The identification of the resulting plot and its agreement with the corresponding plot which can be derived from the comparative analysis of the variants of living tales may prompt analysts to conclude that the natural process of wear ends in the reformulation of a kind of Urform, or Normalform.[1] In the vestiges that have long lost the enchanting spirit of the Märchen, there remains the mere action as a spine, a fractured skeleton of which the living, flesh-and-blood organism, composed over the ages by societies, communities and personalities, disintegrated in the course of unfavorable conditions. And, as in the magic tale, it is this lifeless spine that the gifted storyteller resuscitates, equips with new motifs, and embellishes with personal aesthetics. Narrators I knew often bragged about their abilities of not needing more than an idea to spin a long story.

Three factors: (1) the general, ancient form of expression, then, (2) the flexibility that facilitates the plot to carry new meanings, and finally, (3) the ritual nature of storytelling all contribute to the stability of the tale. As Walter Anderson has suggested, society forces the deviant storyteller to approximate the best possible forms (Anderson 1951).

The skeleton, sometimes as a whole, sometimes only as rudiments, appears as the most stable, oldest and most tenacious element in the tale tradition. It must be the most crystallized, adequate expression of primeval human thoughts. If it is correct that the essentially unchangeable Märchen plots are the construction of the essentially unchangeable human constitution, then we have here the elementary thought expressed by the tale and its creator or shaper, the human being.

The skeleton-like quality itself is another of the factors that give the plot-outline its force of stability. Its vague, unspecific schematism makes it adaptable to problems of all ages, diverse worldviews, social systems and individuals. And finally, if it is true that the tale is the appropriate expression of certain distinctive ideas, it can be also assumed that these ideas were maintained because society tolerates their communication mostly in the framework of the tale, conceived unanimously as "untrue." It is well known that storytellers in Hungary and elsewhere like to use "lie" as a synonym of the word "tale" (Petsch 1900), and that tall tales are often used in the introductory and closing section of the Märchen (Dégh 1944: 130–139). At the same time, however, the formulaic opening and closing sequences and the jocular interjections of the narrators indicate that in a way, as a tacit consensus, bearers consider the tale as something that somewhere and some time may have truly happened. And this is actually correct: the tale – not necessarily the narrated content but its expressed social message – is true. But this truth is protected by the accepted "untrue" nature of the tale.

If this observation is acceptable, it becomes clear that the storyteller can best express "forbidden" ideas while avoiding social censorship by performing under the protection of the socially acceptable rite of storytelling. What can protect the storyteller better from the odium resulting from expressing certain truths than keeping to traditional plots that embody the ritual of storytelling with unambiguous clarity.

These facts are at easy reach for observation and study, although little has been accomplished so far by folklorists in developing a specific ethnopsychological method of tale research that would aim at the mystery of the birth and continuity of the Märchen. The works of C. G. Jung and his disciples merit here particular consideration as in Max Lüthi's review of Hedvig von Beit's monumental work on tale symbolism (von Beit 1952–1957; Lüthi 1958: 182–189). The importance of folkloristic consideration of psychological features in folk narratives was also stressed by Jan de Vries (1954: 34–41) and Kurt Ranke (1958: 660–661).

To observe the dissemination of the tale is difficult in the present and even more difficult retrospectively in the past. But patient examination of a community may permit insight into amazing perspectives. In the village Kakasd, where I have conducted systematic research for eleven years, storytelling today is still a living, highly regarded social practice. In addition to several less recognized and numerous occasional storytellers, I have found two superb, creative personalities. Illiterate Mrs. Zsuzsanna Palkó, born in 1881, won the title Master of Folk Arts in 1954 for her performance of seventy-five Märchen; her nephew, György Andrásfalvi, born in 1908, is a no less effective community entertainer. Both have their own audiences and their well established repertoires. Both narrators learned more than fifty percent of their tales many decades ago from three well known and widely respected storytellers; most of the rest they have learned at the same time and at the same locations. Their teachers, the three master narrators, became custodians as well as further disseminators of the traditionally accumulated stock of stories during the twenty-five to thirty years of their narrational activity. Most of this corpus lives on partly in the repertoires of Zsuzsanna Palkó and György Andrásfalvi, partly in abstracts in the telling of average raconteurs, and partly in rudiments, bits and pieces in the minds of passive bearers of tradition. Although both of the star narrators claim adherence to ancient tradition, it is highly probable that their versions of the original tales have been heavily influenced by read and heard variants before being reformulated by their own creative fantasy. In my experience in traditional villages, core community repertoires are relatively small but extremely tenacious. New materials cannot be easily absorbed; it is more common that innovation comes from the restoration and reinterpretation of old elements that had been in latency sometimes as long as half a century.

Systematic fieldwork in small communities led me to the realization that the local evolution of a tale essentially agrees with the world history of that tale. This observation is a new proof that general regularities in the life of the folktale can be recognized by the observation of communities geographically and temporally in close proximity to us. Focusing on this microcosmos, the distinctive performances of individual storytellers hold the key to understanding the nature of the tale.

In no other form of folk poetry does personality play such an important role as the folktale. Beyond the fact that narrators recite in prose and are free to manipulate their stories at will, in contrast to epic singers whose main technique is to keep their story within the confines of verse rhythm, meter, and melody, the art of storytelling requires many skills. Factual knowledge, creative imagination, the gift of formulating and structuring the intricate web of episodes into an enrapturing story, and sensitivity to adapt to audience expectation are the abilities that qualify the narrator to fulfill the mission of entertaining. A great number of such artists have been discovered by recent Hungarian folklorists (Kovács 1958: 453–466; Ortutay 1955: 5–89).

We do not lack characterization of storyteller types in the international literature. Many schematic descriptions and listings are available to us. Authors classify storytellers according to diverse principles, such as their preference of kinds of folktales, their techniques of performance, and psychological personality type, gender, educational level, class and occupation. Russian folklorists offered the first classifications (see Asadowskij 1932; Čičerov 1946: 29–40), but characterization of storytellers is also attempted by Banó (1939: 6–9), Ortutay (1940: 17), and Uffer (1945: 10–15, 19–21). We need more thorough and detailed analytical characterization on the basis of the total corpus of tales which individuals possess. We also need to know how these individuals acquired their tales, and how they shape and formulate and perform their texts under the influence of personal motivations and social situations. In fact, we need to study the storyteller's life and creativity the way literary historians study poets and novelists. To study personal creativity of storytellers may enlighten us not only about how personal variants originate but also what function the tale can fill in the life of the person.

In a strictly formulaic poetry like the tale, personal creativity is strongly controlled by convention; yet for the gifted original thinker, a relative freedom is accessible to express personality within the rigid limits the genre imposes and society enforces.

The first rule of creativity is that the narrator makes an aesthetic decision in choosing the pieces of his/her repertoire. The future storyteller, like every human being, familiarizes him-/herself from earliest childhood with the inherited traditional knowledge of the community. In the course of time the storyteller knowingly or unknowingly selects from this material following his/her own instincts or responding to the pressures of the community and builds a repertoire that satisfies his/her ambition and pleases the audience. During my field observation in the village Kakasd, active narrators shared the inherited body of tales of the previous generation in about equal measure. Evidently, this sharing cannot be regarded as accidental. Knowing the narrators, one must realize that personality plays a leading role in who chooses what tales. For example, Mrs. Palkó, a widow who raised thirteen children, prefers tales about innocent suffering heroines in which she can elaborate characters and ordeals using her own personal experiences (Dégh 1955–1960, I: nrs. 4, 15, 16, 28, 31 and 49). Pandur, a half-blind narrator prefers tales in which heroes lose their eyesight and are healed miraculously (Dégh 1940: nr. 7;

Dégh 1943: nrs. 30, 33 and 42). Not always is elaboration of personal experience that explicit; in most cases the symbolic language of the tale provides the teller, perhaps unawares, a mode for expressing personal feelings. Repertoire analysis can instruct us also of negative behavior: which tales of the communal heritage are known but not adapted by the narrator? Complete tales as well as motifs, episodes and formulas need to be considered: which are used, avoided or altered? Which of the tales in the narrator's repertoire are continuously changed and which remain almost verbatim the same over a lifetime?

The repertoire of Péter Pandur contained 107 tales at the time of our meeting in the early 40s. Over the next 15 years he added only obscene Schwänke and anecdotes, all of which he learned in the pubs of his new environment, far away from his original homeland. Meanwhile, perhaps under the influence of the audience in the receiving community, he radically transformed a part of his tales, while others he kept unchanged, true to the word. His taste, his preference of pieces in his repertoire has also changed. For example, he forgot the title of one of his favorites (a peculiar formulation of AaTh 463*, "Young Nagy Sándor" (Dégh 1943, II: nr. 30), and when I reminded him, he told me another favorite but entirely different story. He also modified his version of AaTh 1536D* (Whiteshirt and Drawers), adding elements from 1507A. On the other hand, three other tales – The Wise King (AaTh 875); The Three Young Counts (656*) and The King Whose Eyes Laughed and Wept (314) – had not changed. Perhaps the structural difference between these stories is the cause of the variability and invariability of single items in a narrator's repertoire – Pandur kept telling them and they were equally popular. It seems some tales are easy to vary, while others have more consistency.

The structural building of the tale is also characteristic of the creative processes of storytellers. The traditional tale plot at the disposal of the narrator permits the enrichment of his tale by free combination of affinial motifs. Thereby, by omission of a motif and substitution with another from a related tale, or a change in the order of linking episodes together, the tale deviates from its regular destination. If such personal modifications in the building of the tale meet communal approval, new type-ramifications may emerge and effect the birth of whole type-families with essentially identical, stable motifs.

The relationship and common origin of the tale AaTh 403, 408, 425, 706 and 707 seem likely because their variants cross each other constantly and because their blendings are more common than their keeping to their separate type outlines. The common motif stock of these separate tales mutually influence each other; there are examples of tight interwovenness of 408 and 707. Interestingly, Mrs. Palkó tells all five related tales, and as far as content episodes are concerned, she keeps them separate from each other. However, there is a great overlapping in the description of similar situations in the actor's monologues and dialogues, and her characterization of mental states.

The two analytical Hungarian tale type indexes (by János Berze Nagy 1957 and Agnes Kovács 1987–1990) indicate only a few multiepisodic magic tales or novellas whose outlines follow the Aarne–Thompson construct. In more recent collections we find the tendency of tellers to formulate their own tales by clustering several episodes or motif-complexes of diverse tale types. It is no rarity to find the combination or integration of elements from five or six types, and the number of new redactions is growing conspicuously. For example, of the ninety Hungarian variants of AaTh 301, seven local redactions can be discerned – five distinctively Hungarian, one ethnic Romanian, and one South Slavic (Kiss 1959: 253–268). It would be a worthy task to investigate the motif-combination of AaTh 467 in which the sky-high tree appears as culture specific in Hungary and appears most frequently combined with 552, 302, 301, 400 and 530 and 531. Comparative analysis could show what role the tree motif played in the history of Hungarian folk culture (Dégh 1978: 263–316; Kovács 1984: 16–29).

Within one and the same community the same tale may coexist, sequencing motifs in diverse ways. Diversification of the constructs apparently originates from the personal preferences of individual narrators.

The worldview and the demeanor of storytellers are revealed by the way they connect the world of the tale and the world of everyday reality. Märchen elements appear both in the daily life of villagers and in the world of magic; they are as real as they are unreal. Yet the scenes of the action are separated from each other. The adventure usually begins in the real world that is left behind by the hero who undertakes a journey that transforms him/her through testing adventures to find fulfillment in the world of the tale. During the journey, the hero can return to reality at any time, for shorter or longer periods, as he really is a wanderer between worlds (Ranke 1958: 623). Elements of magic and enchantment enter first as aliens in the village environment, to set the action of the narrative plot into motion, but gradually, as the hero distances himself from his homeland and approximates the other realm, the world of enchantment takes over, dominating, setting new rules that become the norm, the everyday. Reaching the destination, the hero loses contact with the reality of the past. In the dreamlike land of the Märchen, reality is as slight as magic in the real world at the departure, although its importance is not less than that of magic. The hero maintains his realistic features throughout his adventure, through his ascent of power and afterward, always staying in essence a real person; this reality check endows the audience with insights into and understanding of the Märchen.

The ways the storyteller proportions various elements of the tale world give another opportunity for inventiveness. For example, introducing the initial situation, the narrator disposes of several formulas and may dramatize village misery by recalling and elaborating sufferings and injustices he/she has endured, simultaneously characterizing the position of the hero and launching his daring adventure.

Giving account of mythical and magical occurrences in the everyday village life preceding the hero's voyage also functions as a reality crossover element for the narrator. I am not only thinking here of tale types that are genetically traceable to deeply rooted belief concepts and may coexist locally with legendary formulations that keep the tale variants active agents of local folk belief, as for example AaTh 365, 506, or 507. More impressive localizations appear in other kinds of magic and novella tales. Many narrators like to add legend-like episodes that are regarded by the villagers as "true stories." Storyteller György Andrásfalvi begins his favorite tale, the Twin Rods, AaTh 303 (Dégh 1955–1960, II, nr. 64) with an episode of magic conducted by the village witch. Also, Mrs. Palkó likes to speak of the village witch who is consulted by her royal heroes in distress; another narrator, Lajos Molnár, has a simple peasant woman relieve the young prince from the evil eye by magic. But realistic features are contained not only in the parts of the tale that occur in the real world but also in the world of magic: they reflect the worldview of the narrator.

In addition to storytellers who are inclined to rationalize fantasy, many embroider the magic part of the Märchen with added fantastic elements; they even present reality within an ambiguous clair-obscure framework. For example, listening to the life history account of András Albert, a Transylvanian lumberman, the outsider may wonder how to distinguish fact from fiction, poetry from lie, and how to regard the relationship between pseudology and storytelling. The folktale requires a conventional normative equilibrium between reality and fantasy, and exaggeration of either one is regarded as unusual, giving the narrator a marginal status on the borderline between tale and literature.

The degree of identification with the story and its hero also distinguishes narrators from each other. For some, the tale is a subjective experience, a complete adaptation of the hero's personality and viewpoint; the narrator struggles and suffers with the hero, is killed and resuscitated and rises victoriously above evil opponents, like Zsuzsanna Palkó, depicting the fate of banished queens deprived of their children. The objective storyteller, on the other hand, depicts the ambiguity of the two worlds with calculated sobriety without getting involved and succeeds in giving an effective performance by the method of "impassibility" and "impersonality." Andrásfalvi in his version of the Two Brothers tale (AaTh 303) displays a sensible distribution of real and unreal elements. In the tale that begins in the village milieu, the hero leaves his family because of an internal conflict and departs, entering the magic tale world. But his adventures bring him back three times until at the end, he meets his twin brother in the tale world where both succeed.

Personal characteristics of narrators also appear in the way of telling. Not much has been written yet about the general style of the Märchen and even less about the personal style of individual narrators, despite the fact that recent discovery of skilled performers shows the great importance of such stylistic diversity. I find it not true that the difference between the folk and the literary tale is that while the folktale is the description of a string of uninterrupted actions without artistic intent, the literary tale stagnates at points with description and subtle characterization of actors and their acts (F. Ranke, 1938: 19–130).

The personal style of the narrator – irrespective of people who are more epically or dramatically inclined – is best manifested in the way tellers handle episodes of their tales: which do they elaborate, extend, embellish, abbreviate, or omit? How far does the narrator preserve traditional formulas or modify or break away entirely from given structures. Frequently, we encounter gifted storytellers who apply conscious tricks to increase the effect of their performance. They slow down the pace of events, repeat episodes retarding the outcome, stretch the audience's expectation by describing physical and mental features and disposition of actors, insert dialogues and monologues before action, and characterize situations and landscapes, often with a personal touch. Such is the case, for example, in certain stories that stress tension toward the happy outcome by retelling the same episode several times: when the advisor of the hero tells it, when it happens, and at the final showdown, when the hero or his representative reveals the truth.

The stylistic elaboration of storytellers often leads to considerable expansion of the text: transcribed variants of the same type may run from half a page to 50 printed pages without the inclusion of new motifs or episodes. It is no rarity that Hungarian storytellers extend their tales for hours, even all night long, and not merely because the narrator becomes superfluously verbose. Through stylistic replenishments, gifted narrators often convert a plain, structurally and episodically weak story, – an awkward and pointless fragment – into a masterpiece. Sometimes a single idea is enough to challenge the talent of ambitious storytellers. Mihály Fedics told Ortutay that he who knows a couple of tales, can make a hundred of it if he has the talent (Ortutay 1940); and Ferenc Czapár, a Sára fisherman, has revealed to me his secret of composition:

> It went on for a week or so, that I finished a tale. That can begin with anything. Table, plate, as it comes. The tale is, you know, like a young sapling. It grows, develops, you prune it, graft it, clean it, it will grow leaves, twigs and fruits. A new life develops, like that of humans as well. Who knows what it will be? This is how the tale is. Once I began a tale about a young lady, that she found a box. She picked it up, looked what is inside, she opened it. It was a dragon. He grabbed her and took her. What happened after: I told it for a week. This is how the tale goes: as we want it, only it has to have a basis, afterwards anything can be added.

The continued maintenance of stories is the result of generations of diverse types of narrators, and the current popularity of village storytelling is very much attributable to this diversity. No matter how much their creativity is controlled by tradition and how much they are influenced by their audience, creative storytellers are the ones who modernize and renew the folktale tradition to make it attractive for current consumption. Their suggestions result in type combinations, new type blendings, new ramifications, the formulation of ethnic subtypes, and new local and regional redactions. Peasant society, however, often rejects overly bold attempts at modification; tradition prevails over innovation if it does not carefully follow traditional – often conservative – ideas. In modern post-war Hungary, society has gradually undergone great changes due to industrial and technological growth, urbanization, and the transformation of the old class structure. The changes have radically altered the life of villages and individuals, while the living corpus of folktales continues to preserve traditional conventions. Although modern concepts appear in tales – Péter Pandur's princess treats the hero to espresso coffee and cognac; András Albert's dragon swallows an express train, and Mrs. Palkó's king receives a declaration of war from his enemy by telephone and telegrams – these adaptations remain on the surface and do not affect the essence of the tale. The messages of the tale remain unchanged, wonders are still conceptualized as belonging to the sphere of traditional images and remain uninfluenced by the everyday wonders – like radio and television – encountered by people of our time.

Within the framework of faithfulness to tradition, however, exceptional narrators I called "form-breakers" can exercise their skill in front of an enraptured audience. These narrators choose to be different and break the conventional frame and create new tales by combining traditional tale elements in an unusual and unexpected way. Some unconventional pieces can be found in the repertoire of narrators who otherwise are faithful to tradition while the repertoire of others consist almost exclusively of irregular pieces. Part of these tales are cast within the usual frames but differ conspicuously from other variants, that is, only in their essential elements do they conform with the known variants of the type and fit only in general terms into the international type system. Other parts, on the other hand, seem to constitute a new tale even if its composite motifs are listed in the Motif Index. Among the unusual form-breaking talents are farmer Lajos Molnár of Csenger, whose tales are unique novelesque compositions (Ortutay, Dégh and Kovács 1960, II: nr. 122 and 123), András Albert, lumberman from Csikszentdomokos (Transylvania), whose robust fantasy, personal experience and literacy results in intensification of magic in magic tales (Dégh 1965a: nr. 3 and 7); the half-Gypsy Lajos Ámi, illiterate ranger from Szamosszeg (Erdész 1968) and the Gypsy bricklayer Ferenc Kis from Mátészalka (my unpublished collection 1963) share the skill to turn Märchen-narratives into prose heroic epics.

Strangely enough, gifted formbreakers have only recently been acknowledged. It is possible that similar narrators have always existed but that the researchers appreciated only the faithful bearers of tradition, not those who recreated the tales they acquired. These did not fulfill the expectation of the collector looking for Aarne–Thompson models, and were dismissed as individual formulations that deviate from the canon and unnecessarily "water up" the story instead of observing tradition. Maintenance of type models, replication of literary abstractions were sought as expressions of communal creation. We find it exceedingly important to explore original narrators and study their role in and influence on community repertoires.

Tradition, however, used by storytellers and more or less modified by form-breakers, is not an abstract, metaphysical concept. Tradition is manifested in the taste and social, moral, and religious conceptions of its bearers in the small and concrete storytelling community of the existing society. The personality of the storyteller is influenced mostly by the immediate environment representing all society, commonly by its directly expressed expectations and criticisms. Thus, from the viewpoint of storytelling, community is a condensed society. If we recognize that the immediate small community consistently guides, stimulates and curtails the individual storyteller, then, continuing our previous thought, we may suggest that the storyteller is not only a personality but the condensed community.

The seemingly impossible task of observing how the tale performs its social function in general can be realized by researching small groups and their representative storytellers, not only as individuals but as representatives of society.

Thus I conclude that the basic questions of the genesis and function of the tale can be approximated best by the study of personalities. As a further step beyond cultural-historical and philological study of tales, I regard as essential the study of emergent manifestations of live storytelling through the exploration of the community broken into composite individuals, primarily the storytelling personalities.

BIOLOGY OF STORYTELLING

1. Term and Definition

Although the word "biology" has been put to only limited use in narrative study, it denotes a research area of great complexity. "Biology" indicates a significant switch of focus in scholarship, from text to context. The term signals a change in concentration from the static view of artificially constructed and isolated oral narrative sequences, to the dynamics of telling and transmitting stories from person to person and from people to people, through means of direct contact, interaction, and resulting processes responsible for the formation and continual recreation of narratives.

It was Carl Wilhelm von Sydow who first made the point that "scholars have failed to study the *biology* of tradition." He criticized early folklore schools for their preoccupation with the origin of disseminated traditions and their complete disregard of the manner of dissemination. He charged the Finnish School with applying the migration theory "generally and exclusively," limiting its area of inquiry to the country of origin instead of examining the manner of tale dissemination. Von Sydow exhorted researchers to focus on transmission through active and passive bearers of tradition, and to use thorough field methods in collecting oral materials found in local communities and distributed by travelers (von Sydow 1948: 11).

Whether or not they were influenced by von Sydow's suggestions and criticisms of the Finnish School, narrative scholars displayed increasing dissatisfaction with tale philology, the study of texts printed on paper and divorced from their life-giving sociocultural background. The Finns, in their routinely applied methodology of tale study, were satisfied to remain within the limits of generic comparative analysis, investigating accidentally captured and unevenly distributed versions of endlessly varying oral narration. Thus, critics began to feel that research writings necessarily reflected individual impressions rather than documentable facts. It was found that describing units of narrative content and form – genres, types, subtypes, episodes, motifs and other constituent elements – was an arbitrary scholarly exercise based on insufficiently and inaccurately collected materials. In such cases, type and motif classification could not help reveal the true extent and nature of narrative. Critics also felt that folktale philologists were not interested in the spontaneous creativity of folk narrators as expressed in the variation of stories, but rather in the accumulation of identical narrative sequences reinforcing the fixed type outlines. Most early collectors trimmed off the "superfluous garrulity" of individual tellers, maiming the natural flow of the living tale. Working with artificial texts, researchers could not satisfactorily conceive of the form, style, and meaning of stories, and could not even approximate their ultimate goal: the reconstruction of the original "archetypes" through comparative analysis of temporally and spatially distributed materials (Ortutay 1972b: 231–240; Dundes 1964: 39–40; Georges 1972: 325–330; Holbek 1965: 158–161; Jason 1970: 285–294).

Although it was Axel Olrik who in his influential article, "Epische Gesetze der Volksdichtung," first formulated the concept "Biologie der Sage" and "Biologie des Märchens" (Olrik 1909: 3), the term "biology" is used primarily in the German-language narrative studies, where it was first employed to denote ethnographical descriptions of observed storytelling. Hertha Grudde, Otto Brinkmann, Machtilda Brachetti, Karl Haiding, and Gottfried Henssen, to name just a few, were first noted as Märchenbiologen, presenting narrative repertoires of individual tellers and communities. Will-Erich Peuckert remarks,

> Wir sprechen heute gern von einer 'Biologie' der Sage, und dem Volkskundler liegt daran, das Wo und Wie des Sagenerzählens und das Alter, Geschlecht und Handwerk, Herkunft, Heimat und das Wessen ihres Erzählers zu ergründen. (Today, we like to speak of a 'biology' of the legend, by which the folklorist means ascertaining the 'where' and 'how' of legend-telling, as well as the age, sex, occupation, background, homeland, and spirit of the teller.) (Peuckert 1959: xviii.)

On the broader European scope, Max Lüthi refers to the "sogenannte [so-called] *Märchenbiologie*" as a specific means for investigating [die] "Persönlichkeit der Erzähler . . . [die] Rolle des Märchens und Märchenerzählens im Dasein des Einzelnen und der Gemeinschaft . . ." ("personality of the narrator . . . the significance of the Märchen and Märchen-telling for the individual and for the community"), and lists a number of representative European collections (Lüthi 1976: 109). Shortly thereafter, Lüthi assigned an even broader spectrum to his *Märchenbiology* concept. He documented his new definition with a rich bibliography, which expanded from edition to edition (Lüthi 1976: 89–108). In addition to his former emphasis on the participants in the storytelling community and their relationship to narratives and narration, Lüthi's expanded concept includes the study of the processes of tale formation, variation, decay, and regeneration, as well as the interaction between the tale and the social systems from which it comes.

Depending on their specific scholarly affiliations, proponents of *Märchenbiology* have termed their methods ethnographical, functional-anthropological, sociological, or socio-psychological. Although Lüthi discusses *Psychologie des Märchens* under a separate heading, other scholars incorporate psychological approaches in their studies of the narrative event. Among such approaches are the investigations of the use of psychological testing to determine transmissional processes and studies of the psychological background of the interplay between narrators and their chosen stories (Dégh and Vázsonyi 1975; Dégh and Vázsonyi 1973: 50–54; Pentikäinen 1978: 9–10; Burns 1972).

2. Homo Narrans *through the Ages*

From the time *Erzählforschung* ("narrative research") established itself as a special field of knowledge, scholars were busy uncovering sources from the past. From different parts of the world, documents were gathered which attested to the existence of noted storytellers who entertained their respective audiences with appropriate stories, through which they gained recognition and popularity. Since classical antiquity, names of raconteurs have been revealed, as well as the nature, and sometimes the content, of their stories. It was learned that different cultures and social classes established different conditions and uses for storytelling, and, accordingly, granted various statuses to the narrators. Narration was reported everywhere and on all sorts of occasions, festive and everyday, intentional and accidental. In an historic overview, stories were found to be at home at African tribal gatherings; the campfires of Indian big game hunters; Middle-Eastern coffee houses and courts of law; the households of European royalty and nobility; the dining halls of monasteries; the hostels of itinerant artisans; roadside gatherings of merchants, beggars, and other travelers; children's nurseries; the camps of migrant harvesters; funeral wakes and marriage ceremonies; the firesides of farmers; the pubs and general stores; the path to the market; the pilgrimage to the shrine of a worshipped saint (Bolte 1921; Dégh 1969/1989: 63–119). The functions of telling a story, as well as of listening to it, were found to be as multifarious as the occasions. The story-telling session might

serve as pure entertainment and delight, or provide relief from boredom, diversion for the troubled, escape from bleak and hopeless reality, respite from the torturous thoughts of sleepless nights. It might
also serve practical purposes: edification, dispensation of moral and
ethical advice, or teaching of history and religion. The social value of
stories varied according to their effectiveness, as did the esteem in
which specialists in different kinds of stories were held. While, for
example, women's tales were confined to the households to entertain
small children, wisdom-tale tellers acquired political power with their
skills. Witty jesters and masters of the long adventure tale became
priceless servants of oriental and medieval European rulers; and those
experienced in supernatural encounters shaped their adventures into
stories which enjoyed the spellbound and awestruck attention of fellow villagers. In view of the great diversity of narratives – ranging
from brief and factual personal experience accounts to long, elaborate,
artfully shaped *Märchen* – created by tellers in different historic epochs,
one might remember Kurt Ranke's words, "das Erzählen von Geschichten aller Art einem der elementarsten Bedürfnisse menschlichen
Wesen entspricht" ("The narration of stories of all kinds fulfills one
of the most basic needs of human beings" [Ranke 1967b: 9]). Ranke's
concept of *homo narrans* as "die Summe aller erzählenden und tra-
dierenden Menschen" ("the sum of all story-telling and tradition-bear-
ing people") sets for the *Märchenbiologist* the task of penetrating to
the core of the problem and seeking an answer to the fundamental
question: what messages are so essential to mankind that they keep
being converted into artistic metaphors and conveyed through face-
to-face oral narration? (Ranke 1967b: 9.)

3. Early Recognition of Narrators

It cannot be said that storytellers and their art remained unnoticed
by collectors and ignored by theorists. From the beginning of scholarly
research, since the identification of Frau Viehmann (the teller of about
thirty tales in the Grimm collection), many raconteurs have been recognized. The modern reader of the field notes, papers and correspondence of the Brothers Grimm will be impressed by their arduous
search for skilled tellers, their collecting strategy and their enlisting
of the aid of friends to capture the precious stories of the genuine
folk. During the nineteenth and early twentieth centuries, quite a few
collectors followed the example of the Grimms and recorded the names
of their informants. Some, like Ulrich Jahn and Wilhelm Wisser, identi-

fied the name, age and occupation of each teller in their storybooks, but seldom accompanied this information with an indication as to which story belonged to whom (Jahn 1891; Wisser 1926). Though Reinhold Bünker identified the illiterate street cleaner Tobias Kern as a man of admirable memory and a contributor to Bünker's tale collection (Bünker 1906), and though Lajos Kálmány compiled a volume of seventy tales by farmhand Mihály Borbély (Kálmány 1914), not much else was said about these narrators to help the reader understand the teller and his art. There were even far fewer scholars who introduced their tale collections with more detailed ethnographic descriptions of tellers and telling in their local settings. Giuseppe Pitre's vivid description of Agatuzza Messia and John Francis Campbell's account of some impressive narrators (Patrick Smith, Lachlan MacNeill, and others) were among the notable exceptions (Campbell 1860–1862).

That early scholars did not realize the significance of individual narrators and their products is no surprise. Rather, they viewed the tellers as the preservers, retainers, indeed the passive vehicles of the tales, which were themselves considered to be cultural universals. The early target of study was not the individual's original invention within his own cultural frame, but the communal folk spirit as a repository of survivals from previous stages of human civilization. For the Grimms and the mythologists, the folk preserved the rudiments of German prehistory; for the British anthropologists, they retained the relics of early civilization. The "folk" (i.e., the contemporary European peasant) and the "savage" of other continents were abstract entities, and so was the tale, the product of communal creation. Therefore, raconteurs were appreciated more for their remarkable memories and adherence to a tradition presumed to be ancient than for their creativity and innovative talent. Thus, research goals influenced the principles of data gathering. At that time, the often-emphasized care for trustworthiness in collection meant only the accuracy of the content, not the literal reproduction of individual tellings. The statements of Edwin Sydney Hartland and many others sound misleading in their insistence that documents be gathered

> direct from the lips of the illiterate story-teller, and set down with accuracy and good faith. Every turn of phrase, awkward or coarse though it may seem to cultured ears, must be unrelentingly reported; and every grotesquery, each strange word, or incomprehensible or silly incident, must be given without flinching. Any attempt to soften down inconsistencies, vulgarities or stupidities, detracts from the value of the text, and may hide or destroy something from which the student may be able to make a discovery of importance to science. (Hartland 1891: 21.)

Continually, scores of collections show that collectors accepted the Grimmian principle of editing and retouching texts. It was often stated that the dedicated scholar must deeply understand the folk so that he can recreate the "original," even from awkward scraps obtained form peasants too ignorant to put them into appropriate shape.

4. Theory and Methods: The Russian School

For various reasons, scholars of later schools – plot philologists, as well as form and content analysts – did not, and still do not, view individual versions as unique and independent creations, as do *Märchenbiologists*. The linguists and formalists use composite plots, or the literary variants they happen to find in printed collections, for analysis of levels of surface and deep meaning, form and structure.

For the *Märchenbiologist*, the primary data appropriate for scientific research can be obtained only through exacting fieldwork: the faithful recording and the observation of creative processes of storytelling.

Theoretical as well as methodological principles of *Märchenbiologists* have often been traced to Émile Durkheim and later French sociologists as well as to the functionalism of Bronislaw Malinowski and A. R. Radcliffe-Brown (Bascom 1954; Oring 1976: 67–80). However, folktale scholars in Europe were far more strongly influenced by the modest booklet of Asadowskij which presented the personality of the Siberian Natalia Osipowna Winokurowa. Asadowskij had previously published her tales in Russian. In this German monograph, Asadowskij gave an account of the special orientation of the Russian school of folklorists, from the late nineteenth century onward. For the Russians, epic singers, tale tellers and other folk artists became the focus of research. To determine the creative processes of oral art, Russian scholars recorded the same text repeatedly over a lengthy period of time from different persons, and related the tales to the social milieu from which they had sprung. From 1908, N. E. Onchukov's collection was the model for certain systematic tale studies. Onchukov and his followers aspired to show how tales live in society through the activity of individual carriers, and to demonstrate that they are not, as had previously been held, the products of an impersonal *Volksmassendichtung* ("poetry of the folk masses" [Asadowskij 1926: 11]). What Asadowskij thought to accomplish by this approach was

Einblick in das Märchen und seine Entwicklung und in die Bedingungen der Erhaltung des Märchens in dieser oder jener Gegend zu erhalten und die Typen der Erzähler festzustellen (... to gain insight into the *Märchen* and its development and into the conditions which govern its existence in this or that region, and to determine the types of narrators.) (Asadowskij 1926: 13).

Yuri Sokolov and Mark Asadowskij summarized the results of the Russian approach, classifying narrator types according to their specific repertoires, narrative styles, and performing artistry (Sokolov 1938; Asadowskij 1960).

5. Trends in Germany and Elsewhere

Meanwhile, folklore fieldworkers in different national schools of Europe began to study the relationship of tales and their tellers, attempting to record entire story repertoires and appending to the texts brief sketches of the lives, social roles, and narrative styles of the narrators. Nevertheless, these sketches were more descriptive than analytical. In Germany, in the early 1930's, Julius Schwietering's disciples initiated a trend in the sociology of folklore. They followed their teacher's direction that he outlined in an address in 1934. To understand folklore, he said, not its forms as isolable objects must be studied, but the way they function within the totality of life:

> Nicht das Lied, sondern das Singen – singen als handhaben von Wort und Weise – oder das Gesungenwerden – nicht die Erzählung, sondern das Erzählen, oder Erzähltwerden – nicht die Volkstracht, sondern das Tragen oder Getragenwerden einer Tracht . . . (Not the song but the singing – to sing as composed of word and melody, and to being sung; not the story but its telling or the process of being told; not the folk costume but the wearing or being worn of a folk costume . . .) (Schwietering 1935: 68.)

Some monographic studies acknowledge individual bearers, though mainly as contributors to communal property. Like others, Machtilda Brachetti regarded the Märchen as "Gemeinschaftsdichtung, weil es die Kollektivpsyche einer Gemeinschaft widerspiegelt" (". . . communal poetry, because it reflects the collective psyche of a community" [Brachetti 1930: 202]). On the other hand, Gottfried Henssen claimed that the over-appreciation of the community had led to the neglect of the individual. He recommended systematic fieldwork all over the German-speaking territory, focusing on the local community-and-teller repertoires and on their meaning and significance to the bearers. He also emphasized that such undertaking would make it possible to show how tales originate, spread, and change, among different regions and subgroups. As Henssen has expressed,

Nicht die Erfoschung des Erzählgutes an sich, sondern die Erforschung des Volkscharakters durch das Erzählgut . . . [ist] das
Endziel. (Not the investigation of the narrative item in itself, but
rather the investigation of folk character through the narrative item
. . . [is] the final goal.) (Henssen 1939: 137.)

His suggestions and model research inspired a whole generation of followers.

In the meantime, von Sydow's principles were more influential in
Scandinavia and in northern Europe than elsewhere. Carl-Herman
Tillhagen's penetrating study of Dimitri Taikon, the Swedish Gypsy
narrator, is an impressive example (Tillhagen 1948). Von Sydow was
instrumental in the establishment of the Irish Folklore Commission
in Dublin, which accepted his principles of collecting. James Delargy's
summary report on Celtic storytellers and their art is an excellent
document of personality-oriented fieldwork in Ireland (Delargy 1945).
The archived and partly published Irish materials await their future
analyst.

6. Sociology of Storytelling in Hungary

Despite several contributions to *Märchenbiology* from various coun-
tries, only one systematic school has been established: that of Gyula
Ortutay (Ortutay 1940). Essentially, Ortutay aimed at goals similar to
Henssen's, but the Hungarian's sources of inspiration were different.
In his study of the tales of the 86-year-old, illiterate Mihály Fedics,
Ortutay acknowledged not only the influence of Asadowskij's work,
but also his debt to Cecil Sharp's thesis on folklore transmission and
classicist Károly Marót's theory on the use of tradition by oral artists.
Ortutay was also influenced by Malinowski's call for authenticity and
by the fieldwork methodologies of the rural sociology school of Dimitri
Gusti. Ortutay stated his aims in clear terms:

> What I consider my principal task is to observe the lot of the sort
> of creative individual that was able to emerge in the conditions of
> the older, strict community order of Hungarian peasant society and
> culture: to what extent the individual was able to exercise his crea-
> tive powers through the traditions sanctified by the community;
> and how far the development of epic material handed down from
> generation to generation can be influenced by personality and talent,
> factors whose creative role we have no right to ignore even though
> that popular [i.e., "folk"] culture which grows up and changes under
> the strict discipline of the community appears to be so much against
> personality. It is the special tensions prevailing between the person-
> ality and the tradition preserved by the community that gives us

the clue to an understanding of the essence of popular [folk] culture, and a one-sided emphasis on any of the factors may well lead us astray. (Ortutay 1972b: 226–227.)

The essence of Ortutay's approach to *Märchenbiology* was in-depth fieldwork developed successively by the authors of the series *Uj Magyar Népköltési Gyüjtemény*: eight distinct monograph studies and tale repertoires written under his editorship.[1] Fieldwork was conducted through recording, intensive interviewing, and participant observation in natural setting, with three basic foci of operation:

1. The narrator's personal life and education, the nature and acquisition of his repertoire, his art and performing behavior.
2. The community, in terms of (a) the locality's sociocultural design and (b) the tale audience membership and participation in authentic performance.
3. The community repertoire and the dynamics of transmission: observation of creative processes through repeated recordings of different tales from the same persons, and through recordings of the same tales as told by various individuals, and transmitted from generation to generation.

This intensive tripartite micro-analysis of the relationship between narrator and audience during an authentic tale-telling session was performed in different ways, depending on the nature of the specific cases encountered by the eight monograph authors. In an evaluation of results, Linda Dégh pointed out that research oriented toward the act of storytelling might bring us closer to the solution of such basic questions as: which powers are at work to create, maintain and vary tales, and what do tales mean to those who create, maintain, and listen to them? Even if diffusionists could perfect their method and use more dependable materials, they would discern only general tendencies in variation and spread, not concrete answers as to how transmission is performed, how meaning and functions are changed through the life history of the tale (Dégh 1960: 28–29). Reaching out beyond the confines of small communities, Ortutay was particularly influential in the study of transmission processes in oral cultures. In his criticism of diffusionist, formalist, and philological studies of texts, he suggests that

'. . . the dialectical unity of the individual and the communal in oral tradition might illuminate processes of social and creative psychology, indeed, the rules of folklore aesthetics. . . . Our central question in the philology of oral transmission is . . . how the individual and communal dialectics are manifested through the types and variants in creation, what are their proportions, how do they determine formal and content elements of poetic creation. (Ortutay 1965: 7.)

An international symposium initiated by Ortutay in 1969 focused on
the problems of developing such a "philology of oral transmission"
(Voigt 1974).

7. Recent Research in Europe

During the 1960s and 1970s, European tale scholarship routinely
adapted some principles of *Märchenbiology*. Scores of accounts cropped
up describing the "globale Erforschung des Erzählens als soziale und
kulturelle Erscheinung" (". . . global investigation of narration as a
social and cultural phenomenon") (Bîrlea 1973: 450). Identification of
tellers and their sociocultural environment are now found in the introductions to increasing numbers of collections, such as those by Alfred
Cammann, Károly Gaál, Siegfried Neumann, Dov Noy, Charlotte
Oberfeld, Antonín Satke, and Daniel Fabré and Jacques Lacroix (Cammann 1961, 1967, 1973; Gaál 1965, 1972; Neumann 1967a: 274–284;
1970; Noy 1963; Oberfeld 1970; Satke 1958; Fabré and Lacroix 1974).
Some exceptional narrators with large repertoires (of 250 to more than
500 narratives) have been introduced by Sándor Erdész, József Faragó,
Olga Nagy, Jaromír Jech, and others (Erdész 1968; Faragó 1971: 439–
443; Nagy 1978: 473–557; Jech 1959). Through systematic questioning
over a period of ten years, Juha Pentikäinen identified and analyzed
an uprooted narrator's inactive repertoire and her capacity for recall
(Pentikäinen 1972: 127–131; 1978). In *Folktales and Society*, I made a
monographic description of a storytelling community, focusing on
the narrative occasions, the formulation of the community repertoire,
and the personal styles of active tellers (Dégh 1969/1989). Such
research led to the recognition of further perspectives in the study of
tradition and innovation, and of the role of national and ethnic values
(as described by Mihai Pop and others). Several of the scholars supplemented their *Märchenbiology* methods with some applicable aspects
of anthropology, social psychology, sociolinguistics and linguistic
structuralism.

Tendencies of current orientation were well represented at the Sixth
Congress of the International Society for Folk Narrative Research in
Helsinki, 1974.[2] Most of the speakers reported case studies of repertoires of individual narrators. In my commentary, I pointed out that
the greatest merit of the "depth study" suggested by Pentikäinen for
repertoire analysis lies in the carefully planned strategy of collecting,
interviewing, and informally observing the teller over a long period
of time.

8. Research in America: Anthropologists Look at Folklore

American narrative scholars acquired their training from anthropology, which developed efficient fieldwork techniques in the study of native Americans and tribal societies on other continents. Although anthropological fieldworkers recorded myths, legends, and other prose accounts as well as native autobiographies (Langness 1965), live telling situations were of little interest to the scholars. Folklore texts, for them, were valued mainly as "a part of culture" (Bascom 1953: 286). Most of the materials were obtained through the aid of interpreters and logically arranged for publication by scholars without any account of the telling situation or identification of the tellers. Representatives of the "personality and culture" trend were not interested in the artistry of their informants but rather used stories as test materials to discern patterns of native psychology and behavior. As Eric Wolf noted, "What anthropologists lack in their endeavor is exploration of human creativity" (Wolf 1964: 48). Nevertheless, Franz Boas and his disciples did not ignore native artists and their products. Boas suggested "we have to turn our attention first of all to the artist himself" (Boas 1927/1955: 155). Ruth Benedict stated her interest as being in both the "themes folklore elaborates and the literary problems of the Zuni narrator" (Benedict 1935, vol. 1: xxi). She gave valuable guidance to folktale scholars by arguing against the doctrine of communal authorship and for the narrator's originality and freedom to create in the context of traditionalism.

In recent years, folklore-oriented anthropologists also yielded some notable contributions to *Märchenbiology*. John L. Fischer, for example, summarized the advantages of applying sociopsychological methods (Fischer 1965). Melville Jacobs subjected eight Chinook texts to elaborate style and content analysis. Although the teller's name was mentioned, Jacobs' interest was not in her art but in the oral literature she mediated (Jacobs 1959). British anthropologist Ruth Finnegan was the first to offer an expert descriptive account on African storytelling in the introduction to the texts she collected (Finnegan 1967). Perhaps the best work in this category is Daniel Crowley's study of creativity in Bahamian storytelling, an absorbing description of individual and person style: *I Could Talk Old-Story Good* (Crowley 1966).

9. The Place of Narration in American Folkloristics

It was Richard Dorson who first recorded tale repertoires from American narrators. Dorson, who emerged as the founder of American folkloristics, was also the first to record tale repertoires from different American folk groups. Inspired by both European tale scholarship and American anthropology, Dorson was successful in developing a method for the study of American folk culture. He realized that narrational conditions in America are distinctly different from those found in Europe and among the nonliterate on other continents. As he pointed out, American civilization is composed not of one unified culture but of "a score of ethnic, regional and occupational subcultures." Therefore, no ritually formalized storytelling could be established to transmit a stable body of narrative. Instead, subgroup raconteurs emerge and produce more informal stories within their own "wide variety of folk groups, from tradition-directed pockets to other-directed societies in American life" (Dorson 1960: 28–29). Dorson convincingly documents his observations with a large number of his own narrator-oriented text collections, which also serve as models to a newly founded tale scholarship in the United States with special emphasis on occupational, regional, ethnic, and racial group repertoires. American folklorists follow his method of observing, recording, and publishing materials.

Meanwhile, a group of theory-oriented young scholars demanded more penetrating descriptions of living folklore. They defined folklore as " . . . an artistic action. It involves creativity and artistic response . . ." (Ben-Amos 1971: 10). In an effort to effect the emancipation of folklore from anthropology and to dissociate themselves from the historic-geographic method imported from Europe by Stith Thompson and Archer Taylor, they set themselves the standard of gathering types of folklore which were more fitting for scholarly scrutiny than those which previously had been accumulated by self-taught fieldworkers in America and by anthropologists among primitives. In essence, they echoed the criticisms of European *Märchenbiologists* and developed ideas and methods similar to those of their transatlantic counterparts.

American researchers benefited from the observation of William Hugh Jansen and others. Jansen, a fieldwork-oriented scholar, called attention to (1) the classifiability of tale performance situations and performers, and (2) the necessity of distinguishing between the esoteric and exoteric qualities of folklore (Jansen 1957, 1959). Further clarification of the "field" followed with Kenneth S. Goldstein's systematic fieldwork textbook (Goldstein 1964, 1967a, 1967b). Goldstein elaborated some attractive fieldwork conditions – such as the "natural context" and how it can be induced by the fieldworker – and considered the possibility of duplicating the techniques of laboratory experiments in studying storytellers. Alan Dundes argued for the study of "the ethnography of the speaking of folklore" (Dundes and Arewa 1964: 71), a new concept inspired by sociolinguistics, to change the earlier "mistaken emphasis in folklore upon the lore rather than upon the folk" (Dundes and Arewa 1964: 70). Very much in accordance with the principles of European *Märchenbiology*, Dundes insisted that "folklorists must actively seek to elicit the meaning of folklore from the folk" (Dundes 1966: 507), through the collection of "metafolklore" or "oral literary criticism": the folk interpretation of lore.

In search for a conceptual framework for the description of live folklore processes, this group of folklorists, recognized by Dorson as "contextualists" (Dorson 1972: 45–47), went beyond the search for linguistic models describing verbal behavior. They applied the concepts of small-group, face-to-face interaction and role-playing from behavioral sociology, as well as rhetorical methods of describing strategies of artistic expression from literary criticism. Moreover, they borrowed some aspects of symbolic anthropology, analytical psychology, and communications study.

Few of the contextualists, however, waded into the context of real storytelling communities. Robert Georges claimed to have switched research focus "from folktale research to the study of narrating." Georges defined his term "storytelling event" as "an entirely different concept – a holistic rather than an atomistic concept – of a complex communicative event" (Georges 1969: 317). His ideas were further clarified by Dan Ben-Amos: "The telling is the tale; therefore the narrator, his story, and his audience are all related to each other as components of a single continuum, which is the communicative event" (Ben-Amos 1971: 10). Elli Köngäs-Maranda observed that contextualists tend to focus so heavily on the process of actual transmission that the storyteller is only one agent among the many (Köngäs-Maranda 1976).

The theoretical considerations forwarded by these American scholars have not yet been tested extensively in concrete field study. Their influence to date can be discerned in Barbara Kirshenblatt-Gimblett's dissertation on the performance of narratives in the Toronto Jewish community, a suggestive experiment employing linguistic and behavioral models (Kirshenblatt-Gimblett 1972). Ben-Amos's *Sweet Words*, on the other hand, is a technically perfect general description of storytelling rather than the realization of the theorists' goal of minutely describing a "storytelling event" (Ben-Amos 1975). In a general assessment of the "contextualist" contributions found in *Folklore Performance and Communication*, Dmitri Segal noted that there are unexpected lacunae in the authors' bibliographical backgrounds (Ben-Amos and Goldstein 1975). Although European and Russian *Märchenbiologists* have paid specific attention to the storytelling occasion, Americans have ignored the work of the continental scholars. The Europeans had already differentiated between stylistic traditions and attempted to determine the influence of the performance ambience on the form of the text (Segal 1976: 367–382).

Currently, there is an increasing awareness of the need for problem-oriented, fieldwork-based research. Dealing with people and their traditions, Henry Glassie summarized the general feeling: "Current scholars often concern themselves fashionably with theory for theory's sake. But theory matures in dialectic with reality, and the critical faculty which enables theorists to judge, test, and develop their thought comes through consideration of real people and things." (Glassie 1975: 163.)

Scholars utilized suggestions from both European *Märchenbiology* tradition and American contextualist approaches. Holistic descriptions of storytelling events appear in the works of Ilhan Basgöz, Linda Dégh, Barbara Kirshenblatt-Gimblett, Sylvia Grider, and many young folklorists. Following the guidance of Hermann Bausinger into the realm of informal storytelling in the modern world, and following Dorson's example of studying specifically American forms – legends, yarns, urban and ethnic jokes, dialect stories, and immigrant narratives – experts began to explore new conditions of narration. They found and described storytelling in college dormitories, youth camps, general stores, bars, factory cafeterias, train depots, old folks' homes, and a variety of occupational, social and religious group meetings as well as in impromptu get-togethers held expressly for the sake of storytelling.

To date, the American school has described principally two kinds of storytelling: legends and personal experience narratives. Legend-telling study, aimed at the testing of Dégh and Vázsonyi's theoretical hypotheses, has been conducted by Dégh, Gary Hall, Sylvia Grider, Elizabeth Tucker, Janet Langlois, and others. Most of these works were published in the sixteen volumes of the journal *Indiana Folklore* (1968–1984). These studies resulted in a new definition of the legend as a debate (Dégh and Vázsonyi 1973). In the study of personal experience stories, following the groundwork of Siegfried Neumann, Ilona Dobos, and Richard Dorson, distinct types were identified as "fight stories" (Leary 1976: 27–39), "family misfortune stories" (Brandes 1975: 5–18), immigrant reminiscences and autobiographical narratives

(Dégh 1975), and specific stories on the members of dangerous occupational groups (McCarl 1976: 49–66; Thorne 1976: 209–217).

It can be stated that the *Märchenbiology* method of storytelling research is helpful in discerning the goal and meaning of narratives in modern society, as well as their sociocultural functions and their traditional and innovative elements of content and form.

THE NATURE OF WOMEN'S STORYTELLING

It has been repeatedly stated through history by authors of many persuasions that storytelling is a preeminently feminine occupation. Without specifying the kinds of stories, authors claimed that women by nature and by vocation, as mothers, nurses, homemakers, and domestic workers, narrate to children, adolescent girls, and their own female associates. Although women may learn stories from their fathers and brothers, and may also invite men to their winter evening work-circles for story entertainment, it historically has been their family role to narrate. Women use their diverse kinds of narratives for diverse purposes when addressing their household audiences. In addition to pure entertainment, stimulating laughter, excitement, emotion, or fright, women's stories discipline and socialize children and teach girls proper behavior in preparation for future life-roles as well as comfort adult women in their daily domestic drudgery.

On the other hand, sources indicate an equal number of male storytellers who perform for mixed audiences or exclusively for work and leisure gatherings of men (Dégh 1983: 116–128). Several authors observed that women are more creative in lyric genres, whereas men excel in elaborate epics, the Märchen in particular (Böckel 1913; Katona 1980: 317–318). In fact, as reported by field researchers in traditional communities within the classic Märchen-distribution area of Europe, Asia, and immediate contact territories and faraway colonies, storytelling can be considered a par excellence male occupation. It is migrant workers who exchange stories at distant working places and temporary residences and who further embellish and disseminate their repertoires while on the road and back to their hometown. Marginal men – exiles, beggars, peddlers, discharged soldiers and preachers – were welcome guests treated generously by village families in exchange for stories, as were the craftsmen who did necessary repairs while entertaining the women-folk at the fireside. The arrival of itinerants thus highlighted the dull winter life of villagers (Dégh 1969/1989: 356–357). This "wissende Leuten," "Durchreisenden" (Asadowskij 1926: 24), were the men from whom N. O. Winokurowa learned the majority of her tales (Asadowskij 1926: 27–28). Indeed, most of the other noted female narrators who became community entertainers beyond the confines of the family also gave credit to the men who brought their stories home to the family circle. More fathers and grandfathers than mothers and grandmothers are referred to as sources of prominent female personalities (Delargy 1945: 7, 23) such as the East Prussian Trude Lenz (Tolksdorf 1980: 28), the Bucovina Székely Zsuzsanna Palkó (Dégh 1969), Mária Fábián (Sebestyén 1979–1986), and the Transylvanian Klára Györi (O. Nagy 1978), to name some of the most recent.

Nevertheless, these facts would not suggest male prominence over women in narrating but rather a certain functional division in sex roles, given by family and occupational distinctiveness. Thus, in discussing the concept of female folktales, two main issues may be raised:

1. What is the distinctive role of women as tellers of tales?

2. Do women develop a specifically feminine repertoire to serve their female audiences?

The woman appears as the natural storytellers through her traditional position in the family dating back from classical antiquity, arching over subsequent historic epochs, social systems, and religious ideologies, and cutting across folk and elite groups of complex civilizations. The image of the woman-narrator seems both ambiguous and mutable in different situations. Prior to the Grimms, commentaries refer to "Ammenmärchen," "contes de ma mére l'oye," "contes de vieilles et de nourrices," "Mährleins mütterchen," etc., and signify the low public opinion and discreet nature of both tellers and stories (Bolte and Polívka 1918–1932, Vol. 4: 41–94; Schenda 1983: 28–30). The women's tales are plain, naive, unremarkable, and unpretentious, tied to everyday private occasions in which hired domestic servants and wet nurses entertain, put to sleep, discipline by rewarding or, in turn, scare young children. Yet the elite authors were deeply impressed by their childhood memories and enthusiastically reported their first exposure to nursery tales. Diaries, private letters, and literary works express admiration for narrating nurses, upgrading their image and turning them into literary models. The reported repertoire of stories was a miscellany of genres: fable, formula tale, Schwank, exemplum, Märchen, horror story, supernatural and religious legend, not infrequently also from written sources, as well as occasionally invented or personally experienced. Nevertheless, the Märchen – magic or novelesque – became the recognized and fashionable pastime story of women. During the 18th and 19th centuries, not only the telling of nursery stories was reported but also the exchange of "Weiber Märchen" among spinning, quilting, and knitting women. On the other hand, urban elite ladies killed their boredom with "winter tales," enjoying each other's company and narrating skill. Among the known raconteurs were the mothers of Pushkin and Gorky, the grandmothers of Tolstoy and Dickens. Goethe's mother was particularly noted as a narrator. Her way of retelling newly learned pieces is featured in her letter from 1807. "Ich habe mir die Geschichte (von Fortunatus) zusammengezogen, alles überflüssige weggeschnitten und ein ganz artiges Märchen deraus geformt" (Bolte and Polívka 1918–1932, Vol. 4: 79).

The Märchen, that is, the "conte des fées," or "contes merveilleux," as a feminine literary genre was already established since the time of Perrault. A line of women authors popularized the Märchen in France in the course of the 18th century, to the tastes of the feudal aristocracy as well as the educated urban classes. This specific Märchen became the tool of child and adolescent women's education, intended to supply "Kinder mit Normen und Geselschaftsmodellen dass sie sich vorstellen konnten, durch Verdrängung und Konformismus ihr eigenes Glück zu finden zu zivilisieren" (Zipes 1983: 57). No wonder that by the time of the debut of the Grimm brothers, sophisticated tale-enthusiasts knew that tales belong to women and the household. Thus, the Grimms named their scientifically intended collection *Kinder- und Hausmärchen*, and presented it for the broader urban elite as an "Erziehungsbuch" to be used selectively for their children. This made perfect sense because for the most part, both collectors and narrators were women who learned their stories from other women in their childhood home. The most cherished Märchenfrau of the Grimms, the widow K. D. Viehmann, was also presented to fit the image of the old nurse storyteller. The collection, as a whole, identified as "Gattung Grimm," did not, however, deviate from the miscellany of earlier household narrators. It included magic tales, novellas, Christian legends, chain and catch tales, lies and Schwänke. It is quite remarkable how little there was in this rich treasury for mothers and nurses actually to select for the bedtime entertainment of youngsters following the advice of the Grimms. While Bolte and Polívka list a total of 18 titles of children's stories (1918–1932, Vol. 4: 472), later authors also identified the "Warn- und Schreckmärchen" category (Rumpf 1955; Zipes 1982: 15–18) intended for child control. Along with the rest, meant to be good reading for women of all ages and retelling material, the *KHM* became the ultimate sourcebook for the Märchen disseminated in the world.

The seemingly anachronistic Märchen was given new lease on life by the editorial hand of the Grimms, successfully incorporating and solidifying the whimsically floating oral folk tradition of previous centuries in a structurally and stylistically balanced and standardized literary form. While consistent and multiple media dissemination of this standardized stock of narratives helped reinvigorate fading peasant tradition in the industrial age, it also helped turn the Märchen in the 20th century into a socially significant educational institution. Educators and child psychologists recognized overt and covert meanings of tales and their beneficial effects on personality development (Bühler and Bilz 1961; von Franz 1972; Piaget 1929; Bettelheim 1976) and encouraged storytelling in public schools and at home. Drawing on the Viehmännin-model, and exploiting a relatively limited selection of booktales from Perrault, Grimm, Andrew Lang, Hans Christian Andersen, and the Thousand and One Nights (Dégh 1983: 118), a new cast of professional and lay female storytellers emerged, mostly in Germany, France, and the United States. Young audiences were the primary recipients: story hours were instituted for different age groups of children and adolescents in daycare centers, kindergarten playgrounds, summer camps, schools and libraries, and furthermore for gifted, handicapped, delinquent and other special groups. The storytellers – educators, counselors, librarians – availing themselves of materials from special sourcebooks (Eastman 1926; Ireland 1973; Clarkson and Cross 1980; Janning 1983; Betz 1983), obtained their training in narrating courses and workshops in teachers' colleges and university library schools (Baker and Greene 1977). Their goal was to provide entertainment, broaden experiences, instigate desired values and ideals, and keep alive cultural heritage. Beyond storytelling for children, there is a growing, nostalgic interest in the reintroduction of the Märchen to adult urban audiences as a more human substitute for mass media entertainment. Female raconteurs are known to perform at clubs, resorts, art programs, military camps, retirement homes, etc. Storyteller Felecitas Betz describes her way of restoring modern-day "Märchenerzählgemeinschaft" by telling (or reading) Buchmärchen creatively when addressing different groups of listeners (Betz 1983: 113–125; Görög-Karady and de la Salle 1979). The Europäische Märchengesellschaft has held annual international encounters for storytellers and researchers – laymen, artists, and scholars – since 1956 to maintain Märchen-tradition.[1] Storytelling-guilds began to multiply at the same time in the United States, with a predominantly female membership, between ages 20 and 70. In celebrating the bicentennial anniversary of the nation, the Smithsonian Institution launched a festival movement and also established annual weeklong storytelling festivals with competing members. The art of storytelling was also taught through radio programs.[2]

Innumerable local groups study and practice narration at weekend get-togethers[3] and communicate through newsletters and magazines.[4]

Their repertoire includes international classical forms as well as local oral stories, learned or spontaneously invented, by narrators of both folk and elite extraction. Development of genre specialization may be observed between the sexes: the Märchen and the ghost stories became almost exclusively feminine, whereas men became the tellers of jokes, lies, and humorous and adventurous occupational and personal narratives (Dégh 1983: 120). If mothers and nurses nurture children of both sexes with Märchen, there is a considerable division in narrative preference past the Märchen-age. Traditional Moslem society prescribes that adolescent boys stop listening to female tales and join their elders in devoting themselves to pious life, engaging in the narration of saints' legends and exempla (Abdelsalam 1983). Even without such strictures, boys reject the Märchen repertoire which women continue to use for feminine audiences beyond childhood in modern urban society (Stone 1975b, 1983). This repertoire consists of narratives about the adventures of female heroes from rags to riches.

But, in reference to our second question, can we speak of tales with specifically feminine themes, told by women to other women? In traditional societies, two groups of narratives have been identified as tales of women: (a) complex magic and romantic tales with women protagonists, and (b) Schwänke in which the education of young women is offered by humorous exempla, criticizing socially unacceptable conduct. Additionally, (c) a much less-seizable category, relevant to both old-fashioned rural and modern urban societies, has only recently been discovered by *Märchenbiology* and performance-oriented fieldworkers: autobiographical episodes of great variety circulating among women groups outside the household.

(a) In a worldwide distribution, the Aarne–Thompson index lists 92 heroine tales compared to 207 hero tales, twice as many, whereas the Grimm collection, a secondary source for the modern urban tale repertoire, contains 44 heroine and only 70 hero tales (Stone 1975: x). A further increase of heroine tales and decrease of hero tales in storybook selections during the last century indicate that the Märchen has become more and more a woman-oriented genre, addressed to girl education and socialization beyond the unisex Märchen age of children. If Märchen-heroines previously exhibited a variety of characteristics in the tales in which they had starring roles as mirror images of male protagonists (such as in AaTh 327, 328, 510/532), tricksters (874, 875, 879, 882), shrewd manipulators, achievers of power (881, 884, 888, 890, 940), in our time, women seem to be more popular in their submissive and helpless roles. A small but extremely popular repertoire of tales evolved and persist with innocent beauties in the title role. Their fate is to be abused, tortured, banished, persecuted, corrected, and reformed, in order to conform to the female image of patriarchal family systems. Subservience, patience, endurance, passivity, devotion, and industry are the virtues of women in Aschenbrödel, Schneewittchen, Dornröschen, Rapunzel, Froschkönig, Rotkäppchen, Frau Holle, Gänsemagd, Sieben Raben, Hansel und Gretel, and others (Lüthi 1962/1980: 135–136; Stone 1975, 1983; Dégh 1983). The almost symptomatic acceptance of these role models by women has been noted by feminist authors as well as psychiatrists (Berne 1973; de Beauvoir 1953: 12, 163, 177 ff.; Dowling 1981; Meyer zu Capellen 1980: 89–119).

On the other hand, the repertoire of traditional rural female storytellers does not show the same attraction to the same group of tales (Fabré and Lacroix 1974). As a randomly selected example, drawn from the Märchen repertoires of Hungarian women community raconteurs, no such preference is indicated. Zs. Palkó (Dégh 1969/1989) told 16 heroine and 22 hero tales, M. Fábián 23 heroine and 61 hero tales (Sebestyén 1979–1986), and Julie Szöke-Tót 16 heroine and 27 hero tales (Dobos 1962). Two of these women gave their sources as their fathers or other male relative and the third her grandfather and his old cronies. The ratio is similar within the repertoire of men: Péter Pandur narrated 19 heroine and 20 hero tales (Dégh 1943), Lajos Ámi 26 heroine and 58 hero tales (Erdész 1968). This conforms with the international distribution in the AaTh index. Alessandro Falassi's description of a storytelling event at a Tuscan veglia further weakens the exclusivity of female hero tales as Frauenmärchen. In the company of adults and children, feminine tales (AaTh 333, 403, 440, 510A and 510B in three versions) were recited by two women, a man, and a grandson (Falassi 1980: 30–70).

(b) In general terms, Schwankenerzähler are held to be men (Neumann 1964: 91–102); nevertheless, female work and leisure groups enjoy as much joking as their male counterparts. Male village jokesters have a choice of sexual jests at their disposal to entertain and tease young married women, while older women spice dull manual work by exchanging dirty jokes among themselves. Except for jokes told by extraordinary women of comic talent (O. Nagy 1978: 475–557), however, the feminine Schwank repertoire is what Ágnes Kovács characterizes as "girl-raising tales" (Sebestyén 1979: I, 366), passed from woman to woman in the family. As a child, M. Fábián was often instructed by her relatives with didactic tales for young girls: "Mind you, the same thing might happen to you" (Kovács 1980: 377), and women at evening gatherings often request some of their favorite pieces (Dégh 1969/1989: 316, 320–321). These themes are more variable locally than AaTh numbers would suggest, satirizing bad conduct of newlywed women and girls of marriageable age. The targets of ridicule are laziness combined with ignorance of feminine duties (AaTh 822, 902, 1371), stubbornness (1365), vanity (902), bad manners (1458), gossipiness (1381 D), stupidity (1387, 1450), and bodily defect (1456, 1457). By their very nature, these stories can easily be adjusted to local events and are open to improvization.

(c) Narratives of a personal nature, featured in terms of life history episodes or current experience accounts, belong to the contemporary interests of folk narrativists. Earlier, though, more attention was paid to the experience stories of mobile men than homebound women; and except for solicited autobiographies, or analytic reconstruction of life histories of outstanding personalities (Pentikäinen 1978), little is known about this most functional, spontaneous female form. Personal stories began to attract attention when post World War II industrial growth forced rural women out of their villages in search of jobs elsewhere. It was found that peasant women released from household obligations easily adjusted their narrative competence to absorb new experiences. Some women, inspired traditional storytellers among them, developed new repertoires of personal experience accounts drawn upon the most memorable events of their past everydays from childhood to adulthood, highlighting episodes of first love and family life; they also drew upon new adventures experienced during migration and work (Dobos 1962, 1978, 1981). The audience – work and leisure companions, likewise displaced from their hometowns – shared in the exchange of life experiences, satisfying their need to express the longing for their lost homes, their desire to integrate into a new group, and the need for cultural learning and entertainment. Similar narratives have also resulted from other types of temporary or permanent detachment (Tolksdorf 1980), employment in other countries, and emigration in modern urban America. Closely related to the upsurge of the Feminist Movement in recent years, women's associations have emerged as political action groups for women's rights. These groups have developed their specific "collaborative" folk narratives, a new brand of women-stories declaring women's claims in the public arena. Susan Kalčik (1975: 3–11) describes a unique genre developed in conversation at consciousness-raising rap-group sessions. Other female conversational storytelling appears to be less organized but nevertheless spontaneously therapeutic, such as rape stories circulated among the abused who seek solace in each other's company. Within the broad category of crime narratives, on the basis of 400 items collected from women in Brooklyn, Eleanor Wachs (1988) gave a detailed account of the nature of stories told by victims of mugging, rape, and robbery as a shared "warning system" among women.

Evidently, women's Märchen cannot be defined simply by relating to one type of tale told by women to other women. It must be considered a mutable concept, subject to change in time and space. Researchers analyzing the Märchen repertoire of traditional peasant women saw the feminine nature of the Märchen not so much in the choice of themes but in the stylistic featuring of their stories. When Asadowskij spoke of the "besonderen Eigenschaften der Weiblichen Volksdichtung," he meant "die liebevolle Schilderung des eigene weiblichen Lebens . . . in den von Frauen erzählten Märchen sich die Herrschaft des Gefühlvollen Tones geltend macht" (1926: 61). With reference to earlier Russian collectors, Onchukov also observes that "women have their own 'womanish' ancient tales . . . in relating any tale, a woman involuntarily reflects in it that which especially interests her, everything that touches her everyday mode of life. The woman storyteller, relating a folk tale, among other things, always describes in detail and with special fondness the everyday life that she knows so well, as well as the life of a woman" (Sokolov 1938/1966: 414–415). Furthermore, "the special social and everyday conditions of the life of the woman . . . have placed their imprint on the tales which were related by women" (Sokolov 1938/1966: 416). It thus is not the preference for heroine tales that makes a Märchen a woman's Märchen but the elaboration, stressing the feminine point of view in any kind of Märchen. This has been illustrated by Asadowskij, discussing Winokurowa's narration; by Dégh (1969/1989: 208–211), discussing Mrs. Palkó; by Á. Kovács, comparing Mrs. Palkó and Mrs. Fábián's different ways to use and manipulate their life experiences in tale construction; and by Adams (1972), comparing Winokurowa and Palkó to Tzune Watanabe's featuring tales. By comparing versions of the same tale type told by men and women, we may be able to isolate specific male and female subtypes of the same tale, as has been suggested by El-Shamy and Swahn (El-Shamy 1979, 1984; Swahn 1955). The Snake Prince tale as analyzed in chapter 9 of this book exemplifies how the gender of the teller may be decisive of the variant's orientation.

MANIPULATION OF PERSONAL EXPERIENCE

Before raising questions concerning a theory of the personal experience narrative, thought must be given to its definition. This is not easy since there is hardly any definition, classificatory principle, or specificity pertaining to the whole or constituent areas of the discipline of folklore. Not one single law explains the emergence, persistence, and decline of folklore products without calling for reservation because of numerous nonfitting exceptions. In view of the increasing numbers of exceptions, one begins to doubt the possibility of imposing any kind of law. This is nothing new. It has been noted by others, particularly those who recognized the arbitrariness of genre terminology constructed by scholars (not the folk) and applied liberally to fit diverse purposes of analysis and interpretation. (Abrahams 1976a; Austerlitz 1976; Ben-Amos, 1976; Honko 1976; Voigt 1976.)

None of our definitions seems to be entirely satisfactory, not even the most venerable and unanimously cited can go without some qualifying, cautionary note such as "mostly," "usually," or "generally." Those who enjoy cynical word-play and paradoxicalness could conclude that the only dependable law of folklore is that it is not governed by a dependable law. Perhaps the only method to find an acceptable compromise of terms and definitions would be to obtain an oversized bag in which there would be sufficient room for all related concepts and synonyms to be placed and from which those found dated, useless, or mistakenly included, could be easily eliminated. In other words, instead of narrowing and tightening, categories should be broadened. Such housecleaning is necessary because the themes, perspectives, existential conditions, and above all, the vehicles of folklore, are radically changing almost daily and leading us to new discoveries. As Henry Glassie has suggested to us, "Each generation must state the definition anew, debate it afresh, because folklore's definition is not factual and free of value. Its virtue is that it is charged with values, saturated with opinions . . . " (Glassie 1983: 128.)

Burdened with these thoughts, let us turn to the problem-complex surrounding a currently much-talked-about genre: the personal experience narrative. If it is much talked about among folklorists, there must be a reason. After all, academic fashions, like other cultural phenomena, are products of pertinent social conditions. With the personal story, as currently conceived, we face major problems of definition, description, and delimitation. At this time, only thematic categories are available for scrutiny, and there is little else to examine for a more comprehensive orientation into essentials. While classifications are suggested, and thematic categories and subcategories are identified by scholars in ever increasing number, the whole domain of experience accounts remains vast and uncharted.

The degree and nature of interest in personal narratives is indicative of developmental phases of folk narrative study and also the increasing willingness of folklorists to adapt theories and methods developed by other disciplines in their approach to narration. At an early stage of theorizing in the late 1920s and 1930s, scholars with literary training and interest in the arts aimed at basic or simplex forms of expression in order to trace the evolution of complex oral and literary narratives. Wesselski, Peuckert, and von Sydow traced the generic background of the recognized traditional genres – the *Märchen*, the *Schwank*, and the *Sage*. (Wesselski 1931; Peuckert 1965, von Sydow 1934). They identified such elementary forms of prose communication as *Bericht*, *Memorate*, *Chronikat*, *Geschichte*, and *Mitteilung*, "by which a *Geschehen* turns into a *Geschichte*" (Peuckert 1965: 11). Jolles' morphological-behavioral system of genre-hierarchy, on the other hand, isolated *Memorabile* and *Kasus* as similarly factual accounts. The reinterpretations and refinements of Jolles' *Einfache Formen* (Jolles 1930) and Berendsohn's *Grundformen* (Berendsohn 1921) culminated in Bausinger's triplicate scheme of the "everyday narration" as basic story formulations of the happy, the hilarious, and the dismal, leading to the three basic structures of Märchen, Schwank, and Sage (Bausinger 1958, 1975). At the same time, Ranke's interpretation of Jolles' *Geistesbeschäftigung* concept (K. Ranke 1967a, 1967b) led to the generalization of the "homo narrans" idea and the notion of narration as an elementary need. Ranke's comparative analysis of genre-relationship has shown that isolation of pure genres is impossible and that in real life, neatly defined genre characteristics merge and overlap; everyday facts of personal nature may be significant ingredients in all fictional forms. While Ranke shows transition of themes from one genre into the other due to change of cultural conditions and environments (Ranke 1965), concepts of "mixed" or "transitional" forms are being introduced by theorists disturbed by the accumulation of unclassifiable stories by a new generation of fieldwork-based scholars. The fragility of genre-boundaries and the profusion of narratives that do not fit the conven-

ient archival drawers labeled to fit established terminology were documented at the Liblice conference of the International Society for Folk
Narrative Research in 1966, and yielded more subcategories and transitory forms (*Fabula* 1967: 9). Nevertheless, the measuring scale
remained the Märchen, the Schwank, and the Sage, whether they are
regarded as antecedents of these analytically established genres or as
substitutes and equivalents, emerging in the post-peasant period and
reflective of new conditions in the industrial world.

There was never any doubt that the exchange of personal, or personalized experiences of a factual nature, always existed. Early written
and printed documents: diaries, memoirs, private letters, chronicles,
sermons, and newspapers attest to the fact that narration as a social
act contained more "everyday stories about sickness and death" than
elaborate folktales (Schenda 1983: 27). Occasionally folklore collectors
have also noticed these casual and trivial reflections of folk mentality
without finding them worthy of publication along with the classic
forms they were determined to find.

The turning of the tide occurred during the postwar period as a
result of certain factors: (1) in the new era, ethnographic fieldworkers
were unsuccessful in locating archaic folktales in the modernizing
villages and resorted to the more informal "true stories," so named
by the bearers. Notwithstanding diversity as to the meaning of "true"
as objectively or subjectively factual, the social relevance of this class
of stories attracted scholarly concern; (2) a new interest in the social
function of narrating discovered the storytelling event as a complex
forum of exchange between tellers and listeners, producing great
diversity in genres; (3) recognition of the ethnographic value of personal accounts containing information on the life, work, and worldview of individuals and the community prompted fieldworkers to
systematically record autobiographical stories. (Röhrich 1976b: 1080–
1085; Dégh 1975; Schenda 1981a, Schenda and Böckli 1982; Lehmann
1983.) Realizing the fact that one finds only what one is looking for,
predictable genre-orientation was replaced by open-minded search
for any form of narrative communication. Histories of life experiences,
people's own reflections on experienced reality, and reaction to
encountering, creating, and being affected by events became inexhaustible sources of folklore in the modern world.

A fairly recent interest on the part of social scientists in the culture
of the "everyday" is broadening the scope of research into the genre
while also complicating the quest for an unambiguous definition of
the personal narrative. "Everyday" is defined in terms of being the
opposite of holiday, contrasting the ordinary, monotonous, bleak routine work and life with the extraordinary, different, joyful, festive,

recreational and adventurous (Greverus 1978: 93–94). In this dichotomy, everyday has no culture, creativity, or celebration in traditional
frames. Nevertheless, narration is viewed as an everyday activity.
"Personal narratives are situated communications and, as such, provide compelling evidence of the versatility of the genre as well as the
centrality of 'storying' in everyday life," observes Robinson (1981: 85).
According to Konrad Ehlich, the everyday of narrating is a real everyday, in which narrating is one among the many activities performed.
Ability of telling everyday stories was not suppressed by literary
(professional) recounting for a passive audience (Ehlich 1980: 18–21).
The elevated artistry of Märchen, Schwank, and Sage is contrasted to
everyday stories by Bausinger as Sunday wear is to everyday clothing
(Bausinger 1975: 323).

It is now time to ask, what are the common defining elements of
the personal experience narrative identified by the following terms:
*alltägliches Erzählen, Alltagsgespräch, Alltagsgeschichte, Bericht, Chronikat,
eigene Erlebnisse im Alltag, Erinnerungsgeschichte,* folk talk, *Gegenwär-
tiges Erzählen, Geschichten aus eigenes Leben, Geschichte, Geschehen,*
informal narrative, life history narrative, life story, memorate, *Mitteilung, parole quotidienne,* personal story, personal narrative, spontaneous experience story, story, and true story? More could be added to
this rather monotonous and repetitious list of variables signifying that
the story in question emerges from an everyday segment of someone's
life. In addition, there is a large body of literature on this genre stressing functional, performative, formal, stylistic, or content features of
specific subclasses, applying linguistic, semiotic, literary, psychological, sociological, anthropological analyses and interpretations ably
summarized by Sandra Dolby-Stahl (1985: 65–67).

The most consistent elements are contained in Dolby-Stahl's succinct
definition: "The personal narrative is a prose narrative relating a personal experience; it is usually told in first person and its content is
nontraditional" (Stahl 1977: 20; 1989: 12). There may be additional
elements, such as that the genre is "unartistic" and treats "facts as
facts." However, I will limit the discussion to the "personal," "prose,"
and "nontraditional" aspects in order to consider their implications,
meaning, and validity.

"Personal" appears twice in the definition. Who is the person who
narrates and why is the narrative personal? Memorate analysts have
yielded to a more liberal interpretation of the concept. Accordingly,
personal does not necessarily mean the first teller's experience but
also includes that of a second, third or later member of the chain of
tradition-bearers (Pentikäinen 1970c: 112–115). By the reference: "I
heard it from the friend of a friend," the story retains its personal

nature as much as if the teller had stated: "This happened to me." This liberty is welcome. However, the narrative may not be the third or fourth but the umpteenth link in the first-person style narrative which may have been switched into the third-person form for some reason, only to resume its original first-person form at a later date because the teller chooses to identify with the account. Thus, first person as experiencer cannot be a firm element of the definition. Dolby-Stahl herself cautions that the telling is "usually" and not in all cases in the first person. In her latest essay on the personal story, she restates and further elaborates her understanding of the "personal" component. In search of the meaning created by the raconteur addressing the listener, Dolby-Stahl builds on her own field observation and stresses the private and intimate nature of the genre, using the term "personalore" (Dolby-Stahl 1985: 59–60). This limitation to discrete family and close-knit friendship circles certainly fits Virtanen's case of telling spontaneous paranormal experience accounts as expressions of the teller's emotional ties to the addressees (Virtanen 1976: 340; 1990). But even other sensitive themes do not allow us to generalize. In her discussion of "bereavement stories," Gillian Bennett points out that "they are capable of showing the ways that private experience is shaped into public form, through the means of traditional attitudes and expectations" (1985: 96). Most articulate tellers of their life experiences that I have met enjoyed sharing well-rehearsed episodes with the public. However, a Canadian couple confided details of their tragic life to me, a complete stranger, just because I happened to be a passerby who could not commit indiscretion and betray confidentiality (Dégh 1975: 158–222). They thus felt safe to release their burden, as if they had given it to the wind. Another woman volunteered to record her life history on a tape, alone, addressing me as if I were present. At the end, she authorized me to publish it in whatever form I chose. These examples show that creative individuals may also tell intimate stories to complete strangers.

"The personal narrative is a prose narrative." Again, in most cases this is so: but in others, it is not. In my study of rural American and Canadian ethnics (Dégh 1979b), I have encountered lengthy personal stories in verse form. An informant recited his poem about his wife's adulterous affairs with her boarders and the painful divorce proceedings in strictly personal terms. Another informant related his exploits as a hobo in ballad form, and a third man related a vision he saw in his dream, again in verse form, and recorded it in his diary. What aim would be served by denying the status of personal narrative to these rather awkward poems which are as detailed and banal, so to say prosaic, as an everyday event?

"Its content is nontraditional," or "its traditionality is limited to the context of personal or private history which spawned it" (Dolby-Stahl 1985: 48), is the most problematic element in the definition. To tackle it is to open a can of worms. Is there anything in this world without tradition? By definition, nontraditional things could not have happened to anyone (Dégh and Vázsonyi 1974). Is emigration to America traditional? The immigrant went through immigration procedures: his papers were examined; his health checked, as is customary. But was all this new to him? By no means; he had heard about it from generations of earlier emigrants' families in his hometown. Is then his story personal or traditional? The personal part of his account can hardly be regarded as a genre-identifier. . . . "But there was a fat lady on the boat whose denture fell into the soup . . ." Is this personal or traditional? If we consider only unprecedented occurrences as constituents of personal narratives whose content lacks traditionality, the concept of personal narrative must be limited to a very few exceptions which would be difficult to recognize as a distinct genre. To justify the specification of the "nontraditional," not only the content but the manner of its telling should also be unique – never heard before. But then, how can we call this product folklore? Perhaps we can, since there are two other folklore attributes – oral telling and the nonprofessional status of the teller. But are these really *sine qua non* attributes?

Personal stories are often told by professional authors, politicians and entertainers, alternately using oral, written, and other media of communication. Ultimately, the definition of the personal narrative has to drop the "nontraditional" element.

But even if content could avoid being traditional or conventional, its textual, situational, and social context, its manifest performance in performer-audience interaction cannot. The telling of a personal narrative is a social act, as is any other narration. It has its rules and strategies. Tellers reach their appropriate audience using communal (traditional) means to succeed in their goal: personal gratification, identity presentation, status elevation, or other, while the listener's expectation is met. This means that the manner of telling, the choice of words, phraseology, stylistic turns, emphases, must follow the local etiquette, fitting the referential framework shaped by tradition.

What then is nontraditionality? Albrecht Lehmann suggests that the successful everyday story must combine traditional and individual elements (Lehmann 1983: 32), while Oldrich Sirovátka diminishes the uniqueness of the personal story by saying that individuals elaborate on a theme which corresponds to communal lives and expresses communal views by using communal means (1975: 664). The appeal of these stories is that they highlight episodes of the average lifespan

which could have happened to anyone. The history of life may appear
as a multiepisodic narrative, though more often than not it serves as
a frame to any mono- or multiepisodic story. We may go so far as to
say that tradition contributes effectively to individual life histories
and that people themselves adjust their lives to fit the model set by tradition.

Bausinger has observed lately that purely personal unique motifs
were always a part of any traditional narration, and the degree of
their significance depends on the function of the context (1980: 274).
With personal experience stories, the function of the social context is
crucial.

There is no way to classify the kinds of experience stories even in
thematic terms. It is enough to say that any part of life history, from
cradle to grave, including great turning points or insignificant details
in family life, occupation, entertainment, celebration, religion, crisis,
illness, and travel, may provide material for elaboration into a narrative. It has been noted that in the traditional patriarchal society, men's
stories focused on experiences faraway – military service, labor migration, whereas women's concerns were homebound – love, marriage,
family life. In modern urban society, specific narrational exchanges
have been reported from occupational, religious, social and political
action support groups oriented toward particular goals. As byproducts
of these associations, the most varied materials have been collected:
conversion stories of newborn Christians; birthing stories of expectant
parents; narratives of consciousness-raising rap-sessions of gays and
lesbians, and of women; victims of crime and urban violence; therapeutic confessional products of people in interactional analysis; and so
on, and so forth. The open-endedness of categories has been observed
by Charles Keil, " . . . there is an academic imperialist tendency at
work here, a mystification that turns every group's expressive life
and every individual's personal experience narrative into grist for
the folklorist's mill. Even if we calculate just one personal experience
narrative per person, the planet's proven narrative reserves are stag-
gering, and the folklore empire will never suffer a scarcity of
resources" (1979: 209).

As I have already noted, researchers of the everyday stress that by
their very nature, personal stories are factual, unremarkable, unartistic
and average, just as is the talent of their tellers (Lehmann 1983: 62–
63; Jeggle 1978: 81–126). The evidence, however, shows just the opposite. Published material presents a great variety of highly elaborate
stories about narrow escape, disaster, embarrassment, improbable or
fateful coincidence, absurd, humorous, mystic, supernatural, and horrible encounters that approximate the realm of fiction. Highlights of

Everyman's life appear as moments of reversal from monotony and drudgery. They are cherished as precious gems which help people capture public attention for a moment and attain a sense of importance. Indeed, their authors regard their creations with pride. With personal stories the teller not only claims authorship but also plays the role of participant and eventually that of the central hero entering the limelight for the moment.

Evidently, much depends on the personal skill of the everyday raconteur. In many cultures, polished speech is a learned skill – a part of enculturation and much appreciated (Bauman and Sherzer 1974; Bauman 1977). But not everyone is articulate and able to tell about even the most memorable event in his life. Others can turn an unremarkable incident into a fascinating story. People may be appreciated by their peers because of one single account which, by constant repetition, undergoes individual sharpening and refinement with the help of community suggestions. My query after traditional tellers of magic tales often ended in the home of the performer of one single personal story which was highly acclaimed. Besides one-story people, however, there are truly recognized masters who can create fascinating narratives from everyday local events, and are as popular as specialists of Aarne-Thompson type tales. It seems this contingent is an integral part of individual and community repertoires.

Julia Tóth became a personal storyteller when she moved from her native village to the industrial city. Her new audience did not appreciate her traditional magic tales. Nevertheless, everyone liked her touching stories about her sufferings as an orphan, hard labor on the farm, forbidden love, forced marriage to an older man (Dobos 1962, 1978: 175, 200) which she narrated to the other women with whom she shared residence in the company's dormitory. The Transylvanian Klára Györi won high community esteem for her more than four hundred humorous narratives about factual village affairs involving herself and others (O. Nagy 1978: 474–558). Emigrants who were able to tell their autobiographies and polished their accounts by repeated telling (as did retired farmer Joe Tarr) developed a patterned, formulaic structure framed by a conceptual projection of accomplished life (Dégh 1975). Pierre Crépeau has argued that the immigrant life history follows the cultural transformation of the teller in terms of rites of passage in which temporal progress provides coordinating structure to the content (1978). There is no justification for separating personal experience stories from other forms of narration to which they are symbiotically related. Orienting ourselves to group-life, the function, the purpose, and the meaning of storytelling (and not to singled-out items) may be considered as witness depositions (Loftus 1979). The stories contain a reasonably reliable confession or information of at least one, not necessarily first-hand and not necessarily immediate, eyewitness. This makes them so valuable to social history and sociology (Kohli 1978; Schütz and Luckmann 1984). The structure and patterning of these narratives is determined by the laws, customs and cultural knowledge of society (someone's own life or that of someone else). We have all heard people say, "My life is like a novel," meaning really that their experiences could provide raw materials for a novel. But in fact, an extraordinary life history need not be written: it also can be told or even acted out (Carr 1986: 61). Those who are familiar with the works of Erving Goffman on everyday behavior and presentation of self (1959, 1974), or who have read James Peacock's article on "life as narrative" (1969) and the theory of ostension (Dégh and Vázsonyi 1983: 5– 34), will know that life is a work of art – a narrative, a drama, or an imitation – in itself. It is traditional, not only by the biological rule of inheritance but also because what took place, what the narrator-creator-imitator did, was possible only within the existing and folkloristically sanctioned system of social conventions.

THE LEGEND TELLER

Legend tellers do not exist in the same sense as tale tellers, epic singers, balladeers, dancers, or musicians. There is no stage for them and no social recognition for their recital skill. Legend is not considered an art of personal inspiration to be performed for the enjoyment of an attentive audience, but rather it is a specific area of knowledge on which the narrator can offer information. It is not the story that counts, but the message it conveys. The message shapes the story in a way that makes sense and attracts interest.

As early as 1937, Matthias Zender made some insightful comments concerning legend tellers, regarded by villagers as curious characters, "originals." Only a few people can tell fifty to two hundred tales, but almost everyone knows several legends. Zender distinguished people who cannot narrate but are bearers of beliefs and are important as believing listeners. Equally important are the doubters, who have never seen anything supernatural and would deny even natural facts that border on the incredible. Legend tellers, continues Zender, are sensitive and extremely serious people who while narrating relive their experience, making it realistic and persuasive to the listener. The legend teller may be knowledgeable and experienced, he/she may be a recognized expert in certain areas and develop a large repertoire of legends, but he may also gain respect for being involved in one single but overpowering legendary event that affected or completely trans-formed his life. This person keeps repeating (and varying) his narrative throughout life. He may be an accidental recipient of an experience, a victim or beneficiary of circumstances, or he may be an active seeker, a hereditary bearer of a message. (Zender 1937.)

It often happens that the legend teller becomes initiated into one area of extranormal knowledge through one crucial experience and thereafter remains a lifelong specialist, associating with people of similar interests. An example here is Ruth Loux, an Indianapolis real estate agent and specialist in PSI. Her encounter with an illiterate Tennessee mountain woman who occasionally turned herself into the sixteen-year-old intellectual Little Joe determined her future (McNeil 1971: 216–245). Support groups arise among those who share out-of-

body experiences, life-after-life travel, UFO abduction, or spirit possession experiences. Because of the marketability of such phenomena,
some individuals take the limelight in star roles on television programs
and in the popular press. There is no limit to the possibilities. Some
inspired legend tellers – or psychics – may become authorities, police
consultants in difficult criminal cases, and advisors to powerful politicians having to make important decisions. "An astrologer dictating
the President's schedule?" was a scandalous disclosure of Nancy Reagan's long-term reliance on heavenly signs and the advice of psychic
Joan Quigley (*Time*, 1988, May 5). Mrs. Reagan did not do anything
unusual. She followed the time-honored tradition that has guided
emperors and war lords through the ages. From classical times, the
oracle of Dodona and the haruspices of Rome enjoyed privileges and
exercised considerable power, just as latter-day prophets, clairvoyants
and fortune tellers influenced such famous and infamous rulers as
Czar Nicholas II, Stalin, and Hitler in modern times.

Investigators of ghostly disturbances have risen to prominence in
the same way. They call themselves ghost hunters, ghost busters –
the superb Hollywood farce *Ghostbusters*, with actors Bill Murray and
Dan Ackroyd, enhanced the ambiguous social position of haunted
house exorcists in America – or exorcists, depending on which occult
establishment they belong to and how they interpret the role that
gave them notoriety through their services to homeowners. Books,
movies, public lectures, interviews in the press, on radio and television
highlight their experience, lending credibility to basic haunted house
legends. Ed and Lorraine Warren, the ghost hunters of the famous
demon-possessed Amityville house (Brittle 1980), and Hans Holzer,
the occult scientist and ghost tracer (Holzer 1973, 1974), are among
the most successful in communicating traditional legends through
several media.

Nevertheless, the majority of those who encounter legend experiences remain private, withdrawn, within the family. There is a large
contingent of individuals with legendary experience who are invisible
because they have no way of finding compassionate friends ready to
listen to them. Such were the people – men and women, old, middle-
aged and young – who responded to my inquiry on haunted houses
in Indiana. My correspondents, who generously assisted in my attempt
to map the locations of haunted places, gave me detailed ghost stories
(some with the floor plan of their own residences to help me place
the apparitions) but did not sign their names or give me their addresses
for fear of embarrassing their families or of publicizing a secret that
would render the haunted house impossible to sell. The letter writers,
some of whom recorded their stories and sent me the tapes in an

envelope, were genuine legend tellers but socially isolated misfits, delighted with the opportunity to go public and reveal their secret without causing any harm and being identified. Many of them felt it important to warn the public about the supernatural invaders from whom they had suffered so much torture. One young wife wrote:

> Dear Linda Dégh, I read the writeups in the *Elkhart Truth* about ghosts in the Elkhart area. Reading about this had made me uneasy. It has been on my mind and I lost two nights' sleep. For years I have been troubled over the experience I had . . . I feel if I could tell the citizens of Elkhart I might get some psychological relief . . .

After eleven handwritten pages containing seven legends, she ends with this:

> Some people in Elkhart know that house I'm talking about. But for my family's sake I can't reveal our names. But for the Elkhart residents ghosts are not a laughing matter. Be careful. Some are not friendly. Amen. Thank you. P.S. If you drive down US 20 West at night and no one is home and the light is on upstairs you have seen what others have seen. And parents please listen to your children. For I still have scars from it. The last line I wrote is for the public, if you ever print this somewhere.

Despite the high probability that the majority of legend-bearers may remain invisible, the visible minority is strong, vocal, and sufficiently organized to influence the social consciousness of modern society and to draw attention to its propositions. Proponents of legendary subjects and beliefs tend to establish their own institutions. Groups are formed, bringing together tellers and audiences. In other words, practitioners and disciples together form a bond to communicate, circulate, and perpetuate the main message of their legend. Members of the group (prophets, gurus, charismatic leaders of clubs, sects and cults, shamans, witches, spiritualists, psychics and their followers, activists and representatives) establish the appropriate social context and networks, and stabilize the text while they also multiply it by continued retellings. Together they help it to spectacular proliferation and variation. Occult institutions infiltrate our world, educate the general public; their terms and concepts become commonplaces and banalities even among the least interested.

The legend teller is telling the truth. He does not confabulate and is careful not to deviate from the facts he knows. He gives all the supporting information he can find to satisfy his audience's curiosity. He depends on the support of audience members who are also familiar with the case and are ready to assist with additional information. Since the narrative is situated in the real world, in human time, and is about events involving everyday people and capable of happening to anyone, it is both valuable and helpful in dealing with the dangers of human life.

Recognized traditional Märchen-tellers conscious of their craft are careful to distinguish legends from tales. The legends they tell appear to be marginal in their repertoire, as first-hand learned true events that may be part of their life history. They know that their audience appreciates high-flying fantasy in the formulation of tales but that the audience would not tolerate artistic embroidery of the truth they believe in. It is one thing to tell a Märchen, to enjoy the liberty of creating a fictitious story, and another thing to tell a legend and reproduce reality. None of the village storytellers I personally knew included their legends in their repertoires. On the whole, these legends were more autobiographical, not for public storytelling. The legend tellers do not make the story; the story makes them, and this is why they are appreciated by their community. But this description does not necessarily fit the urban storytellers who do not have the innate sense of mission and responsibility to their community or *ad hoc* audience. The legend they choose to tell is just another piece to add to their *oeuvre*. Without personal commitment to a cultural tradition, they create their repertoire for public (stage) performance or publication. As entertainers, they are guided by their own tastes; they liberally select from traditional and literary sources, usually recasting legends into a romantic fairytale format.

But whether the legend teller is dedicated and self-consciously public, or hidden and private, anyone may tell a legend occasionally, without particular personal interest or involvement, merely repeating something heard. As a matter of fact, there is hardly anyone who has never experienced the air of legend and the compulsion to tell about it to someone. The "numinous" touch (Otto), the "sublogical" disposition (Marót), the Ergriffenheit (Burkhardt, Jung), or the simple "déja vu" are very common factors that may explain the legend teller's creativity, even if he or she is only an occasional translator of one single experience into a legend. The real legend teller, however, is a believer, actively attracted to the uncanny, outrageous, mystic, absurd, anomalous phenomena erupting unexpectedly from normal everyday situations, forcefully telling him or her that things in this world may not be as expected.

Janet Bevis, a remarkable young woman with a large repertoire of precognitive experiences, told me how she was initiated into the realm of hidden, supernatural dimensions, and how she reacted to her visions, the topic of her legends. Born and raised in a midwest American farming community, she inherited the local belief in the supernatural. Her grandmother was a bloodstopper and a healer, and her mother had premonitions; she also spoke to the dead. Her first experience occurred at fourteen, when a red light streamed toward her in the backyard, without a sound. Then shortly afterwards, she saw a star approaching and disappearing. Four years later, a cigar-shaped UFO flew over while she was driving home from work. Her fourth encounter with the unknown came while she was at home in bed with her two younger sisters. She was reading a book about the supernatural when the light began to flicker, and little toys fell off the shelf. She did not think much about it because her mother used to tell her about "strange things," so she believed it was nothing extraordinary. "At a young age, you believe in ghosts and stuff – it's exciting, you laugh, joke about it with your friends. I thought perceptions, visions are fun, I was ambitious. I wanted to become famous as a schoolgirl. Being different from others." Her fifth supernatural experience happened when she gave birth to her first child: Jesus appeared to tell her that her baby, who was injured at birth, would go to heaven and everything would be okay. Later on, she was exposed to both negative and positive encounters. She was haunted and tormented by the evil spirit of a witch and revenants, while she also enjoyed developing the skill of precognition. "When things began to happen to me I felt, this is a gift from God. I can help by knowing what's gonna happen." Watching TV gameshows, she knew the answers before anybody else; at a football game she stopped the rival team from winning; she could mentally force a slow car to get out of her way, and her kids cheered: "Wow, Mom, that's neat, you can do this. I can't believe it. Man, that's neat!" She told herself: "Keep tryin' Jan, keep tryin'. Keep working these powers, the sooner you get these powers perfected, the sooner you will be able to save someone from dying . . . a real purpose in my life . . . this is it, this is really it. God's given me the special gift . . . I was just overwhelmed and excited inside . . ." But when she envisioned disasters, she could not stop them from happening and this had really crushed her. Like many other inspired legend tellers, Janet struggles between what her urban-industrial environment taught her as normal and rational, and what she perceives as being based on her family heritage. Torn between certainty and doubt, she fears for her sanity. She ponders the likelihood of accounts she hears during her daily activities or what she experiences personally in a vision or a dream, and she formulates an opinion ready to express when the occasion arises. But when she finds no support from her pastor and her husband, she is desperate.

. . . I got to the point where I thought that I'm really going to die. The pressure, the weight on my chest, the depression was spreading more rapidly . . . I said to my husband . . . to please help me. I said: "You got to help me. I'm losing my mind, I can't handle it anymore, I don't know what to do, I'm losing my mind." And he said: "Jan, you're right, you're losing your mind . . . you are the most craziest person I met in my life." I said: "Bill, I'm not crazy, you heard the crashings, you witnessed the things that happened . . ." He said: "Yes, you're a witch, you're crazy, you're nuts . . . you need psychological help . . ." (Recorded in 1987, a section from a long autobiographical narrative.)

If legend tellers can step out of isolation and find their allies, they usually appear as undecided seekers, curious about proof and disproof. Feeling the urge to tell the story, they would submit their positions to debate. The experience is easy to view as not unique and not "unheard of." Nowadays anybody who reads the newspaper or watches television is educated in the occult and knows its terminology enough to qualify and place a vision in the context of "scientific" language, which is different from the traditional. When it occurs, the individual can feel comfort in experiencing something that others did and talked about. What he or she saw was not a spook but an astral body, an apparition, an earthbound spirit or a poltergeist; not a fireball, nor a spooklight, but a space alien or a UFO; and if persons could not catch their breath at night, they were possessed by earthbound spirits, not plagued by a nightmare or the Old Hag (Hufford 1982).

Institutions form around legendary messages and bring together kindred souls to give them comfort in association, raising their self-awareness and dignity. At weekend PSI encounters, regional conventions, and spiritualist retreats, one may meet representatives of diverse groups and take stock of the great diversity of legend tellers united by the common context of belief – in what? – not necessarily defined. The groups are presented by separate booths at the convention grounds, where one can chat with visitors, collect pamphlets, and meet initiates. It is an interesting crowd: professionals, amateurs, members, commited supporters, novices, and unaffiliated accidental guests with mild curiosity.

At a psychic fair in 1987, I talked with three people at the local cafeteria. Each belonged to a different legend conduit, although they had coffee together and listened to each other's stories with interest. All three spoke with confidence, adding their interpretations to assure me they were not amateurs. The language was professional, borrowed from reading in parapsychology and other esoteric fields. But they regarded their gift or knowledge not as that of professionals, whom they viewed critically because "they package their gift to fool others and make a profit of it."

Iris Murphy, 47, of Indianapolis, claims she has a well-developed second sight. She was born that way. She wears glasses because she does not look at people but into their souls and that scares them. When she was four she knew what was in the Christmas packages under the tree and what was going on. She had a vision when her best friend was in danger. She explained the nature of her expertise, without telling a story.

Machinist Jerry Teiffel, 62, of Connersville, Indiana, believes in UFO's.

The most unusual thing I ever saw was something that took place about four years ago. This thing I saw was just before dark, one summer evening, and where I live, is about a quarter of a mile from where my dad lives. And just before dark, the sun just went down and I went to my dad's house. And he was gone but my brother was there. And he was doing something with the tractor. And I just stood there in front of the house. We talked a little while. And my two sons came up on their bicycles. And we fooled around a little while, then we started to walk home, which is quite a while away. As we got to the house, there is a hayfield and there was a fence on each side. The field was not perfectly leveled, kind of sloping. And at that time of the day it's usually very quiet, you know, no wind blowing at all. And it was beginning to get dark. We walked over this field. There was a little mist of smoke, six inches in diameter across the field. Now, something had to pass over the field and we never did know what it was. In other words, we missed seeing something by possibly a minute. If we had come down, got away from the house a minute sooner, we would have seen what made the smoke. It looked like exhaust . . . You ever seen a small motorcycle when a boy takes off on it and leaves a trail of smoke behind it? That's what it looked like. Except it . . . on one side of the field. It was going perfectly horizontal, on one end of the field it is, some telephone wire, but on the other end of the field was high it was down within five feet on the ground. And the trail of smoke went over, over the fence, and right between a couple of trees. Now of course, we know . . .
(Did it smell?)
Ya, it had a smell like castor oil. Do you know how castor oil smells like? We've been to some car races, I suppose smells like castor oil. That's what it smells like. We did not hear any noise at all. All was a trail and the smoke, possibly exhaust, and we saw that. I mean we smelled the odor of castor oil. That's all. In other words . . .
(What did you say to each other when you saw it?)
We was . . . we was discussing this trail of smoke over there, we walked over in the field where it was and by the time we walked over, the smoke started to spread out. And we walked over these trees where this thing went under it, had to be pretty small however large it was because these trees were pretty close. Went over to see

it, maybe if it was a UFO, maybe some of the trees would have been burned, you know, passing through the land. We did not find any trace.

(At that time, did you know already that there are UFO's?)

Oh ya, ya, a lot of other people had been seeing them. Like I said, all we saw is that smoke before dark. If the wind had blown we probably would not have seen it. I thought there must be something to it. I knew it could not be a motorcycle thing in the air. It couldn't be that. No other explanation, something had to make the smoke, something had to make the smell. We didn't know what it was. I was very disappointed. I would certainly like to know what that was.

(Do you believe in other unexplainable things?)

Ya, I'm not too much interested in ghost stories and mediums and things like that but there's many other things. ESP. I'm much interested.

(Did you have an experience?)

Yes, one fourteen years ago . . . (Another story followed.)

Don Worley (51, Noblesville), the third person in the group, specializes in ghost stories: "apparitions" as he calls ghosts. His account broadens our view of the legend complex related to the ritual visit of haunted bridges by young adults.

Don became interested in the ghost stories told (and experienced) by couples parked under the bridge and decided to investigate the truth behind them. A plumber by profession, he said this:

> I have this hobby. I am naturally curious and try to understand things. That's why I am interested in an apparition of someone. I find out who lived there, and a lot of things about life, see? I came into this hobby because these objects project light beams in the area. Lit up the whole cornfield and barn and everything . . . so I began to talk to people.

He talked to ten people who saw the ghosts, and he read newspapers about drownings thirty-three years back, in order to identify the earth-bound spirits and the connections between them. Finally, he went to see for himself.

> I live near this place and I have lots of time to track it down, to find out what the truth is. It's Dublin, Indiana, on Route 44, a bridge, a very spooky place . . . Three different couples parked at this really spooky-looking place, the Screaming Bridge they call it.[1] And then, this thing came around the headlights of the car, ran across the road, and what they saw was a skirt and a blouse and white glow, looked like hair or a scarf . . . One boy did not get to look because his girlfriend got scared and hollered, and he stepped on the gas and they left . . . I still did not believe in ghosts then really, you know, I had to see this myself. We went down there, me and my nephew, one night, and we parked there under the bridge. And I

seen . . . first . . . it was such a moonlit night. It was a bad night to watch for ghosts because it washed out lots of colors . . . About a half hour . . . hour later, I said to my nephew: "Jack, there's someone on the bridge." There was a figure there. Took a few steps, then hurried off the bridge in front of us. She had a skirt and a blouse on.

After talking to local people, Don found out who the restless revenant in skirt and blouse was: a girl named Jeanie. Under the care of a domineering sister who "chased off her boyfriend," she did not want to live, so she drowned herself. There was another "Jeanie's ghost" Don learned about from the locals: a little girl phantom, who in life saw an angel, predicting that she would die in childhood. The third "earthbound spirit" was a mother who drowned "because she lost her little girl in that car wreck at the roadside." Don ended our conversation by saying that "This is not folklore, this is fact, as many can testify." "I have good news for you," he added. "If Jeanie's ghost is there, I know who she is, then we all, like that, we all become spirits." Not many legend tellers make it as clear as Don that ghost stories are optimistic promises to mortals of eternal life. Said Don:

Earthbound spirirts are seen by psychics. I am as psychic as a fencepost . . . One lady came to my house with a problem – someone is looking from across when she is home alone at night. I found out, her husband is very jealous and she is psychic, so she picks up his thought when he is away. Once he touched her on the neck, that's when she went into hysterics. I investigated many things ever since.
(How do you investigate?)
I take the tape recorder, talk to many people, asking a lot of questions.
(Why do you do that?)
Look, I am fifty-one, I am not goin' to be here for long. I want to know the truth. Things that I can find out myself, not what I read in some book. That's why I've done this. I did not believe in haunts, but it fits right down there. I found out about an old haunted dresser that cracks and pops when anybody dies in that family since 1910. I believe the witness, an elderly lady that would not go tell me all this story for anything if it were not true . . . Did you read about poltergeists? You should talk to the lady who moved to seven homes, was haunted for fourteen years. She lives in Hamilton, Ohio. Course I can't give her address, I don't think she would be in the mood to talk to you.

Evidently, Don wants to be prepared for life after life.

Some go to religion – I was in church for seventeen years. I don't think that's wrong either but I go a little further than that . . . They stress what they want to stress, the Bible, the New Testament, but I want to know where I'm going.

(Do you believe in UFOs?)
I didn't see UFOs but my wife and daughter did, and they would
not lie to me. But I saw more, I was rewarded by seeing apparitions
we will be . . .

These excerpts from a much longer conversation show three types of
nonprofessional legend tellers who are actively seeking answers to
their particular experiences by going to occult meetings and by check-
ing out stories, almost as folklorists do. They contextualize their legends with as much precision as any traditional legend teller would.
They are proponents, participants in the legend conduit in search of
more understanding about the spirit world.

Once I spent a Sunday afternoon with an "occult-seeking" private
circle. As I was told, the house on the west side of Indianapolis where
the Psychic Holiday was held was recently exorcised. Members, with
heated zeal, narrated supernatural experiences. At the end, listening
to too many legends, beliefs, wisdoms and philosophy, I asked the
man who seemed to be the leader: "Could you please tell me what
it is you believe in?" "In everything," came the answer, "you name
it, and we believe it." This honest statement (later I heard it again
and again) should caution us that there are possibly fewer "things in
heaven and earth than are dreamt of" in the philosophy of a latter-
day Horatio. It seems more people's minds are *omni-credens* than we
imagine. Who opts for which legend-establishment, who wanders
from one to another, and who keeps allegiance to several can be
discerned from personal life histories and psychological personality
analyses. The bottom line is a question of belief.

This composite picture of the legend teller was drafted from bits
and pieces of current materials. The personality dedicated to legend
is actively present in all layers of modern society, and in its networks,
divided according to age, sex, and social, occupational, and recreational groups. The person chooses to listen to and pass on legends,
seeking out the appropriate conduit of people of the same mind (Dégh
1979a: 124–126). Although there is a clearly distinct repertoire carried
by the conduits of diverse groups within the social networks, these
repertoires are closely related and interdependent. With the aid of the
mass media, the legends spread as fast as news is aired, crossing all
boundaries, alternating channels of communication, mixing and merging stories, producing more and more variants at an increasing speed
by the innumerable nameless as well as identifiable legend tellers.
We cannot speak about the legend as an oral folklore genre anymore
because the coexistent vehicles of communication together shape
them. A new variant of the classic legend "The Vanishing Hitchhiker"
would be influenced by versions told orally, printed as a daily paper's

news item, a magazine short story, a parapsychological report in a popular science publication, a headline and feature story in a tabloid, played as a pre-adolescent girl's seance game, calling up "Mary" from the bathroom mirror, an actual visitation at the site of Mary's grave at Halloween, listening to the ballad version on a commercial phonograph record, or making drawings of the story as a school assignment.[2] In the past, we were too preoccupied with "genuine" "oral" texts and did not pay particular attention to the multimedia variants in the background of emergent texts. We cannot afford this shortsightedness anymore because a new version cannot be interpreted without the comparative and contrastive analysis of its predecessors in any possible manifestation. Legend tellers are not choosy about their packaging: the relevance and appeal of the message is what matters, not the trimmings.

Part Two

WORLDVIEW: BETWEEN FANTASY AND
REALITY

THE WORLD OF EUROPEAN MÄRCHEN-TELLERS

1.

At the age of 74, Mrs. Zsuzsanna Palkó, illiterate master storyteller (Dégh 1969/1989), encountered face-to face the world of fulfillment of her tales. As a recognized narrator of a traditional peasant community in a multiethnic environment, she often depicted the wonders experienced by her tale heroes, but her inspiration came from internal rather than external experience. One morning, though, Mrs. Palkó received a telegram notifying her that she had been granted the distinguished title of Master of Folk Arts by the Hungarian government and that she would be taken to Budapest by car for an official ceremony in her honor. Aunt Zsuzsa had never before received a telegram, but her tale heroes did. Her real-life connections with government agencies came by means of the village crier or the mail carrier who brought unpleasant and unappealable decrees, reminding her of her obligations toward superior powers, whereas kings and emperors in her tales proclaimed war and summoned members of their Parliaments by telegram. Mrs. Palkó had never ridden in a car. She traveled by wagon when she peddled cabbages, onions, and rugs or hauled timber with her sons; or she rode in flea-ridden boxcars crammed with job-seeking seasonal laborers. In her tale, however, it was the dragon who drove a car behind the fiery war-hammer he had flung ahead of him to signal his arrival to his wife.

When the lights of the approaching Hungarian capital appeared in the darkness of the night, the storyteller saw "myriads of stars that came down from the skies" to welcome her. She later saw the "miracles" of the city and identified lower-middle-class comfort with the wonders of the magic tale. The second-rate hotel in which she was put up was a "palace" in her eyes with crisp, dazzling-white bedding and a full-size mirror on the cupboard. Only shaving hand-mirrors were available at the general store in her village, and she was stunned by the sight of her own reflection because she had never seen herself in full. The walls of Fairy Elizabeth's castle, on the other hand, had been covered all over with mirrors. Likewise, mirrors lined the mangers of the millionaire factory owner's stable in her tale so that the horses would have better appetites from seeing reflected how the other horses ate. Her hotel room was on the fifth floor, the same height from which the princess watched her royal father hire the swineherd in the tale – how come there had been no elevator in the palace such as this? Mrs. Palkó had never seen one, and she rode up and down to see how this magic worked and how it would fit into the reality of the magic world of her tales. She walked the streets with great amazement, crossing the hanging chain-bridge arching over the Danube – very similar to the one Mrs. Palkó had described in a tale, about a bridge built overnight by the fairy wife of Fisherman Joe to fulfill the impossible command of their cruel landlord. Mrs. Palkó examined the high-rise houses and the public buildings of the city and thought she recognized in them the miraculous city of the tales. When she was taken on a sightseeing tour, she saw the Millenium Monument composed of the statues of the sacred medieval kings of Hungary. The gallery of armor-clad, helmeted heroes impressed her, especially those on horseback: they bore the symbols of royal power because they were closest to the image of the feudal ruler stereotyped in traditional magic tales.

The royal palace upon the hill, still like a gigantic ruin ten years after the war, looked down on the city. But for Mrs. Palkó it seemed the three-hundred-window golden palace of her tales had come true. "Does the king live here?" she asked respectfully. But the real highlight of her enchantment was at the House of Parliament where the celebration took place. Aunt Zsuzsa was given a pin and a document as well as money: she had never seen such a big sum before. She was honored with a reception and a buffet, and fine-looking ladies and gentlemen urged her to take from the goodies, but she could not swallow anything. The folks were "more like angels than people," and everybody was anxious to talk to her. The whole setup strikingly resembled the finale of wonder tales embroidered by Mrs. Palkó's artistic style. Newsmen were among the guests, and a broadcaster with a tape recorder asked her to tell a tale. She started one of her favorites for the "royal" audience. The situation reminded her of the one she recounted about: the slandered and banished queen returns disguised as servant girl and is asked to tell a tale at the spinning bee of the false queen. The experienced narrator was not annoyed when the listeners lost interest in her long story – the reporter ran out of tapes – she was used to varying degrees of interest in her own community and was overwhelmed with joy by being the focus of attention, even if only for a short while. In addition, Aunt Zsuzsa was eager to learn more of the Parliament which she had so often described in her tales as the scene of war declaration and the administration of justice, and the meeting place of kings, princes and high nobility. "Does the king work here?" she asked while closely examining the slender columns of the gracious Neo-Gothic building, the heavy deep-red velvet curtains, the huge silver candelabra, the sparkling crystal chandeliers and the precious gem-and-gold-studded decorations, treasures contributed by rulers through the ages. She did not expect to hear that there was no longer a king, that Hungary was a People's Republic under Communist dominance, governed by a presidential council: this news would have been meaningless to her. Lost in thoughts, Mrs. Palkó did not listen to people around her anymore; she was alone in the miraculous world of a reality of her own. Throughout her stay in the city, she identified her tale concepts in real life, matching reality against the background of a deeper, subjective truth. "This is where Little I Don't Know could have lived," she whispered. "His palace is just like the one in which King Lajos was reared. . . . and, oh yes, there is the telephone, like the one the palace guard had at the gate when he reported to the king that a guest was arriving, but he didn't know if it was an emperor or a king . . ." Mrs. Palkó actually found reinforcemenrt for her belief in the miraculous world of the tale by discovering and identifying experienced miracles of the city.

Not all Old World storytellers had the opportunity to directly experience the enchantments of the capital city as did Zsuzsanna Palkó, and not all were able to readily establish a link between the city and their tale universes. But Mrs. Palkó certainly was not the only Hungarian Märchen-teller who interpreted urban experiences in terms of peasant tales. This phenomenon was characteristic of East and Central European peasant narrators, for whom life of the real world was determined by their system of labor and struggle for basic subsistence, and for whom everything outside of the village everyday belonged to the extraordinary, magic tale-world. In the following pages, I will illustrate the dichotomy between the two worlds as shown by the balance of factual and symbolic ingredients constituting magic tales.

2.

The magic tale as known from field collections among European peasantries during the 19th and 20th centuries was shaped in oral tradition

by different classes of the agricultural population in varying degrees,
depending on their social conditions. This communal creation of the
European peasant folk reached its most polished form at the time the
feudal system was transformed by the advancement of capitalism.
The tale resisted the corrosive forces of social and economic change
and kept its popularity as long as traditional village conditions persisted. On the basis of earlier prose genres, literary adaptations, and
continuous retroaction with related epics, the folktale appeared as the
most representative narrative genre that appealed to its bearers even
when its themes seemed anachronistic to outsiders. Its artistic framework, style, well-balanced episodic structure and clear logic – that is,
all the known linguistic implements that make an exciting adventure
story – made it possible to construct and convey existential messages
otherwise not possible to express.

Peasant society in East Europe emerged as part-society, dependent
on the national elite (Redfield 1960; Wolf 1966; Potter, Diaz and Foster
1967); and its tale, in every respect, reveals this relationship. Themes,
images, characters, scenery, speech formulas and techniques of narration were set within the framework of normative interaction between
folk and elite, displaying the complexities and the hierarchical nature
of this relationship that erased traces of original authorship. The creative process of tale-formation, however, changed considerably due to
the interest of the elite, particularly when the discipline of folklore
emerged. Eighteenth-century romanticists discovered the tale as a
naive literary art, the God-given inspiration of the ignorant European
serf-peasant, the innocent agriculturist and critic of urban morals, and
publicized it reshaped in the fashionable Baroque style – as it should
have been, they thought, had the peasant had proper education. Following this literary sterilization of the tales of wet nurses and discharged soldiers, the Grimm brothers and their followers, for almost
a century, did exactly the same thing. Later on, folklore as an independent discipline was founded and began its career with the study of
the European Märchen, known at that time only in romanticized,
rewritten form as "communal art," separated from original authors:
the individual oral performers, makers of versions of traditional tales.
The early folklore schools investigated the origin and dissemination
of tale plots, not what they meant to the people who transmitted them;
thus, the texts used for cross-cultural-historical comparison were
abstracted, containing only the most common content elements, isolated from their social and cultural relationships.

European folktale scholars today can only retrospectively deduce
the processes of Märchen formation because reliable recordings before
traditional peasant conditions began to crumble are unavailable. Folk-

lorists had witnessed the passing of the magic tale, which was unable to accommodate ideas and expectations in the industrial age. It was to be expected that the tale would begin to decline first in the technologically advanced, urbanized countries of West Europe in the wake of the 20th century. Folklore genres have their own fates and life spans. While magic tales could not easily be adjusted to the urbanization of their natural environment, others – like jokes and anecdotes – were easily adapted. Under certain conditions, the ballad made a comeback under new impulses, whereas the legend lived on to experience a never-expected renaissance in the world of electronic communication. The hostility of an industrial lifestyle to the folktale was noted by Stith Thompson, who remarked that fairy tales did not cross the Ocean with the immigrants to North America. Indeed, those who carried their tales over could not find a suitable audience in the tenements of mining places, company towns, and factory settlements of urban America. The boarding house, the factory canteen and the saloon were no substitute for Old Country firesides, village pubs, spinneries, and lumberjack camps. If not for the impact of the booktales of the Grimm brothers and Andrew Lang, Disney cartoons, and commercial advertisements, tales would not be known in America at all.

The last resort of the peasant tale is in rural East Europe, where old-style agricultural conditions persisted until the end of World War II. Modernization of farm production came abruptly and administratively as part of the imposition of the Communist ruling system, not as a consequence of natural growth. Changing labor conditions, however, could not transform the traditional worldview and lifestyle of the people overnight. Even modern technology, which offered more comfortable living and working conditions – like electrification, fertilization, and inoculation of farm animals – met resistance and hostility on the part of peasants who trusted the routine of their ancestors and were suspicious of "blessings" from above. And even if farm machinery and new techniques were grudgingly accepted, and modern homes replaced open-chimneyed, mudwalled adobes in the course of time, a similar adjustment could not be made in people's minds. Peasant men and women who had reached maturity in the old system were unable to change their *Weltanschauung*, religious belief system and tale ideology. As long as the generations that lived under the old conditions survive, tales will still be told in East European villages. They will also be passed around within the peer group and eventually to children and grandchildren (Dobos 1962). Nevertheless, the generations born or raised in the new system will not be able to transmit the tale tradition to subsequent generations. There is a gap here for those who enjoy freedom of choice of career in a new urbanized-industrialized socioeconomic order. The message of the tale, remaining on the plane of obsolete peasant existence, slowly becomes irrelevant. In other words, the Märchen necessarily stays within the confines of traditional peasant culture, unable to compete with the multiple forms of entertainment – radio, TV, movies – replacing its function in post-peasant society.

One might raise the question: how did the tale survive for so long in peasant-based agricultural countries? How could it have kept its social prestige as the exclusive form of oral prose literature after its actual themes became hopelessly anachronistic even within the artistically crafted frame? If its fantastic and naive symbolism could retain its attraction and prolong its life in a system progressing toward the total destruction of old peasant values, why could it not find a form in which to survive? Had the underlying social reality of peasant life not changed for eight hundered years as much as it had changed in three recent decades? The answers lie within the cultural-historical relationship between folktales and society.

The East European tale dialect represents a specific regional redaction of the composite European form. This is largely due to continual cultural contacts and ethnic mergers between neighbor peoples who are often linked together by a common political-historical fate on the one hand, and a similar peasant social structure on the other. Hungary occupies the central area within the region, hence its tale corpus plays the role of a homogenizing cross-cultural link, offering a schoolbook example, a representative sample for the researcher. Ethnographers often stress that the Hungarian people are retaining their prehistoric Ugric-Turkic heritage, sandwiched between Slavs and Germans in the center of Europe. At the same time, its position also made Hungary a mediator of culture between East and West. This cultural blending can be seen in the coincidence of tale elements from the East and the West and can account for a remarkable wealth in magic tales. Some tales did not travel further in either direction, and several Western tale types acquired specific formulation in Hungary, retaining their acquired forms even after being adopted by East European neighbors.

Within the Hungarian language territory, most of the Märchen were collected from farm workers, the progeny of manorial serfs employed on the large estates of aristocrats, the gentry, or the Roman Catholic clergy, specifically in the northeast, east, and southeastern parts of the land. Standing on the lowest rung of the social ladder of peasant society, these farm workers shared their misery with ethnic minorities in the same region. They also shared with them their fascination for the miraculous world of magic tales. The contact zones of the border areas happened to be adjacent to regions of the neighboring countries

where peasant life was similar and the same tales were equally popular. The largely bilingual, or even trilingual, itinerant seasonal farm
laborers served on estates of lords in the Ukraine, Galicia, Romania,
or Hungary in turn. Their exchange resulted not only in the dissemination of Hungarian ethnic tale types but also in the enrichment of the
tale stock of such multi-ethnic areas as Moldavia, Transylvania, the
Subcarpathian Ukraine, and the East Slovakian region. Cross-cultural
ethnic tale studies convincingly showed the nature of Märchen adaptation among the peoples of East Europe and marked out the trends of
modifications resulting from ethnic diversity.

A case in point is the Hungarian ethnic tale "The Tree that Reached
to the Sky" (AaTh 468). It is by no means a unique story invented in
Hungary; it is a representative of common European collaboration.
The tale combines complete sequences of three well-known magic
tales: "Three Animals as Brothers-in-Law" 552A; "The Grateful Animals" 554; and "Ferdinand the True and Ferdinand the False" 531. The
tale also includes a number of more or less elaborate motifs. The
distinctive ethnic feature of this tale is in its frame: the hero climbs
up a high tree whose invisible top bears another world. This is where
he can pick the rejuvenating fruit for the sick king and this is where
he finds the stolen princess whom he rescues. This frame (the young-
ster's ascent and descent on the tree) has connections with the prehistoric shamanistic religion of ancient Hungarians and their linguistic
kindred; the motif of tree-climbing in order to communicate with
supernatural beings continued to exist as a folk religious motif in
Hungarian history, reinforcing the incident in the tale. The story is
evenly spread in all regions of Hungary and was adapted by German,
Slovak, Serbian, and Gypsy minorities as well as by the people of
proximate regions in Austria, Serbia, Romania and Slovakia, Ukraine
and Moldavia, but nowhere else. It is remarkable that the performance
of the climbing of the tree measured against the parallel timetable of
the growth of the crops from planting to harvesting by the young
hero was also adapted in most of the variants outside of Hungary.

Some tale plots are more suitable for accommodating actual concerns of the narrator than others. Folktale scholars in the past took it
for granted that the tale does not allow descriptive details on account
of the fast-moving action. We know now how untrue this is, having
learned more about the elaboration of plot and episode details from
narrators. The tale is not an impersonal account of events, lacking
emotional involvement and compassion on the part of tellers and their
audience. In fact, the realistic portrayal of situations, the narrator's
conscious use of his or her life's experiences, is an expected addition
to the objective and factual tale plot outline. This personalized elabora-

tion of the plot brings it closer to the audience and makes it viable and flexible. These passages, fillers between formulaic plot episodes, are improvized by the narrator. Not only are these contributions of individual narrators important in creating new personal, regional, and ethnic variants of tale types; they are an integral part of tale performance in traditional communities. The formation of the specific East-European redaction of three international tale types shows this variation as follows:

(1) The Aarne–Thompson index "The Three Stolen Princesses" (301) has two subtypes, while in East Europe five distinctive redactions can be identified through embellishments, multiplication of tests, trials and intrigues, description of antagonists, labor contract, and execution of chores: cleaning, herding, cooking, chopping wood, etc., taken from the storyteller's lived-through labor experience.

(2) The male-version of the Cinderella story, as identified by both Lajos Katona (1912) and Stith Thompson (1946), is a specific East European product composed of three familiar European types: "Cinderella (510), "Goldener" (314) and "I Don't Know" (532). The plot itself invites elaboration of situations to make them feasible and palatable for local audiences. The three-page storybook version that was read to Zsuzsa Palkó some thirty years earlier seems a dry abstract to her tape-recorded story which extended to thirty-six pages in print. She rehearsed this tale mostly at wakes where it took her all night to entertain the attendants. Her plot invites extension particularly in describing the dual personality of the hero: an innocently banished and victimized child and a trickster, a destructive *enfant terrible* (Görög et al. 1980: 13). The paradoxical character is a weakling, almost dull-witted, doing everything wrong out of pretense because he is actually a fearless warrior in hiding. Most of the details feature I Don't Know's execution of household duties and his senseless devastation of the master's property. This duality of character reflects perfectly the dichotomous worldview of the tale, leading up to resolution of the ambiguity of the hero's character and biography – he emerges as the redeemer. Narrators of this tale are at liberty to fit in their personal experiences; variants often feature domestic employment. Kitchens, service quarters and employers appear, and expert descriptions are given of bread-kneading, cooking, horse grooming, and the duties of a kitchen-help, turkey herder, gardener, and stable boy.

(3) The tale type 407B "The Devil's (Dead Man's) Mistress" is widely disseminated throughout East Europe. Rooted in vampire and revenant belief, very much alive particularly among East and South Slavs and Romanians, its lasting popularity can be attributed to the parallel coexistence of its legend version. The tale (fiction for its

bearers) is supported by the legend (true or not true to its bearers, but dealing with some question of reality). The story begins in a normal village scene, at a girl's spinnery, the place of courtship. The heroine, embarrassed for not having a date, unwittingly summons an evil spirit (or the devil himself), and is pursued and tortured by the suitor until the prince rescues her. The girl's journey to happiness begins on the village scene; she runs away for fear of the evil revenant; and the tale, well into the world of the tale, continues with a focus on escape from the returning dead, a common fear of villagers in East Europe.

3.

If peasant Märchen were developed from earlier oral and literary narrative forms, how far back can we reach? European ethnographers interested in the relatively self-contained peasant culture focused on conditions they could trace back to the turn of the century by systematically questioning members of the oldest living generation. Unfortunately, reaching back to the memory fragments of the elders does not help us pursue the magic tale as much as it helps cartographers or material culture specialists. As a matter of fact, already during the second half of the nineteenth century, collectors were tolling the bells over the vanishing of traditional folklore; the twenty-fourth hour had come, they warned: cities, railroads, factories, and enforced school education might soon devour what was left. Experience since then, however, has taught folklorists that folklore does not "die out" without a trace. There never was a stable, self-sufficient folk society that produced a perfect folk literature. Folklore was always a product of changing social conditions: as society changed, so did its folklore. Each epoch had its characteristic folklore that in time lost its significance and was replaced by other folklore more fitting in a new era. Thus the magic tale, like other folklore genres, made its career through different stages of development from inception to a peak and a decline. To intepret the magic tale as an expression of the European peasant, we have to reach back to the socioeconomic conditions underlying the world order presented in the tale.

Even a superficial glance will show that the scene of the magic tale narrated by a contemporary storyteller is set in the age of feudalism, regardless of its earlier or later formulation. Its best symbols were chosen from the properties of the feudal system, during which the tale obtained its essential shape that survived the abolition of serfdom. The feudal system persisted in East Europe at least a century after it was abolished in West Europe; and even afterwards, the liberated serf had no choice but to continue working on the estate of landowners under similar conditions until the end of World War II. This fact explains the stabilization of the feudal setting of magic tales.

Serfdom in the countries of agriculturally based and industrially underdeveloped East Europe was abolished between 1848 and 1864. After the legal liberation of serfs, an era of secondary serfdom began. Only the landed serf could benefit from liberation by his right to increase his land ownership through free enterprise. However, the great masses, manorial peasants, cotters and landless farmhands freed from legal bondage, lost the security enjoyed within the unjust feudal system. Although they could move freely, their chance of employment was uncertain, and they could no longer expect support from the lord and the manorial village community. At the same time, large estates remained the bases of the economic order because industrialization progressed slowly as the fundamentals of capitalism – roads, railroads, land drainage, industrial plants and towns – were in the process of planning. Construction opened job opportunities for the peasant man-power which had lost its means of living in the village. The new construction workers essentially remained peasants; their home base continued to be the village where they returned after working hours and where their families continued to live under the old rules, produc-ing household supplies in the old way. At the turn of the century, mining and manufacturing industry started to pick up. Skilled workers were imported from foreign countries, and unskilled labor became available for the liberated serfs. These proletariatized peasants, half-way between town and village, worked in season; when they were laid off, they returned to the village to earn their bread as harvesters on the estates.

Nevertheless, the peasant masses could not find jobs in industry. Those who possessed a few acres could not prosper and maintain their status as small holders because their land diminished in the hands of subsequent generations. Soon they went bankrupt in the new order and joined the steadily growing body of agrarian laborers that worked on the large estates, the homesteads of the nobility, lease-holders, and the clergy. Although the farmhand worked on contract with the estates and could legally move from one landlord to another, in practice this was impossible because the masters protected their interests against those who served them. The agricultural estate serv-ant had to maintain a humble attitude and put the services of his wife and offspring at the master's disposal for free in order to keep his job. Thus, the master and peasant relation remained serf-like. The peasant family was paid in kind and in shared crops, and its income was hardly enough for basic food supplies. The farm worker had to learn that this was his fate; nothing could be done about it. The irreconcilable opposition between lord and peasant is the order of the world, and it is the peasant who has to bend.

There were few ways to escape. There was religion: mystic, ecstatic sects proliferated as a last resort. Jehovah Witnesses, Nazarenes, Shakers, Fasters, Exorcizers, Seven-Day Adventists founded their local chapters. The members, without exception, were large-estate farmhands. One sect rooted out fruit trees to divert interest from earthly goods in the hope of gaining eternal happiness in Heaven. Profound religious zeal blended into the archaic system of folk belief that also was fundamental to the worldview of the Märchen, unaffected by enlightenment and popular education. For the lethargic, who lost hope of a rational solution, there was the miracle of the tale, in which the little swineherd could conquer the dragon, marry the daughter of the king, and become a king himself. Of course, one rational way to attempt an escape remained: emigration. Until governments curbed mass exodus, America was also a kind of "other world" where the poor might divert their destiny. Seventy-five percent of seasonal workers of the Upper Tisza region experienced this adventure but returned disillusioned. The 79-year-old Lajos Feka, whose tales I recorded in his home village in 1962, told a story about his trip – very similar to the adventures of a tale hero. He emigrated in 1909 and returned in 1914. For him, America floated on the ocean. When whales move in the water, the earth shakes, buildings collapse, and golden-haired mermaids come to the shores of New York City and sing to the people. This much remained of his attempted escape.

Hungarian students of peasant society described the agricultural laborer class as the largest and lowest of peasantry. Folklorist Gyula Ortutay characterized the ideology of this class as serf-like, meaning that for them "the order of social classes and power relations is final, unchangeable; the system of obligations, services and rights in their interrelations cannot be altered" (Ortutay 1972a). Studying storytellers and their tales, he concluded that "folktales show us most eloquently the definitive relationship between peasant culture and peasant existence," and that "present-day folktales reveal to us the consciousness of peasants." In his discussion of the personality of storyteller Mihály Fedics, Ortutay observes a combination of "the serf's ambiguity between subservience and rebellion" as manifested in Fedics's personal life as well as his tales. Fedics was a hired man all his life, deeply religious and a believer of supernatural power and magic knowledge. While humble and obedient, he also participated in peasant protests and walkouts. As he mentions in his life story, he even dared to beat up policemen. He spent eighteen months in America working in a factory, but this experience had completely slipped from his memory. Ortutay cites two tales representative of Fedics's serf-peasant attitude: the first is a version of AaTh 1000, "Anger Bargain"; the other is about a farmworker whom God favors more for his prayers than for his work on the landlord's estate. The magic tale, then, reflects the world-view of its bearers, peasants in the course of the late 19th to the late 20th century, when socioeconomic conditions anachronistically preserved labor relations of the patriarchal feudal system.

4.

The folklorist who makes his appearance on the main street of a Hungarian village, with his overnight bag, tape recorder and camera, has to push his bike through the hilly trails of the subsiding, sandy, wagon-wheel-worn, dirt road. After having walked six to twelve miles from the railway station to the place known to the area for its good storytellers, he or she will see nothing unusual. No swineherd is in sight on the nearby marshy pasture, playing his flute to make his pigs dance to cheer up the little princess who cannot laugh. No royal palace lies on the rocky hill above the village, and no dragon tries to steal the mid-summer sun that has just reached its noon position in the sky. No golden and silver forest lines the outskirts where the iron-nosed witch turns people into stone, nor does a magic talking filly await to be redeemed from the garbage pile from behind the stable. Except for the barefooted ragamuffins who follow the stranger on his or her stroll among the small thatched-roof adobe houses and who are to be his first contacts by posing for pictures, the place seems deserted. Except for the pounding of the laundry by some tattered women in the backyard and the distant hum of the thrashing machine, signaling that the men are at work in the fields, there is silence. The miraculous world of tales lives only in the minds of the people, stronger than reality itself. The stranger passing through will also become a part of this miraculous world. The community is deeply involved in tale fantasy. But not now; not in the busy season when they cannot afford to listen to tales without risking their subsistence. It is not easy for the folklorist – an idler among hard workers – to become accepted. Ortutay described his first face-to-face encounter with the villagers in 1933 with these words:

> There is deep suspicion and grave worry in the eyes of the peasant as he looks at me. The cow was wronged by the evil eye, the wheat

had been spoiled by rust, half of the potatoes are rotten. The woman is expecting. In the room with its stamped-dirt floor, an oppressive smell of sweat rises towards the ceiling. "Is it a song that the young gentleman wants? Whatever will the gentlefolk be wanting next?" The poor folklorist, who had imagined his summer days in such bright colors during the winter, crumpled in his chair. He looked at the picture of the Blessed Virgin smiling fixedly at him from the wall. He was silent and began to feel shame. Very deep shame.

Tales are told when they can be afforded. Village work parties at bean- or corn-shelling, spinning, or feather-stripping time, sweeten dull manual labor with the enchanting words of the storyteller. The men, home from the fields, relax on the porch with neighbors and exchange tales to forget worries and regain their energies, soul and body. During long winter nights, tales prosper among harvesters whose bread basket empties before the next harvest. Most poor people cannot stay in their village for the whole year. As sharecroppers, they move with their families to the farmstead of their employer. Opportunities for storytelling are given by a variety of communal works – in the fields: planting, gleaning, hoeing, pruning, digging and harvesting; in the barn: shelling beans, shucking corn; on the pasture: herding animals; in the stables: taking care of animals. And if work procedures are inappropriate for storytelling, tales flourish during the breaks and after working hours, following dinner, until people fall asleep. For fishermen, lumbermen, and herdsmen, far away from home and family, the tale was once the only diversion from everyday drudgery. Likewise, factory hands and construction workers, railroaders, and enlisted soldiers exchanged tales in their barracks after retiring. Others, like intinerant craftsmen, tailors, cobblers, tinkers, peddlers and beggars bargained for accommodations at peasant homes in exchange for their fireside entertainment: telling tales.

Our research shows that storytelling as a work-related activity is the art of poor peasants in East Europe. The village offers opportunities for the performance of other kinds of entertainments, but it does not allow enough time for group togetherness to unfold long magic tales as in isolated work camps outside the village. But the tales are imported to the villagers who learned to enjoy listening to them and who lived under conditions favorable to listening, learning, and refining tales. Without exception, known East European storytellers are poor people: house servants, farmhands, sharecroppers, vineyard, tobacco and melon-horticulturists, rangers, night watchmen, itinerant merchants, peddlers, beggars, construction workers, roadbuilders, miners, fishermen, lumbermen, herdsmen and the like. As a rule, they entertain their peers with tales. Members of other classes of peasantry do not share their interest. In fact, wealthy farmers do not tell magic tales.

Hungarian landed peasantry whose ancestors enjoyed communal and individual privileges during the feudal system belonged to the lesser nobility or the full-section owning, serf-farmer class and were later elevated to middle-class. However, they retained their peasant lifestyle – hard work and thrift for the sake of increasing land holdings, with a conscious pride of being peasant and an aspiration to move up and share in political power. Farmers did not attend the storytelling sessions of their day laborers, but with the jovial indulgence of masters in a patriarchal relationship, acknowledged their workers' "naive" pastimes. Their attitude was always characterized as sober, rational, no-nonsense, enlightened. Their par excellence folklore genre was the Schwank and historical legend; their concern was local and national history with a profound interest in the history in which their ancestors had played a role. They were the loyal guardians of customs and local rituals: baptisms, weddings, and burials were turning points for the display of wealth and power; and the preservation of traditional costumes meant maintenance of cultural identity. Well-to-do farmers did not care for magic tales; they denied having time to waste on such foolishness fit for children. In light of the farmer's year-round work rhythm, there was a strict schedule that could not be violated – it was regarded as immoral to idle when work had to be done. The farmer lived to increase his wealth; he had no time to travel: he stayed in the village, remained earthbound; his land was his world. Storytelling occasions of poor people were also governed by the farmer's ethic in that narration was permissible only at winter leisure time, at communal work when listening to stories helped people stay awake and work more, or during work breaks. Storytelling was strictly prohibited when the story could interfere with work.

The former nobleman and the former manorial serf retained fundamentally contrary attitudes towards the fantasy world of the tale, but unusual conditions that lead to a change of the social hierarchy do not cause immediate ideological change. When the Bucovina Székelys were relocated to West-Hungary in consequence of political events during World War II, poor sharecroppers with large families received handsome properties, while the powerful old landowners with no children at home were allotted only smaller plots. "Who were big in the Bucovina, are big now," said one of the storytellers, whereas the wife of a former farmhand expressed her joy over the change in a song:

Hálistennek megfordult a világ
Szegényekböl lesznek a jó gazdák.

(Thanks to God, the world has turned;
From poor people, big farmers have grown.)

And change indeed happened: the residents of the poor section of the Bucovina village who earned their living by seasonal work on manorial estates raised the prestige of storytelling. What they practiced at leisure in their tenements gained social significance in the village: storytelling became a preferred entertainment at wakes and other important social gatherings.

Why was the magic tale the classic genre of oral narration among the poor? Because its overt and convert content and messages were meaningful for them in many ways. Primarily, the tale is a career story of a single individual, a story of ascent from nothingness to power that anybody can attain. It is easy for the poor to identify himself with this character and to identify the tale hero's antagonists with his or her real-life antagonists. The conditions favorable to magic tales are poverty, oppression and backwardness, insufficient general education, and historical consciousness. Tales flourish among illiterates or semi-literates whose admirable ability to recall and orally compose declines with book education. Peasant tales also display an ignorance of history, geography, and natural science – what children learn in school. The philosophy, morality and religious belief, the concepts of what is right and wrong in tales, collide with what was taught in the village grade school. Justice obviously is on the side of the hero with whom the narrator and the tale-audience identify.

Since the time of Friederich von der Leyen (1911), many folklorists have said the tale is the wish fulfillment of poor peasants: daydreams coming true. It was also found that the tale conveys social criticism of social injustice and inequities between rich and poor, powerful and powerless, oppressor and oppressed; it speaks what otherwise cannot be expressed, and symbolically it destroys the unjust social order to the satisfaction of the poor.

The basic opposition set up by the magic tale functions as the core guideline and driving force of the heroic adventure for the bearers of the tale. But the narrative sequencing of pairs of oppositions in progression is not the invention of European peasants. Magic tales cannot be derived from social injustice alone; many psychological and physical features, individual dispositions and inequalities may contribute as much to the tale conflict as social differences. This fact is all the more true because many tale episodes – featuring sibling rivalry and conflicts of beauty vs. ugliness, luck vs. unluckiness, and cleverness vs. silliness – predate the feudalistic features of old-fashioned peasant society. Nevertheless, actors and circumstances of the feudal order work as perfect symbols in the tale mirroring peasant conditions.

5.

In its own terms, the magic tale tells about the humble hero's wanderings between two worlds. These two worlds represent two extremes: "our world," the world of joyless, hopeless, laborious everydays that is familiar in its realities as well as its unrealities to everyone; and "their world," that of the powerful, the happy, the rich. At one end is the village and at the other is the city. The narrative is built within the framework of the voyage of the hero from village reality to the desired reality of a projected world of hope – in Jolles's term, where the world is featured as it should be, following the rules of a naive morality (Jolles 1930: 241).

It is easy to follow the travel of the hero from the known to the imaginary world and to survey the important features and stations of his progress in showing how a bridge is built between the conflicting worlds as an ultimate goal of the genre. If the hero's career reflects the real and the imaginary life-span of the tale bearers, we can also understand the adventurous voyage between the worlds as a sequence of conflicting manifestations of these worlds. The ambiguity is always there from the beginning to the end, but on different levels and in different proportions. There is as much wonder in the presentation of the real world as there is reality in the world of fantasy.

The progressive plot of the Märchen is simple and clear. It begins in the village, the desolate place of sufferings, continues in the transitory world, becoming progressively more unreal, marked out by challenge and testing of character, and ends in the fantastic setting of fulfillment. In relation to details, however, it is hard to distinguish real from unreal – after all, the hero is a real human being and his negotiations are all realistic. The three worlds are depicted in the imagination of peasants and feature peasant concerns and existential problems in both factual and symbolic terms. The three worlds are well patterned and strikingly contrasted while not quite isolated from each other. Actors cross the boundaries of the different worlds without difficulty, and it is even possible that the worlds blend into each other.

The construction of the narrative of György Andrásfalvi's masterpiece version of the Twin Brothers tale (AaTh 303) is a model example of the (1) parallel, (2) transitional, and (3) contrasting worldviews as they occur in the subsequent stages of magic tales in general (Dégh 1960: 114–141; German translation Dégh 1962: 356–383). The account begins with a peasant couple gathering hemp on their plot while their only child sleeps in the shade. A strange thing happens: the couple finds two boys rather than just their son. This is not a tale miracle yet; the environment is the peasant world where such an extraordinary event is admissible. Like orderly villagers, the couple seeks help from the mayor to find the parents of the second child. No one claims him, so the two like identical twins are brought up together. They are fine boys – everything seems in order; but the mother cannot rest until she finds out which of the two is her real offspring. She consults a "wise woman," as any villager would, and is advised to perform an act of divination to find the answer. This still belongs to village routine. But the act of "witching" triggers the transition into the other world. The foundling (he is going to be the hero) learns his origin from his jealous brother and leaves home to try his luck. Here the story does not yet depart from the real environment; the leave is just temporary. The hero enters the service of a witch to acquire a magic horse and a sword: tools for heroic adventure. He gives his treasures to his brother and serves three more years for the same pay. He returns home to the family but is restless and leaves again, entrusting his life token – a knife driven into a tree stump – to his brother. He arrives at the royal city which is in mourning for the princesses taken by the dragon in exchange for water. The hero lodges at the goose pen of a poor widow outside the city and acts in a double role, changing his identity by the mere switching of costumes. He enters the service of the head-cook of the royal kitchen as kitchen help. He chops wood, fetches water from the well, scrubs floors and scours pots. Afterwards he goes to the old woman, dresses in his princely attire, saddles his horse, grabs his sword, kills the dragon and returns to the kitchen in his kitchen-help outfit before the princess he rescued returns to her father's palace. This dual performance represents two levels of simultaneous Märchen realities within the environment of the royal city. But this complex episode is not uncommon in related tales of lowly heroes and heroines. The outcome is obvious: the hero wins his reward. But his brother is still at home. Here the narrator inserts a flashback that reveals what induced the teller to share the heroic adventure. The boy at home helps in the communal building of a barn for a neighbor, and afterwards the participants celebrate with a dance party. This typical local custom of the narrator's home village is an excellent setting for the contrast between the real and the tale world. While the Gypsy band plays and the merrymaking is at its highest, the life token in the tree trunk starts to bleed, whereupon the second boy puts on his hero's outfit, saddles the horse and takes to the road to rescue his brother. His voyage is similar but shorter and ends with his marriage to the second princess. The wedding reunites the conflicting worlds: the parents move to the royal town where the twin brothers share in ruling the two kingdoms they have freed.

6.

Within the frame of the action, several key features enhance the feudal-patriarchal atmosphere of magic tales – too many to discuss in detail, but some examples will suffice to illustrate the point. The paraphernalia, accessories, properties, social types and relationships between people recall medieval conditions and provide for the necessary distance, the otherworldliness that attracts the tale audience. In addition to its established content episodes, the tale describes scenes, landscapes, cities, buildings, the looks of actors and their costumes with traditional formulas, not the narrator's own images. Dialogues that characterize the speakers are formulaic as much as the description of the beauty of the princess and the hideousness of the monster. Beauty and goodness, evil and ugliness are convenient bedfellows. When I asked fisherman János Nagy, after his thorough, almost passionate characterization of the wife-snatching seven-headed monster Hollófer-nyiges (assumably from the biblical Holofernes), I asked him for more detail: how were its heads placed on one neck? How could it eat lead-dumplings with fork and knife? How was it able to live a family life? These answers embarrassed the respected storyteller. It turned out that he never thought of visualizing the images of his stories: he simply used and embellished the formula. The miner Joe Minárcsik was defensive when I asked about how could the manikin wrap his seven-times-seven league long beard around his waist. "I saw it like now," he said, using the closing formula to discourage my curiosity. "This is how I heard it." Yes, indeed, storytellers respect their teachers and do not question their formulas. It was exceptional that Zsuzsanna Palkó identified her formulaic tale scenery and heroes in Budapest, the city she had never seen before, as she tried to establish a link between them and the reality of the two worlds of the tale.

The use of costumes and props in magic tales calls to mind the staging of a theatrical play; the stereotyped action and actors and the artistic transposition of reality are the limelight of the stage. The outward appearance signals identity, and switching costumes means a change of status: in medieval times people's attire marked their status, occupation, and age. In the tale, the life history of a hero is told in stages of transformations into different identities, often not in the real sense (humans into animals, plants, or objects) but by simply putting on another dress. The ash-girl, Cinderella, the Little Goose-Girl, Fleaskin, turns herself into a sparkling beauty; Little I Don't Know appears as a brave in copper, silver, and gold uniform defeating the dragon while posing by day as a turkey herder, dirty and smelly with a tripe hiding his golden hair. He also makes the princess lovesick when he enters the king's dance or the Sunday church service in his princely outfit. The dressing-up scene for the final showdown at the king's palace gives the imaginative narrator plenty of opportunity to embroider details. The bridal gown of the princess, the radiant attire of the hero from gold-spurred boots to gilded royal headwear, the diamond-studded saddle of the horses and the red velvet-lined coach display the deep impression of traditional images of royal splendor. The tale about the Clever Peasant Girl (AaTh 875) shows the real significance of dressing up. In Péter Pandur's version, the prince intro- duces the herdsman's daughter to his father, requesting that he approve their marriage. "No, under no condition," he replies. "What do you think? To marry the worm of the earth? Get out of here and take her away; her head does not fit the crown." But the prince does not give up. He summons the chambermaid and his butler, sends them to the store to buy royal garments and jewelry for his bride. "The chambermaid dressed up the cattleman's daughter, who now looked like the queen of seven kingdoms." As she appeared before the king again, the old man jumped from his throne in enchantment: "You see, my son, this girl suits you; this is the one I like. Come my dear, let me kiss you." Young Julia Puskás concluded her tale about the Soldier Girl (AaTh 884B) – the story of the banished wife who defeats the enemy and saves the life of her royal husband in solder's uniform – with the following comment: "From that time on, she ruled because he almost lost the country to the enemy and became just a bum."

Another characteristic feudal element of the magic tale is its social and human relationships. Not only does a strong hierarchy govern the relationship between the ruler and the ruled, the monarch and his subjects, there is also a rigid power-submission relationship between the different classes, depending on rank and economic status. The poor peasants, merchants, and craftsmen display obligation and humility towards the wealthy, as do low-ranking officials to their superiors. On top of the power structure is the king, an absolute ruler, punishing and rewarding subjects whose lives are in his hands, as shown in the rhythmic, formulaic address of a king by the hired hand

(hero): "Mighty king, I submit my life and my death to your disposal"
("Felséges királyom, életem, halálom kezedbe ajánlom"). When the
king hires the lowly hero for a herding job, he warns him: "If you
succeed, my daughter and half of my kingdom will be yours; but if
you fail, the hangman will take care of you." When a soldier reports
to the king that he has seen a duck turn into a fairy, the king replies:
"If you lie, I will have your head separated from your trunk. But if
you speak the truth, I will reward you." As in the Middle Ages, the
king in the tale can order the execution of his faithless wife, disobedient
daughter, treacherous brother, and betraying companions: he can
decide life or death. But not only is he an infallible and ruthless judge
of right and wrong, he is also a patriarch on fatherly terms with his
subjects. He himself hires and fires his house servants, herdsmen, and
seasonal laborers and is concerned with their welfare. He talks to
them like a jovial father, addresses them "dear Son," and is addressed
"my father, King." This cordial relationship is extended to the family
of the king and the servant. The royal family attends church services
with the servant, whose parents enjoy the king's support in need as
they also share his disgrace. Similar social ties control relationships
between employer and employee on the lower ranks in the tale hierarchy down to the classes within peasant society. As in other respects,
the *Weltanschauung* of the tale combines the feudal with the village
hierarchy: the image of the king corresponds to that of the rich farmer.

The same hierarchy regulates relationships within the Märchen family, peasant or otherwise. The father is the domestic equivalent of the
king: he has the power and authority to ordain the fate of his wife
and children just as the king ordains that of his subjects. The father
runs his household the way the king runs his kingdom. The father
negotiates marriage contracts for his sons and daughters according
to his interests. He tests their ability and courage and sends them on
dangerous missions. In the initial episode of a group of related hero
tales, the king tests the ability of his three sons who want to undertake
a task, and only the youngest proves to be competent. In one of János
Nagy's tales, the father slips into a bear's skin, and it is only the
youngest who does not run screamingly from the palace. In another
tale by József Fejes, the king flings his sword at each of his three sons
to see which one has the stamina to stand by and wait until his wrath
diminishes. The father can punish disobedient children by banishment
or disinheritance; he can torture and mutilate them or put them to
death. In a group of heroine tales (510B, 706, 707), the widowed king
wants to force his daughter into an incestuous union, and when she
flees, he makes all effort to find her and destroy her. The father's will
must be fulfilled even after his death; otherwise he will return as a

malevolent spectre. The father does not tolerate rivalry; he throws his only son into a dry well when the boy tells him about a dream he had – that he would become so great a man that his parents would hold a towel and a washbowl for him (AaTh 517). In Mrs. Palkó's version of type 450, the children run away because their father wants to eat them – having learned about the good taste of human flesh.

In this patriarchal family context, the wife does not fare better than the children. The girl is the prize of the hero – that is, the symbol of the real prize: the kingdom of her father. Her role ends here; she becomes a wife, a passive servant and blind executor of her husband's wishes. She desperately tries to defend and protect her children, but she usually fails, like the mother of the king in Mrs Palkó's version of type 706 who cannot prevent the expulsion of the queen with her two gold-haired sons. The wife is obligated to her husband even if he mistreats her. Adultery, even the slightest suspicion thereof, draws cruel punishment, banishment, torture, mutilation.

In this rigid patriarchal system of the tale, the fate of male hero and female heroine does not differ much. The division of labor in the peasant family assigns equal responsibilities to male and female children from an early age. In the family enterprise they have their important roles; they are responsible for herding, planting, picking, gleaning, doing household chores, and caring for smaller siblings. They mature into adulthood while enduring the same kinds of work and tests of abilities as the tale hero or heroine. The childhood of either the servant girl who steals the treasure of the witch (AaTh 328) or the swineherd who kills the dragon (AaTh 300) is the untold given in the biographical adventure story of both male and female heroes.

Tale society is basically agricultural, thus, occupation, duty, and socially valuable behavior must further activities that serve agricultural production. Young heroes and heroines are experienced in farmwork and their worth is measured according to the quality of their work. They are rewarded according to their thrift and industry and punished according to their failure in agriculturally important tasks. Like the marriageable village girl, the heroine of the tale must be healthy, strong, diligent, and thrifty so that the young couple can make a living. Laziness is regarded as the worst vice of Märchen characters, and is duly punished in tales. The services performed by the hero in the household of the king is identical with the household duties learned growing up in a peasant home. The hero and the heroine, on the road to a happy end, are hired on contract to a powerful boss. Skill in tending, grooming, grazing, and herding domestic animals is a prime virtue; by taking good care of livestock, they acquire experience and the friendship of magic helpers and magic objects whereby they can pass dangerous tests. The hard tests for combating adversaries are usually agricultural. In a particularly well-liked East European tale (465C), the lord gives impossible tasks to his serf because he wants to destroy him and take his fairy wife. In Joe Fejes's version, the lord orders the serf to plough down a rocky mountain, level it, plant wheat, grow it, harvest it, thrash it, grind it, make bread and have a freshly baked loaf on the table next morning. Likewise, the serf is ordered to plant grapes, tend them, make wine and have a bottleful on the master's table by morning. The third task is to clear the forest, chop the trees, make firewood and pile the dried logs up on front of the lord's house by the morning. Impalement or breaking on the wheel – the classic medieval modes of execution – are the punishments the serf may get if he cannot deliver.

In a number of tales, earning the "daily bread" is a matter of great concern. Sowing the grain, shielding the parcel of land with the sprouting wheat – meaningfully called *élet* (life) in Hungarian – from wind, hail, drought, frost, and rust, appear often in tales. In one story, the sons of a poor man must guard the wheatfield of their father and catch the thief, a fairy who steals the ears. In another, the ogre steals the Sun to kill the crops and starve people. The dragon ties up three winds but lets the northern wind blow and freeze the crops, forcing the king to give him his daughter. In realistic details, the narrator Lajos Molnár describes that by harvest time: the wheat would not yellow. "The king could not sleep. It was before harvest time, there was no wind and the wheat would not ripen. People could not see why, why is there no wind to ripen the wheat. They watch it today, they watch it tomorrow. They wonder, isn't it true, as the old people used to say it, that wheat ripens when the wind blows? But the corn also needed rain badly, it should have eared by now. But there was no wind to bring the blessing of rain . . . Fall came, they did not need to shell the corn, there were no ears. They could not sow because the earth was dry. Winter came – on St. Andrew's day there was so much frost that the potato froze in the clamp. The north wind blew; it was so cold that whoever had a dog carried it in his lap outside to have it bark. Only the king was not hungry. He still had wheat and corn from last year."

Harvesting on contract is also an important Märchen topic as creative narrators elaborate. The contexts of the international tale Anger Bargain (AaTh 1000) and Strong John (650) are particularly suitable for embroidery with real-life experiences of farmhands. These are, in fact, experience stories in which the tale action is not particularly eventful, and the stress is on labor relations. The shrewd sharecropper and sometimes his companion undertake a harvesting job on contract.

The master thinks he can get something for nothing, but he is out-witted; and the bargain ends with his losing everything he has. The opposition of employer and employee is present in all tales, but the explicit change from poverty and humility to wealth and power by naked force occurs only in this type family. "Father," asks the young enterpreneur before preparing himself to make a deal with a master, "have you always been so poor?" "Yes, my boy. I was born poor and have to die poor." In contrast, the son answers: "I have to work, father, to fight, so it will be easier to live."

Peasant misery is aptly described by many gifted narrators in the opening episode of their tales, as if they were pouring out all their complaints into one dramatic staging of the initial situation. The bleaker the poverty-stricken village, the more uplifting the journey of the hero. Does the Märchen remedy the injustices peasants had to endure? Ideally, the story corrects unfavorable rules of the existing order in favor of the tale audience. Reward and punishment occur in tales but not necessarily according to the official code of ethics. Rich and poor, master and peasant are opponents in the tale; and justice is served when the two trade places. This reversal has nothing to do with the character of the actors as in two variants of the same tale (AaTh 1536A) told by Péter Pandur and Zsuzsa Palkó, respectively. In the first, a starving peasant family adopts a smart orphan boy who systematically raids the pantry of the rich neighbor. As a result, the excessive number of children (thirty-six), die of overeating: the rich farmer is drained of his wealth and the poor becomes rich by virtue of having only one enterprising child. In the second variant, the loyal older brother inherits the fortune while the delinquent younger brother is excluded from the father's will. The young man systematic-ally empties the house of his brother pretending that the thief is the returning dead mother who cannot rest because she did not give her younger son his due share. Division of the property restores peace between the brothers. The ruthless moral of the tale is summarized by Pandur at the end of his tale: "The poor man made a great fortune and the rich farmer lost all his fortune and fell on evil days."

The basis of this tale-justice is deeply rooted in the existential prob-lem of old-fashioned peasant society: land-ownership for self-subsis-tent farming. To be farmers on their own and not to have to serve others made farm laborers cross the ocean and work in industrial mills twelve hours a day on a starvation diet until the money for a piece of land could be saved. The need to increase the farmland so that it could sustain the family led to systematic poisoning of old people with arsenic, painstakingly dissolved from flypaper and served in whiskey. To keep the farm from crumbling during the 1920s and the 1930s, peasants exercised birth control until whole communities died out; large farmhouses collapsed because no one remained to inherit them. To survive in traditional peasant society, caught halfway between truth and hope for a miracle, a rigid and ruthless law had to be enforced. This system of justice is mirrored in the dichotomous world of the magic tale.

7.

The magic tale can be studied from several points of view and can be conceptualized as the conduit that carries many meanings. Its sketchy outline invites artistic creativity, conscious and unconscious utterances as well as reflections of the narrator's personal ideas. My purposes were (1) to point out that the magic tale as a genre expresses individual and communal concerns of traditional peasant society, and (2) to show how the direct observation of tale communication and variation can reveal motivations and causes of social change. Tale motifs that feature real conditions and project an alien world from elements of experienced reality allow us to identify the genre as a heroic journey from the real world to the unreal world of fulfillment through the overcoming of dangerous obstacles. The plot structure accommodates the narrator's identification with the hero, even fosters an assumption of the heroic role and journeying with the hero. The magic tale is goal-oriented and satisfies its bearers because it fulfills the goal: to close the gap between the real and the unreal, between this world and the other, and to elevate the poor to power. To be sure, not all poor people – perhaps just one, who may be the storyteller him- or herself. The folktale hero, the poor servant boy, the goose girl, the simpleton third prince, scoffed at by his pompous brothers, and the exiled, mutilated wife – each reconciles the irreconcilable ambiguities between the two worlds.

Folklorists have studied the magic tale since the time of the Grimm brothers and have developed several methods and theories of approach for its exploration. Many questions have been asked: where did the Märchen originate, why is it so widespread and durable, why is it so stable and so variable? Does the tale tell something else than what it overtly tells, does it has a deeper meaning to our unconscious soul? What kept the feudal-patriarchal character of the tale persistent, why have peasantries developed this particular genre, why did it become the classic conduit of peasant complaint, and why does it disappear in the post-peasant era? Our ethnographic survey of the magic tale told by East Central European peasant storytellers during the last century gives some ideas about the close proximity of tale and experience. For the peasant, the magic tale is the symbolization of reality, the telling of one's life story in the language of enchantment.

Enchantment – dream fulfillment – is a need of everyone, and tales or tale equivalents appear in all cultures and all layers of society. Tales of some sort have always been used in preparing children for adult life. But is there a replacement for the peasant tale in modern urban society? Leaving the traditional form and the etiquette of face-to-face storytelling, is there a replacement for the lost art in the new environment? New media create their own vehicles to transmit traditional themes. Dime novels, cartoons, illustrated magazines, tabloids, movie and television plots often tell similar happy-end career-stories, constructed according to similar structures and patterns. Only the environment and the characters are different; and, to be sure, the storyteller is replaced by an invisible professional entertainer, feeding into a passive mass of recipients who absorb but do not germinate continuity of the peasant tale.

Trying to find continuity among peasant labor-force immigrants in the New World, I had to recognize that emigration terminated people's attraction to magic tales. Most of my informants could give valuable information about storytelling in their native village; they even mentioned tales they could vaguely remember. Detached from their home base, their acculturation had been completed in two steps. During the first, the rural-peasant lifestyle had been transformed into urban-industrial life; during the second, people from different regions of their old country united into national minority enclaves, surrounded by multiethnic settlements. In this situation, the immigrant generation retained its old peasant worldview but not its pertinent stock of tales. The narratives they created for themselves, though not transmitted to the first American-born generation, used concepts and images of the magic tale to interpret the miracles of urban-industrial magic in America. Unlike Mrs. Palkó, who walked in amazement for the first time in Budapest, the immigrants Mrs. Hévizi in Gary (Indiana) and Mr. Molnár in Toronto could not juxtapose concepts of the tale with their urban experiences. But in their artistic use of personal experiences – being treated to a meal in a fancy restaurant in Chicago, visiting the airport where a grandson had made his first flight, working as a maid at a millionaire's mansion, cooking in a Greek restaurant, tale-like accounts emerged. Television shows and magazine writing about Hollywood stars and beauty queens also featured tale-like stories; however, retired farmer János Albert of Kipling told me he watches TV movies regularly – but only the pictures, not the sound. Why not? "Because it bothers me. I do not understand what they are saying, but I feel good about seeing the beautiful people and the luxurious palaces, cars, and jewelry. So I can make up the story for myself." Thus, for the unadjusted immigrant generation, after sixty years of residency and accomplished affluence, traditional tale elements come back in a new context.

THE MAGIC TALE AND ITS MAGIC

There was a king called Amarasakti who ruled in peace and glory in the city of Mahilaropia. Only one sorrow spoiled his pleasure: his three sons did not want to be educated. Amarasakti summoned his wise men to seek their advice: how could the lazy princes quickly be taught the basis of *Niti* – the wise conduct of life? The counsellors agreed that it would take many years, unless Vishnusharman, the famous eighty-year-old Brahman, would help. It came to pass that the sage promised the king he would make the princes masters of the art of wise living within six months. If he failed the king could humiliate him by displaying "his Majestic bare bottom." Vishnusharman did not force the boys to learn grammar and read books about religion or the practical matters of everyday life. Instead he taught them eighty-six tales. This was how he fulfilled Amarasakti's wish and transformed the princes into wise men.

Panchatantra is a five-part work that contains Vishnusharman's stories within this frame tale. It is one of the earliest documents illustrating the notion running through scholarly study of the tale and its history,[1] that the tale has the power to mold human character – a conviction that has remained unchanged to this day.

The distinguished personalities – the *vanas vulgi fabulas* as the *Acta Sanctorum* calls them – who have given tales serious consideration, range from Herodotus, Plato, and Strabo to Jean Piaget (Piaget 1929), Charlotte Bühler (Bühler and Bilz 1961) and Bruno Bettelheim (Bettelheim 1976). Folktales are studied by students of comparative literature, religion, history of art, linguistics, anthropology[2] and folkloristics[3]. They are also analyzed by specialists in teaching, sociology, and psychology.[4] Their power has been analyzed and exploited by the church (Moser-Rath 1964) and even by the military. After the defeat of the Third Reich the Allies blamed Nazi bestiality on the influence of the tales of the Brothers Grimm, and it became illegal to publish them (Kamenetzky 1977: 168–178).

Attitudes have changed over the centuries; depending on the period and social class, they have ranged from disdain to reverence – but never indifference. The feudal elite feared the tale: they saw it as fomenting unrest among the peasants. So did the clergy, who thought the worldly happiness achieved by the hero of the tale might distract people from seeking happiness in heaven. Tales by expert storytellers served as diversion from everyday concerns for kings dosing off in their bedrooms just as for sharecroppers in their camps after the working hours. The telling of tales over thousand and one nights saved the life of the fictitious Queen Sheherazade in the literary story of the Arabian Nights. It earned a night's rest for Irish and Siberian wayfarers who told stories night after night and were accommodated at friendly farms in return for the entertainment they provided. Storytelling was a sacred ritual for Swedish gypsies, miracle-working magic for Romanian mountain shepherds, therapy for Athabascan Indians (Rooth 1976); it had a variety of different functions in other cultures, the tale itself remaining essentially the same.[5] The tale as we know it in the western world (or more accurately in its original homeland between Ireland and India, whence it was carried by waves of migration to other continents) is the most appropriate vehicle for conveying the essential messages of humanity. This fact is supported by the tale's variety of usage, degree of appreciation, antiquity, and wide dissemination. Its formal features, for example, context, narrative situation, audience response, method of telling, and so on, play a decisive part in determining the genre and help us to understand its effect and ultimate aim. Everyone knows that folktales begin with an unmistakable introductory formula. In languages examined by folklorists it appears something like "once upon a time" in English, "*es was einmal*" in German, "*il y avait une fois*" in French, "*era una volta*" in Italian, "*zhyl-byl*" in Russian, and "*egyszer volt*" in Hungarian (Bolte and Polívka 1918–1932: 13–15)

Although this convention, both as sign and stereotype, tells us that what follows happened some time ago, it indicates that the statement, and indeed the story itself, should not be taken at face value. This is more apparent in traditional folk culture, where master narrators use lengthy rhythmic runs to indicate that the tale they are telling is not true (Dégh 1944: 130–139). Even before the narrative begins, it is clear that to appreciate it one should be neither gullible not inflexibly agnostic, but rather cultivate a state of mind achieved by the "voluntary suspension of disbelief," as Coleridge so aptly phrased it. As a conventional formula, the introduction is intended to convey the notion that the story is both true and untrue. It is one of the most important and characteristic features distinguishing the folktale from related prose genres and is supported by other paralingual, kinesic, and proxemic signs.

Everyone, including nursery-school-age children, knows the way a story should be told, with crescendos and diminuendos, exaggerated onomatopoetic imitation and non-vocal signs, all making the clear statement: "Pay attention! A tale is being told." Formalities accompanying the tale-telling event resemble theatrical signs (Eco 1975: 34) surrounding a performance on the stage. The building it takes place in, the sounding of a gong, the switching-off of lights in the auditorium, the turning-on of theatrical (non-natural) lights, the raising of the curtain and other formalities – even the smell of the scenery – tell the audience that what they are watching is a play, a representation (Osolsobe 1971: 35), not the presentation of real people and real events. Signs preceding the accompanying storytelling – the tale signs – serve the purpose of making the fictitious nature of the story immediately recognizable and valid for the whole performance. They appeal to the senses and provide a feeling of relaxation. The audience knows what to expect: a wholesome adventure story with a predictably satisfying outcome. The tone of storytelling is so unique that it can be recognized even without understanding the words. In an early expressionist drama, Grandfather entertained his grandchildren with a tale they called Number Tale. It went like this: "one, two, three (slow recount), four, five, six . . . (pause) . . . seven, eight! (dramatically), nine, ten, eleven, twelve (mysteriously), thirteen, fourteen (defiantly) . . ." and so on. Believe it or not, no-one was bored. Reacting to the tone and in spite of the nonsensical text, the listeners became absorbed in the familiar recital of a traditional magic tale.

The many different techniques used for telling tales in a natural setting seem to indicate that the ritual of storytelling is almost as important as the text, symbolism, and meaning of the tale, which is rooted in the individual and collective subconscious. If, as I think, this supposition is true, it supports the contention that the tale and its form are a very successful folk product, polished and perfected over thousands of years and satisfying the desire for wish-fulfillment (the satisfaction of the desires of id, ego, and superego) in a discreet and disguised form. Anyone who listens to the tales after he has passed the magic-animistic age of childhood feels that the adventures, magic rescue, transformation, and well-earned victory of the hero are not genuine, that is, not completely true in the accepted sense but only "once upon a time," beyond the Seven Seas, in the world of the tale, where the characteristic *claire-obscure* sheds light on all that it wants to reveal, and hides all that it wants to conceal. And the listener, setting aside his suspicions, is able to experience the forbidden without the embarrassment he would feel if he had to admit that the tale, or even parts of it, concerned himself.

Anyone trying to analyze the form and content of the tale in terms of folklore, psychology, and sociology needs to realize that its seemingly surface features of form and style are in fact fundamental constituents. Apart from acting as stylistic formulas and introductory and closing cadences outside the action of the tale, the traditional stereotyped formulas, dialogue, description, characterization, and repetition within the text of the narrative act as tale-qualifiers. Indeed their rhythmic recurrence within the tale signifies that the narrative is unfolding and more is to come.

In popular usage the term "tale" covers the entire province of oral prose narrative.[6] In the same way, disciplines not committed to the accuracy of the folklorist label a variety of folk and nonfolk genres as "tales," including stories written by professional authors for children, to be told by mothers or read by themselves, even if they contain little which resembles a tale.[7] The separation of nontale narratives from the main stock of tales is necessary not because of professional pedantry but because they are related in terms of origin, age, purpose, function, form, and worldview. The only common denominator which seems to justify the blanket treatment of disparate genres is the fact that the word "tale" is related to the verbs "to tell" and "to talk." Most native systems of classification identify the tale and other prose forms with telling or talking because, like most folklore genres, they are, or might be, communicated orally in face-to-face contact, even if they are nowadays more and more often disseminated through other channels. But this in itself does not make everything that is orally narrated a tale.

Broader use of the term "tale" may be due to the influence of the Grimm collection *Kinder- und Hausmärchen* on the general reader. Nevertheless what the Grimms called *Märchen,* and what posterity more cautiously called *Gattung Grimm* (Jolles 1930: 219; Berendsohn 1921: 2), covers a wide variety of folktales and their subcategories, as well as folk narratives of a different kind. Among the two hundred and ten texts are animal fables, exempla, fabliaux, Christian legends about saints and miracles, etiological and mythic-demonic legends, tales about lying, jokes, anecdotes, chain-tales, catch-tales and horror stories, as well as what are known as *Märchen*, i.e., a lengthy and heroic adventurous journey from deprivation to fulfillment, through trial, danger, and suffering, acted out and counteracted with magic helpers and enemies.

A clear and unambiguous distinction between the genres of tale and nontale would be possible only by carefully defining each one. There have been many attempts to do this, none very satisfactory.[8] It is questionable whether, thanks to the lack of a fixed oral prose tradition, such a distinction could ever be made. But, apart form the difficulties of categorizing folklore prose, one has to remember that most artistic creations – including folklore – can be fully defined through themselves, by displaying the original object, almost like the scholars at Lagado's Grand Academy in Swift's *Gulliver's Travels* (often described as a children's tale), who did away with words and communicated by displaying things.

Even without a satisfactory definition we can identify the most representative, classical category identified in the Aarne–Thompson system "Ordinary Folk Tales" (Nos. 300–1199) and contrast it with the *Kontrastgattung* (Lüthi 1966: 22–48), the mythic-demonic legend. Both share a common stock of elements used to express entirely different points of view. Both are basic forms of oral prose fundamental to human expression.

This type of legend can often be distinguished from stories about the explanation of natural phenomena, or historic events and the deeds of famous people. They need to be separated from belief legends (*Sagen* – legends proper), which seldom deal with issues crucial to everyday events. They do not appear spontaneously in daily life but rather from time to time in connection with special events embodying the past and commemorating the concerns of past generations. This is why we call them inactive or extinct legends or defervescent legends because, like extinct volcanoes, they are not heated by life-giving warmth or strained by internal forces. Who wonders, or indeed cares, whether King Barbarossa still slumbers in his subterranean cave, or whether George Washington really chopped down his father's cherry tree; neither would have any effect on one's daily life (Dégh and Vázsonyi 1973: 8–11). On the other hand, the legend about the Hoohman who roams around to harm couples in the Lovers' Lane (Dégh 1968b), or about Resurrection Mary, the phantom hitch-hiker on the Chicago freeway, who might ask for a ride from any lone driver,[9] or about the spook in our bedroom closet are highly relevant to the world as we know it.

The active legend is based on vigorous and living belief. This does not mean that the tellers of such legends necessarily believe them, but rather that they must take up a stand for or against. The belief pattern is very broad and ranges from total acceptance to downright rejection. Taking sides is an inherent feature of the folk legend, for the tale does not require belief or disbelief in the ordinary sense of these words (Dégh and Vázsonyi 1976: 93–124). The legend states explicitly or implicitly that its message is, was, or can be believed. Someone, somewhere, some time ago believed in it, so it cannot be relegated to the "once upon a time" and "Never-Never Land" category.

If someone describes the appearance of a female ghost dressed in white in a moonlit cemetery, a case of clairvoyance, of telekinesis, or an encounter with Bigfoot, the listeners will have to take sides. One will say, "Yes, I believe it," another "No, I don't believe it" or, often, "I'm not sure if I should believe it." Any story of this kind, whether or not it is factually true, will make the narrator's position clear.

On the other hand, if we are told that "once upon a time" the kiss of the Prince woke Briar Rose from her deathlike slumber, the Frog was disenchanted by the princess and turned into a prince, or the swineherd cut off the seven heads of the dragon with one blow, then there is no need to take sides. Any discussion or elaboration of truth or untruth would seem absurd and contradict the role that society has assigned to the tale. Anyone trying to buy a round-trip ticket on a magic carpet will interest the psychiatrist as well as the folklorist, and anyone explaining to other adults that magic carpets do not exist as a means of public transport would provoke the same response.

A typical audience of adolescents and reasonably normal adults will adopt different attitudes towards the tale and the legend. The earthling who leaves behind everyday reality with its causal order of gravity, time, and space to take a short journey into the magic world of the tale, governed by one-dimensional magic rules (Lüthi 1966: 8–12) so different from ours, returns enriched by feelings of fulfillment, poetic gratification, and catharsis. The legend experience is quite different. Its magic captivates suddenly and unexpectedly. It penetrates everyday life, dividing the world into the profane and numinous. The legend tells us we can never be safe because extranormal powers may interfere with our lives at any time. The earth we know as our home is not entirely ours, the logic which guides our thinking may be uncertain or invalid; we cannot trust our senses, and even scientific instruments are unreliable. Conversely we have to believe incredible truths, masters we do not know, phenomena we cannot understand, and laws whose validity we cannot ascertain. These are the messages of the legends that are all around us in our present-day, urban-industrial world. They are told almost everywhere where people meet: in student halls or residences, at children's slumber parties, in factory cafeterias, hospital waiting rooms, old people's gatherings, and at church meetings, in complete contrast to the rational electronic age in which we live.

People are attracted and fascinated by the magic of the legend. They visit frightening places, haunted mansions, cemeteries, Halloween houses, and join in hunts for ghosts, vampires, and monsters. They learn new legends from cinema and TV films, cartoons, comic books, paperbacks, and sensational press reports of UFO landings, magic healing, activities of well-known clairvoyants, preachers and witches, and by purchasing mail-order talismans of Lady Luck and other occult props and potions through classified advertisements (Dégh and Vázsonyi 1979: 64–66; Snow 1979: 44–74).

If humans are visitors in the world of the *Märchen*, the legend is an illegal alien on earth, a malicious and hostile intruder. Perhaps horrified people should stage a walkout, carrying placards of Cinderella and Snow White and chanting "Dracula, go home!" But of course we know very well that the public would do exactly the opposite. It would be too much of a digression to quote all the polls taken from time to time by different institutions showing a steady increase of interest in the legend and its horrors. It will be enough if I quote my own findings from questionnaire-based research in which about one thousand individuals between the ages of 15 and 70, living throughout the United States, stated their knowledge and belief in current legends; many did not remember a single tale.[10] Nearly all those interviewed had visited frightening places in their neighborhood and many insisted that the experience had reinforced their belief. Beliefs are based on some kind of testimony, and those who hold them received their information directly or indirectly through a legend. From the folklorist's point of view, not only is every legend based on belief, each belief represents in itself the conclusion, compressed content, and summary of the legend underlying it (Dégh and Vázsonyi 1974: 239). The increase in beliefs, cults, and pseudo-science can in this sense be equated with the proliferation of legends.

Fluidity of form and flexibility of content mean the legend can adopt any unusual theme of current interest. The tale is a consistently structured story, triggered by some unpleasant event, and with a guaranteed happy ending (Sirovátka 1969: 330–331). It has to be told in full, from start to finish, since the constituent parts would not in themselves make sense. The legend, on the other hand, has no consistent form. It need not start at the beginning nor be told in full. It may be fragmented, even limited to one incident or reference that represents or serves as the whole. A legend may be hesitant, awkward, polished and at the same time highly subjective and emotional. It is a disturbing account of some experience over which teller and listener have no control. It signals danger and personal threat, making both teller and audience feel involved. The tale does not openly describe our own anxieties; the legend does. The tale cannot happen to us; the legend can.

Today the proliferation of legend narratives coincides and perhaps relates to the decrease in tales. Of course, media-oriented and mobile urban society cannot sustain the relationships needed for traditional storytelling. Ghost and horror-story collections outnumber storybooks on the American market, and consequently the modern American reader does not know more that ten or twelve magic tales – mostly those popularized by animated films and TV shows.[11] Paradoxically, however, this scarcity does not mean that the images in the stories, and their magic, have been greatly curtailed. Magic, enchantment, impossibility changing into possibility, sudden and unexpected pleasant quirks of chance, justice triumphing over injustice, the attainment of simple, everlasting happiness, the fulfillment that is not so much concrete individual tales as the tale itself in abstract – all demonstrate that the object of suspended disbelief has not lost its power. We are witnessing a phenomenon of tale dissemination which seems, in effect, to be following Ricardo's classic rule that the rapid circulation of a little money produces the same inflationary effect as the slow circulation of a lot of currency. Fragments of magic tales – typical incidents, images, figures and formulas – reassemble like debris left after an explosion, to fit essential needs adjusted to contemporary society on the basis of a common understanding of what they represent and symbolize, and live on as strongly as ever. The Frog becomes a Prince, Jack in the Beanstalk, the Little Goose Girl, the Lazy Spinning Girl, Rumpelstiltskin, the Wicked Stepmother, the Seven Dwarfs, the Spirit in the Bottle, the Fountain of Youth, magic mirrors and wands, Cinderella's slipper, talking horses and birds, Kind and Unkind Girls, the Enchanted Castle, and the Youth Who Learned What Fear Is: the whole magical *Landschaft* (Peuckert 1965: 69) is part of our thought processes, and we encounter the familiar signs in many different forms. We see the magic of the tale in plots of romantic novels that we like to call tale equivalents (Bausinger 1971: 235–237) because their structure, forms, and themes resemble the adventure plot of the magic tale (a cowboy rescues a kidnap victim and marries the millionaire's daughter, or a poor office girl marries the boss) in variants to be found in the media, e.g., puppet plays, musicals, cartoons, and commercial advertisements,[12] as well as in stylistic phrases and metaphors. If it was the Grimms who spread magic tales throughout the world, Walt Disney stereotyped roles from everyday life after the characters in folk tales (Stone 1978).

The modern world is filled with the unreality of the legend masquerading as reality and its aggressive magic which becomes part of life, creating a feeling of numinosity without promise of relief. Humans, striving to attain harmony, do not reject out of hand the satisfying magic of the tale which provides that needed sense of relief. The magic of the legend introduces the world of unreality to reality and makes one doubt the rationale accepted by society. But it does not make it clear that it approximates to some other social consensus in place of rationality. In this sense the legend is the genre of irrationality whereas the tale, which expects listeners not to confuse its magic laws with reality, represents rationality. If the legend posits a gloomy and alarming question, the tale provides a comforting, reassuring and uplifting answer.

THE APPROACH TO WORLDVIEW
IN FOLK NARRATIVE STUDY

Description, definition, delimitation, and clarification of the subject and the objectives of disciplines in the humanities – folkloristics among them – is a constant concern. There are no established facts that satisfy all seekers, there are no theories that cannot be challenged – not only because human conditions change and what was true yesterday may be untrue tomorrow but mainly because the scientific observers themselves create the subject of their study and reach conclusions guided by their culture-specific impressions and chosen goals. Throughout its history, our field has been shrouded by an air of uncertainty, and its representatives have always felt the urge to reexamine and revise its basic tenets. Each generation of folklorists has set its own agenda to rethink earlier definitions. Controversies and heated debates have enlivened the pages of journals and the august assemblies of academics. Our generation of folklorists, more than ever before, has seen great structural and ideological changes in the order of the world that made many of the postulates and aims of our discipline hopelessly anachronistic and its research tools and methods useless. No wonder the reconsideration of concepts is an ongoing process.

I regret to say, however, that nowadays some kind of inertia is surfacing in those debates. There seems to be more stagnation than creative progress. More and more, folklorists weary of critically rereading the accumulated body of scholarship of the past, shop around for new ideas, for a new beginning, by borrowing from other disciplines while ignoring those developed within folkloristics by subsequent generations of scholars. That is to say, instead of establishing continuity and building on disciplinary tradition that would strengthen our field, they are ready to bury the past and begin on a tabula rasa. This is why we read so many "new directions," "rediscoveries," and "reinventions." Dismissing issues raised before, we are encouraged not to read, but to forget the past, to start afresh on the wings of borrowed theories and methodologies. General editors often reject articles that treat themes and use methods not in vogue, and they urge authors to develop new ideas. The youngest generation of folklorists expect their teachers to guide them to new directions and present the latest inventions at professional meetings. And the new ideas come in cycles, focusing on celebrated authors of other disciplines, losing power as soon as a new trend is suggested by opinion leaders without coming to a resolution concerning the "new" trend. During the 1960s and 1970s, earlier scholarly attempts at data gathering, classifying, comparing, and chronologizing were dismissed as entirely useless. The new critics found archives obsolete, storing improperly collected texts, worthless for scholarly attention. Modern-minded innovators did not see the purpose of compiling more variants of the same story when so many already existed (Jacobs 1966a; Dundes 1969a). They were not interested in origins and the intricacies of the evolutionary-devolutionary tendencies of text (Dundes 1969b). While a group of American and Finnish folklorists made an admirable joint effort in 1986 to update the comparative method in folkloristics (Georges 1986; Dundes 1986; Honko 1986; Goldberg 1986; Jones 1986), other scholars continued to apply nonfolkloristic approaches to narrative analysis. Disclaiming the validity of comparative text philology, so-called "contextualists" turned their focus from folklore texts and their performers to acts of communication as processual events inspired by behavioral scientists in anthropology, linguistics, sociology, and psychology (Dorson 1972: 45; Bauman 1983: 362–368), leaning more toward collective than individual creativity. The humanistic focus that distinguishes folkloristics from the social sciences is blurred by these borrowings. Disrespect to our own intellectual tradition, omitting the materials gathered by previous generations, erodes the goal and threatens the integrity of the discipline, making questionable the right of existence of folkloristics that is as old and venerable as the much-admired other disciplines. Do we really want to change paradigms? The recent exploitation of the interdisciplinary nature of folkloristics and the emphasis on its liminality betwixt and between neighbor fields[1] is particularly alarming. It seems to oppose the concern of folklorists with tradition, which is peculiar, as among Nordic scholars the term "tradition-research" is used interchangeably with "folkloristics" (Honko 1983: 13–22). But while innovation-seeking critics stress traditionality, they also try to substitute ideas born in alien research contexts and intellectual trends for those built brick-by-brick within the domain of their own study experience. (As a characteristic example of experimentation, see Siikala 1990.) By assessing the benefits of and the time wasted on the application of fast-breaking and fast-fading trends over the last thirty years, we may wonder why we are so eager to admire those who reinvent the wheel by simply replacing old terminologies with fashionable new ones (e.g., Briggs and Bauman 1992: 131–172). Remember the wisdom of the proverb about choosing the old key over the new (MI Z62.1.), applied in AaTh 313 and 425, to reinstate the abandoned and forgotten bride?

Folk narrative study as the oldest systematic field of folkloristics developed and tested scholarly methods and approaches to accommodate research needs for its other fields. At recent scholarly discussions held under the aegis of the International Society for Folk Narrative Research, specialists reexamined methods of collecting and classifying, approaches to analysis – comparative, structural and functional – and contemplated the usefulness of basic concepts: tradition, variant, type and oicotype, personal creativity, meaning and cultural identity. It was the elected executive boards that decided on congress themes, broad enough and liberal enough to accommodate the interest of its international membership and to keep abreast at the same time with evolving trends of inquiry in the human sciences.[2]

In the course of discussions, the folk narrative stock has broadened considerably because field collectors recording community repertoires found a greater diversity in narratives than previously noted. Observed live narration led to the introduction of the concept *homo narrans*: the idea that the *homo sapiens, faber,* and *ludens,* is by nature also a narrator. And if so, what kind of stories do humans tell? Basic or simplex or cultural forms had already been identified in relationship with the Grimms' genres *(Gattung Grimm)* and gained general acknowledgment by folklorists when Jolles submitted his morphological categories that, as he claimed, resulted from the verbalization of distinctive mental (spiritual) attitudes of a creative force. Elaborating this idea further, behind formal, stylistic and gestalt features, Ranke saw above all, the genres as formulations of conscious or unconscious psychomental manifestations that speak for the spirit of human creativity. Each form, even each repetition of the same narrative content, constitutes a creative process and functions as a distinctive expression of happiness, desire, fulfillment, laughter, fear, or awe. Therefore, Ranke claims, the study of narrative genres is basic for the understanding of human beings (K. Ranke 1978: 46). I would like to cite here his words:

Die verschiedene volkstümlichen Erzählgattungen auch verschiedenen Grundbedürfnissen der menschlichen Seele entspringen . . . Solange der Mensch die Welt empfindet, denkt und bildet, solange er vor allem in seiner Sprache Welt schafft, solange wird er seinen verschiedenen Emotional – und Mentalprozessen die ihnen gemässe Ausdrucksform gegeben haben. (Ranke 1978: 30.)

Along the same lines, expanding the narrative repertoire with texts which fit the classical categories only in part, Hermann Bausinger introduced the forms of the *Alltagsgeschichte* (everyday story, that is personal experience story and its structures, schemes, and patterns) (Bausinger 1958: 239–254). He also viewed these forms as products of the creative conceptualization of the basic messages they impart: that is, the ways the world is featured in them as benign, wish-fulfilling, horrible, or ridiculous. Are not these pioneering authors dealing here with worldview when they see the emergence of genres – narratives – as resulting from diverse conceptualizations of the world? If we may speculate about the *Aussage*, the kernel, the literal and symbolic meaning of stories, we may recognize that the view of the world has been fundamental in genre identification for these and other folk narrative specialists. These scholars were not thinking of the text in isolation but rather the text as the product of someone's personal creativity within a social milieu. Thus, genre as an ideological product was conceived before discussions about a folkloristic genre theory even began.

The transcontinental dialogue about genre identification that developed from the late '60s by and large distanced itself from the aspect of worldview. Leading American and European folklorists were seeking the linguistically, aesthetically identifiable and researchable narrative units, structures and patterns that can be interrelated in a developmental continuum, charted and studied interdependently as a system. Analytical scholarly type constructs, so-called "ideal types," were contrasted with native or ethnic "natural types" – the fixed, general abstracts versus unfixable myriads of local variables – essentially by Lauri Honko and Dan Ben-Amos (Honko 1989: 13–28; Ben-Amos 1976b: ix–xlv; 1976c: 214–242). In another proposal by Roger Abrahams (Abrahams 1976b: 193–214), genres were placed on a scale according to the degree of involvement in the performance of texts. The quest, as Ben-Amos has admitted most recently, was "to settle, once for all, the babel of genre terms in folklore," and it failed. Necessarily so. Much wasted energy went into the effort to force generic diversity into the straightjacket of ideal types, only to come to the conclusion others had made without so much ado: " . . . instead of constructing a unified artificial system, we better explore the diversity of terms . . . they do represent the views and ideas of the people who tell the stories, sing the songs, and cite the proverbs" (Ben-Amos 1992: 25–26). What a detour to return to the worldview constructed by bearers of folklore as a target of folkloristic research. It seems to me we spend too much time muscle-flexing, preparing research tools, forming principles, setting standards and theorizing before looking at our data. The data is what reveals to us how people feel and think about themselves, and the world around them is manifest in folklore genres through the personal interpretation of individuals who tell them. We should not seek easy order but rather the disorder of diversity. An attempt to do so was made at the Ninth Congress of the International Society for Folk Narrative Research in Budapest in 1989 when the plenary session entertained the main theme: emergent forms of modern narration (Röhrich and Wienker-Piepho 1990).

Although the obscure, vague, and general term "worldview" (or *Weltanschauung*) seldom appears as a major research goal in folk narrative study, one way or another it is addressed in all descriptive and analytical studies of stories and their tellers. I am inclined to believe that the vagueness needs to be maintained to allow for a broader spectrum of how narrators think about themselves and the universe. But what are we talking about here?

When folklorists speak in general terms about worldview, folk-idea, ideology – any kind of reaction to stimuli by the surrounding environment (Dundes 1971a: 93–103, Mullen 1978: 209–220; El-Shamy 1967), they mean the sum total of subjective interpretations of perceived and experienced reality of individuals. Any human action is motivated by such a perception. It contains beliefs, opinions, philosophies, conducts, behavioral patterns, social relationships, and practices of humans, related to life on this earth and beyond in the supernatural realm. Worldview then permeates all cultural performances, including folklore. Narratives, in particular, are loaded with worldview expressions: they reveal inherited communal and personal views of human conduct – this is their generic goal (Dégh 1981: 45–78). Bearers of narrative tradition as much as seasoned researchers know and anticipate how a joke, an exemplum, or a ballad to be performed is going to characterize the world, yet we cannot single out one type of worldview or deal with all expressed in one narrative or one telling. Scholars in anthropology state their distance from the people they study when they speak of a separate system of thinking, or a system of meaning unlike that of their own. They use their own common sense imagery to conceptualize the world in contrast with the analytical otherness of their subjects. Folklorists are more specific in their interpretation of worldview expressed in the confines of folklore utterances than anthropologists, whose description is more encompassing and inconcrete, sometimes overlapping with culture, ethos, behavior, cognition, magic thinking, etc. Worldview for folklorists is not an organizing factor but rather the contextualizing, localizing, concretizing element that turns the global into local, the empty formula (Honko 1984: 273–281) into meaningful reality, and the traditional episode into a familiar occurrence. That is to say, worldview is not an abstraction but part of an active and persuasive elaboration of the traditional material, the framing of the folklore text by its *ad hoc* formulator, who fits it into the cultural-conceptual system of its audience. This adjustment is seldom a conscious strategy of the bearer of folklore tradition but rather a matter of natural and mostly unconscious internalization of an attractive content. It is also an interpretive vehicle, inseparable from the content of the text and its context. This idea is particularly important for the folklorist who collects emergent forms of folklore directly in order to understand the complexity of the creative process. Turning now more specifically to the worldview of the magic tale, we might remember the authors who gave us the best clues to its conceptualization. They suggested that we explore the magic tale as an ideological construct.

The enchanted world of the Märchen has fascinated many scholars from a variety of disciplines for more than a century. Interest developed not only in stable plots literalized by the Grimms but also in plot constituencies: episodes, characters, and images. Enchantment, supernatural agents, transformation, magic, and animistic, totemistic features were explored and traced to belief systems and early social institutions. Tales as relics of desacralized myths were also attributed to projections of dream images and fulfillment of desires. Literary analysts interested in the art of storytelling considered tale elements as symbols and metaphors, linguistic formulas and stylistic devices. The tale also was considered as an evolutionary scheme replicating the history of social institutions as well as the stages of child development. These approaches inadvertently contributed to the study of worldview. However, following Jolles's characterization of the Märchen as guided by a naive morality that contradicts the rules of the real world and adapts another in which things happen not as they normally do but as they should (Jolles 1930: 240–41), some prominent Märchen philologists did more than that. They addressed the question of worldview more directly with penetrating text analyses and illustrations. These works, guiding one through the maze of piled-up worldview fragments, laid the groundwork for further study and challenged scholars to make a new order. The authors I have in mind described in diverse ways the tale and its world by contrasting it to the legend and its world, thus characterizing both "basic forms" of the act of traditional narration. Röhrich's landmark book *Märchen und Wirklichkeit* (Röhrich 1974) shows that the different conceptualizations of reality in tale and in legend constitute the main difference between these genres. Lüthi, on the other hand, argues for stylistic differences between the two. But with Lüthi, style speaks for an underlying behavioral distinction between tale and legend and a different imagery of humans and their world in both (Lüthi 1966: 47–56). For Lüthi, the tale is a humanistically oriented genre, with the hero and the heroine as dominant figures at the center, whereas the legend deals with the intrusion of the "totally different" into the human world. Ranke sees the Märchen as subjectively unbelievable, focused on the wanderings between the worlds of a central hero, as opposed to legend which is focused on a subjectively believable experience (K. Ranke 1978: 16–17).

A remarkable, undeservedly overlooked essay by János Honti (1937, English transl. 1975) has major significance for a new exploration of worldview in magic tales. According to his thesis, documented with supporting materials, humans through history have lived in a dichotomous tension between practical reality and the reality of the Märchen world. The world of the Märchen, according to Honti, existed before Märchen were invented and lives on outside of the Märchen: it makes life livable and the burdens of practical life tolerable. Borrowing the idea of the romantic poet Novalis (Friedrich von Hardenberg 1772–1801), "alles ist ein Märchen," Honti suggests the omnipresence of the tale world in human thinking: world history and the history of the Märchen cannot be separated from each other; the tale is everywhere, indisputably and ineradicably accompanying and influencing practical reality. Humankind's elementary objective – to shape, interpret and make the world livable – is achieved by internalizing it, writes Honti. This world arches between two extremes: from the technical and the logical reality of practical life, to the reality of intellectual life, religion, and the arts. The tale-world takes multiple and ambiguous turns. Potentially anything is possible, without limitations. However, in its display, passes, not boundaries, bridges not walls, resolutions not entrapments are typical of this world. How is it possible that the virtuous poor man cannot turn into a ferocious monster and the heroine cannot be devoured by the dragon? The creator of the tale does not take anything from the world of unlimited possibilities but selects the most reasonable, desirable or tolerable. The roads of the tale lead through death to resurrection. The history of the tale and the world history of human destiny cannot be separated from each other, Honti concludes.

The authors mentioned so far depended on literary texts and discussed the worldview of traditional tale types rather than the specific worldview of storytellers featured in their tale versions. Although they all recognized the importance of narrators in shaping the tale-world, they theorized on the basis of literary texts. It will be the task of the Märchen biologist[3] to explore the real significance of worldview.

I believe the key is the individual at the inspired moment of telling a tale to his or her customary audience.

We speak about two worldviews here: the one inherent in the traditional type, and the other, the specific worldview of the narrator. Evidently the individual's worldview is revealed already by his or her choice of stories from the available repertoire and further shown by the creation of new variants. Juha Pentikäinen speaks of Marina Takalo's worldview tales – "a specific tale category" – which he identifies as having "some *weltanschaulich* meaning." That is, these tales uniformly reflect the fatalistic and rationalistic Weltanschauung of the storyteller, representing 32 percent of her repertoire. (Pentikäinen 1978: 267, 333.)

We should not speak here only of tale types and their internalization by the narrator but also of the personal additions, interpretations, observations, descriptions, and commentaries as 'oral literary criticisms' (Dundes 1966) which are added to the formulaic content sequence of the tale. Intensive text analysis of this sort has never been a specific objective of Märchen scholars. In fact, few scholars have ever suggested attention to the creative process in tale construction that would take improvized details along with traditional content motifs and episodes into consideration (Dégh 1972; Bronner 1992). It may be true that formulas are applied without the endowment of personal meaning and appear as mere repetitions of respected tradition. Experienced storytellers know the rules of storytelling: that adventures must be repeated three times, that phrases and dialogues may not be changed but must be kept verbatim even if they do not make sense or do not seem particularly appealing to the narrator, and that the specific formulations of respected ancestral storytellers must be kept intact. For example, Zsuzsanna Palkó, one of the greatest Märchen-tellers that ever lived, recounts the three-times-repeated dialogue between the banished wife turned turtle-dove sitting on the window-sill and her gold cross on the neck of the substitute bride as follows: "Do you sleep my little gold cross?" And the gold cross on the neck of the false queen answered: "Not much!" And she asks: "How does the prince do?" "He slumbers like a prince." "And the queen?" "She lies kicking about the house like a bestial whore." (Dégh 1960: 50–51.) Asking what does she mean by that, she shrugged her shoulder: "I don't know but this is how I heard the story goes."

Experienced narrators, nevertheless, also know where they have the liberty to insert personal commentaries without disrupting the harmony of episodic sequencing. The tightly structured complex tale that allows little leeway to express personal feelings also can be manipulated by the sensitive narrator without breaking the rhythm of the

prose. Beyond "asides," digressions to impart information to the listeners (Georges 1983; Basgöz 1986), the storyteller usually takes advantage of transitional cadences or turning points in the narrative where
the speed of action can be slowed down to describe the milieu, to
introduce and characterize the actors, and to use personal experiences
and observations to internalize and interpret their actions. The introductory and the closing episodes, departures and arrivals, heroic tests,
torture and suffering of heroes are particularly sensitive to worldview
expressions. At these points, the speed of sequencing action upon
action slows down to permit description appealing to the compassionate audience. Therefore we may benefit from comparing variants of
identical tales told by acknowledged community narrators repeatedly
at different occasions. Of course, any human action is fueled by worldview. One can only agree with Gregory Schrempp that "worldview
motivates and shapes attitudes and behavior, and therefore human
action is unintelligible apart from it". Thus, our study of the folktale
as a human product and its specific versions as personal acts of creation
can show how the world is featured by this genre: what is the genre-
specific image of the world? For better understanding, components
of the ideological construct of worldview need to be discerned from
complete tale texts, not just the type and motif sequence and connecting technical devices. Also, non- or semi-traditional details, *ad hoc*
elaborations complementing the story, reveal more of the fundamental
function of the genre than the more or less stable content elements.

HOW DO STORYTELLERS INTERPRET THE
SNAKEPRINCE TALE?

The Search for the Lost Husband, the basic adventure story of a woman, is shared by a number of magic tales identified by researchers as self-sufficient types, subtypes, or regional oicotypes. These separate narratives subsumed under AaTh 425 A to P and 430, 432, and 441, developed through continual repetition, variation, and spread in time and space. They also gained independence from each other while remaining dependent on the same stock of narrative formulas. By the choice of prominent oral storytellers, literary authors or both, subculturally or ethnically distinctive types evolved which creatively exploited affinial elements for culture-specific as well as individual reinterpretations of the main story.

Depending on personal interest, many research options are at the disposal of folklorists and related social scientists to explore this tale complex or tale-family and its ramifications. The text to be studied may be the cross-cultural, composite "Normalform" (Anderson 1923: 403) (an analytical construct), an influential literary version (crafted by Apuleius or the Grimm brothers), a regional redaction or a subtype, the local variants of a community, the individual formulation of one storyteller, and so on. The purpose of study may also be diverse: discernment of origin and avenues of diffusion by comparative text analysis, search for universal, subcultural, and individual levels of meaning, interpretation of the metaphoric language of the tale by psychoanalytical, sociological, and ethnographical approaches. Relatively speaking, we are fortunate because AaTh 425 is among the very few monographically researched complex tales. Most scholarly attention, however, has been paid to the identification and distinction of separate motif-sequences constituting the text of individual subtypes rather than the levels of meaning of the tale to its bearers. Monograph studies of Ernst Tegethoff (1922), Inger M. Boberg (1938), Jan Öjvind Swahn (1955) and Georgios Megas (1971) appear as stepping stones on a newly trodden path supporting hypotheses of origin and dissemination by increasing the stock of variants to cover relevant

European regions. The result summarized by Megas (1975), who added key data from the Mediterranean area, reinforces earlier speculations that 425A, the most prominent and widespread subtype, represents the oldest and purest form of the tale. This is none other than the story of Cupid (Amor) and Psyche, a mythological-metapho-rical narrative episode of the novel *Metamorphoseon* by Apuleius. Does it mean that this web of oral tradition has literary roots? Indeed not, the claim is that Apuleius used folk elements as modern fairytale authors do today and that these elements can be traced back to the early Mykenean mythopoetic age. According to Megas, some of the oldest ingredients of the tale were not used by Apuleius but continued to live in tradition and appear in widespread modern European variants.

Looking at 425A, the primary subtype, isolated by Swahn from fifteen other subtypes, the number of texts is impressive. They were neatly classified and mapped by several scholars in addition to the monograph authors who incidentally captured and uprooted them from their ethnographic reality, cutting off their existential lifeline only to attempt tentative, cautious (and often contradictory) conclusions. But how convincingly can conclusions be drawn from several hundreds of texts if variants are virtually limitless?

Without criticizing conclusions resulting from cross-cultural comparison on the basis of plot-outlines, I will try to do a less ambitious, more down-to-earth fieldwork-based assessment of text formulations in the hope of discerning some of the meanings of AaTh 425A that are not easy to deduce from the abstract plot outline. Regarding each telling of a variant as a unique event that only in the eyes of the scholar-beholder is linked up with the international network of variants, I will argue that the variant created by a narrator is the product of the ethnographic present. The personal text not only shows the narrator's ability in formulating a story from the available plot episodes, his or her way of making the world of fantasy palpable by connecting it with the world of everyday's reality; the told story also mirrors the narrator's specific conceptualization of the world and its affairs: his or her cultural and personal meanings. Most importantly, the main implementation of storytellers concerns subjective characterization of the tale actors: compassionate identification with the actions of some and vehement disapproval of that of others. The storyteller is never neutral but emotionally involved when featuring the personality of the cast. The tale does not tolerate disorder; it makes order in chaos and sense of nonsense, complements fragments and clarifies absurdities resulting from shifts of meanings during the process of transmission – otherwise it could not be told and survive. Each telling of a tale is also a reinterpretation, and an updating, having its broader basis in the ethnic redaction.

If sociocultural conditions influence the formulation of meaningful oico-types, then the oicotype-models are used by individuals to express their own meanings within socially sanctioned formulas. These meanings are important, although they do not appear necessarily in narrative motifs overtly causing radical revisions in the content, but rather marginally as commentaries, accompanying the plot. They are expressions of opinions, sentiments, featuring characters and situations, as the story action evolves. In other words, the small details, the seemingly insignificant, sometimes trivial, spontaneous personal illuminations and elaborations of tale events situate the narrative according to existing social norms and keep the story itself relevant to its audience. The storyteller's personal creativity usually manifests more in such subjective additions to the plot than in the invention of new episodes. It is precisely these nuances – connections between content episodes – that make a folktale a folktale. Violin virtuoso Isaac Stern told his admirers after a recent concert at the Indiana University campus in Bloomington: "It is not the notes but the connections between the notes that make great music." This may be true of the performing arts in general, storytelling among them. Not the content motifs but their interlinkage make great Märchen.

The Hungarian ethnic redaction of the Cupid and Psyche type is remarkably consistent and displays relatively minimal borrowing from other subtypes – even less with other types about abused women and female wanderers between the worlds. Earliest mention of the tale comes from the eighteenth century, but the first text appears only in 1822 and is followed by others from all parts of the country. The forty variants available to me (I was unable to consult materials in the Hungarian Ethnographic Archives to be incorporated into the Hungarian Folktale Catalogue now in progress) are helpful in establishing the plot outline; nevertheless, thirty texts were useless for close scrutiny because their collectors or publishers drastically edited their version. They made them "pure," devoid of any allusion to sex, euphemizing the bridal night episode, frequently even eliminating consequential pregnancy and childbirth. All texts were told by illiterate or semiliterate villagers, but only twenty-six (nineteen men and seven women) were identified by name, none by economic and social position within the hierarchy of peasant society.

The Hungarian ethnic plot outline is as follows:

1. Royal (land- and castle-owning) couple suffers from barrenness. Desperate queen (blamed by husband) prays to God to give any child (boy), even if a snake. Sometimes she is cursed by old woman (a witch) to bear a snake.

2. Snakechild is raised in concealment hidden from public eye.

3. Snakechild swells to enormous size and thickness rapidly. He demands his mother get him another king's beautiful daughter.

4. Mother negotiates for the marriage partner and lures the girl from her parent's home to the invisible prince.

5. Girl is locked into the room of the snakeprince. Sometimes there are two reluctant girls who show disgust and are slain by the prince; the third is kind and submissive, resigns to her fate.

6. Girl is impregnated. Prince shed snakeskin by night but wears it by day.

7. Girl seeks advice from village witch (wise woman) on how to get rid of the snakeskin – or her mother-in-law suggests burning the skin.

8. Prince reproaches wife for not being patient until he is free from the curse that made him a snake, and leaves. The condition of reunion is to plant a grain of wheat and a walnut, water them with her tears until she can bake a bread and a walnut cake. This will take seven years; then she can start her voyage of another seven years with the token food to find him. He places an iron hoop on her body and curses her not to be able to bear her child until he touches her belly. She drops her blood on his white shirt with the curse that nobody should be able to remove the stain until she can do the wash.

9. The voyage. Sun, Moon and Wind, sons of sisters who pity the girl, guide her to the kingdom (castle) where she snakeprince resides. She is given three golden objects (usually distaff, spindle and yarn of gold).

10. Snakeprince is married to another princess and leads the pleasant life of kings; goes hunting every day, returning in the evening.

11. Girl, 14 years pregnant, driven by remorse and weary of travel, is employed as washwoman. For the price of the gold objects, she bargains with the princess to let her spend the night with the snakeprince. Twice he is drugged with sleeping potion and does not hear her wailing to relieve her from her burden. Third night, butler tells him what he overheard. Prince spills the wine into his bath.

12. Reunion. One or twin gold-haired boys are born. The princess discovers the family idyll in the bedroom: the 7-year-old children play with a ball and their beautiful parents watch them.

13. Judgment. Punishment of princess (and her mother, a witch who advised her) by death for substituting for the first wife. Metaphor of the retrieved old key's priority over the new.

This plot outline includes all elements that make the tale coherent and logistically comprehensive for bearers of the same culture. The variants follow it more or less closely; some are more inclusive, others less, depending on personal choice, knowledge and taste, or momentary mood. Some texts show deviation that blurs the main tendency. For example, two variants have a poor woman, not the queen, as the hero's mother, or poor girls as the chosen wife. Two other variants show treachery and intrigue that unite the snakeprince with the second bride. In all cases, the animal bridegroom is a snake except for a pig (three times), the lowest of domestic animals in the eye of peasants, and once a greyhound, the country gentleman's precious pet animal, "tough-skinned, black-freckled." The snake has a descriptive name: Kigyóbőrű Kis Király (Snake-skinned Little King), Kigyó Jancsi (Snake Johnny), Királyfia Kis Miklós (Kingson Little Nicky), Kigyó Sebestyén (Snake Sebastian), Kigyókirály Kis Jancsi (Snakeking Little Johnny), Kigyóbőr (Snakeskin), Kigyókirályfi (Snakeprince), Kigyófuvó Szép Jánoskám (My Snake-Blowing Beautiful Johnny). The miraculously growing thick snake that holds up its head to whistle and to communicate, as portrayed in this tale, is alien to the snake image prevalent in Hungarian folk belief and legends. It seems to belong to the earliest elements of this tale as suggested by Megas, ascertaining its universal symbolic character (Megas 1971: 199).

In essence, the events of this tale are based on the archaic patriarchal peasant order. Three particularly important ideas operate as pillars on which the story rests its institutional authenticity. The first is the expectation that the first-born will be a boy and not a girl. Implicit also is the fear from unnatural birth (deformity) that traditionally causes suspicion concerning the new mother's background because such mishap occurs as a punishment for evil supernatural connection.

The second pillar on which this tale rests is the institution of arranged marriages. It is the parents who arrange the marriage of their children, serving family interests without caring for the partners' attraction to each other. "They get used to each other like we did," was the usual argument. Until the end of World War II, as in the tale, it was the mother (or a female relative) who bargained as her son's agent for the girl, who was explicity sold by her parents to maintain economic well-being and social status. In the language of the tale, the virgin princess, like any young girl to be given into marriage, is trapped in the bridal chamber, which is also the scene of the first encounter of the couple. Curiosity, fear, anger, and passion alternate while they get acquainted and negotiate their identities, testing each other's sexuality, capability of love, tenderness, and care. This is what the core of this ethnic subvariant of the Cupid and Pysche tale is: consummation of marriage and its consequences.

The third idea is at the conclusion of the tale and concerns the ambiguity between male drive toward polygamy and freedom from family ties and the Christian concept of monogamous marriage.

The settling of the conflict between the two wives is the most cumbersome part of the story. Individual storytellers, guided by their sense of marital fidelity, try somehow to resolve the apparent double standard. But none of the solutions offered by individual narrators fits smoothly. Without explicit reference, it seems clear that the prince has remarried after abandoning his pregnant wife. Sometimes storytellers do not even mention a woman in the other remote royal castle or if so, it is the relative of the prince or an older queen who is in trouble and needs help. In a version by Ágoston Fábián, the prince escapes to his original home, leaving room for speculation concerning the cause of his enchantment. In another formulation, the woman (with her witch-mother) is similar to the substitute wife who destroys the heroine in AaTh 408 (The Three Oranges) and related tales. Her actions – employing the heroine as a washwoman, buying her gold toys for an absurd fee – reveal both a spoiled whimsical princess who needs to have everything, and a trickster who uses a sleeping potion on her husband to protect her interest. But this is obviously just a joke, because who would see a rival in the deformed pregnant women of fourteen years, whose body is kept from exploding by seven iron hoops, in the formulation of master storyteller Péter Pandur (Dégh 1943, I: 262–271). She is addressed as "auntie" by the chambermaids, while in Mrs. Palkó's rendition (Dégh 1955–1960: 137–154), she is smelly and filthy and cannot be employed anywhere else but the laundry. The second wife seems loyal and protective of the huntloving carefree prince. There is an elaborate description of how she pampers him, what choice food and drink he gets at the royal table, how he is bathed, rubbed dry, put to bed and lulled to sleep in Pandur's version. In Mrs. Palkó's text, she shows mild contempt against the wash woman as she pushes her into the bedroom with the words: "Go, sniff his asshole." The poor woman explicitly requests permission "to sleep with your husband," in Lajos Ámi's version (Erdész 1968, II: 18–26); she is allowed to do so in exchange for the precious spindle contemplating that the "worst she can leave behind her is a flea." In Pandur's story, she is angered and saddened when she sees the newborn babies and the beautiful wife in the bedroom, and she reproaches the prince for not having given her children: a failed marriage indeed.

Somehow the wickedness of the second wife is implicit with the situation. The otherwise dissimilar variants of Mr. and Mrs. Fábián (Sebestyén 1979–1985, Vol. 2: 9–16, 267–272), share the Magic Flight motif (AaTh 313): the restored family has to escape with the help of magic objects. But no matter how storytellers characterize the second wife, she is doomed by the single fact that she has taken – usurped – the place of the suffering heroine who has all our sympathy. She must be punished for administering the sleeping potion, says Aladár Kovács (G. Nagy 1985:1, 311–317), or simply for being the second wife. Cruel punishment by torturous death is conferred upon her by public acclaim at a hearing set by the high court. Questions are posed: "Who is worth more, the sworn or the unsworn?" (Mrs. Palkó. A second marriage is always "unsworn," according to the Catholic canon.); "the real or the unreal?" (Ámi); "the old or the new?" (A. Fábián). As in similar folktale situations, the substitute wife condemns herself as worthless and guilty. Her removal is a necessity; the sentence has to be passed so that order and family equilibrium can be restored to satisfy the rigid folktale justice. There is only one notable exception. In Pandur's text, the rival queen is transformed from villainness to benefactress as she discovers the royal identity of the laundress. This is in accord with Pandur's subservient attitude toward nobility. She and her king host the glorious family for a month until the heroine recovers and feels strong enough to travel back home.

The in depth study of personal variation and interpretation of the ethnic versions by practicing storytellers may be the key to a better understanding of the basic message of this (or any other) tale. Limits of time do not allow me to offer the penetrating analysis necessary for such an enterprise, but even a modest sample can give an idea of research potentials.

The Bucovina Székely repertoire contains three variants of AaTh 425A and were told by Mrs. Zsuzsanna Palkó in 1959, and Mr. and Mrs. Ágoston Fábián in 1979 and 1982, respectively. Only Mrs. Palkó referred to her source. She heard it from an older woman when she was fourteen, not from any of the respected community narrators. Yet the tale became one of her most cherished repertoire pieces which at seventy-four was among her longest and most elaborate. I recorded it at her house when she entertained her usual audience of adult neighbors, after all the children were asleep, on a cold winter night. This tale was among her favorite feminine tales in which the sufferings and abuse of women are the main motifs – not only that of young heroines, but also mothers, mothers-in-law and their compassionate supporters, and servants mistreated by other women and male kinsmen: fathers, husbands, and brothers. The crucial three episodes in this tale are interlinked by the heroine's sense of guilt for failing as wife and mother and her acceptance of the blame, humiliation, and submission to penance. In the opening scene of the story, the king blames the queen for not having a child, a son, whereas she commits the sin of supplicating God for a son, no matter what, even a snake. She knows this is a sin that embarrasses her husband. As soon as her wish comes true, she prays: "My God, I sinned. God blessed me with this ugly animal. What will my husband tell me if he finds out? Even more, strangers if they find out that the king has a snake son?" They do not call the priest to baptise the child: "No one should find out ever." They were "sad and ashamed." In the description of the queen's negotiation for the prospective bride on behalf of the snake, Mrs. Palkó realizes the absurdity of the situation. "I don't know what was the world like then, that the father allowed his daughter to go with the queen so that if she likes him, she will stay." The queen and the king treat her to dinner, let her rest while the girl can hardly wait to see the prospective groom. "She trembled from excitement." The tension grows in the narrator's description: "Let's go, let's surprise him." As they open the door, the snake lifts his head. The girl asks: "My, what kind of snake is there?" "This is our son," answers the queen. She reasons with the girl: "He loves you, he does not want to hurt you, he wants to marry you" . . . "be patient with him, you won't regret it, he will be good to you . . . ."

What follows is the hyperbolic description of the bridal night. The girl is trapped; windows and doors are locked. She fights, tries to escape, throws herself against the wall and cries, "I am to lay with him in bed? I would rather kill myself than be with this disgusting beast." The snake tries to soothe her, but for a week she keeps running around crying like a lunatic without eating or sleeping, all in vain. Exhausted and hungry, she accepts the food and lies down to sleep. But when she wakes, "the snake crawls up to her side in bed. She screams so that her eye popped out of her head: 'Go away you ugly beast, don't touch me,' she cries, but he kept consoling her: 'Please, allow me to lay with you. I won't hurt you.'" The king and the queen jumped out of bed: "Our son is killing the girl!" They dash in, find nothing wrong, only that the snake crept up to her side in the bed. They close the door and leave the couple alone. The masterful narration of Mrs. Palkó dramatizes the passionate reconciliation of the first encounter of the lovers in exquisite prose, ending with the girl's total resignation to her fate. After a peaceful slumber, she wakes, finding a "beautiful prince in bed with her . . . she never saw anyone like him, not even in her dream . . . where did he come from? She looks around. No trace of the snake . . . she was happy. She took delight in her lover . . . she was (immediately) in the family way . . ."

Mrs. Palkó's version places the transformation of the girl in the bridal chamber into the center of the narrative. Her femininity fulfilled, she became a woman: wife and mother. Yet in the following episode, seeking advice of a witch (wise women are commonly consulted by people in her village) on how to get rid of the snakeskin is the disobedience that results in her abandonment. She has to suffer and do penance in order to regain her status: from homeless servant to royalty, from banished pregnant exile without a husband to wife and mother.

Mrs. Mária Fábián's version follows closely Mrs. Palkó's outline, although she denied having heard it from her. Mrs. Fábián is the celebrated current storyteller of Kakasd. As a member of the Kakasd Folklore Ensemble, she rose to national fame telling stories to adult and juvenile audiences upon invitation. She inherited her storytelling skill and philosophy from her father, Rudolf Györfi, whose critical attitude toward Mrs. Palkó's style and choice of tales is noticeable from her remarks. Mrs. Fábián, now in her mid-sixties, began telling tales to fellow women workers at the cooperative farm. Her talent was much appreciated and won her a new job as nanny in the daycare center where until her recent retirement, she told tales to preschool children. She adjusted her large repertoire (170 tales were recorded and published) to the juvenile audience according to her puritanic standard of child education. She eliminated all sexually oriented, obscene, vulgar, impolite, disrespectful, careless, or sloppy expressions. Her ambition was to raise the next generation as loyal Székelys to maintain traditional ethnic values expressed in the particular language dialect inherent in folktales.

The text I recorded was told to children put to bed after lunch for their afternoon nap (another version was published by A. Sebestyén). The main characteristic of this version is that while it follows Mrs. Palkó's episodic sequence and repeats sentences word for word, sexual allusions are carefully excluded. The queen in this version adopts an orphaned baby snake that crawls into her lap asking for pity. When the snake wants a wife, the queen visits the other country's royal family with the picture of her husband as if he would be the suitor. The bridal chamber scene is similar to Mrs. Palkó's without the mention of the bed, the pleading of the snake, love or impregnation. The burning of the snakeskin appears here as the guilt shared by the queen and her daughter-in-law: the king raises his voice in anger because of the loss of his son. The second princess appears as a rival who aspires to become the wife of the prince. The resolution is without conflict: the wife arrives with the bread and the walnut cake; the prince takes a bite and they flee together on a witch's broom.

Ágoston Fábián, aged husband of Mária, does not like his role as shadow of his famous wife. He grudgingly yields, if he is in a good mood, to recalling tales from his days in the military. His version is close to his wife's, but its focus shifts. It is a poor man who adopts the snake and takes it home to his wife. This beginning logically links up with AaTh 560II (The Magic Ring) in which the poor woman begs the king for the hand of his daughter, and the conditions are impossible to fulfill without magic help. The snake in this version is from fairyland, capable of magic acts, and when his wife burns his skin, he goes back there. She must wander for ten years. Upon arrival, the fairy family is hostile to her, so they escape by Magic Flight (AaTh 313). No allusion to sex, second wife or the voyage – this tale argues clearly from the male point of view.

Péter Pandur's 1942 version deviates considerably from that of the Kakasd Székelys. Although the plot outline is identical, the narrator's turbulent personal life, exposure to a great variety of rural and urban environments and occupations leave their mark on his text. Leaving his Transylvanian home at a tender age, he served in the households of aristocratic and noble land-owning families. During World War I he was an officer's servant, then a cook's help in the canteen. Later he worked on construction sites and at the railroad, dug wells, gathered herbs, delivered mail. He married and settled in a village 30 kilometers north of Budapest, where he always remained a stranger, a cultural exile. As a poor man, blinded by an accident, he and his native-born wife acquired housing only in the Gypsy district where he was appreciated for his tales by his cronies in the pub. I recorded his Snakeprince story twice, first in shorthand and fifteen years later on tape.

The queen in Pandur's story is cursed by an old witch who is slighted when after church service she distributes money among the poor. This causes grief, pain, and embarrassment, but the queen is not blamed. They advertise for a nurse. Simple girls get nauseated by the sight of the snake; only a princess, former girlfriend of the queen, volunteers for the job. Pandur elaborates how she feeds the snake with a bottle, how he grows up to be nineteen or twenty. The "marriage" then is described. The snake shakes his skin off, when one evening he sees the girl undress and prepare for bed. He sits at her side and tells her about the curse of which by her kindness she disenchanted him. He also proposes to her. "I feel very much in love with you and hope you also love me." He proposes they marry right then without a clergyman to keep the secret. They live like man and wife for a while, until she tells him: "My dear, I feel I am going to be a mother." He warns her not to reveal the secret and warns her what is going to happen if she does. As time passes, however, the king and the queen notice her condition and start to pressure her: "What is this? You do not go anywhere in this world, no man sets his foot in here, how come you are pregnant? Tell us, we won't leave you alone until you confess." She resists for a long time but finally she tells them. The queen, dressed in poor woman's clothing, wanders from village to village to find a wise woman (witch) for advice. In Pandur's argument, the burning of the snakeskin is a must so that an open wedding can be held and so that the couple could socialize with other princely couples and live a normal life. The skin-burning is also detailed: buy a special coal-oven, hide it behind curtains . . . etc. Unlike in other variants, Pandur elaborates the wandering of the prince. He runs away, gets poor man's clothing not to be recognized while his mother takes to bed and his father sends the army after him. He walks until he reaches another kingdom where he introduces himself to the king, explains about his ordeal. He is invited to stay. His identity restored, he is treated like a family member. When the seven years' pregnant wife takes to the road after her husband, she assumes the clothing of her chambermaid and takes jewelry and money with her. The rest follows closely the plot except Pandur's inclusion of butlers, hunters, chambermaids, footmen of the royal household in the supporting roles. In this story the queen is supportive once she discovers that the disguised woman is a princess and the wife; there is no sexual rivalry. Pandur's story rests on a scheme of transformation through the change of clothing: the rich and powerful become poor and homeless only to regain original status. Male and female servants are described as they are waiting at tables, respectfully reporting to their masters, loyally supporting them and grooming them. Like Pandur's other tales, this one also reveals the impact of his early experience as a count's waiting boy in his conceptualization of royalty, power and wealth. This experience also was basic to his selection of words and formulation of sentences in the dialogues of the high-born actors. There is no ambiguity in this variant, and no one is blamed for the curse or the skin-burning. The narrator is compassionate with every actor except for the witch who enchanted the offspring. But she is just triggering the tale event and has no function. All ends well without any punishments.

Lajos Ámi, a Hungarian Gypsy night watchman, was 62 when his unusually large and 'form-breaking' magic tale repertoire was discovered. He claimed to have learned all his 280 tales from an Italian sergeant during World War I. His embroidery was so much exaggerated, breaking all accepted rules of narration, that his fellow villagers called him a liar. His variant is actually a fragment and places the hero, "a poor lumberjack," in the center. There is no enchanted prince;

the story opens when the hero, János, curses his wife not to be able to bear their child until he touches her with both arms. He leaves for an adventure, offers help to a queen whose husband lost his kingdom to Sweden, China, and the Soviet Union. In exchange, the queen promises him half of the land if regained, but he wants her for his wife. She packs him food for the battle, and in three installments, János beats the enemy by kicking and slapping the soldiers, and shouting insults to their nation pride. He marries the queen. He lives the life of kings, hunting in the royal woods. When the overdue pregnant woman offers her merchandise to the queen in exchange for sleeping with her husband, she consults a witch and follows advice to drug him. With the help of a "cinderboy," who reproaches him for playing the king when he in fact is only a lumberjack, János encounters his wife. Seven years passed; a seven-year-old boy and girl are born. The second wife and the witch are executed. In Ami's tale, the first wife plays a subordinate role. She does not violate a tabu; she does not have to do penance. The husband is the agent, the restless, hungry for adventure; he is so much obsessed with career orientation that he in fact forgets about his family and his responsibilities.

What the personal formulation of the above few prominent narrators shows us about the meaning of AaTh 425 may be further explored through the examination of the cast of characters. Tales are biographical epics with a central hero whom the narrator shapes with compassion, with whom he or she identifies. All others play supporting roles which are also projected subjectively by the narrator: with compassion or with rejection, never with sober objectivity. The rating of the two sets of characters in the Hungarian subtype is the following:

Women:

Queen: bears unnatural child; follows bad advice (burning the snakeskin).

Adviser (a magician, a witch): without malice gives bad advice concerning the burning of the snakeskin.

Heroine: meek, innocent and submissive princess brought to the snake by queen, is impregnated, burns snakeskin whereby she is cursed and suffers abandonment. Deprived of royal paraphernalia and degraded in rank and looks, searches for husband. Reunion and restoration to rank is achieved with the help of three old women and their supernatural sons.

Donors: mothers of Sun, Moon, and Wind, give heroine three gold objects.

Second wife: queen, sedates husband before granting permission to heroine to sleep with him in exchange for gold objects.

Chambermaids: render household services in the castle of second wife; negotiate for gold objects; accommodate heroine as washwoman.

Men:

King: nagging queen for not bearing him a boy; scolding wife and daughter-in-law for burning the snakeskin and making his son leave.

Snakeprince: aggressive, demanding: forces mother to negotiate for princess, demands secrecy from wife; abandons her for disobedience without mercy, and sets cruel conditions for possible reunion; resumes a pleasurable and carefree life elsewhere as king and forgets completely about first wife.

Helpers: Sun, Moon, Wind assist the heroine.

House servants, footman, butler: render service to Snakeprince in the second wife's castle. One tells about the nightly visits of his first wife.

The newborn children: one or two gold-haired boys or a boy and a girl seven-year-old when they are born.

As one reads this case of male and female characters, the nature of interdependence between the sexes in the course of events becomes clearer and helps us understand another, maybe more general, maybe universal level of the meaning of this story. Above I already gave a plot outline that was based on the forty Hungarian subcultural variants. But is this outline accurate? That is, is this outline identical with what is meant by the narrators? Is there more to add to the cultural meaning and within it, the personal meaning of the storytellers?

In his monograph study, Swahn observes that AaTh 425 "developed almost exclusively in a female milieu." Without being able to show the "sex distribution of tradition-bearers," he found it striking to note, "to what a great extent this tale has been cherished by female storytellers – it is only in the case of subtype O, the 'male' form of the tale, that male storytellers regularly appear" (Swahn 1955: 437–438). This is not the first time that a distinctive male and female folktale tradition is mentioned (Dégh 1985: 211–220). But since researchers both in cross-cultural comparative text studies and in field-based ethnographic collections failed to provide for documentation, the distinction remains an impressionistic comment, not an established fact.

One certainly may look at the Amor and Psyche tale as a version of the feminine tale biographies. It is a segment of life history wrapped in an artistic narrative, featuring the critical transformational phase of the woman's life: marriage, subordination, acceptance of domestic service and fulfillment in motherhood. Yet this is only half of the story very much dependent on the other half: the story of the Snakeprince. In this case, it is a longer story: unnatural birth, starting life as a misfit, regaining normalcy by marriage, searching for adventure, and return. In fact, the two biographies make one interdependent story about the establishment of the asymmetric relationship of man and woman in marriage. The woman, gentle, submissive, domestic, industrious (even her precious gold toys are household tools: distaff, spindle and hemp); the man, aggressive, enterprising, and promiscuous, does not confirm to his role without conflict. The woman who desperately wants a child to fulfill her prescribed role – motherhood – makes a sinful wish; she is guilty. The woman who tries to get away from the forced marriage and slavery is guilty; the woman who wants normalcy restored and burns the snakeskin (in fact, resents secret sex relations and wants to be lawful, coming out of the closet) is guilty. So is anyone who supports her – her mother, mother-in-law, and the village witch. (It is interesting that the village witch or wise woman – healer, midwife, marriage broker and adviser – is a stock character in this tale, although her help is disastrous. As a representative of village reality, to whom women in need turn, however, she is important in situating the plot.) So is the second wife unacceptable by church canon of the leading faith, Catholicism. The woman's domain is the home where she serves the husband and raises his sons; her procreative capability is her main worth. The man, on the other hand, is powerful and free of ties. He takes the reluctant girl by force, then, and for disobeying his orders leaves her and orders her to leave after him in pursuit while he also ties her with impregnation. She becomes his property for good but he has no obligation to her; he is free to establish new family ties.

Recounted in specific cultural terms, the story reflects the universal opposition between "domestic" and "public" roles of woman and man. She is dependent, he is independent in their union. Ironically, however, as this tale tells us most clearly, it is the woman who is active, even dynamic, while the man is passive. She initiates, he reacts. In the Cupid and Psyche story, women are the doers. Men make demands on women, order them around, coerce them to fulfill their desires, threaten them and abuse them if they fail to please them. Men do not have tasks to perform, no challenge to meet. The Snakeprince mobilizes women to serve him. Like a playboy, he leads a carefree life; horseback riding, hunting are his pastimes – the luxury of the landed nobility in the eyes of Hungarian peasants – and when he is back home, a gang of cooks, chambermaids, butlers, and waiters assist to make his feasting, breathing, and sleeping pleasurable. He seems so passive and helpless that women must help him. He seems unaware of intrigue around him; if it were not for his observant footman, he would never notice his first wife lamenting at his bedside. This tells also something of female efficiency and male inefficiency.

Does AaTh 425A speak from the vantage point of the woman? This tale in Europe belongs to the favorite repertoire pieces of both male and female narrators, but because storytelling in traditional peasant villages is a distinctively male occupation, the female story is not biased by either sex's rendition. In the patriarchal family system which the tale mirrors, the division of sex roles is taken for granted. It is up to the narrator's personal interest to take sides. This is forcefully illustrated by the variants of Péter Pandur and Zsuzsanna Palkó. I am inclined to agree with Asadowskij's observation that it is not the content but the style, the internalization of the incidents, that make a tale feminine or masculine (Asadowskij 1926).

In 1975, Megas published the following synopsis of the Amor and Psyche tale:

> The basic scheme is easy to recognize; it always concerns the marriage of a girl to a mysterious being. The duration of the marriage depends on respecting a prohibition; the young wife disobeys the prohibition and the husband disappears; she prepares herself and sets out to find him. She suffers terrible pains but at the end is reunited with him. (Megas 1975: 464.)

This story skeleton was deduced in the spirit of the Grimm brothers; it fits the traditional educational role of folktales administered to adolescent girls in the petty burgeoise household. "Obey your husband, fulfill his desires, do not fight back. Don't think for youself because if you do, you will lose him. Being left alone means loss of status." This is, in essence, what the tale told to future wives communicates. It does not make much difference if the tellers are men or women because their way of thinking is equally governed by the social order in which they live. Our analytical reading of the Hungarian ethnic type and its personal variables does not support the lexical content outline of Megas. The careful examination of other regional subtypes may show further tendencies and crystallizations to lead us to more meaningful subtexts and universals incorporated by this tale.

THE CRACK ON THE RED GOBLET,
OR TRUTH IN MODERN LEGEND

Friedrich Ranke's 1925 definition of the folk legend has generally been accepted for many years. According to Ranke, "the folk legend is a popular narrative with an objectively untrue imaginary content" (Ranke 1969: 4) and "by its nature claims to be given credit on the part of the teller as well as the listener" (Ranke 1969: 3). Since Ranke's time, fieldworkers have assembled a more representative, scientifically recorded corpus of legends which indicates that both of his statements need revision. Nevertheless, Ranke's definition lingers on, and questions concerning its validity have been raised only recently (Georges 1971: 1–19). The authors of this essay in particular tried to demonstrate that "although objective truth and the presence, quality, and quantity of subjective belief are irrelevant, it is all the more relevant that any legend . . . makes its case. It takes a stand and calls for the expression of opinions in the question of truth and belief" (Dégh and Vázsonyi 1971: 301).

Speaking of the currently observable modern legend, this essential feature becomes more conspicuous because legends now focus more on paranormal, horrible, bizarre, and thus controversial encounters which demand, by their nature, statements of opinion from the members of legend-telling events. The legend is more conversational than other genres, and a true legend-telling event is not therefore the solo performance of one accredited person to whom the others passively listen. It is a dispute – a dialectic duel of ideas, principles, beliefs, and passions. It resembles strongly the theological polemics of the Age of Reformation and Counterreformation in its topics, methods, and atmosphere. Peuckert wrote of it as the conflict of two worldviews, two belief worlds (Peuckert 1965: 35).

Belief, however, is a matter of gradation. "You believe more in one idea that the other" wrote Åke Hultkrantz (1968: 80). Albert Wesselski (1931: 24–53), too, noted the ambivalent nature of legend belief, saying that the legend is "half believed." On a scale running from total belief to total nonbelief, there are numerous grades. But the real opposite of belief is not an indifferent, impartial, more imaginary nonbelief but rather another active belief which disproves the first. We will identify such belief as "negative belief" and the legend based on it as "negative legend." If, for example, someone were to relate the legend, reduced here to its minimum, for the sake of simplicity, that: "Monday morning the house on N. Street was haunted," or, in a fuller form, "I believe that on Monday morning the house on N. Street was haunted," the proponent would qualify as a believer. If, on the other hand, someone were to state: "I do not believe that on Monday morning the house was haunted," he would be looked upon as an unbeliever. In most cases, the sentence could be reformulated, without the modification of its essential meaning, as follows: "I believe that on Monday morning the house on N. Street was not haunted." In this form the proponent shows himself to be a believer even if the belief is preceded by a negative sign. He is the counterpart of the previously mentioned individual, and thus a participant in the dialectics of the legend process. In his disclaimer he does not use rational counterproof, and accordingly, his disapproval does not divert the legend from the legend conduit[1] that progresses frequently from the believer to the negative believer and vice versa. Therefore, in such cases we will use the label "negative legend" instead of "antilegend," which has been proposed by folklorists[2] to denote narratives that discredit an account expressive of another kind of belief on the basis of a negative belief.

The following are the basic variables of the legend considered in relationship to belief:

Positive legend

I believe that	on Monday morning the house on N. Street was haunted.

Negative legend

I do not believe that	on Monday morning the house on N. Street was haunted.

Or, in a more candid phrasing:

I believe that	on Monday morning the house on N. Street was not haunted.

The situation is entirely different if the opponents derive their statements not from belief but draw evidence conceived as objective and correct according to the norms of society. In this case the statement might be called antilegend.

Antilegend

I know that it is not true that   on Monday morning the house on N. Street was haunted.

Or:

I know that it is true that   on Monday morning the house on N. Street was not haunted.

The real difference between the antilegend and the negative legend is not that the teller of the former refers to knowledge, cognition, observation or facts. This kind of reference is often made by the mediator of both positive and negative legends, although not necessarily with the use of the same nomenclature. What matters is that the denial in the antilegend was not conceived in the "legend climate," as Peuckert (1965: 34) expresses it, but in a "rational climate." With its rational emphasis, the antilegend does not substitute one belief for another but intends to attach and destroy the legend as a whole. Legends are, according to Peuckert, "documents of the wrestling of a magic or mythic *Weltanschauung* with that of the rational, the sensible."[3]

In the case of the spook of the house on N. Street, as well as many other common legends, the representative of rationalism will obviously seldom find objective proof because of the nature of legend situations. But this example can be abandoned for another that shows more aptly this analysis.

There is a legend transmitted to college freshman by sophomore girls mainly in September and October as a part of the newcomers' initiation into group membership. It is about a young college girl who goes on a blind date with a fraternity boy to a party at his fraternity house. The boy slips a Spanish fly (cantharides) into her drink, and she is seduced (Greenberg 1973). *Consumer Reports* in 1972 informed its readers that, according to scientific tests, "cantharides is not an aphrodisiac, despite it popular reputation." This communication could be the basis of an antilegend:

Positive legend

I believe that   cantharides is an aphrodisiac and a boy seduced a girl by mixing it into her drink.

Negative legend

I do not believe that   cantharides is an aphrodisiac and
                                         a boy seduced a girl by mixing it
                                         into her drink.

Or:

I believe that   cantharides is not an aphrodisiac
                                         and a boy did not seduce a girl
                                         by mixing it into her drink.

Antilegend

I know that it is not true that   cantharides is an aphrodisiac and
                                         boy seduced a girl by mixing it
                                         into her drink.

The antilegend, based on socially accepted objective knowledge, cannot be classified with the regular legends. The antilegend did not originate in the atmosphere in which legend-creating forces can act. On the contrary, its tendency is destructive to the legend; under normal conditions, it does not venture forth on the legend conduit of either positive or negative believers. It does not belong to folklore, just as an incidental, contrary opinion of another expert that cantharides is indeed an aphrodisiac would also not belong. However, it does make a difference if, for example, in the course of a discussion between believers and nonbelievers, the antilegend becomes refuted in a way other than by an argument on the basis of a contrary belief. The new formation thus created perhaps does not have to be named – either seriously or humorously – "anti-antilegend." The double denial would convert the much traveled story into a secondary positive legend:

Secondary positive legend

I do not believe that it is not true
that   cantharides is an aphrodisiac and
                                         a boy seduced a girl by mixing it
                                         into her drink.

That is:

I believe that it is true that   cantharides is an aphrodisiac,
                                         and a boy seduced a girl by mix-
                                         ing it into her drink.

One hopes that the given nomenclature with the pertinent schemes is not too reminiscent of scholasticism. The intention is to make a clear distinction between, on one hand, positive and negative belief, and, on the other, nonbelief based on positive or negative cognizance. Although nonbelief might also be a vehicle of legends – legend accounts might be appended to a nonbelieving statement – and occasionally might help a legend to pass from the sender to the receiver, nonbelief is seldom an active part of the legend formation process.

In the foregoing, we mentioned knowledge, cognition, observation, and facts as being contrary to the objectively unestablished legend belief. Our reader may wonder if we are thereby giving free play to the principle of Friedrich Ranke and others with whom we have already taken issue (Dégh and Vázsonyi 1971: 282). By no means do we suggest that the legend statement is definitely untrue and that, consequently, the counter-statement is definitely true. It might happen that the legend belief coincides with the truth and the contrary knowledge turns out to be untrue. It is possible, we propose, to believe the truth and to know the untruth. Moreover, it is possible to doubt both. The legend belief does not have much to do with plain reason and common sense; indeed, in most cases, it can defy them successfully. One person's belief might be the conviction of another, and vice versa. People, for example, earlier believed without any scientific evidence in many curative methods which medicine verified later. Following the verification of such practice, the cure belongs equally to rational medical science and to irrational folk belief. Dundes (1961: 37) wrote: "The homeopathic magic of many cures has . . . been found to be the scientific basis of immunization through inoculations . . . There are true as well as false superstitions." If, let us suppose, research can verify, or has already verified, certain paranormal phenomena, folk narratives about such phenomena will invariably remain legends. It is not the scientific cognition of experts that will verify them for the legend-producing folk but the sustaining folk faith, the dialectics of positive and negative belief. The legend is able not only to defy reason but also to extricate itself from its unwanted support. In general, it remains unaffected by friendly or hostile encounters with reality.

The most organized, guileful attempt of the antilegend to invade the legend belief system in the modern world has come from the occult sciences, parapsychology in particular. This realm of knowledge/belief attained academic status when, yielding to Margaret Mead's proposal, the American Association for the Advancement of Science admitted the Parapsychological Association to its membership in 1969. Currently, about 100 colleges in the United States offer courses in parapsychology and related fields. Parapsychologists or paranormalists, as Professor Joseph Rhine, the path-breaking pioneer of Duke University calls himself and his followers, are mostly concerned with clairvoyance, out-of-body experience, psychokinesis, and precognition. They contend that such phenomena are caused by natural forces and dissociate themselves from researchers dealing with the supernatural. Nevertheless, the growing prestige of parapsychology inevitably spreads over a great many occult explorations, movements, and business enterprises. Hence, in consideration of the relationship between legend belief and truth, the current position of parapsychology has to be taken into account.

With reference to factual observations, precision instruments, and elaborate theories, researchers state that what had been considered before as the concomitant of semiconsciousness (*Dämmerzustand*), illusion, gullibility, accidental circumstances, or the product of creative fantasy is, in many cases, true. That is to say, this area of knowledge does not try to disprove the belief contained in legends and does not only reach conclusions independent from, but identical with, belief, as some other disciplines occasionally do. Instead, it enters an alliance with belief and proves it. The memorates – the apparent evidences of fabulates – not only theoretically but also practically figure as testimonies in the system of parapsychology. Parapsychology rates paranormal phenomena, the subject of most contemporary legends, as truth; hence it accepts pertinent personal narratives as objective reality reports. Folkloristically speaking, it attempts to liquidate the legend itself as a genre or at least transfer it from the category "legend" into the category "true story." However, is parapsychology successful in this attempt?

There is a red goblet on the mantlepiece of our living room. It is shaped like a graceful tulip; two deer in rich gold dust were painted on it by a skilled craftsman some time in the Biedermeier era. A small crack on its upper rim is hardly noticeable. The crack probably lowers the goblet's value somewhat, but for us, this minute flaw makes the goblet special. It is the source and the bearer of a legend. The antique glass is a gift from Mrs. D., the wife of an affluent retired Hungarian farmer of W., in Canada. She gave it to us as a souvenir, a token of friendship, and also because she "does not like broken things in her home." Broken glass might cause bad luck. Besides, she had wanted to get rid of it for a long time anyway because of the ominous story of its crack. Mrs. D. received the goblet from a favorite aunt in the Old Country and brought it along when she emigrated; for decades, it stood with other knicknacks on a shelf in her china cabinet. One day, not so long ago, she thought she heard a soft clink from inside the glass case. When she looked to see what was the matter, she was horrified to see the sudden fracture on the goblet. Of course, she sensed what it portended, and a letter came a week later with the sad message confirming her fear that her aunt had died the same minute the glass cracked. "I do not believe in such things," she told us, finishing her account, "but in this case . . . there must be something to it . . . maybe. She died right in *that* moment. What do you say?"

The life token motif – death of a person indicated through the mysterious self-destruction of a related object – is as universal (Motif E760–67) as the multifarious notions about death portents that signal the death of a faraway person to a beloved kin (Bächtold-Stäubli and Hoffmann-Krayer 1927–1942: 1000–1003). Mrs. D. was probably aware of the fact that her experience was not unique. This is why she said, standing in front of the china cabinet with the goblet in her hand, that she does not believe in *such* things. She did not say that she does not believe in *this* concrete phenomenon that she herself observed; nor did she say that she fully believes it, without having any second thought. She was hesitant, undecided about what to think. Her conclusion was that there *might* be something to it. She expected us, outsiders representing the judgment of society, to advise her. "Who knows?" was our response. We still think it was the best answer under current circumstances of scientific knowledge. It deserved a nod of assent from Mrs. D.

Taking all things into consideration, the problem of the cracked goblet might be of interest to quite a few people besides the parapsychologists – for example, the husband who wants to learn more about the personality of his wife to increase his understanding of her views. It might also be of interest to the family doctor in his treatment of Mrs. D.'s eventual nervous complaints; to the antique dealer concerned with the preservation of perishable old glasses; to the glass manufacturer who wants to know why glass objects sometimes crack without direct impact; to the woman herself in view of her own sensory and extrasensory perceptions; to the minister because of the possible conflict between official religion and folk belief; to the friends and relatives of the dead and the living woman; and, in general, to all who desire to believe, to hesitate, or to disbelieve. There is only one category of people uninterested in the mystery of the cracked glass, provided they choose to remain within the limits of their profession – the folklorists.

Strictly speaking, however, Gerhard Heilfurth (1967: 31) has already gone beyond this limit. In one of his books, he commented: "The [paranormal] phenomena recently became the object of research in parapsychology." This sounds like a factual remark, yet one can deduce something from it. By putting this sentence into a folklore study, he declared that parapsychological research is relevant to folkloristics. Others are even more explicit: Fritz Harkort (1968: 103) cites his own precognitive dreams; Leea Virtanen (1976: 345) claims to rely on an unknown power in acquiring information. It seems that some folklorists believe that parapsychological or any other of the occult researches can be instrumental in the future formulation of standpoints of the discipline. Can this really be true?

For the sake of simplicity, let us assume that the numinous[4] quality so much emphasized by many contemporary legend scholars will be totally clarified in the near future. Let us assume that researchers will be able to measure the presence of paranormal energies with the help of a brilliant new invention, the numinometer, which will perform with *deca-numen* precision. In this way, they will find out that a part of the perception attributed to hallucination, daydreams, error, fantasy, or overstatement are real facts. They will verify that paranormal experiences are concerned not with delusions but with functions of formerly unrecognized senses. But they will find this for only a segment of the range of paranormal experiences, and not for all of them. The visions of psychotics, the sensory errors of normal people under great emotional strain, or the innocent exaggerations of raconteurs will nonetheless, again and again, be manifested. But if these phenomena do not cease to exist, and if psychology does not lose its validity beside parapsychology, then neurotics, dreamers, ravers, and narrators will continue to tell ego stories that parallel the accounts of people who command extrasensory perception. There will be no apparent difference between them. Both kinds of tellers will allude, as before, to testimony of their own eyes. And of those who pass the accounts on, some will state under scientific warranty that a paranormal phenomenon actually had occurred at a particular place at a particular hour, whereas others will continue to refer to trustworthy old Uncle Steve who experienced it himself.

It is questionable whether a truthful report of real experience is more persuasive than the product of robust hallucination or vigorous fantasy. André Gide (1949: 5) noted an unpublished story by Oscar Wilde about the man who used to entertain his fellow villagers with his enticing lies at nightly get-togethers. Once he told about a faun he saw playing the flute in the forest and a troop of woodland creatures dancing around. Then he told about three mermaids he saw on the seashore, combing their green hair with a golden comb. But once the man actually saw the faun and the woodland creatures in the forest and the mermaids on the seashore! When, as usual, the villagers asked him: "What did you see?" he answered: "I saw nothing." Evidently, Wilde's narrator belonged to that brand of people whom truth does not inspire but embarrass. We do not think such people are very rare.

Ultimately, legends will survive the attacks of the occult sciences. A legend will arise whether the paranormal phenomenon actually took place or not; the result of the event will be legend with, without, or in spite of the assistance of parapsychology or any other scholarly assertion of truth. It will move on through the legend conduit whether or not it is true. It seems possible, however, that the number of legends that will antagonize the modern discipline will multiply in the future. These negative legends will probably claim that the cases described by scientists were not real. Accordingly, there already are floating legends that suggest that people have not been on the moon at all; we could read in the newspaper about a Southern farmer who took his son out of a school in which such ridiculous, nonsensical tales are taught as truths. We also were informed that the axis of the Earth was altered by the underground nuclear tests; thus the predictions of astrology are no longer valid. In this vein, Uncle Steve is still the most trustworthy witness for the legend recipients who live in the "mythical climate"[5] and will continue to stay in it for awhile, if not forever. The Southern farmer is more prepared to hear the fiddle tune of David accompanied by St. Cecilia from the moon than the televised reports from the astronauts.

So far, parapsychology has had only one significant effect on folkloristics. It seems to infuse new authority into the concept of the "objectively untrue" postulated by Friedrich Ranke and his followers. From the viewpoint of legend theory, there is only one reason to investigate whether the paranormal phenomenon featured in a story has or has not really taken place, and that is when some kind of inference can be drawn from the result of the investigation. There can be only one inference; namely, that if the event really happened, the narrative that tells about it should be treated differently than the way it would be treated if it had not happened. Here we have the old, often refuted definition element in a new shape (Dégh and Vázsonyi 1971: 282–286).

Obviously, Ranke's "objectively untrue" and von Sydow's statement (1934: 75) that legends "cannot have happened" were not rejected by all authors. Moreover, some see the legend as "solidified rumor." Gordon Allport and Leo Postman (1947: 162) conventionalized versions of accounts that were originally rumors. According to Tamotsu Shibutani (1966: 155), this is a misconception that is derived from the presumed falsity of orally transmitted phenomena. Scott Littleton (1965: 21) states that in the definitions "from Max Müller to Malinowski, from Hartland to Bidney," the first, basic criterion is almost always "the extent to which a narrative is or is not based upon objectively determinable facts or scientifically acceptable hypotheses." Burkhardt

(Isler 1971: 3) says that it is not reliable to assert that, by definition, legend contents are in any case objectively untrue, because they would disclaim *a priori* the existence of spirits. That is to say, the legend does not cease to exist as a legend just because it deals with "objectively true," or occult, phenomena.

This is, however, acceptable as a principle that concerns not only paranormal phenomena but also any legend subject. It need not be proven that legend tellers, unless they are persons of unique encyclopedic knowledge, cannot have ample information of all possible legend topics. The legend is frequently identified, after von Sydow, as *Glaubenfabulate* (belief fabulate); this view actually narrows the concept of the legend. Even if we believed that legend tellers can obtain proof through laborious search on whether a certain event has objectively taken place, what kind of attitude do we expect from them? If they found that the account was untrue, should they pass the story on, offering as true what they know is untrue? If, on the other hand, they found that the account is true, should they be exercising a senseless restraint and be silent about it? This is the behavior not of *Homo narrans* (K. Ranke 1967b: 4–12) but, indeed, of the pathological liar. An even more demanding criterion is the one that requires a "scientifically *acceptable* hypothesis" (Littleton 1965: 21). The word acceptable implies the capability of independent and correct judgment. Such skill cannot be expected from the legend recipient, who later assumes the teller's role. Since objective facts cannot govern the recipient's attitudes, the concept of truth or its elevated form, the scientific hypothesis, is irrelevant to the determination of the legend.

The rapid accumulation of successive events, the modification of ideas, the discovery of new facts, the repudiation of old ones and their rehabilitation, are processes that can hardly be followed by the average educated person, or even the scientist. The common awareness of the folk develops and changes in continuation with, and often parallel to, scientific accomplishment, sometimes in opposition to and even independently from it, under the impact of diverse factors. This, however, does not imply the "knowledge of objective truth" and the acceptance of "scientific hypotheses." On the contrary, common knowledge incorporates this information very slowly, almost reluctantly. Humanity hardly ever stepped over the confines of geocentrism.

The mutable judgments on objective truth, therefore, have neither theoretical bearing on legend nor do they have any practical effect on the worldview of the legend. What was born as a legend, within the "legend climate," what was transmitted as legend and received as legend, or, in other words, what traveled through the legend conduit in society, stays a legend even if its content turns out to be true.

Shibutani (1966: 156) cites the example of a historic personality's legendary accounts, which do not differ significantly from documentary records. Likewise, a story spread as incontestably true cannot be classified as a legend only because its content turns out to be untrue – unless, of course, it remains alive after it is generally disproved. It will be enough to call to mind the usually inscrutable objective truth of historic legends, but a couple of examples of contemporary legends should further illuminate this point.

An acquaintance, who is an enthusiastic rumormonger and legend teller, related the following story: Once a bachelor prepared to take a bath in his apartment in a highrise building. He had undressed, the bath water was running, and he was prepared to step into the tub when he heard the newsboy throwing the paper against the front door. The man opened the door slightly and looked out to see if there was anyone around. Seeing no one on the stairway, he stepped out and stooped down to pick up the paper. In the same moment, a draft slammed the door behind him, and the bachelor stood stark naked on the stairway. Not knowing what to do, he pressed the doorbell of the nearest neighbor, who was shocked to see this lunatic and would not let him in. So he tried something else, running amuck between the floors while the bath water flowed in a small stream from under his door. After several adventures, the janitor came to his rescue. As is usual, our informant gave details concerning the accident location and also named the credible source. Shortly afterward and for weeks thereafter, we kept hearing the same story with slight variations. After a while, it started to fade. No doubt, this was a typical urban legend that spread and evaporated quickly. A year later, we encountered the story again printed in the Russian novel *Twelve chairs* (1961), by Ilf and Petrov. The legend, believed to be local, appeared in almost the same form. Evidently, this was the source of the versions we had heard. The credible modern urban stories were most probably siblings of the several-decades-old Russian story and therefore objectively untrue.

Soon after this experience, our accomplished legend narrator surprised us with another credible story. This time it was about a young hothead who took part in a political conspiracy during the late 1950s. When he was about to be apprehended, he tried to save his skin by illegal flight across the Hungarian border. He did not make it, so he secretly returned to Budapest, where his widowed mother hid him in her two-room apartment, all the while spreading rumors that he was dead. There the young man lived for years. When someone rang the bell, he crawled under the bed or stepped into the closet. He never dared to talk aloud, cough, or even breathe or sneeze vigorously for fear that the neighbors or an occasional visitor might notice something. One day, after five years had elapsed, he could not stand it any longer. He ripped open the window and started to yell, scream, and cry so that people on the street gathered beneath him; the young man had a fit. An ambulance was summoned and he was taken to the psychiatric ward of a hospital. He is still there. As a tragicomic epilogue and conclusion to this well-dramatized story, it turned out that he had no reason for his seclusion, for he had been granted amnesty years earlier. When our informant waited for our reaction, we just smiled knowingly, because we recognized the original, the *Urform*. It seemed obvious that this was a simplified, actualized oral retelling of Sartre's drama, "The Condemned of Altona." Our informant vehemently protested. He insisted that he knew the mother and had met the son. Actually, they had been neighbors when they were children. He could also name the hospital where the man was treated for his nervous breakdown. Our informant acted just like any ambitious legend teller attempting to make his story sound truthful. After having heard the same story repeated by others with the same claim for credence, we followed up the leads. It was true. Two witnesses, the mother of the legend hero and the doctor who treated him in the hospital, said so. This legend – what else could we call it – was actually true. After almost a decade, we again came across the legend in a news report in the *Indianapolis Star* of May 6, 1972.

> Moscow (UPI) – A Russian who collaborated with Nazi invaders during World War II has emerged after hiding for 20 years behind his mother's stove, it was reported yesterday. The newspaper, *Soviet Byelorussia*, said P. L. Lavnik, now 48 years old, went into hiding after the war while his mother spread rumors he was dead. He came out of hiding, the newspaper said, in response to a government offer to pardon collaborators and army deserters.

The Louisville Courier-Journal of March 17, 1968 (p. 2) reported a similar and even a longer-lasting hiding story:

> San Fernando, Spain (AP) – Juan Rodriguez Aragon, 67, who locked himself up in his house when the Spanish civil war started July 18, 1936, has surrendered to the authorities, the Spanish news agency, Cifra, reported. Aragon, a carpenter when hostilities began, told officials he was afraid the political articles he used to write in a local magazine might bring reprisals. Cifra said his family used to tell friends Juan had disappeared. Authorities indicated he would be questioned and then released since there were no charges against him.

Are these all corrupted versions of the Sartre drama? Or did the Budapest folk legend reach the Soviet Union and Spain in ten years?

Or are they factual occurrences? No matter what the truth is, the legend did and will recur. Hiding, after all, is an even older, more elementary concept than stories about hiding.

Here is a third story in which truth and untruth intermingle within even greater complexity. The original story is a model of the classical historic legend. All children in Budapest know this story, although none can tell where they learned it. Perhaps parents communicate it to their children as part of their enculturation. It might once have also been printed in an elementary school reader. In other words, the legend is common knowledge to everyone who was born and reared or who lived for a while in the Hungarian capital. It is about the Chain Bridge, the first to connect the two parts of the city, which is divided by the Danube. This bridge, decorated with two lion statues on both ends, was built in 1842 by Adam Clark, a British engineer. At the opening ceremonies, Clark proudly stated that he had completed his work to perfection – not even a nail was missing. A cobbler's apprentice delivering boots to costumers happened to pass by and heard what the engineer said. "The lions have no tongues!" yelled the boy in front of the audience of eminent townspeople, whereupon the embarrassed builder jumped into the river and drowned. It is commonly known that the story of Adam Clark's suicide is objectively untrue. He did not jump into the Danube but lived for a number of years after returning to England; he even built several other bridges.

At a recent international folklore conference, one of the coauthors related this example during an informal talk with friends, who agreed that legends might not even need a special occasion for their communication. They can be part of a group's common knowledge, a group whose members cannot remember when and how they learned them. M. M. related that the same story had a similar currency in his native Ljubljana [Slovenia], which proves that the story is not a local legend, but a migratory one. "The punchline of the account is that the lions actually have their tongues in their mouths," commented T. D., of the University of Budapest, robbing the narrative of its epic credibility. In discussing the case further with Hungarians, we decided on a second punchline: "The lions have no tongues." We definitely remembered this as the truth. The debate would have been easy to resolve, since the lions are still at the abutments of the bridge, but we did not expect folklore theory to benefit significantly were the dispute settled. But our friend in Budapest did not leave it at that. She climbed up the platform, photographed one of the lions at close range, and sent the picture to us. There was a tongue in the lion's mouth. This came as a surprise, so we continued our inquiry whereupon we unearthed a new legend: the city council recently ordered the originally missing tongues to be made. We do not pursue the matter any further. This is enough to demonstrate the many facets of truth in legend. Even this plain story could be transformed from legend to negative legend, to secondary positive legend, to antilegend and again, to legend.

Thinking of less tangible topics, such as the paranormal that so many hold as the main subject of modern legend, we still insist that, in terms of legend process and social functions, it makes no difference what was or will be proven by factual knowledge. Likewise, it is irrelevant whether the legend narrator acquired the ingredients of his account through ESP or by telephone.

What happens if, instead of on weak reality, one legend belief impinges upon another equally powerful legend belief? In such a case, a peculiar phenomenon can be witnessed. There is an unwritten code of procedure that offers the proponent of the positive legend, mostly the believer, a technical advantage over the teller of the negative legend, representative of a more rational worldview. The positive legend teller can use formally unobjectionable arguments, such as "I have seen it myself," "It happened to my father, " or "I heard it from a trustworthy friend." On the other hand, the teller of the negative legend can bring up only vague generalities, such as "I have not seen it," "There are no such things," "This is just a superstition," "Such things do not exist anymore," or "Such things cannot happen here."

Such statements, which pay no heed to the truth, cannot be accepted as proofs by themselves. In rare instances, the negative legend is able to offer proof *vis-á-vis* the positive legend by confronting one belief with another. Mrs. H. of Gary, Indiana, an outstanding raconteur, told about one of her extraordinary experiences. As a young girl, she used to enjoy the cool breeze with her girlfriends on hot summer nights along a brook outside her home town. The place was quite close to the graveyard; the white tombstones seemed to gleam through the hedges, and the girls always shuddered when they walked by, remembering oft-heard ghost stories. One night, terror-stricken, they spotted a white apparition as if swaying in the moonlight on the plank across the rivulet. Will-Erich Peuckert (1965: 58), who asserted that "the bridge, as well as, or even more so the brook, is a place surrounded by the feeling of dread from the Beyond," would not have been surprised to hear that the site was a recognized locus for supernatural encounters in Mrs. H.'s birthplace. The girls, shaken by fear, ran toward the main street. Much later, they found out that one of the local youths had played a nasty trick on them. "So, you mean, there are no ghosts?" we queried. She answered the same way as we did to the owner of the goblet with the telekinetic crack on its rim: "Who knows?"

What does this negative story prove? Nothing more than that there was no ghost in a certain situation at a certain place. Peuckert (1965: 88) cited similar accounts, what he calls *Gegensage* (counterlegend or antilegend). One is about a country sexton who chases away a black sheep, while yelling to the great glee of others: "Get thee behind me, Satan!" Another widespread legend mentioned by the same author (Peuckert 1965: 91), is about the village drunk who lays a wager for a dare with his cronies. He visits a cemetery at midnight, accidentally nails his coat to a grave marker, and loses his mind from fright. Departing from these and similar negative legends, only arbitrary and unjustified analogues could lead to the assumption that, since there were no occult forces or supernatural beings involved in these cases, there could not have been occult forces or supernatural beings involved in other cases elsewhere. That is, Satan did not join another man or another occasion in the guise of a black sheep, and the dead man disturbed in his grave did not grab the coat of another nightly prowler in the cemetery. This kind of negative legend can prove only that there are delusions and that there might be deliberate deceit as well. Nevertheless, this is too weak an argument to upset, at least formally, the magico-mythic belief supported by "evidence."

In the peculiar atmosphere of the legend, the affirmative statement would be the winner over the negative if it were to capitalize only on the advantage of the fallacy of *argumentum ad ignorantiam*: the fact that statements the opposite of which are unprovable seem to be true. However, the superiority of the positive legend over the negative is built on a "legal" basis. "The burden of proving the existence or nonexistence of a given fact lies upon [he] who alleges it" (Kling 1966: 419). Hence, the reason for the "legal" mastery of the positive legend can be attributed not only to the negative legend's inability to provide proof, but also to the fact that the positive legend shows the ability to do so. The legend belief defies rational motive, common sense, contrary knowledge – all things of which the antilegend is made. In most cases it is successful in defying contrary belief offered by the negative legend. It even survives the competition of occult sciences and also refuses their help. The legend cannot use any truth but its own. Once in a while a legend dies. But if it does so, it dies of natural causes and because the time of its demise has come.

As we have seen, the negative legend limits its own validity to a few cases (mostly only to one) and the inferences offered by them are limited as well. The shrunken negative legend example: "On Monday morning the house on N. Street was not haunted" has no further logical consequences. On the other hand, an immense number of consecutive deductions can be derived from a positive legend, such as "On Monday the house on N. Street was haunted." In this instance, we must infer that ghosts most probably do exist. If there were one somewhere at a given time, we can count on another somewhere else at some other time. Yet if ghosts exist, they must act according to the unknown rules of their existence. They can appear whimsically. The worst they can do is cry, wail, moan, knock, rattle chains, throw objects, and hover incorporeally in sheets thus undermining people's faith in the calculable order of things and confidence in rationality and causality, upon which the average person's feeling of the continuity of earthly existence is based. Some of the occult sciences – parapsychology in particular – disclaim dealings with the supernatural and declare that the object of their investigation belongs not in the paranormal but in the strictly normal world. The followers of these trends, however, do not seem to honor the distinction. What the investigators consider as knowledge is turned to belief by the masses, and what is meant as a theory appears as a new vocabulary for old legends. Hence, the social effect of the occult sciences, whether they concern themselves with the natural or the supernatural, does not show notable differences. It would seem that the question of whether that particular ghost did or did not haunt the house on N. Street at that particular time or whether that crack on the red goblet is or is not a psychic phenomenon, has a greater significance than one would have assumed.

This is, fortunately, more theory than practice. People seldom thoroughly examine their own thoughts, let alone those of others. Believers usually do not draw a lesson from the consequences of their beliefs. The plebes occupying room 4714 at the West Point Military Academy who saw the life-sized apparition of a nineteenth-century officer emerge from a wall (*Time*, December 4, 1972: 6), did not unconditionally agree with each other. Some suspected a hoax or looked for another common sense explanation. Others, such as the cadet captain who investigated the event and was "still a firm unbeliever, admitted that the designated point of evaporation, which is normally quite warm, felt icy to the touch." Presumably, the vision was a reinforcement of supernatural belief for some; and there were several cadets who, like so many legend tellers, began their account like this: "I certainly do no believe in such things, but this one I have seen with my own two eyes."

In general, people eclectically select from the treasure trove of folk belief. Some believe in witches but do not believe in werewolves; others believe in werewolves but do not believe in the evil eye. Some believe in the evil eye but do not believe in vampires, or they believe in vampires but do not believe in the return of the mummy. Some do not believe in transcendental inspiration but do believe in precognition. A high school senior in a Canadian rural town, an enthusiast of scientific occultism, explained to us: "There are no ghosts. This is a superstition. But there are astral bodies and it is easy to confuse them with ghosts." In addition, many people believe in their own official religion, which prohibits the belief in witches, werewolves, the evil eye, vampires, living mummies, transcendental inspiration and pre-cognition, ghosts, and astral bodies. Even if believers do not generalize their beliefs, the question to be raised is of great importance. Indeed the *question*, not the *answer*, is essential. The worldview of people is extremely complex and durable. In general, it does not change signific-antly under the influence of some persuasive argument or counterar-gument. Few people of magico-mythical disposition could be turned into rationalist thinkers through the thoughtful advice of a friend, and few rationalist thinkers have given up their reservations about what is commonly known as a superstition under the influence of a legend. Persons who have once had a taste of a belief, no matter how and where, will hardly reconsider it throughout their lives. The attitude toward the legend develops in time into a well-constructed and well-set role and even into a dialogue or a repeated group rite. The cast is remarkably stable; not even the text of the roles is modified consider-ably over time.

In Indiana Harbor, we met an elderly couple who were eager to tell us all the stories they knew. The man specialized in jokes, and his wife was an accomplished legend teller (Dégh 1976). We visited them repeatedly for several years. In addition to the always interesting new stories from their inexhaustible supply, the woman recited each time her favorite supernatural experience. Once, she heard loud sob-bing while she was cooking in the kitchen. She opened the door to see who was crying but could not find anyone outside. Only much later did she learn that her sister's daughter had died at the same time, far away, at the other end of the town. They loved each other dearly, and this is why the old woman heard her dying niece crying. The text of the narrative was almost exactly the same each time. The husband always listened patiently as she unfolded the story – who knows for how many hundreds of times in front of varied audiences of occasional visitors! – and like an actor on cue, he interjected at regular intervals: "Oh, baloney! There are no such things! I don't believe one word of it!" Whereupon his wife responded in due course with such retorts: "Oh, come on! It wasn't just me who heard it. There were two other people here visiting me, and they heard it, too!" At this point, the man became irritated: "They haven't heard a thing. They were just imagining things like yourself!" This ritual wordy warfare took at least five minutes every time. The woman became more and more excited, and the man, more and more stubborn. Then suddenly, without any noticeable reason, the debate would end. Naturally, it had no outcome. How could there have been a resolution if the couple had not been able for decades to come to terms on this matter? The question that apparently played a rather important role in the life of the otherwise peaceful, relaxed, tolerant, and emphatically rational old couple continued to remain a question.

Similarly, no agreement could be reached by a mother and daughter concerning the existence of supernatural being in Crown Point (Dégh and Vázsonyi 1971: 294). The recorded dialogue of the two women could be conceived as a legend-telling session in which the aged mother related her witch stories with remarkable verbosity and eloquence and her daughter, a middle-aged woman, responded with a counterstory to each. The stories and counterstories, the arguments and counterarguments, the legends and negative legends fitted smoothly, so that, if nothing else, the heated and persistent ideological debate seemed to be not an improvised, but rather a well-rehearsed, dramatic act.

It has been found that accidental pairs or groups of people who have no opportunity to learn and rehearse their parts act very much the same way. People gathered at a party, customers standing by chance next to each other at a bar, new residents of a student dormitory, participants of a slumber party, or travelers on a long train trip sharing the same compartment know the essentials of their roles. Each of these actors will faithfully present his or her accepted image assumed for one or more occasions, or sometimes for a lifetime, like the players in a *commedia dell'arte*. Pantalone, the captain, the doctor, Arlecchino, Brighella, and the others all knew what behavior was allotted to them by tradition. Similarly, in the legend-telling groups, stereotypical characters are necessary for the believer, the objective observer, the undecided, the skeptic, the negative-believer, the rationalist, and the others. The stereotypes appear not only as individuals but also as representatives of segments of society, as spokesmen of diverse beliefs and convictions.[6] Nowadays the parapsychologist and his congeners also appear on the stage. They stand for the antilegend, but they involuntarily serve the cause of the legend.

The roles of all actors in the performance also become ambiguous. It is not clear any more who represents whom. Earlier there were backward, unschooled, superstitious, often older people whose firm belief stood opposed to the disbelief of the enlightened, schooled, progressive younger generation. Contrarily, nowadays it is more the young generation who seem to be inclined toward mysticism and belief in the occult. The young promulgate both old-fashioned ghost

stories and modern legends related to growing cults and occult practices and sciences. Their identification with legend is not modest and
defensive like that of superstitious people of yesterday: it is aggressive
and self-conscious. Their arguments are not incoherent and naive but
sophisticated, sometimes philosophical. The legend event is no longer
limited to the narrow confines of small groups isolated from larger
society. Through the intervention of the media, legends reach out to
the masses and make participants of almost everyone in society.

What brought about the change? What technical means were essential to make it happen? How was the dissemination of legend furthered
by them? These questions require further investigation. The study of
the social avenues and functions of the legend, not only as the most
popular but also as the most characteristic folklore genre of modern
industrial society, may lead to new learning about the world in which
we live.

Part Three

CONDUITS OF TRANSMISSION

THE HYPOTHESIS OF MULTI-CONDUIT TRANSMISSION IN FOLKLORE

1.

Folklorists have long been concerned with the nature of transmission of folklore expression. Theodor Benfey, founder of the "Migrational Theory," was the first who opposed the Grimmian concept of the common language family-heritage. Benfey's theory of tale diffusion was utilized in studies without radical changes by the members of the Folklore Fellows association (otherwise known as the Finnish School). On that basis they developed folk narrative research into a special branch of comparative folkloristics. The canon of the so-called historic-geographic method demanded from its adherents the amassing of texts of tales ("variants") which are similar in their basic plots, but different in their particular formulations. The resulting "type" is a hypothetical abstraction deduced statistically from the variants. Scholars measured the extent of space and time in order to trace both the archetype and the narrative's place of origin. In 1913, Antti Aarne summarized the technique of text comparison and listed the kinds of alterations that might occur in the "archetype" in the course of its wanderings without affecting its original plot (Aarne 1913; Bødker 1965: 125; Thompson 1946: 435–436). Ten years later, Walter Anderson published his famous book on the riddle-tale, *Kaiser und Abt*, then the most extensive monograph study of its kind (Anderson 1923).[1] Anderson claimed that he had found the key to the equilibrium between the stability and variability of folk narratives, namely the "law of self correction." In his conclusion, Anderson not only confirmed Aarne's thesis concerning tale dissemination but also suggested that the same law is applicable to other kinds of folklore: songs, proverbs, riddles, magic prayers, and so forth. According to Anderson, there exists a superorganic mechanism by which folklore patterns revise themselves through automatic reinforcement of essential motifs in the unlimited number of continually transmitted variants. That is to say, this "law of self-correction" operates through people who act as vehicles of folklore and who were exposed to the given folklore kinds not once, but many times, not in one form but in multiple variations. This process aids the amplification of deteriorated single versions and the restoration of the stable archetype (Anderson 1923: 397–403). Kaarle Krohn's manual on the research method of the Finnish School (Krohn 1926/1971: 114 ff.) codified this thesis of the "remarkable stability" of folklore forms which explained the ability of traditional narrative patterns to travel around the world while remaining relatively fixed, yielding only to a limited measure of oscillation around one lasting focus. When Albert Wesselski took issue with this postulate of the historic-geographic method, Anderson further elaborated upon his early ideas in an extensive rejoinder (Anderson 1935).

Nevertheless, the unanimously accepted theses of the prestigious folklore school were even challenged by Carl Wilhelm von Sydow, one of the Folklore Fellows. In his criticism he pointed out the fallacy of assumption that oral tradition spreads like the steady current of "a stream in a certain direction" (von Sydow 1948: 17). As early as 1931, von Sydow called attention to the importance of the study of "biology of tradition" (von Sydow 1948: 11). He emphasized that text analysts did not deal with faithfully recorded folklore items but with abstracted, arbitrary constructions that had nothing to do with reality. Folk traditions do not live as common property "in the depth of the soul of the people" (von Sydow 1948: 12); rather, they are subject to individual creativity. All kinds of folk expressions have their active proponents and passive carriers who represent only a limited number of people in every community. What is being transmitted and in what way is highly incidental. With reference to his own field experience in small communities, von Sydow stated that various kinds of narratives "obey different laws for their transmission and spread" (von Sydow 1948: 44). Some genres stay within the confines of a small community and expire in no time; others travel fast and far. A complex magic tale, for example, could hardly spread from village to village since its telling requires special skills and opportunity; its diffusion is also contingent upon the ability of passive bearers carrying it further on (von Sydow 1948: 17–20).

For forty years, Walter Anderson doggedly defended his "law of self-correction" and rebutted all his opponents with alluring rhetoric, while von Sydow's important suggestions remained mostly neglected. The concept of folklore transmission became an acknowledged theoretical notion that was included in many folklore textbooks without essential critical comments (Thompson 1946: 436–438; Weiss 1946: 38; Lüthi 1962: 102–103; Bausinger 1968: 48; K. Ranke 1969: 113). Even those who otherwise disagreed with the Finnish School of Folklore quoted and confirmed for some reason the "law of self-correction" which became a household term in their vocabulary.[2]

The increase of folklore collections which were adequately recorded, containing necessary ethnographic details and social background information, enabled the reformulation of folklore transmission, variation, stabilization, continuation, diffusion and related processes. Representatives of the "Märchenbiology"[3] trend – who study the life and social function of the tale – worked independently of each other and never established a particular "school." Nevertheless, they shared the opinion that regularities of folklore communication cannot be understood without a first-hand observation of the differing kinds of storytelling processes. They recognize the necessity of studying narratives as they are shaped by the interaction of three factors: tradition, teller, and audience. Tradition, in this context, is the sum total of links in the transmission chain which represent the entire sequence of past raconteurs. It underlies the folkloric creation of individuals who are supported and controlled by the audience. Modern folklorists try to explore the regularities of transmission in different kinds of normal field situations. They observe natural and stimulated transmission processes in order to obtain more information of person-to-person textual variation. Among these numerous studies of change, we have found four methodological strategies: (1) recording of a single narrative from the same teller in different situations over a long period of time; (2) recording of the same narrative from different persons in the same community; (3) recording of a single narrative as told by persons who belong to different living generations within a community (Dégh 1969: 49–51, 76–177); (4) confronting storytellers who recite different versions of the same narrative (Goldstein 1967a: 72–84). Inspired by the ideas of Cecil Sharp[4] and his own field experiences, Gyula Ortutay wrote a theoretical study on the regularities of oral transmission in order to account for the maintenance of folklore forms. In the course of folklore variation, Ortutay described and characterized the creative and destructive phases of modification to be attributed to individual initiatives as well as to social circumstances (Ortutay 1959: 175–221).

Not too many general conclusions may yet be drawn from the observation of folklore communication in the natural context. However, we can safely say that investigations neither justify the contention that oral transmission inundates like a stream covering everything, nor support the thesis that the once-established "perfect" form of tradition is perpetuated merely by multiple and manifold reinforcement. As von Sydow had anticipated, the transmission, variation, and retention of folklore might depend on other factors as well, such as the content of its forms or the personalities of its transmitters.

Hence, if the principles which underline the spread of folklore differ from those suggested by Anderson, the question may be raised: is there an experiment that may support another theory?

2.

In an earlier article on certain features of the folk legend, we attempted to substantiate the hypothesis that legends are communicated through a specific conduit distinct from other kinds of folklore expressions. We have termed the line of transmission of legends which was created by affinities between certain people legend conduit (Dégh and Vázsonyi 1971)[5]: "By this term we understand the contact that becomes established between individuals who qualify as legend receivers or transmitters." This definition assumes that there are persons who qualify neither as receiver nor transmitters of legends. These individuals may be the "passive bearers" of legends, to use von Sydow's term (von Sydow 1948: 13–15), or else they simply may not choose to communicate legends. However, the same persons might prefer to narrate one of several other genres and might participate as "active bearers" in one or more different communicative sequences. The forms of oral transmission are as extremely diverse as are people, and the eventualities of affinity between men and folklore are just as multifarious.

If it is acceptable to assume that the legend is transmitted by members of the *legend conduit*, we might as well assume that jokes, for example, are dispensed through the *joke conduit* by a sequence of witty people; riddles pass through the *riddle conduit* made up of riddle fans; and tales progress through the *tale conduit* shaped by the different types of storytellers, and so forth. This assumption is logically plausible and may be supported by careful consideration of the social transmission of folklore. Furthermore, within a single genre, such as the tale, for example, different types, type clusters, episodes, minor incidents, and even motifs and formulas have their own conduit as they all are subject of transmission. Hence, in the following discussion, we propose to use the term "conduit" also to denote a relationship that would be more precisely identified as "sub-conduits" and "micro-conduits." Some of our experiments substantiate the concept of generic conduits, although so far we accept them only tentatively as our investigations are incomplete.

From our suggested rules and the system resulting from the further ramifications of the conduit, we would like to propose the term: *multi-conduit principle*. It would be impossible to determine the number of potential ramifications of folklore transmission as an all-inclusive whole. Similarly it would not be possible to distinguish the embranchment of any of its smaller complexes, for instance, the magic tale.

The overly simplified scheme of the multi-conduit system of folklore communication in society can be delineated as in Figure 1.

FIGURE 1

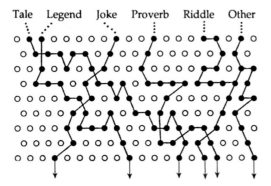

This random selection of various kinds of folklore indicates only imaginary directions and extent of the conduit. As a matter of fact, almost everyone acts as a participant in some kind or another of a communicative chain, but because of technical reasons this fact can be illustrated in only a few instances on this diagram. Each participant of one sequence can be the member of another as well. However, in reality, individual roles can sometimes be easily distinguished. People who prefer to tell ghost stories, for example, are not identical with those who enjoy cracking jokes; rumor mongers are not identical with the tellers of Märchen; and those who mediate the gossip of everyday life are unlikely to tell, let us say, historical anecdotes.

For example, two of the outstanding magic-tale-tellers whom we have encountered in our fieldwork refused to relate legends, being reluctant to claim the narratives "as truth," whereas in their field of competence, they freely used that imagination. It was remarkable to note that both János Nagy of Sára, County Zemplén, and Mrs. Palkó of Kakasd, used the same excuse for not knowing legends. In another instance, one of the bookish village wiseacres can tell only historical legends and holds contempt for those who waste their time listening to old wives' tales (Balassa 1963: 88–89). Sometimes, even man and wife may belong to different generic conduits. A joke teller of high esteem will not stop making disparaging remarks while his wife, an expert ghost-story narrator, accustomed to her husband's objections, continues to entertain her audience without the slightest embarrassment. Mr. I. Cs. of Indiana Harbor, Indiana, told us more than 250 jokes and anecdotes, and his wife is a real treasure trove of supernatural experiences and magic healing events (Dégh and Vázsonyi 1976: 101–122). Fieldworkers are well aware that communities may be subdivided according to the use of the available body of narratives. The active bearers who might be recognized artists, as well as the carriers of a single piece of interest, always find a responsive audience for their folklore message, through the chosen conduit, dependent upon the contributors' taste and interest. Correspondingly they understand perfectly well to whom the message should be passed in order to main continuance of the specific conduit. One can safely say, then, that "communication channels . . . consist of shared understandings concerning who may address whom, about what subject, under what circumstances, with what degree of confidence" (Shibutani 1966: 21). During our field research in the steel cities of Northwest Indiana, we found that old women of the Hungarian ethnic community practiced a normalized sequence of around-the-clock telephone communication to dispense information, gossip, and rumor about sickness, death, and burial of community members. The conduit of death rumor is on the alert day and night (Dégh 1969d: 76). Old ladies do not hesitate to make instantaneous chain calls when they hear about the occurrence, even if it should reach them in the late hours of the night when it is normally considered improper to communicate other kinds of information.

The foregoing examples suggest that our diagram approximates reality by the zigzagged conduits as they run side by side and as they sometimes intersect each other, though they seldom unite because the carriers of different genres are usually not identical.

Although experience shows that one of the basic regularities in the spread of oral transmission is, by and large, expressed by the *multi-conduit principle*, we have no proof to substantiate this. There is no way to follow the progress of oral transmission in society. Even those who have attempted to track the route of a single story, that before their very eyes became popular overnight, lost the entangled threat in a labyrinth. Out of many possible examples we will refer to some typical cases of interest.

A few years after World War II, according to general talk in Budapest, three German soldiers emerged from a cave close to the capital. They were pale and blind, they had long shaggy hair and beards, their nails were an inch long, and their uniforms were filthy – all rags and tatters. According to rumor, these soldiers found asylum in the cave which had been used as a military provisions room during the siege of the city. They did not know that the war was over and remained in hiding for years. Crawling out of the shelter, they exposed themselves to fresh air and sunshine, collapsed, and died. One of the daily newspapers assigned five reporters to discover the story's origin. Police investigators joined the search party which questioned a great number of respondents eager to testify to the truthfulness of the incident. However, it soon turned out that none of the 'witnesses' could offer factual evidence, and the investigators lost interest in the story. The matter was taken up by folklorists who registered the plot as a modern variant of the Kyffhäuser legend ("Friederich Rotbart auf dem Kyffhäuser" in *Deutsche Sagen* 23 by the Grimm Brothers). In another instance, New York City newsmen who pursued the Dead-Cat-Come-to-Justice rumor on its cross-country journey through department stores and police stations failed to confirm its veracity (Jacobson 1948: 44–46). The account about the neatly wrapped remains of a deceased pet cat that kept being returned to its owner until a shoplifter was shocked to death by it had to be left to the concern of folklorists (Dorson 1959a: 253–254). Another department store epic, about snakes shipped in with dry goods from Hong Kong (Cord 1969a: 110–114), was launched in 1969 and has ranged from the East Coast to the West Coast, with newsmen at its heels, heading for a blind alley. This narrative is paralleled by the case of the Stolen Grandmother whose body was loaded on the roof of a Volkswagen (Dégh 1968a: 68–77), and another narrative about a Volkswagen dented by an elephant in a parking lot (Smart 1970: 6–7); interested newsmen are still tireless, keeping on their wild goose chase.

It appears obvious that these folk legends, as any other oral phenomena, are hard to follow as they fluctuate and live in reality. It is even harder to describe them with adequate precision. Hence it is reasonable to assume that laboratory experiments could be more expedient than time-consuming, casual observation in exploring some of the laws of oral transmission. An experimental method of analysis to clarify some pertinent problems can be worked out after the evaluation of previous experimental attempts.

3.

Since the beginning of this century, social scientists attempted to elaborate a method which would enable them to prove or disprove speculations concerning the nature of oral transmission. Most of them were sociologists, social psychologists, or anthropologists, but even some of the not-overly-enterprising folklorists tried their hand in laboratory experiments. Although William Stern was the first to open vistas for

experimental text variation study as early as 1903–1906 (Stern 1903–
1906), the test most suggestive for folkloristics were processed later
(Bartlett 1920; König 1929; Schmitz 1930; Wesselski 1931; Nadel 1937–
1938; Wolff 1943; Allport and Postman 1947; Anderson 1951; Schier
1955; and others). Most of these scholars were concerned with a group
of phenomena that could be subsumed under the category "memory"
(Hunter 1964), the key to the problem of the laws of oral transmission.
The testers in general were engaged in the laboratory reproduction
concerning person-to-person oral transmission and in the measurement of each single movement in the chain of transmission.

We will discuss some of these experiments at a later point; here it
suffices to note some differences between laboratory and real-life situations. For example, under laboratory conditions, experiments in the
crucial serial reproduction are so markedly different from the real-
life process that generalizations based on them are not applicable to
actual behavior. On the other hand, it is almost impossible to observe
sequential reproduction as it occurs in real life. In this respect, Shibutani's words, "Rumor construction rarely occurs in a unilinear chain"
(Shibutani 1966: 101), are an understatement. Even if rumor were in
a unilinear chain, it still would be next to impossible to trace the
avenue of a message, whether deliberately planted or not. Accordingly, there would be no better hope of subsequently tracking down
the progress of a message from its source to a given place.

Accidentally, Andrew Vázsonyi had the rare opportunity to observe
the process of person-to-person communication while serving as a
medical orderly in a Hungarian military labor company shortly before
the outbreak of World War II. His unit was stationed on the border
zone between Hungary and Romania, which had been seized by the
Hungarian Army a few months earlier. The company's assignment
was to remove a section of the barbed wire barrier erected previously
by the Romanians. It was a slow, dull job that required patience and
some care because injury could occur. Some two hundred working
men were lined up along the barbed wire in one single, continuous
straight line at a distance of approximately five to ten feet from one
another. About fifty other members of the company were assigned to
another job elsewhere. The positional situation: "uniform distances
between individuals" resulted from the nature of the work, yet it
brings to mind researches in proxemics (Hall 1968: 83–108). The labor
period was long, and the working site was altogether isolated far
beyond the reach of radio, newspapers, or visitors. No collective dis-
traction was possible: no common singing, social games, playing, or
storytelling could be started. Obviously, the men were eager to hear
anything that could ease their boredom. Rumors that cropped up out

of nowhere every day, and even more than once a day, were received with much attention and speedily passed on.

It was the duty of the medical orderly to walk up and down behind the line and help with his first aid kit those who were injured by the wire. The otherwise wearisome situation of the labor company was ideal for an experiment.

Initially the test had no other purpose than the observation of the mouth-to-mouth spreading of information and its process of distortion. The notion that serial reproduction is conducive to the corruption of messages was well-known. Stern had already stated that chain reproduction as far as rumors are concerned exhibits extraordinary unreliability in oral transmission (Klineberg 1958: 221). In this case, however, extraordinary circumstances made it possible for the experimenter to follow step-by-step the modification of the message, to measure the mechanism of distortion. While working on the test, with his two aides who confidentially agreed to assist, the author soon realized that there was much more he could find out. He did not rely on the accidentally formulated messages but took turns with his two aides in planting them. A carefully selected bit of news or fake news of common concern was launched somewhere at one end or the other of the line, always contacting one among the first or the last twenty men. The topic usually involved major or minor problems of labor service that bore immediate relevance to the daily life of the men. In addition, the author also planted other important items of hearsay that were locally less pertinent, sometimes even jokes and anecdotes. Once the pseudo-rumors were started, the author made a slow walk behind the line. He stopped here and there, asking questions that did not wake suspicion, such as: "Is there any news?" "Was there something interesting?"

Some striking features could be recognized in this specific case of message communication. First, some rumors passed with considerable speed on the line, while others traveled much more slowly. Understandably, news concerned with military service and matters of a local nature spread faster than news that might have held greater importance on a higher level but had no immediate impact on the life of the group. The difference noticed in the two cases brings to mind the observation of Kenneth B. Clark: "An 'affective' paragraph (in prose material) is remembered significantly better than a parallel 'matter of fact' paragraph at an immediate recall" (1940: 61). Shibutani's observation also corroborates our conclusions: messages referring to "Ego-involvement" and messages containing "emotionally neutral materials" (Shibutani 1966: 92) merit varying speeds of internal reception and relay. The attitude expressing emotional involvement was

induced in our case by local and personal news, for example, concerning living quarters, provisioning, disciplinary prohibitions, cessation
of work, day of rest, etc., whereas news of common interest such as
world politics or events of national or international importance seldom
merited much excitement on the eve of World War II. If a rumor
concerned local topics, it reached the end of the front line in about
an hour, because everyone passed his information on without delay.
On the other hand, if the rumor failed to stir emotions, it took a whole
morning or afternoon to drag itself down the line.

But regardless, whether news progressed rapidly or slowly, modifications in the original message appeared as the second striking feature
of message transmission after the tenth to the fifteenth repetition.
Sometimes, significant alterations were introduced at the beginning
of the row after the rumor had passed through just a few transmitters.
While in most cases the message became simplified and abbreviated,
at other times its original meaning changed. Once the rumor had been
twisted to a certain extent, it did not undergo further major distortion,
similar to the observation of Theodore Caplow (1948: 298–302). Had
the author been aware at that time of these findings of Gordon Allport
and Leo Postman (1947: 75, 115, 134–138), he could have recognized
the processes of leveling, sharpening, and assimilation in the conduct
of the rumor, as well as the process of simplification and clarification
that Werner Wolff termed structuration (Wolff 1943: 206). Yet,
strangely enough, in a routine situation as the information traveled
through the line from morning till noon or from afternoon till evening,
the places of distortion could hardly ever be spotted. And even if the
spot seemingly could be located, respondents usually insisted they
had repeated exactly what they themselves had heard and only in
exceptional cases would they admit to 'misunderstanding' what was
passed on to them. Therefore, the question concerning the precise
means of distortion remained unanswered. No reliable information
was obtained concerning the reason for modifications, and there
appeared to be no rule to explain their nature. Of course, one might
generally note that sometimes the changes reflected the desire of the
group or the anxiety of the people involved.

If the foregoing two features of transmission do not allow general
conclusions, the observation of a third phenomenon turns out to be
in retrospect the most significant. Certain messages did not make their
way to the end of the line but stopped at a point and died. As already
stated, in the 'Ego-involvement' situation of hopeless boredom,
rumors would have meant refreshment, a potential contact with the
men right and left, to the laborers tinkering with the barbed wire.
Still, undeniably, it happened that some news here and there had

disappeared. There was only one condition that could explain some of these phenomena.

There were some twenty Orthodox Jews serving with the company, and a strong cohesion held them together in sharing the same *Weltan-schauung* and observing the same religious regulations. They were allowed to remain together and work in a specific segment of the unbroken line. All messages, anecdotes, jokes, etc., had to go through this section. If the material were unattractive or repulsive due to religious reasons, the Orthodox Jews refused to pass it on, and the message became stranded among them. Transmissions halted by the Jews concerned topics of foodstuffs because they were on a special religious diet, and they also did not mediate news about varying kinds of entertainments. Their reaction to such topics was not only indifference but oftentimes vehement opposition. Such characteristics were outstanding and easy to recognize.

In the basic setting, then, the members of the line were both senders and receivers of the message (Figure 2). This ideal situation would never occur in reality, and is only a theoretical construction. Actually, sometimes messages reached the end of the line after having bypassed a few (possibly two or three) of the group members. This happened when one workman of the chain briefly left his working place and

FIGURE 2

passed the message to one of the subsequent neighbors, or when the sender was not on friendly terms with his immediate neighbors, or else, when he knew that they would not be interested in hearing particular information, etc. In our suggested terms we might say that the people who were bypassed did not coincide with the *conduit*; this particular message evaded them (Figure 3).

FIGURE 3

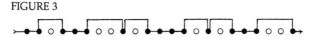

Sometime it happened that the messages were blocked at one point of the line without any apparent reason. The message that jumped a distance of 15–30 feet over two or three people could not bypass a gap of ten to twenty people that occupied 30–60 feet, or in some cases, even more. Normally, information to be sent was seldom interesting enough to deserve such an irregular move. The laborer could not leave his place for a necessarily lengthier period of time, and therefore ten to twenty people served as an impenetrable barrier that blocked the continuation of the message: the conduit ran into a jam at a certain point (Figure 4).

FIGURE 4

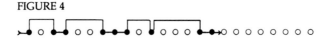

The discontinuation of certain types of information among the Orthodox Jews is easy to explain. Other gaps cannot be explained so easily. In retrospect, today we feel there must have been other occasional and spontaneously shaped clusters within the seemingly homogeneous line (Figure 4). The group, as such, might have existed only for a few minutes as linked together, for example, by one single and accidentally shared *tabu* and then dissolved as the group reacted in diverse ways to other messages. Nevertheless, until such cohesion existed, group members did not extend, for some reason, certain kinds of messages. Consequently, some messages could not reach their potential ultimate destination: the last member of the chain.

A certain phenomenon may be taken as a spontaneous counterproof of the above described assumptions. A sputtering message that did not make its way to the end of the line along the barbed wire from morning till noon might suddenly start to spread very rapidly, provided that it remained topical for the day. This took place during lunch break, when the line disintegrated and the whole company was united into one varied body of workers. After the lunch break ended and the medical orderly could resume his inspection, strolling all the way along the working line that had straightened up as before, he was able to hear the same message by and large almost uncorrupted from practically everyone at the beginning and at the end of the line. Yet he found that various segments within the line were still not affected by the message. These so-to-speak immune islands of men possessed no knowledge of the topic or were acquainted with the subject only in an incomplete or corrupted form. It is quite obvious that rumors progressed rapidly during lunch time as each man could talk to several others while around the field kitchen, and the members of the informed group could further address themselves to whole groups of uninformed people. That the messages became less distorted after luncheon than before the noon meal can perhaps also be explained by Walter Anderson's "law of self-correction" (Anderson 1923: 397–403). This rule seems to be more applicable to the behavior of short messages, rumors – for example, simple, unambiguous and easily verifiable facts, than to the folk narratives originally aimed at by Anderson. It is interesting to note that Shibutani found similar rules specifically concerning the construction of rumors (Shibutani 1966: 140). During the luncheon period, the message in question circulated freely, was reinforced, and was corrected again and again in the memory of senders and receivers.

Correspondingly, the acceleration in rumor dissemination during lunchtime and the enlivened maintenance of the message after lunch was no surprise for the author and his aides. On the other hand, they could not find an explanation for another phenomenon: that messages energetically circulated among most of the people could still remain unknown or known only in a very distorted form to certain other persons. We would like to propose the multi-conduit hypothesis as an explanation for these gaps in communication. In the basis situation, the company, following command, was forced to line up in single file (Figures 1–3). In this situation, the message could not find its own conduit, as there was only one conduit at its disposal. Similarly, the conduit could not meet its message as no alternative message existed. Frequently, these messages became stalled on an inappropriate conduit; and deformed, inappropriate messages resulted. During the luncheon break, however, the situation changed. Each of the men gave his information to whomever he wanted. The resulting conduit was not the product of necessity, nor was it created by lack of choice; it was naturally and genuinely formed. The message was passed on by those who were interested in hearing and telling it. Members of the company knew each other quite well after having spent many months together. They knew each other's taste, orientation, field of interest and knew well to whom to turn, whom to avoid. As Theodore Caplow has noted, once channels are established, diffusion occurs over a relatively small number of well-defined routes (Caplow 1948).

FIGURE 5

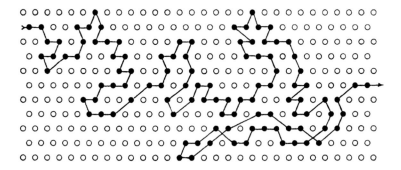

Figure 5 represents the fictive situation during leisure time when the message passes through its hypothetical "natural" conduit. The zigzag windings indicate that the conduit criss-crosses within a group incorporating some people, avoiding others. Those who are evaded might fall into the route of another or even several other conduits. For the sake of lucidity we have, as in other cases, not indicated the possible ramifications, confluences, or blind paths, etc., of this conduit.

Following the lunch break, the natural groups were dissolved, the genuine conduits were torn apart. The participants took up positions at difference places on the work line, as shown in Figure 6.

FIGURE 6

The hypothetical "natural" conduit is marked with (black, respectively dotted) lines, the members of the conduit as above are represented by black dots, whereas those who have not heard or only possess partial or distorted knowledge of the message are marked with circles.

The messages enter, as a matter of fact, a more favorable strategic position than usual because they could spread not only in one direction but would be able also to progress to the right and the left. One might assume that the message with a double impact would certainly penetrate all gaps and become known to everybody. Strangely enough, this did not occur. If gaps in the line were consistently shown in the morning, that is, if individuals or smaller sections of the line only partially remembered the message or remembered it wrongly, as a rule these gaps were not filled during the luncheon break. The multi-conduit principle offers an explanation of this: those who did not coincide with the conduit either did not learn or incorrectly perceived or remembered the proper emphasis of the message. In summary, the case which we have presented might suggest the following:

(1) The velocity of message communication is variable. It is slower if it progressed on a marked-out course and is speedier if it can spontaneously choose its path.

(2) The extent of distortion is likewise variable, but it is generally more frequent and exaggerated if it moves along a designated track than if the message follows a self-appointed spontaneous course.

At long last, after the lapse of a few months, the ever-so-often planted rumor about the discharge of the company came true. Its members re-entered the complex rumor-structure environment of pre-wartime society where it would have been much more difficult to pursue the avenues of gossip and rumor than along the lines of the barbed wires on the borderland of Romania and Hungary.

4.

In a simplified form, the conclusion we have drawn calls to mind the well-known truth that there is nothing to be gained by a forced job. That is to say, what one chooses to do by one's own free will is done better than what one does under coercion. This was never considered by experimenters in folklore, in part probably because a laboratory situation by definition lacks spontaneity. In real life there is hardly an opportunity to observe a *spontaneous* situation which is suitable for *laboratory* tests. The case of the compulsory labor company, previously discussed, is definitely rare. Serial reproduction as it occurs in the course of social interaction would usually be impossible to observe. However, we are not concerned so much with the lack of voluntariness but we regret that those who conducted laboratory experiments failed to account for its absence in their conclusions.

Of the available experiments in transmission of folklore, we would like to discuss in some detail Walter Anderson's *Ein Volkskundliches Experiment* (1951). Anderson's work was based on F. C. Bartlett's psychological remembering-test published in 1920. In spite of Wesselski's contention that Anderson's theory is nothing but an easily collapsible hypothesis blown up into an axiom that does not merit scholarly attention (Wesselski 1931: 156), we feel that Anderson's "law of self-correction" calls for serious scrutiny. Although this axiom has lost much of its theoretical support, it deserves attention because it continues to maintain, like folk narratives themselves, an 'extraordinary stability' in the minds of folklore scholars. One is tempted to assume that the Andersonian axiom is being maintained and perpetuated by some benevolent "self-correction." Among the few *par excellence* ethnographic experiments, this one seems to be the most intensive and certainly the most impressive. Anderson performed his famous experiment in 1947, but according to him, it was preceded by tests in the 1920s. The work reflected rather conservative scholarly conceptions compared to contemporary views. Nevertheless, the experiment created a kind of *res judicata* in the interpretation of oral transmission processes. Among the scholars who take for granted Anderson's law, we find such contemporary theoreticians as Hermann Bausinger (1968: 48), Kurt Ranke (1969: 113), and quite a few others. For example, Richard Weiss (1946: 37–39) and Max Lüthi (1962/1980: 102–103) speak of the self-corrective processes of folklore styles balancing out digressive trends of distortion (*zersingen*). Gyula Ortutay suggests numerous important features of oral tradition but also acknowledges Anderson's thesis and even pays it respect by repeating the experiment successfully with his own students in 1953 (Ortutay 1959: 198–199, 213–214; Anderson 1956). Lutz Röhrich offers some criticism but accepts the ideas as a "mechanical explanation" (1969: 131–132). Kenneth Goldstein also makes comments concerning the experiment. It is remarkable that these and other scholars who authored resourceful modern theories did not challenge the experiment. Even Rudolf Schenda, one of the leading proponents of the modernization of the German Volkskunde trend, resorts to one single experiment-model, that of Walter Anderson (Schenda 1970: 154).

What does this experiment purport? We would like to recapture here the exact meaning of the law of self-correction in the words of its originator:

> In the year 1923 I have laid down the follow Law of Self Correction: "the extraordinary stability of folk narratives is explained by the fact that (1) every narrator had heard the respective *Märchen* (or *Schwank*, legend, and so on), from his predecessor, as a rule not once but several times; (2) that, as a rule, has heard it not only from one single person but from a whole group of persons (and in different versions)." (Anderson 1956: 3–5.)

The experiment performed in order to substantiate this thesis should also be presented here in Anderson's own words:

> Three transmission-chains (A, B, C) were composed each of 12 links (A 1–12, B 1–12, C 1–12). Almost all participants were male and female students of Germanic studies. The chosen text was a Pomeranian devil legend from Swinemünde, unknown to the general public. This legend was once read slowly to participants A1, B1, and C1. On the next day all three wrote it down from memory. Likewise A1 read his script to A2, B1 to B2, and C1 to C2 respectively who then reproduced their version next day as remembered, and so on.
>
> And what is the result of this experiment? . . . Step by step, the text degenerated rapidly and the three final products (A 12, B 12, and C 12) displayed the worst disfigurations, gaps, and additions and resembled each other and the original text only in a most general way. (Anderson 1956: 3–5.)

As stated, Anderson's theory and experiment have retained their appeal to folklorists until this very day. Nevertheless, over the years, they have also drawn some, more or less justified, criticism. Some of the questions raised by folklorists have been answered by Anderson himself. On the following pages we will review the essential comments, with Anderson's eventual responses. Additionally, we will make our own evaluative remarks.

(1) "The selection of the persons used in the experiment," says Kurt Schier, "is contestable" (Schier 1955: 129). There was no selection whatsoever, replies Anderson, as he was glad to find 36 students who volunteered for the test (Anderson 1956: 9).

Testing conditions for German scholars must have been poor in those days, and we can appreciate the eagerness of Anderson to try to do his best. However, if 36 persons are too few for the experiment, it would have been wiser to postpone it to a later date when more favorable conditions could be secured.

What kind of selection did Schier suggest? The tester should have considered the personality of his subjects: their attitude to the experiment and their remembering capability. Above all, Anderson should have determined whether the subjects would have qualified as raconteurs in a normal storytelling community. In his rejoinder, Anderson emphasizes the absurdity of these demands: " . . . I should have subjected some hundred persons to an exact psychological analysis and complicated tests in order to select thirty-six persons to fit into artificially constructed transmission sequences . . . that in reality never could occur" (Anderson 1956: 8).

We did not find any record of Schier's answer to this sarcastic reply of Anderson. But we might answer for him: by all means, Anderson should have performed complicated psychological tests on all one hundred individuals and even many more. "The emotional factors influencing recall cannot be fully investigated through group experiments without considering individual factors" (Wolff 1943: 200). If the experiment does not allow for spontaneity in either the choice of the transmission chain or the message to be transmitted (compare to the situation described in Part III), reality should have been approximated by the tester at least through the application of psychological methods. The real chain of transmission, the *conduit* as we have called it, takes shape in a social milieu of differing individual interests as well as distinctive personal affinities and aversions. The experimental sequence constructed by psychological insight comes much closer to approaching the accidental transmission chain than the one thrown together by the random division of thirty-six persons. Continues Anderson:

> My only principle in the selection of the participants was to find exclusively very intelligent people with retentive memory. Forgetful, puddle-headed simpletons usually do not become students of German studies. (Anderson 1956: 9.)

We certainly do not want to deny that university students need to have ability in memorizing what they learn. Nevertheless, it is debatable indeed whether an intelligent person equally remembers materials which have different values to him. To mention an example, one of our good friends, a professor of linguistics at the Sorbonne, recently asked us to send him texts of a specific type of joke he would like to discuss in his lectures. Our friend enjoys listening to jokes – he also has a scholarly interest in them – but as he asserted in his letter, they evaporate from his head as soon as he has heard them. He is not even a *passive bearer*. Evidently the overall dependability of memory cannot be inferred from someone's profession as the author of *Ein Volkskundliches Experiment* believed.

(2)"The actual circumstances of storytelling communities were not adequately taken into consideration," says Schier. Goldstein agrees with this objection. "The natural context in which tales are told was absent from the experiment" (Goldstein 1967a: 74). Later, Schier adds, "Whoever can tell a story particularly well, will tell it again and again," whereas Anderson flings back his retort: "Does the community know the story only from this one person? How can you be so sure that he tells it better than someone else?" (Schier 1955: 9–10).

Anderson's question sounds as if he assumes that the "particularly well" told story is the version that comes closest to the *Urform*. Also, it appears that he imagines that the storytelling community stages a competitive comparison between the tellers of the variants of a certain story and then decides which narrator's piece they wish to hear repeatedly. This chosen variant, of course, should be the most complete, yielding the least oscillation.

Field experience has convinced us of a simpler and more human kind of behavior with regard to the selection of favorite stories. Naturally, the community is unaware of the *Urform* (or rather the *Normalform*) as defined by Anderson, and might accept a beautifully embroidered narrative as its favorite version. Yet scholars who think in terms of the abstract construction of type outlines would consider it as 'corrupt' or 'fragmentary.'

The type, composed of motifs of available variants, is likewise unknown to the carriers of folktale tradition. Thus the community, as a rule, does not even realize the assumed relationship between deviant variations of the same tale type in the repertoire of different popular storytellers (Dégh 1969/1989: 88–90, 185–186). In their learning phase, storytellers might pick up stories wherever they find them. It is rather a common practice, though, to acquire the basic repertoire from family tradition and later to include selections from the body of tale themes which is available in the community (Dégh 1959: 23–39). Once the narrators put together the pieces of their repertoire, they will shape plots according to their own taste and talents. Interested people will want to hear stories repeatedly, just because they like them, regardless of whether or not they have heard them before. Obviously, there is no way to compare the individual versions created by the raconteurs of a given community. What is then the standard for the better or for the best version sanctioned by a community? Is there such a standard at all? Alan Dundes asks why we have to suppose that the tales need to be corrected. "Only the unquestioned assumption that folktales become incorrect through time can possibly justify the notion that folktales need to correct themselves – granting for the sake of argument that tales rather than people do the correction" (Dundes 1969a: 8). Evidently, there is a correcting tendency performed by what we might call community censorship. The community controls narrators by keeping them from radical deviation. Such a consensus tends to force storytellers to individualize their stories so that the community would no longer be able to identify them as a known tale. Ortutay pointed out in his discussion of the processes of deterioration and corruption that the 'correct' form is always the one that narrators aim at in a given community at a given time and that the subject of the tale fluctuates according to situational changes (Ortutay 1959: 199, 214).

(3) "The temptation legend is inadequate," continues Schier, stripped of most of its viability when removed from its natural context. This is not a genuine local legend, replies Anderson, but rather a migratory legend. Anyway, he contends, for this experiment he has selected a story which was unknown in the environs of Kiel, where most of his students came from (Anderson 1956: 11).

The question of psychological bearings on cultural differences is an important one, whether or not it played a role in the Kiel experiment. At this conjecture, it would be extraneous to draw into our discussion the problem of the transfiguration of culture traits which spread on a natural course from one ethnic group to another. The question here is: how do subjects representing different cultures behave toward experimentally-implanted materials?

Among the many experiments, several are worthy of mention. Ian M. L. Hunter, who has repeated Bartlett's tests, writes, "This story [a legend-like North American Indian folktale] is of interest, since coming from another culture, it presents difficulties to British people because of the strange conventions and beliefs which it reflects . . ." (Hunter 1964: 145). Kenneth Jackson also notes that Barlett's experiment is of little relevance to the storytelling situation because the tale used by him "was a savage one, not a civilized one, and consequently was lacking in the logical international construction of the European-

Asiatic folktale" (Jackson 1961: 58). Dundes comments also on Bartlett's experiment that "One cannot assume that the changes which
occur when members of one culture borrow an item of folklore from
members of another culture are necessarily the same as those which
occur when an item of folklore belonging to the culture is transmitted
solely within that culture" (Dundes 1965: 244). Bartlett considered
typical African cases "in which memory appears to be directly
influenced by social facts" (Bartlett 1932: 240). It turned out, for example, that the exceedingly sharp memory of the Swazi is limited to the
spcificity of cattle, women, marriage, and children – these being the
topics of deepest concern. "The Zulu recalling modes of ancient fighting was voluble, excited, emotional, confident, dramatic. The Swazi
on the same topic was rather taciturn, unmoved, matter-of-fact. But
the Swazi, recounting old stories of diplomacy, where guile gets the
better of might, became more lively, more voluble, gesticulated more
freely, had inward confidence and outward dramatic form. Differences
of this nature, when observed in a particular social group, may have
obvious importance . . ." (Bartlett 1932: 264). "Even the manner of
remembering may be socially determined to a considerable degree,"
emphasizes Otto Klineberg (Klineberg 1958: 228).

S. F. Nadel's experiment has attracted particular attention. His purpose was to "describe certain attempts at attacking, experimentally,
and in the field of so-called primitive cultures, the problem of a possible correlation between diversity of culture and psychological differen-
tiation" (Nadel 1937–1938: 195). Nadel, like other experimenters,
borrowed his model from Bartlett, whose method, which consisted
of description of pictures and reproduction of stories, could be traced
back to William Stern (Klineberg 1958: 228). Nadel noted that members
of the neighboring Nupe and Yoruba responded in a markedly distinct
manner: there was a diversity among the representation of psychological personality types between members of the two tribes; the function
of memory displayed definite divergence.

However generally known that cultural differences motivate human
behavior, it would be extremely hard to determine what magnitude
of cultural differences is necessary to influence the behavior of individuals, and to what extent. It is certain that differences between language,
religion, mythology, education, cognition, as well as other areas of
enculturation, decisively affect human reactions. It should be noted
here that the centuries-old fallacy of "the universal man" which
"falsely assumes that people are intellectually and psychologically the
same in all times, places, and circumstances" understandably still
appears to be a protest against the fallacy of racism (Fischer 1970:
203). Even such a seemingly unexpected factor as climate and tempera-

ture can play a significant role in the achievement motivation of folk stories in different preindustrial societies (Huntington 1915: 612). What then is the extent of influences that can be attributed to cultural background? Presumably, people are quite sensitive in this respect, and a minimal account of background difference might influence their attitudes. In this sense, one might even imply that the devil legend in question could have different impact on the people of Schwinemünde than on the people from Kiel. Nevertheless, this could have been found out from local respondents at the time of Anderson's experiment.

In his cited article Goldstein inquires: "Was the trial item . . . the kind of tale to be found in the traditions of his participants thereby likely to have sufficient meaning to them to result in fuller listening attention, better memory retention, and better communication with the next link in each chain?"

Further on, Schier writes that the experiment with an appropriately chosen *Märchen* might have ended with different conclusions. Anderson replies that he does not believe this, but would welcome a repetition of his test, this time with a magic tale.

This is not the first time that Anderson has encouraged folklorists to repeat his experiment. We do not believe that such a repetition could be considered a genuine experiment. It would be surprising indeed if the procedure performed by use of the same material, with the similar design of the treble human tradition-sequences, would conclude with results different from the original experiment. If the first experiment has substantiated the law of self-correction, all repeated tests would only corroborate the thesis. If, on the other hand, Anderson's experiment had failed to prove the truth of his law, no matter how many repetitions had been performed, it would scarcely strengthen his case. Anderson encouraged the repetition of his experiment on a "carefully selected folktale" because he felt that the principle of self-correction holds true for all genres of folk literature. However, this seems to be doubtful, even if there would be some evidence to prove it true for the magic tale.

Interestingly, Anderson, like Bartlett, experimented with legends. Fieldworkers in folklore can attest that tale-telling and legend-telling exhibit different attitudes. In most cases storytellers and legend tellers have distinct personalities. There are only a few works which discuss the personality of the legend teller (Brinkmann 1933; Uffer 1945; Zender 1937; Haiding 1953; Balassa 1966; Gaál 1965). The village audiences always distinguished them in the traditional site of narration; the tale conduit is not identical with the legend conduit. It is uncertain whether the tale and the legend qualify as identical experimental materials. The rumor and the legend (aptly considered as 'solidified rumor' by

sociologists) tends toward foreshortening (Allport and Postman 1947:
162; Shibutani 1966: 156) as the traditional *Schwank* is often reduced
to a joke (Bausinger 1967: 118–136). Conversely, the tale sometimes
expands far beyond its 'original' size and multiplies through continuous telling by gifted narrators (Dégh 1969/1989: 82–85, 176–181).
According to Werner Wolff, one of the pioneers of experimental depth
psychology, in general every personality finds the most adequate
channel through which he can most conveniently express himself
(Wolff 1943: 194). Correspondingly, those who find that their means
of expression lies in telling prose narratives will find their 'most adequate channel' by specializing in their choice of tales, legends, anecdotes, or other genres. Evidently, it makes a difference whether the
expressed message progresses on the adequate or on an inadequate
channel. There is no *"well-chosen tale"* in the sense that the experimenter
has chosen it 'well.' Rather, the tale-channel – or in our chosen term,
the *tale-conduit*, as a branch of the *multi-conduit system* – is accepted
normally by individuals as the most adequate way of expression. The
conduit would still be subdivided into lesser units. There are tale-
clusters bound together by cohesive affinity among the related plots
wherein single tales are being composed. Furthermore, the single tales
will be split into episodes and the episodes will be split into emancipated incidents that will be moved on toward their complex, further
ramifying *sub-conduits* and *micro-conduits*. The sub-conduits and the
micro-conduits chosen by individuals might be considered as the way
of their suitable expressives. The tale transmitters can express themselves in their own way only if they are allowed to make their own
choice, whereas the "well chosen story" is not picked by the experimenter with all of his scholarly care and competency in the field but
is rather chosen instinctively and occasionally by the narrator.

(4) Schier criticizes Anderson for a "method that is psychological
instead of folkloristic," to which Anderson replies: "Of course, it is
psychological, this is the application of psychological analysis to folkloristic subjects" (Anderson 1956: 11).

This accusation is as unjustified as the author's adknowledgment
of guilt. In 1951, when the quoted sentence was printed, most psychologists already employed more refined tools of experimentation.
Anderson rejected simple test methods at the beginning of his essay
(see part 4 [1]) yet never made any mention of his familiarity with
modern psychology and its relevance to his query.

(5) Schier also objects to the substitution of oral by written transmission. Instead of writing down the texts, Anderson should have made
all thirty-six narrators relate their versions on tape. Anderson's answer
is simple: "I had no tape recorder." But, if he had one – continues

Anderson – he would have also chosen to make the participants write down the story as they remembered it. That is to say, if the individuals had been asked to repeat their story as remembered, they would have necessarily stopped several times, searching for the right word, correcting themselves here and there, inserting later what they had earlier forgotten yet later recalled. They would have interjected signs of trying to recapture the story: "Let's see, how was it?", or "No, it was not like this," etc. Such hesitations, by the way, as Anderson notes, are quite common even with the best storytellers. Emphatically he states that it was his purpose to create an exceptionally favorable situation to induce maximum retention of the text. (Anderson 1956: 12–13.)

Anderson hoped to set up this "exceptionally favorable" situation by allowing the subjects who reproduced the experimental story to put their version down on paper and allowing them time while writing to order their thoughts and correct their text. He overlooked the fact that the oral teller, who interjects his verbally recited narrative: "Let's see, how was it?" or "No, it was not like this," etc., also organizes his thoughts and tries to improve his story, just like the writer who inserts changes into his written text. It is true that there are many people who become confused if they have to perform something verbally in public; nevertheless, it is also true that there are as many people who become confused if they must express themselves in writing. While we know many people who write easily in good style but who remain much below their own standards in fluency, style, and memory when they have to speak, we know just as many others who are enjoyable public speakers, perfect entertainers, but freeze in sight of a piece of paper and can express themselves only very poorly in writing. As Dundes rightly states, "One does not write as one speaks, nor does one speak as one writes" (Dundes 1965: 244).

The authors are acquainted with the editor of a daily paper who never accepts an article from an author who dictated his text to someone instead of handwriting or typing it himself. It is the opinion of this editor that the act of dictating includes uttering sound stresses, gestures, and mimicry. The presence of a second person makes the author theatrical, and renders the written text redundant. He has stated and proven many times that he is able to infer from the style and length of an article whether the author wrote it in longhand or typed it or whether he dictated to someone else. For the storyteller, unlike our editor friend, texts aimed at performance and dramatic effect might be the most suitable. Presumably the storyteller, who is used to speaking rather than to writing, who is used to the presence and responses of an audience, could not reach the same perfection in the solitude of an echoless room.

Moreover, storytellers can be decisively influenced by minor circumstances and less responsive listeners. Once we visited a very old village
narrator and urged him to tell us a story. His ability was so much
linked to corn-shelling that he could not even remember a tale until
his daughter put two ears of corn in his hands. Another time we tried
to persuade members of an outstanding storytelling community to
tell some stories during the busy summer months. None of the best
entertainers could remember the tales that normally flowed without
hesitation at the proper time of winter, in the atmosphere of the usual
get-togethers. These are not exceptional cases. Similar ones have been
reported by folklorists from different cultures (Dégh 1969/1989: 76–
77). It should be emphasized here again (Dégh 1969/1989, Chapters
6 and 8) that the traditional circumstances of storytelling and the
traditional behavior of the storytellers are as important parts of the
tale as the text itself. Walter Anderson's test subjects were not village
storytellers, of course – in the opinion of Goldstein this was a grave
mistake on his part; nevertheless, it could not be known whether there
were potential storytellers among them who were deprived of their
natural skills when diverted to the "exceptionally favorable" obligation of writing. "A loss of situational familiarity may so affect the
unselfconsciousness of his subjects as to result in a process rarely or
never found in a folk community" (Goldstein 1967: 580).

(6) According to Dieter Glade, the process of self-correction is not
the exclusive but just one cause of folk narrative stability. Eclectically,
he lists twelve reasons for stabilization, most of which are beyond
our present focus (Glade 1966: 235–256). Basically, Glade agrees with
critical reservations to the theory of self-correction. He concurs with
Anderson that it was a mistake to use children in such an experiment
as Schier did. However, he feels that contemporary university students
were no better subjects. He suggests that it would have been more
successful to have used genuine folk-narrators, "who are the representatives of a narrative tradition, who have already heard and told many
stories." This opinion calls to mind a comment by Dundes. In his
criticism of Bartlett's experiment, he notes it is a "serious methodological weakness" that the experimental group used for serial reproduction consisted of isolated individuals: "It was not a folk group with
normal traditional channels of communication." Goldstein expresses
a similar opinion (Dundes 1965: 244; Goldstein 1967a: 74).

If critics imply that both Bartlett and Walter Anderson made a
mistake by not performing their experiment with traditional
storytellers, they are not realistic. Some types of storytellers love to
listen to others; they are eager to hear new stories from passive
bearers in order to enlarge their own repertoire and to better serve

the demands of the audience (Dégh 1969/1989: 192–195). But the addition of a new story to his repertoire and the timing of its narrative are entirely contingent upon the whim and will of the storyteller. We feel that neither Bartlett nor Anderson could have corrected this 'error' even if they had wanted to do so. Goldstein is in agreement with this observation. "Since it is almost impossible to obtain the cooperation of the members of the folk society . . . the investigator is forced to substitute members of a non-folk group . . ." (Goldstein 1967a: 72).

If, on the other hand, Glade, Dundes, and Goldstein did mean that this irreparable error undermines the experimental verification of the "law of self-correction," they are closer to the truth. It should be noted, though, that we do not believe the validity of the test depends on the proper selection of individuals. As we have seen, there is no way to design experimental sequences by the selection of the "proper people" if they have to be experienced folk-narrators. Instead, we would like to suggest the thorough analytical exploration of each experimental raconteur with accompanying pertinent circumstantial data which will corroborate the experimental results. Such a procedure, to be discussed later, should serve the aims of experimental folklore better – not necessarily in view of the work of Walter Anderson. The suggested complex procedure might be termed "experimental depth folklore" by the adoption of Wolff's "experimental depth psychology."

(7) "Anderson's experiment did not really test his notion that a narrator receives his material from several sources," writes Dundes (1965: 245).

If Anderson had performed a countercheck and if he had investigated the situational changes that occur when the subjects heard several versions of the legend, his contentions would have been more convincing. Possibly, the available subjects were too few for this and time was too short to run a counter-proof. Yet, as he does not mention any such attempt, it is more likely that Anderson considered his thesis clinched beyond doubt, fully proven by the incomplete test. This accounts for Anderson's eagerness to see his experiment continued and repeated by others without demanding a countercheck (Anderson 1951: 45). This logical error of his is rather surprising. The fact that the legend learned from a single source degenerates in the course of serial reproduction is not in itself satisfying evidence to make us believe that the legend might not have degenerated under different cirucmstances if the transmitters had learned it from several sources. From the observation that a certain event will ensue under certain conditions, one cannot reasonably infer that the same event would not have occurred under other conditions. Causal relationship between events and circumstances cannot be a matter of conjecture to be codified as a 'law'; it must be proven by exacting methods. One should not assume *a priori* a causal relationship between two facts (the distortion and the single source in our case) in an experiment that is set up to find out whether there is such a causality or not. We cannot resist the temptation to quote Walter Anderson when he notes how imaginary critics would chastise him if he followed Kurt Schier's advice: "Excuse me, sir. You might be right with your hypothesis on the principle of repetition and the multiplicity of sources – but your experiment did not convince me in the least!" Something similar is expressed also by Goldstein: "I feel . . . that his [Anderson's] experiments did not prove his case relative to *folk* process and that his indirect proof-by-analogy to *non-folk* process is unacceptable on purely theoretical grounds" (Anderson 1956: 14; Goldstein 1967a: 74).

(8) Experimentation with serial reproduction launched by Bartlett and continued by others disclosed important facts concerning the psychology of memory. Thirty years later, Walter Anderson repeated the experiment using the same technique but applying it to a different theoretical premise. The folklore adaptation of the method was well received; the presentation of serial reproduction was convincing at first reading. In spite of this, the fact stated in the final conclusion – that the story learned from a single source deteriorates when it is passed on because of some reason – usually manifests itself with the first member of the chain. Therefore, further continuation of the serial reproduction is, in fact, unnecessary. Evidently, twelve-times repetition of the experiment exhibits greater divergency, whereas the presentation of twelve texts creates more dramatic effects. This outward attraction, however, is weakened by more serious drawbacks. By its very nature, this kind of experimental transmission from person to person will cause each successive member to obtain a different text, increasingly changed by the preceding subjects. The material is not measurable; consequently the attitude of the test subjects toward the material is not assessable. How can we be certain that the persons in the chain would have distorted the legend as much as they did or even if they would have distorted it at all if it had reached them unaltered? It might happen that the first reteller of the story immediately drops a motif or adds one and totally denaturizes its original meaning, prevailing tone, and symbolism. Consequently, the first transmitter might determine the attitude of the remaining chain members and thus the fate of the whole material. As Schier rightly notes, such a distorted narrative could not persist; it would either be completed or discontinued (Schier 1955: 16–17). Incidentally, it is not certain that distortions in each case necessarily alter the story's original

form. One or several transmission chain members might modify or restore a missing or corrupted motif imported by accident and reinstate the 'correct' form stimulated by an analogy or by the impact of some kind of affinity (Ortutay 1965: 6–7). They also might approximate an archetype or genotype (Szondi 1947; Szondi, Moser and Webb 1959). In other words, one person might restore a narrative that was altered by the preceding individuals. This process is untraceable and immeasurable. Anderson's test is comparable to the joint cooking of the kitchen personnel in a restaurant where the skills of all cooks are being judged by the finished dish already oversalted by the first cook.

Examination of the legend Anderson has chosen for his experiment illustrates the problems we have raised. The legend concerns a nobleman – a girl chaser and a sinner – who is pursued by the devil disguised as a woman. By playing the tune of a song of penitence, the nobleman gets rid of his pursuer and starts a new life. Interestingly enough, the features of the nobleman as a seducer and sinner are dropped in different phases of the successive reproduction. The story loses its main cohesion, its original meaning, its moral basis, and final conclusion. Why did the nobleman get into trouble if he did not ask for it? Why did he confess to his nonexistent sins? Why did he return to piety if he never was a sinner? Evidently, whoever heard the story before the motifs in question were dropped found himself confronted with different intellectual and emotional tasks than one who learned the story afterwards.

The legend, used by the three artificial "tradition chains" set up by Walter Anderson, was transmitted by twelve persons. The experimenter states in the analysis of three final products that the subjects deviated from the original as much as from each other. He also points out that if the chain of transmission had been twice as long – twenty-four links, instead of twelve – the final production would have been even more fragmentary. In Anderson's conclusion, this result is not presented as a speculation but as a firm statement considered as proven by the experiment. Walter Anderson has a good sense of humor, enjoys quoting anecdotes in his arguments, and we feel this to be in accordance with the spirit of debate taught us by this great pioneer of folk narrative research. Yet the ancient anecdote called to mind by Anderson's inference concerns the cashier in a firm who stops counting the banknote roll containing one hundred ten dollar notes at fifty because "It was correct up to this point; the rest must also be correct." Without violating logic in this case, there is no way of deducing twenty-four out of twelve. Even less convincing would be the findings that the experiment should have substantiated: to show us the fate of the regularities in the folk narrative transmission, as they have been handed down by innumerable generations through history around the world.

There is good reason to presume that after a while the process of degeneration will slow down and stop. In a modified version of Bartlett's experiment, Hunter has observed that as the stories grow shorter, content omission occurs less and less frequently, that is, as the transmission-chain continues, "we would have found it settling down to a relatively fixed form" (Hunter 1964: 148). In a real field situation, one might note that there is a definite difference between the extent of variability in the different kinds of complex tales: some might drift away almost beyond the limits of identification, others show minimal oscillation from their core version (Dégh 1960: 28–42). More generally, the process of distortion [Zersagen] (Weiss 1946) usually concides with cultural change and can cause rationalization in certain folk narrative groups. Upon reaching this point, they usually do not change any further.

Had Anderson asked each of his thirty-six experimental storytellers to repeat one and the same story instead of theatrically staging a serial reproduction, he would have noted that not everybody is "forgetful," not everyone distorts the material received from one single source; i.e., there is no exception to the rule. Theoretically, one might assume also that several members in the transmission-chain are capable of passing on the heard item without distortion. Obviously, in an artificially organized experimental chain this could occur only by special accident. If, however, the transmission-chain is not the construction of the tester but the creation of real life conditions, not as an accident but as a rule, a natural *conduit* will come into existence and serve as the means for the transmission of the material in question.

(9) Anderson's multiple-source principle suggests that in storytelling communities the total population is subdivided into audience groups clustered around different narrators. Such a distribution of tale telling would require more time than people can afford to devote to telling or to listening to tales. In real life one can hardly imagine the existence of so many active or semi-active narrators as the theory suggests. This theory envisions a village in which people give most of their time and energy to the restoration of deviating tales to the *Urform* instead of going about their business. Wesselski rightfully questions: "Would then, a Märchenvillage, if there is one somewhere, prove that the narrators – not the listeners – hear their Märchen regularly not from a single but from many individuals not in one but in different redactions?" (Wesselski 1931: 156). Anderson's rebuttal is not too convincing for those who are familiar with the social role of storytellers. He quotes the names of individuals listed as informants

in three printed tale collections from Spain, Russia, and Bohemia (Anderson 1935: 23–26). There is neither reason to believe that the persons who dictated the tales to the editor of these anthologies were raconteurs distinguished in their communities, nor that the given communities were real "Märchenvillages." That regular storytelling was a general attribute of classical European peasant cultures was an erroneous assumption of the first personality-oriented folktale collectors (Banó 1944: 26–33). Data accumulated disproved this and convinced us that storytelling was more usual in the work-groups outside of village communities. In most of the known cases, the flourishing of tales at a certain time period could be ascribed to the coincidental visit or residence of some outstanding narrators in some – but by no means all – rural settlements (Dégh 1969: 79–81).

As we have already emphasized, the items the scholars identified as variants of a single type were recognized by tellers and audiences as distinct and nonrelated tales in European communities we had known. The occasional audiences hardly comprise the total population of the communities. They consist of only those who like tales and have time and opportunity to listen to them. Storytellers who are acquainted with each other as well as each other's repertoire would never borrow stories from one another. Their body of tales is also acknowledged by the community as their own (Dégh 1969/1989: 86–90). An uncodified traditional copyright law regulates their authorship and their manner of story acquisition. They learn from outsiders away from the locals, from passive bearers who retain story sketches or episodes but who would never perform in public, and they inherit stories from earlier generations. Evidently, the accumulation of a repertoire might also mean that more than one teller may have heard the same story from the same person. However, as we have observed, identical stories learned from common ancestors change so much by manipulation of different personalities that the audiences would not be able to detect the identical source. Also, the narrators are mostly unaware of the affinity between their versions. Even if the listeners could detect the kinship between the 'variants' of different narrators, the bearers would not persuade them to combine the versions. The audience influences the narrators and exercises its normal censorship in order to keep the tellers within the general referential framework, as has been described by many authors. Ortutay makes a condensed statement concerning community control (Ortutay 1940); so does Friedrich von der Leyen: "Überhaupt dürfen wir die Zuhörer als ständig korrigierendes Element betrachten" (von der Leyen and Schier 1958: 109). The influence of the audience, however, is not limited to such mechanical services as adjusting the version of one teller to that of the second, the third, the fourth, etc. Rather, the audience strives to keep the narrator's story up-to-date with actual local interests. Community influence, therefore, can be considered as a stimulus for modification rather than as a source of stabilization. The motifs which bind the story closer to reality, the most mobile surface features of tales, are influenced mostly by community suggestions. Sharp's famous term used originally in folksong creation – fits well the storytelling situation and was utilized by folktale scholars: "The suggestions, unconsciously made by the individual singer, have at every stage of the evolution of the folksong been tested and weighed by the community, and accepted or rejected by their verdict" (Sharp 1907: 16). Unfortunately, these functionally vital elements, because they do not always contain registered narrative motifs, remained unconsidered by the different schools of folklore engaged in the construction of analytical tale models.

As our considerstions of this problem rely on our latest field research in a quite limited geographical area, we, of course, cannot draw conclusion which have universal validity in terms of worldwide processes through many centuries. A series of experiments could only throw light on the correlation of tradition, actual social control, group and family inheritance, personality factors, personal and collective unconscious, and other prevalent major and minor forces that contribute to tale formation.

5.

If the objections to Walter Anderson's assertions are acceptable, only one of his conclusions remains incontrovertible: a repeatedly heard text will probably be better remembered than a text heard only once. This is indeed an obvious rule, and the folktale is no exception. One might not even need experimental proof. From the mere fact that the storyteller knows his tale 'well,' one might conclude without any doubt, that he has heard it often enough to remember it. But how much is 'often enough'? Anderson does not give a guideline and this is no wonder. No one to our knowledge has investigated this point of importance, although recently Juha Pentikäinen elicited, by his "depth research" method of inquiry, more detailed information on the frequency of hearing the same story (Pentikäinen 1970b: 106). He resourcefully adopted storytelling community research methods for his study of folk religion. Presumably, Anderson took into account the *average man's* faculty of perception and remembering when he generalized his rule as valid for all kinds of narrators. (He considered the participants of his experiment, as we have noted already, as "very intelligent" people, above the average.)

However, is it reasonable to believe that storytellers are just average people? Are their interest, orientation, ambition, ability of perception, memory, style, taste, and the other attributes necessary for learning, recollecting, and communicating tales just average? Hunter mentions a friend who could reproduce a tale he had heard twenty-nine years ago. "Admittedly, this particular man was a genius, in any meaningful sense of this ambiguous word, and has among many talents the most remarkable long-term memory abilities" (Hunter 1964: 159). Storytellers – the average people of Anderson – are no geniuses indeed. In their field of competency, no one questions whether storytellers possess "unusual capacity for creativity activity" (Webster's Third New International Dictionary 1960). Most narrators are simple, often poor people, agricultural laborers, farmhands, itinerant craftsmen, and the like (Dégh 1957: 99–126). They do their daily chores as anybody else in the local group and would be surprised to learn that they are admired as exceptional geniuses. Yet some among them can display in their particular fields "unusual capacity for creative activity," typical of the real genius.

Since the nineteenth century, folklorists have most admired the gigantic memory of epic narrators. Singers were noted first because of their incredible store of knowledge: the Serbian, Avdo Mededovic, could sing 12,000 lines; the Uzbek, Polkan, recited 20,000; the Kara-Kirghiz, Orozbakov, knew 250,000 verses, and Karalaev, his countryman, knew 400,000 lines (Bowra 1964: 351–56). It might be remembered that Parry and Lord attributed the retention of long epic songs to the memorization of epic formulae (Lord 1960). The equally keen memory of prose narrators was confirmed later when long complex tales could be recorded by electronic devices in full length. The colossal memory of narrators was credited with the ability to "retell a tale heard only once many years ago" (von der Leyen and Schier 1958: 110), to reproduce tales verbatim, to expand tales excessively, and, above all, to accumulate a large body of tales. Among the many outstanding narrators, the Yemenite-Jew, Jefet Schwili, knew 200; the Gypsy, Dmitri Taikon, 250; the Hungarian, Lajos Ámi, 262; the Irish woman, Peig Sayers, 375; and the Czech, Filomena Hornchová, 500 (Dégh 1969/ 1989: 168; Erdész 1968). The complex achievement of Märchen-tellers is, therefore, by numerical criteria alone, extraordinary. It can be said that narrators in general need to have a very good and in some cases a brilliant memory – if only limited to the retention of tales or even to one specific category of tales. This fact is, of course, no surprise. For a long time folklorists have been aware of the fact that those who are accustomed to relying on their memories tend to have a more developed capacity for remembering than those who secure their recall by the use of a note pad. Ortutay has pointed out that besides seven hundred million adult illiterates of the world reported by UNESCO researchers, the great masses of semi-literate agriculturists in under-developed countries still depend to a great extent on verbally communicated folklore (Ortutay 1959: 4). In simple society, including the village of the recent past, oral literature was the only known form of literary expression; within it, the magic tales, the most complex form of artistry, is the most adequate to express basic patterns of the human mind (von Franz 1970: 11). One of the most important qualities a storyteller possesses is memory, enabling him to narrate and to establish a repertoire. Without a good memory, one cannot become a narrator of distinction.

On the other hand, members of the experimental transmission chain discussed in the foregoing appeared to be forgetful. They left out numerous important portions of the material, distorted other parts, and recharged the story with unfit stuffing. The narrators used in the experiment lacked the brilliancy of regular folk narrators. The memory, the style, and the entire performance of these tellers were far below standard. How can such a contradiction exist between two observations: extraordinary capability of remembering in one case, extraordinary forgetfulness in the other? The answer is simple: in accordance with the spirit of the experiment, we have compared two incommensurable performances, that of genuine raconteurs with that of non-raconteurs. We do not mean to argue that the latter were non-raconteurs, because, as Schier contended, they were carelessly selected for the experiment, or because they were not experienced storytellers and did not belong to a traditional folk group. Even if the test persons had the ability of telling stories – and we do not know if they had – they cannot be viewed as storytellers because the experimental situation was not a storytelling event (Georges 1969: 313–328). It lacked all of the criteria.

There are other important features of traditional narration ignored by Anderson. The members of the transmission sequence did not *volunteer* to narrate and were not given the *freedom of choice*. Without these two features of normal narration, tale transmission cannot materialize. The violation of the principle of *voluntary performance* and *free choice* of materials would result in the formation of the *natural conduit* being impeded. In absence of the natural conduit for transmission, it is readily understandable why the tale degenerates. The phenomenon Anderson had observed resulted from conditions other than he thought.

There is no doubt that in a natural environment, the folk narrator volunteers to tell stories. He/she decides to become an entertainer and prepares to capture the attention of fellow members of the community by telling stories either regularly or once in a while. It might happen that the narrator's audience tries to persuade him with some mild jocular pressure, threat, or promise to pay him for his services (Dégh 1969/1989: 74–75), but when he is not in the right mood, he has the opportunity to refuse. Although Anderson speaks of his test subjects as "freiwillige Mitarbeiter," the cooperation of these collaborators was only partly voluntary. For dependent students who must have been rather anxious to please their teacher, it would have been hard to turn down a professor at a German university in the 1940s. This is, however, only a minor violation of the voluntary principle. A more serious mistake was that the students did not volunteer for *storytelling* but for *participation in the experiment*. The two behaviors are basically different. Very few folklorists would deny that the tale is deeply rooted in the human psyche: "One of the remarkable characteristics of folktales is a free exhibition of man's imagination. So folktales are full of man's desires and dreams . . . In a sense, they are a treasure-house of human psychology whether conscious, unconscious or subconscious" (Suziyama, quoted in Lanham and Shimura 1967: 33). Along with their tales, narrators tell many things about themselves, their environments, their small group, the greater society in which they live, and the universality of mankind. This gift is a delicate revelation which not everybody is willing or capable of making.

The decision to tell a tale involves intent to communicate, inclination to perform a certain amount of self-assurance, and as much artistic brilliance as can be brought to bear on the adaptation and the reproduction of a tale. Storytelling is a personal act, whereas the participation in an experimental story transmission is rather impersonal. It is quite possible that there are individuals who agree to such an impersonal act but would never agree to *lege artis* storytelling involving freely improvised recital of a story in front of an actively responding audience and vice versa. Hunter must have thought of this and explained first the details of the experiment to a group of students and only then solicited volunteers (Hunter 1964: 145). However, not even this method is sufficient to make the experimental conditions correspond with those of the real storytelling situation. The person who 'volunteers for storytelling' does not do it abstractedly, in a general sense. He does not accept the role of the narrator once and for all but agrees or refuses to tell tales in each individual occasion. More precisely, he does not refuse the telling explicitly but just refrains from doing so if he pleases. Thus, to secure a completely voluntary basis, test subjects must be familiar with the tale to be reproduced in advance and, like real storytellers, decide only afterwards – by explicit declaration or just by inactive abstention – whether or not they want to volunteer for the experiment. The given tale-conduit can progress only through absolutely voluntary individuals.

Another pertinent point is the narrator's right of selection. Supposedly, every storyteller has heard many tales in the course of the years, many more than he could remember. We have already mentioned the problem of repertoire-selection by folk narrators, each of whom – in spite of the fact that they live in close proximity to each other and that they share a community body of narratives inherited from previous generations – adapts only a portion of these narrative traditions to his own repertoire. They tell some tales spontaneously, others only on the request of their audience, and there are some tales they do not tell even if someone might ask for them. Similarly, they do not mention tales heard but forgotten, or tales not necessarily forgotten but just not wanted to be remembered. The rejected tales may always reoccur, subject to certain circumstances (Dégh 1959). These tales, tale incidents, episodes, motifs preserved in the narrator's mind, as well as the forgotten, rejected invariants (Ortutay 1959: 191–192), constitute an *entity* of the intricate biological heritage impulses, social influences, and personal experiences as a sum total of the narrator's personality. The compilation of a repertoire consists of a series of artistic activities. For the discipline of folklore, "the function of adaptation and the selection and the transformation of the adapted material is essential . . . Creation is manifest here . . . in the selection of the adapted products" (Bogatyrev and Jakobson 1929: 907). The folk artist feels that the selection and adaptation of tales included in his repertoire is an act of creativity even though he does not use this term. The conscious or unconscious creative activity of folk narrators was specifically discussed by Károly Marót in many of his works since 1939 and summed up in *The Beginnings of Greek Literature* (Marót 1956). While on a field trip in the Indiana Calumet-Region, the authors found several manuscript collections of miscellaneous materials jotted down by the owners over the course of several decades. These compilations, very similar to those of traditional singers, consisted mostly of verses and songs that had been heard, read, or chosen from different sources according to individual taste. The sometimes fragmentary or drastically corrupted items were much less subject to the control of traditional audiences in this particularly disintegrated community. After each text, on each page, sometimes more than once, the compiler signed his name: "written by Joe N." Maybe because he changed it somewhat and so he enjoyed something of the pleasure of creation, he considered the verse his own. In the contemporary domain of written literature and codified copyright law, the phenomenon of cryptomnesia which leads sometimes to a *bona fide* plagiarism might also be explained by similar reasons. (It need not be asserted that the conscious or unconscious modification of an art product and the multiplication of its variants is definitely an act of artistic creation. Bogatyrev and Jakobson did not see any basic difference between Molière reworking old plays and folk manipulation of art songs.) The freedom of choice, the selection of an item and its elements, is not only an indispensable condition of storytelling as an act of artistry, it also is an inherent part of it.

On the other hand, the test subjects, who committed themselves to the reproduction of an unknown legend either out of respect to their teacher or because of their scholarly interest, were by definition restricted in their freedom of choice. Thus, the experiment created an exception situation that was similar to the one before the barbed wire barrier produced by the specific circumstances (Anderson 1951, Part 3). As with all kinds of orally communicated messages, tales can move only through their own adequate conduit. While most messages might progress through numerous conduits (as jokes, anecdotes, rumors for example are told by many people), due to their special relationship with the depth of human soul – and naturally also because of the special abilities required from the tellers – tales and legends can find only a few adequate conduits. Von der Leyen similarly observed that tale transmission does not progress through the broad masses but rather through individually gifted storytellers (von der Leyen 1958: 109).

These talented and, of course, voluntary raconteurs might modify the tale at any stage of transmission. It is a matter of opinion whether such alteration should be considered a "mistake," as Anderson contended, or an "act of creation," as Bogatyrev and Jakobson believed (Bogatyrev and Jakobson 1929: 907). "The story recalled by the person is influenced by a wide diversity of circumstances and activities – some operating at the time of interpreting the story, some operating in the interval between receiving and recalling, some operating at the time of reconstructing" (Hunter 1964: 158). In short, the tale that progresses under normal conditions through the normal conduit might more or less undergo changes depending on the narrator's memory capability and numerous other internal and external circumstances including the passing of time. The regularities of the process, if any, have not yet been explored.

Distortions become unavoidable if narrators are under greater or lesser pressures, i.e., lacking a narrational occasion of free choice and spontaneity. In such cases, the well-known mechanisms of mental defense set in for the avoidance of anxiety, displeasure, and painful memories. The effect of such mental defenses is to force out of the awarenesss of the narrator a considerable portion of his tale materials. Under these circumstances, the tale the narrator actually produces will exhibit the effects of forgetfulness, false recollection, and memory errors. In an experiment, children between the ages of 2 and 5 told stories from their "own creative imagination," albeit upon request. Under the conditions the mechanism of defense could be observed by the authors in many cases (Pither and Prelinger 1969). It seems to us remarkable that almost a half century after the publication of *Psychopathologie des Alltagslebens* and more than a decade after Freud's death, Walter Anderson did not even take the trouble to reject this commonly known theory of defense procedure. His possible excuse, that he did not seek the *reason* of the distortion but rather wanted only to ascertain the facts of its occurrence, would not be too logical, as the question to be answered is whether the distortions were caused by normal conditions of life or abnormal conditions of the experiment. The solution of this problem would determine whether it is reasonable to assume that the narrator does not hear the story from many people "wrongly," but from just a few "properly," and whether it is justified to infer that tale transmission occurs through a specific multi-conduit system. Only exacting investigation can attempt to answer these questions. We would like to propose a few experiments whose results might provide some solutions. These experiments would be based on the following hypothetical premises:

(1) Genuine narrators, that is, people who volunteer to tell stories and select the actual items for recital of their own free will (and, of course, have the necessary aptitude), do not forget, and do not essentially distort the tales. Anderson's experiment was not performed in a natural situation and could give us only an indication of the reactions of narrators under unfavorable conditions.

(2) Not everybody possesses the specific skills of a narrator, but most people respond to certain kinds of tales which they will remember well and rarely forget.

(3) The tales that appeal to a certain person (he listens to them, tells them to others, and hardly forgets them) hold profound kinship with each other. This tale-affiliation is both positive – they have something in common not shared by other tales – and negative – they commonly lack something, shared by other tales. (By examining the statements and free associations of the informants, it is not impossible to find that these tale-complexes can form the core of a classification-system which focuses on the tale's local and universal content, symbolism, structure, and relationship with individual and collective unconscious psychic processes.)

(4) Similar personality types react similarly to similar tale types.

(5) Storytellers learn their stories from similar personality types and likewise pass them on to their peers. In the narrational community, the congenial persons are those who listen with pleasure, memorize, and perpetuate the tales. The *tale-conduit* constitutes the sequence of people who display similar attitudes towards one or several tales.

(6) The tale complexes ('Types') consist of numerous tales; each tale consists of numerous motifs, and the motifs consist of numerous elements. Due mostly to personal differences between individuals belonging to similar personality types, the tales often do not spread as closed entities through conduits and sub-conduits, but rather as motif clusters that are broken up into single motifs and are disseminated through *micro-conduits*. However, the continuation of the tale particles through the micro-conduit does not result in ultimate distortion because if the disintegrated tale does not reach a blind alley, it will fit into another conduit. On the other hand, the unimpaired tale progresses in its safe conduit that protects it from any notable pollution.

(7) The maintenance of the 'extraordinary stability' of the tales as messages passed from generation to generation can be explained with the *multi-conduit system*: the communicative chain of congenial individuals.

FIGURE 7

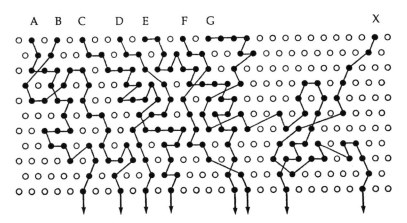

For the above scheme of the multi-conduit system, the groups of circles signify society, and the black dots designate the bearers of single tales (A, B, C, D, etc.) in the society. This diagram (Figure 7), as are the previous ones, is oversimplified and does not indicate that the conduits often merge, ramify, disintegrate, turn into dead ends, etc. The direction of the conduits shown here is of course arbitrary, just for the sake of our discussion.

(8) In general, the laws of transmission cannot be studied with exact analytical methods in normal field situations. Goldstein performed an experiment under the conditions of a normal field situation in 1959–1960. Because of its specific nature, this interesting test cannot be repeated, but its result might be utilized for further orientation (Goldstein 1967a: 72–82). Insurmountable obstacles, like temporal and spatial distance between the informants, the difficulty in locating them, and other complications make such exacting observation impossible. Concrete experiments are needed, as well as careful re-examination of existing theoretical considerations and discernment of the regularities under scrutiny. Quite a few critics have questioned the lag of folklore behind related social sciences (Jacobs 1966a: 423–427; Jason 1969: 410–413); Georges 1969: 313–328); and some have explicitly stated that concrete experimentation is the most neglected domain of the discipline (Dundes 1965: 246; Schenda 1970: 154).

(9) The experiments must correlate the variation, digression, and maintenance of tale texts with the personality of storytellers and other relevant factors. In addition to the more or less unavoidably impression-istic methods of tale analysis, some objective approaches must be employed as well, for instance the statistical study of structural elements of word frequency, and the application of the statistical contingency method recommended by Thomas A. Sebeok (1957: 130–140). Similar objectivity has to be employed in the description of personality. The postulate of 'personality study' in folklore, specifically in the study of the folk narrative, has been recognized but some of the numerous publications concerned with the personality of storytellers commit a logical error. These deduce the personality of the informant from his own accounts (repertoire, worldview, function, biography, etc.) and then evaluate the information in regard to his personality. Contemporary experiments must break away from this vicious circle. The biased evaluation of the impressionistically collected field material has to be substituted by objective depth psychological investigations, i.e., by the exhaustive examination of folklore materials of individual informants and the profound exploration of their personalities on the basis of adequate testing. We believe that this kind of confrontation of personality and certain folklore phenomena will yield new insights into laws of folklore transmission.

6.

On the basis of the assumptions described and summarized in the foregoing, some explorations were made in Hungary by the authors during 1962 and 1963. Although our aim at that time was only preliminary information-gathering, and the experiments we conducted were more or less improvised, they yielded some conclusions worthy of mention.

Most of the chosen test persons were professional writers who share a similar socio-cultural background, educational experience, and focus of interest, and who represent the closest parallel to village storytellers in urban society.

The narrative to be reproduced was a lengthy, recently recorded, complex magic tale, unfamiliar to the listeners. For this reason, more effort at remembering was required in the retelling of this story than of the text used in previous experiments. The Oedipal elements, frightening incidents, and religious motivations of this particular *Märchen* were outstandingly suitable to act forcibly upon the emotions of the participants. (The experimental tale was The Blackmantle, AaTh 507A, discussed in Dégh 1969/1989.)

We tried to simulate reality as much as possible in the experimental situation. Linda Dégh took the opportunity of one of the common social gatherings that resembled normal get-togethers of a village folk-group to read the text to the casually assembled 10–15 authors and their spouses.

The next day we asked individually each of those present at the reading whether they would be willing to repeat the tale and let us record it for an experiment we would like to do. We withdrew the invitation if someone hesitated, using only those eager to partake in the experiment. This way we wanted to ensure the *voluntary participation* of real storytelling events at least, if the principle of *free choice* could not be applied. After the taping of the versions, we asked each respondent to subject himself to a psychological test. The Szondi test, employed by the authors for this experiment, is well known in Europe but enjoys less popularity in the United States. If our explorations were to be continued, we would not insist on the exclusive use of this test. Depending on suitability, we might use others in place of or in addition to the Szondi test (Szondi 1947; Szondi, Moser and Webb 1959). The records of the tests were evaluated by an independent psychologist.

The results, even if they are tentative, seem to confirm our hypothesis. All voluntary test persons reproduced the tale practically without a flaw. It should be remembered that in previous experiments of Anderson and others, each re-teller distorted the material that was much shorter and simpler than our *Märchen*. The fact that hardly any corruption took place in the repeated story substantiates the voluntary principle presented in 5: 1 of this essay. If this principle had been disregarded, similar types of distortion would have occurred as in the Anderson experiment. Naturally, the peculiar memory features of outstanding raconteurs also contribute to this phenomenon of fault-less remembering as discussed by us, in part 5.

It is also noteworthy that half of those who reproduced the tale under the stated conditions and who were subjected to a psychological test displayed the features of one and the same personality type termed hysteroid, according to the adapted terminology. (This term is Szondi's *hy-Triebfaktor*. Szondi's theory takes into account the inherited *"familiäre Unbewusst"* as well as the personal and the collective unconscious. According to Szondi, personalities are divided into four vectors subdivided by eight factors. In our 1963 experiment we used Szondi's terminology.) The fact that all of the personality types who took part in our experiment were hysteroid might be incidental and does not justify further generalizations. Nevertheless, even the few completed experiments seem to support our contention that there is internal relationship between similar tale types and similar personality types as stated in part 5: 4.

We suggest that folklore experiments aided by exact psychological testing can be successfully performed in a laboratory situation which approximate real spontaneous transmission in its basic principle. The triplicate study to be performed by a well-qualified team should consist of exact measurement of text variation, depth exploration of narrators, and the administration of psychological tests. The description of projected experiments would exceed the limits and the goals of this essay. In case the relationship between the tested tales and the personalities of the test persons can be established by the experiment, psychologists might perhaps utilize these repeatedly explored tales as the basis of a personality test (see the Märchen-tests of Charlotte Bühler and Josephine Bilz [1961], the I. P.A.T. Music Preference Test of Personality and the Humor Test of Personality [Cattell 1966]). Pilot experiments were started under the sponsorship of the Research Center for the Language Sciences at Indiana University in the summer of 1971.

Should it turn out in the course of the experiments that personality, social conditions, cultural adherence, and other significant factors have no measurable impact on folklore transmission, this would mean that either different experiments or another explanation should be sought to answer the question we have raised. If, however, the experiment would show otherwise, it would corroborate the hypothesis that the multi-conduit system is a valid factor in folklore transmission.

IS THERE A DIFFERENCE BETWEEN
THE FOLKLORE OF URBAN AND RURAL AMERICANS?

The first Anglo-Saxon colonists built their New England (Yankee) cities and the southern county prototypes. Later the immigrants of diverse ethnic origins from Northwest-Europe arrived by way of the Great Atlantic Migration and formed their own communal settlement prototypes essentially in the Middle-Atlantic, the Appalachian, and the Middle-West regions. These groups also established the so-called "open-country neighborhoods" in which family homesteads or farm-steads were administratively united into townships.

Following the industrial revolution causing the phenomenal rise of immigration from Central, South, and East Europe, new and larger industrial settlements were founded with populations of greater ethnic and cultural diversity. Around the turn of the century, mines, oil-, railroad-, textile-, steel-, and the auto-industry emerged and grew in rapid succession. The job-seeking new arrivals had to build their living quarters in close proximity to the working places, wherever room was yielded around the smoke-blowing factory chimneys, blast furnaces, docks, and the network of railroad tracks. The traces of the variable types of settlement enclaves can still be found behind the back alleys of modern highrise buildings of large modern cities. A dynamic succes-sion of decay and boom – construction of ghettos and slums, and respectable neighborhoods for peope of high-, middle- and modest income – surrounded the downtown-core, the center of business life (Handlin 1951; Hansen 1960; Gordon 1964; Warner 1963; Arensberg and Kimball 1965).

Over the brief history of the population of the North-American continent, the last phase, the industrial explosion, was the shortest and most decisive. During this phase, the total population became endowed with a uniform body of mass-produced cultural goods. These goods superimposed and more or less blurred sociocultural differences. Singular and simple community traditions were easily discarded for goods that accommodated everyday needs conveniently, and eased the hardships of cultural adjustment to American life for those who were already alienated from their imported ethnic heritage.

The foreign traveler who mounts a Greyhound bus to voyage through the land may easily be impressed by a great uniformity of how small and large cities are structured. All towns begin with the gasoline stations of the same companies, motels of the same chains, and franchises of the same fast-food restaurants. Drive-in movies, discount stores and supermarkets dot the main street that exits off the interstate highway and leads through downtown, to the town-hall in the middle of the square, dividing eastside and westside, only to continue past identical businesses in a reverse order on the opposite side of town. Behind this consolidated uniformity, however, communities represent extreme diversities. And since the cities were originally composed of small cultural units expanding far beyond the metropolitan area, ethnic and regional diversities persist latently in the cultural memory of the dwellers despite the homogenizing effect of the industrial mass culture.

American settlements are so young and often so short-lived that emotional attachment to birthplace or original family home can seldom develop and carry over to generations. Most of the time, old people remember the founding and naming of places; place-name legends proliferate even though close proximity to facts and the lack of historical depth limit the soaring of poetic fantasy (Stewart 1956; Rennick 1970: 35–94).

Commercial motivation also shapes the character of settlements. Real estate entrepreneurs buy land and project its parceling for the specific development of industrial and rural residences, recreational and retirement homes. They build townhouses, single family homes, apartments, and condominiums for people of all economic brackets, ages, and occupations. The real estate agency announces the project and circulates the map of the future settlement. The map shows the neighborhoods, transportation routes, the sizes of the lots and houses, and the future locations of schools, churches, banks, hospitals, working places, clubhouses, and sports facilities. Sales strategies are aggressive: potential buyers are invited for a pleasant vacation with free travel, local transportation, accommodations, meals, and gifts on condition of listening to an agent's promotional speech. In about ten years the plan becomes reality – a sample "boom town" is for example Fort Lauderdale, Florida, with more than 100,000 inhabitants (Burgess and Bogue 1967: 15–114). But not all real estate speculators' plans become reality. In 1910, Gary in Northwest Indiana was projected to become "the city of the Century" and dwarf Chicago. Instead, the boom town

of the steel industry that settled sixty diverse ethnic labor-force population groups became known as "the sin city of the century" because
of its high crime rate (Moore 1959).

Living in a new, unexplored and vast land means the loosening of
family ties; job seekers abandoned their primary settlements for better
opportunities: mobility of the population became more characteristic
than the solidification of permanent communities. Breaking natural
ties and moving on to a new place were not traumatic experiences
but steps toward furthering one's career, moving upward on the social
scale. The neighborhoods, characterized by class, professional and
ethnic distinctiveness, functioned as temporary holding grounds;
workers were not setting down roots but waiting for a new move as
their companies transferred them from place to place between the
Atlantic and the Pacific coasts. A progression of family lifestyle also
developed: newlywed couples moved from rented apartments to family homes that were then substituted by bigger houses as more children
were born; but at the end of their career, parents replaced their suburban houses and gardens with apartment or townhouse living. Their
children are even more mobile and enterprising. In pursuit of their
luck, like modern nomads, they wander through the country. Children
as a rule leave the family home at eighteen, if not earlier. When siblings
settle at remote places from each other, accepting membership in
diverse communities, family ties become loose, limited to occasional
and incidental reunions. Two typical customs were generated from
this situation quite consciously in defense against the disintegration
of the American family much bemoaned by illustrated family magazines and church organizations. "Homecoming" is an occasion to visit
hometown on a sacred calendar day or sports weekend (particularly
college football or basketball). But most importantly, Thanksgiving,
ostensibly the commemoration of the first pilgrim settlers of the United
States, has become an intimate dinner gathering of kin on the last
Thursday of November. Kinfolks ritually consume a meal of turkey,
dressing, pumpkin pie and other dishes symbolizing family and
national sentiments. In another effort to build cohesion between generations of relatives, the widely dispersed descendants of an ancestor
gather in a "family reunion" at the homestead or community recreation
center nearby. The family reunion is a carefully planned and organized
institution maintained primarily by people of small towns or farming
communities. The organization committee consists of an elected president, vice-president, secretary-treasurer, a genealogist-historian who
registers members of a family tree. Appointed members provide for
correspondence, publicity, accommodations, food and drinks, music,
child care, door prizes, gifts, and so on. It is no rarity that two to five

hundred descendants show up for such a late summer muster, eating, drinking, and playing together at a state park close to the founders' original location (Swenson 1989).

In pre-industrial America, as in West Europe, agricultural settlements were characterized by self-sufficiency, strong solidarity, and isolation from urban centers. But group cohesion was already diminishing at a time when railroads and train tracks were being built. The upswing of the auto industry and affordable prices for transportation vehicles, particularly during the 1950s and 1960s, resulted in the gigantic expansion of American cities and the further weakening of kinship ties (Larrabee and Riesman 1964: 255–292). The downtown area of cities for a while became the centers of trade and official businesses while the inhabitants, weary of the noise and polluted unhealthy city air, moved their residences into the "green meadows" of the suburbs. Retailers followed them, opening giant shopping malls to accommodate their increasing need for durable goods. Former residences of the inner city deteriorated and became the mass-shelters of the urban poor; other homes, abandoned and left in disrepair, were bulldozed and replaced by highrise modern tenements surrounded by parks and playgrounds. The escapees from the inner city moved into new attractive residential areas developed by real estate companies, thus expanding the city itself. Suburban living became a new ideal on small settlements annexed to industrial areas. These "villages" bore names recalling the British model, giving status to the colonists: Hyde Park, Southampton Courts, Hawthorne Manor, Kensington Gardens. The British predilection for naming cottages and family dwellings also influenced real estate developers who christened residential areas with names like Maple Crest, Hilltop View, Walnut Grove, Lakeview Village, and Swansea Lake. Stylish, high-tech dreamhouses surrounded by manicured lawns, decorative shrubs and trees created an idyllic atmosphere of closeness to nature characterized by Riesman as "suburban dislocation" (see also Wood 1958 and Donaldson 1969).

These havens nostalgically recalled the past and were crafted in imitation stone and brick. However, modest replicas of old farmhouses, castles and mansions in Tudor-, Georgian-, Empire-, French Provincial-, and Colonial styles reflect only the ambition of the new colonist and are not meant to last as a family estate. They will be sold as soon as they outlive their practical use and the children move on. Such suburbia is ostentatious but homogenized, without personal touch (Donaldson 1969: 59–77). More modest were the housing tracts financed after the Korean War by the Veteran Administration, GI Bill, and Federal Housing Agency, whose standardized floorplans (necessary to pass federal inspection) resulted in an even more noticeable homogeneity of housing style. This type of home was aptly described by poetess Malvina Reynolds and popularized by singer Pete Seeger:

Little boxes on the hillside
Little boxes made of ticky tacky
Little boxes on the hillside
Little boxes all the same.
There's a green one and a pink one
And a blue one and a yellow one
And they're all made out of ticky tacky
And they all look just the same.

Whatever their architectural style, the village-like settlements are not always immediately linked with the city; their continued maintenance, improvement, or decay depends on population changes linked to local economic conditions. Because of the rapid turnover, suburbs cannot overcome the initial cultural dissimilarities of its residents. Aside from practical, organized activities, cultural cohesion cannot develop, build human relationships, and turn symbolic communities into real ones. Whereas the traditional European peasant is the bearer of an uninterrupted flow of cultural tradition, the uprooted American colonist or immigrant, wherever he settles, is a pioneer who has been forced to free himself or herself of old values in order to survive. Farmers of the colonial period had to work hard to break up and clear the wilderness in the virgin land (H. Smith 1970) and turn it into prosperous habitats so that their descendants could become agricultural entrepreneurs. Later arrivals of peasant origin became urban-industrial laborers: Americans who completed their careers as suburbanites. Historians, sociologists, and folklorists had described the American acculturation process as converging toward an urban/suburban uniformity, a fact supported by the life histories of both farming and industrial settlers (Handlin 1951; Gordon 1964; Klymasz 1973). This fact explains why the urban- industrial lifestyle has a dominant impact on modern American folklore.

The proximity of life in the city and in the country resulted in a gradual decline of older traditions. If regional and ethnic subcultures were able to preserve and creatively enhance their inherited traditions through decades of relative isolation, not even practical conditions secure the traditions today. Although the raw materials of folklore of every community consist of imported and indigenous materials, the imported survivals turn hopelessly senescent because of lack of social support. Grandparents have no opportunity to transmit their folklore to their grandchildren because they do not live together anymore; old neighborhoods fondly remembered as sites of lively community togetherness have long since dissolved.

Of course, exceptions exist. Some forms of folklore – particularly those approximating professional art and attracting general audiences (like instrumental music, lyric and epic poetry) – can flourish in the urban-industrial world. Continuity can also be observed in community festivities of social, historical, and religious rituals: these play an important role in contemporary American folklife. One could say these commemorative celebrations are specific manifestations of people's desires for a place under the sun: roots, ethnic identity, and group-solidarity. Small regional and ethnic communities, without any out-side stimulus, reconstruct long forgotten or never-existing customs and rites to forge their distinctiveness. For example, the Wisconsin Swiss of New Glarus produce a Wilhelm Tell play every summer on an open-air stage with the appropriate alpine landscape and grazing cattle in the background; the inhabitants of Switzerland County in Southern Indiana celebrate wine-harvest in the fall, tasting imported wine from Switzerland. The number of visitors of the "Beast of Busco" festival in tiny Churubusco, Indiana (pop. 2,000), increases by several thousand each year. This community of working class families and farmers annually celebrates the legendary appearance of a giant turtle in the small lake. The festival originated in a Chicago reporter's article about a local legend in the early 1940s. As curious visitors began to arrive, the story began to shape and develop. Over the years, the telling of the legend has grown into a spectacular procession-play. The proud citizens whose community was "put on the map" by this publicity have paraded ever since, carrying the statue of the Beast around the town and providing a full day of entertainment for the crowd (Gutowski 1992). A common feature of ethnic and local festivals is that the performance is directed both toward an outside audience and themselves, for the reinforcement and reassertion of group iden-tity.

Other folklore forms appeal in other ways. Traditional occasions for storytelling have long expired – if they ever existed in America where the Märchen was communicated more by the print media than by oral tradition (Christiansen 1962: 58). The urban elite formed asso-ciations and guilds to institute storytelling festivals, and educators and librarians also exposed children to oral stories; nevertheless, tales and tale-equivalents among the masses are more naturally communi-cated by the media. That the worldview of the Märchen lives on, and that its heroes and magic transformations are deeply rooted in the minds of modern people, is well documented by its widespread popu-larity in diverse formats. Popular fiction, cartoons, and movies adapt and vary the best-known tale types; and commercial advertisers capitalize on the public's deep familiarity with the magic tale. The good fairy offers a certain brand of toothpaste to the girl who suffers from mouth odor; the enchanted prince is disenchanted from his monster shape by wearing the famous brand of jeans; Cinderella, instead of scrubbing, can in no time apply a special floor wax; the magic wand removes the stain from the bride's wedding dress; the consumer becomes king after tasting the right kind of margarine; and a heavenly messenger drops the perfect ziplock bag into the lap of the helpless homemaker. Tale motifs – situations, magic objects, supernatural helpers, villains, heroes and heroines – represent rudimentary survivals of the magic tales but at the same time, are deeply ingrained in the minds of modern people as essential elements of cultural knowledge. The motifs recall the story that we internalize. Schenda reminded us of these "folklore concentrates" that are omnipresent in our industrial everydays (Schenda 1992: 27–28).

Various kinds of humorous narratives – anecdotal personal experience accounts – are also among the typical repertoires of modern Americans. Another domain, not less complex but more accessible for analysis because of its visibility and proliferation among the masses, is the legend, the most viable genre in the industrial environment of American cities and the countryside. Mass communication in the age of electronic efficiency and increasing mobility of the population has not curtailed legend tradition. On the contrary, these two factors have played a decisive role in the communication of folklore materials, especially legends, legend kernels, and legend fragments. Unlike traditional folklore, this material is not limited to small and homogeneous local groups; the media encompasses all society. Consequently, identical folklore materials, legends and legend-particles among them, are communicated to the whole society whereby a common knowledge unites members of all social groups. Because of their relevant attractive themes, easy reportability, compact style, and fragmentary nature, legends are easily picked up and speedily disseminated. General knowledge of the legend stock therefore grows day by day and functions as a common foundation for the formation of local oral tradition (Dégh and Vázsonyi 1978: 253–272).

The American legend body is rich and displays direct links to European forms. Peasant immigrants imported the folk belief systems underlying their legend stock (Hand 1963a: 43–48). But if we observe that diverse immigrant groups imported diverse kinds of folklore – for example, the English were poor in Märchen and rich in ballads and legends – we may also add that legendry was diversly distributed among groups of colonists and immigrants. From the onset, travelers, educators, spiritual writers, and authors of diaries reported stories about witches, demons, partnership with the devil, treasure hunts, evil eye, second sight, headless hunters, poor souls, and ghosts in farming settlements and ethnic neighborhoods. Because of the brevity of local histories, origin legends and hero-legends are less prominent. However, local historians often combine facts with orally spread local legends. For example, William Monroe Cockrum gives vivid account of the conjurations of a witch in South Indiana during the 1830s (Cockrum 1907). A whole community was under her spell. She stole the milk of cows by milking the towel in which she had stuck pins named after each cow, until a man of experience caught her in the shape of a black cat. The man melted a silver dollar for a bullet, forcing the witch to resume her human shape so that he can shoot her (Dégh 1970: 236–238). Folklore fieldworkers later recorded similar stories, but cases of modern witchcraft gained widespread attention when they began to appear on the pages of the daily press. Accusation of bewitching is no rarity among reported court cases. For example, an Associated Press news story in October 1966, gave nationwide coverage to an Italian case of black magic in the industrial town of Akron, Ohio. In the story, a mother and her daughter were accused as perpetrators in the death of a man named Maenza who bewitched their family. Ima Miraglia, the 49-year-old woman, and her 24-year-old daughter Rosemary accused the victim of being responsible for the illnesses and deaths in their family. The women named a spiritist who advised them to make the necessary steps following a dream the daughter saw. The women insisted that all they wanted was to injure, not to kill Maenza in order to call the attention of the police and make their complaint concerning his conjurations more palpable.

The press particularly spotlights ghosts that haunt houses in both the city and the countryside. "Chicago's No. 1 in my opinion," writes Richard T. Crowe, who conducts a five-hour, 100-mile Chicago Ghost Tour. "Chicago has such a rich variety of ethnic groups and blends, so Chicago ghosts represent every culture and every walk of life. The best of the world's ghosts are represented in Chicago. We've got Polish, Irish, Italian and Jewish ghosts and all the ghosts have the unique Chicago flavor" (MacDougall 1983: 147). Some newspapers advise people who complain about their haunted homes as does the *New York Post*'s 'Dear Meg' column (Dec. 21, 1982). Supernatural belief is perpetuating belief in the supernatural (MacDougall 1983: 157).

The industrial environment does not alter the underlying ideology of traditional legends. Their adaptation to modern living conditions follows the rhythm of the tools of advanced technology. Cars, motorboats, trucks, farm machinery, trains, airplanes, household appliances, radio, television, tape and videotape recorders play an important role in legends set at interstate expressways, parking garages, hotels, motels, supermarkets, highrise buildings, drive-in restaurants, offices, schools, and dormitories as well as in old houses, barns, cemeteries, ruins, country roads, chapels and bridges far away from residential areas (Dégh 1971: 55–68; Dégh 1973: 45, 47). The reason legends can remain essentially unchanged is that they address eternal problems of everyday realities. The car probably most influenced the modernization of legendry. Many ghost legends refer to a car wreck that occurred long ago, as does the classic and extremely variable, ubiquituous Vanishing Hitchhiker (Brunvand 1981: 24–46). Automobile excursions often lead to extraordinary experiences (Dégh 1968a: 68–77). The driver is often pursued by a crazy killer or an evil supernatural being (Baker 1970: 163–189; Cord 1969b: 47–54), and the interior or exterior of the car can also become the scene of gruesome events (Degh 1968b: 92–106). It is common for people to seek a legendary experience, to go to the designated place and see for themselves what people are talking about. Young people particularly like to make the daring trip together to haunted sites where they conjure up the dead to replay the tragic event (Dégh 1969b: 54–89). Cemeteries and city apartment houses can also be the scenes of legendary sightings. According to one story, a young man moved into an apartment after an older man appeared in his dream and told him to do so. The same older man, a former business associate of the young man's father, haunted the place because he had hidden his money there and could not rest. This traditional legend was printed in a comics serial called "Grimm's Ghost Stories" (meaning really 'grim') (1972 nr. 7. Poughkeepsie, New York, Western Publishing Co.). Stories of haunting are commonly known, and the presence of previous inhabitants in homes is the common theme of many legends. The similarity of legends in the city and in the country can be shown by the following two examples:

(1) The ghostly bus tour to Chicago's favorite sites in the spring of 1973 stopped at eleven places. The participating audience was familiar with the stories and recited and discussed them during the ride. They visited Resurrection Cemetery, the habitat of Resurrection Mary who in her white ballgown tries to get into cars at Willowbrook Dance Hall to be driven home. On Division Street, a white-clad Spanish woman looks for her lost children. On the near North Side, gangster-phantoms haunt the place where in 1920 a mass murder was committed. At a playground, site of the restless grave of the forgotten Indian chief Pottawatomi, children are scared away by the weird noises. Whoever rents a room on the ninth floor of the Corydon

Hotel has to share it with a woman with a transparent body. A hospitable old couple offers room and board to the tired traveler, but the next day the house is nowhere to return to for offering thanks. Everybody knows that All Saint's Night is celebrated by the ethnic Catholic congregations of Chicago: at St. Rita's Church six phantom monks read the mass at midnight. At the same time, the statues of saints bleed in St. Adrian's Church (*Chicago Daily News*, April 7–8, 1973).

(2) The inhabitants of rural Brown County, Indiana, comprise a predominantly "WASP" community, opposite to the ethnically and racially mixed, mobile folk of urban Chicago. The sparse population is widely scattered, makes its living of agriculture, cattle breeding, lumbering, or from work in nearby urban-industrial plants. Talks with forty-six average settlers yielded seventy-five legends (Thigpen 1971: 141–215) that can be divided into the following thematic categories: personal encounters with spirits at an old, abandoned farmhouse, twelve personal identifications of ghost houses; a rich cycle of legends about a grave in a small cemetery: a white- or black-clad woman sits on a tree stump watching over her child's (husband's) grave, but whoever she catches will end up in a crash on the way home; a heavenly messenger appears to the pious as proven by photograph; the legend of the "headless woman" looking for her baby killed in a train accident is related to several railroad bridges and is combined with other disaster legends; ten stories tell about the deeds of the famous gangster John Dillinger, in connection with robbing the Bedford bank. None of these have specific features to distinguish them from the types heard in Chicago.

Remarkably, only five traditional witch legends were told in Brown County. On the other hand, respondents knew most of the horror legends popular among high school and college students. At the time of the fieldwork (1972), rumors about a protector spirit, "The Watcher," were prominent without being shaped into a full-fledged legend. The twenty-one or so legend-fragments about "The Watcher" seem to be influenced by comic book images and ideas of popular spiritualism and Satanism. The "Watcher," a supernatural father figure, warns and protects hippie youth groups picnicking in the woods of Brown County from the wrath of conservative farmers (Thigpen 1971: 147–171).

The latest legends popular among young people borrow from counterculture. They tell about dope pushers and their victims, heroic escapes and tricks of smugglers and users. A number of horror stories about real dangers – sex murderers, lunatic asylum escapees waiting with their ax or knife for their prey in dark stairwells, alleys, parking places, dormitories or summer camps – are told by young women

(Dégh 1969c: 55–74; Roemer 1971: 1–16). Another category of scary legends is consumed by young boys, particularly during camping. Giants and monsters roam about the campground in these stories, threatening the safety of boys who do not stay with the group and are lost in the forest (Leary 1973: 174–190). A new phenomenon inspired by science fiction is "Frog City," a mystery house that looks like a farmhouse from the outside but where spies and outer space aliens experiment with tools for future warfare. Intruders will be pursued and driven off the road by a car whose motor is always running in the garage.

These few examples may be sufficient to show the similarity of the ideological background of Old World and New World legends, and to illustrate that separate categorization of legends known in rural or urban areas would not be possible. Individual legends emerge from their own immediate environments and mirror the concerns of people's everydays. Contemporary legends cannot be related directly to specific city or country groups; they permeate the entire society. Legend-telling may occur at any occasion in any social group, among women and men of all ages, of all professions. Group solidarity can also be expressed by communally sharing one single legend. For example, two legends – particularly popular in the 1960s and 1970s on college campuses among young women during their freshman year – were regarded as remedies of fear and tension while adjusting to college life. One of the legends, about a girl who was lured to a fraternity house and then innocently drugged and seduced, is usually told by sophomores to test new initiates at sorority houses (Greenberg 1973: 131–158). The other story is about two roommates scared by an ax-murderer on the loose. One is safely inside but in a state of shock from the noise of scratching fingers at her locked door, while the other is desperately trying to enter and is being murdered by the hatchet-man outside. In an interesting experimental study, the transformation of six freshmen's variants is evaluated. Reciting the legend about the Hatchet Man at night, while sitting around a table with a candle burning, the conversation ends with screams, running back to their rooms and locking their doors in fear. Later the fear subsides, and the story slowly turns into a joke. The girls stick cards on each other's doors: "Sorry I missed you! signed Hatchet Man," "Just wait, I'm here! Your loving Hatchet Man" or just simply "H. M." By the end of the year the story is discontinued, having worn out its original purpose (Grider 1973: 1–32).

The body of current legendry is evenly spread all over the country with the assistance of the mass media. Ever since Orson Welles' famous radio play "War of the Worlds" was broadcast shortly before the outbreak of World War II, and thousands in great fear ran for shelter from the Martians out to destroy the planet Earth, folklorists have recognized the stimulating effect of radio and other forms of mass media on the simultaneous dissemination of legends. It was also recognized that during slow seasons when reportable sensations are sparse, the news media use legends as fillers to substitute for real horrors. Today television is the major distributor of legends. The mass media is also responsible for the body of current legends through their selecting, reconstructing, and reinstating old legends, propagating new legends while suppressing and terminating others. Heeding mass media reports, hundreds of people grabbed their guns, clubs, knives, and flashlights, and waded through the dark forests of Michigan where a mother and her 16-year-old daughter were allegedly attacked by a seven-foot-tall hairy monster; their car was dented and the girl got a black eye. Large crowds stood in the Bronx, their eyes fixed on the picture window where Virgin Mary's image appeared at the apartment of a recent immigrant woman from Guatemala. Publication of legendary accounts may have economic ramifications: department stores accused of selling imported knitwear in which poisonous snakes allegedly hatched and killed customers sued the newspaper for millions of dollars for loss of business (Mullen 1970: 214–228). Evidently, mass media and folk tradition influence each other.

But we already knew that before. The publication of the *Deutsche Sagen* by the Grimm brothers reinforced ongoing legend tradition. The interchange between oral and written material, however, has not been regular but only incidental and has occurred in slow motion, over the lifetime of generations. In contrast, there is little temporal distance between modern legends and their mass-mediated versions.

For example, if a reader picks up the telephone in the morning to notify the local newspaper about an event that contains a potential legend kernel, the story can be printed in the evening edition so that residents learn about it the same day. If the story is interesting enough, the local radio station may broadcast it and the local television station may show pictures of the phenomenon. It is possible that the local event may get the same-day national, and even international, attention. Going through so many hands, the event already has several variants at this point. Next day, another reporter can hear an oral version and inform his paper about it, so that next day the reader is exposed to another variant; this blitz-like transmission continues and becomes impossible to follow through all its courses. How can we know who launched the story first, what its original form and content was and how it was disseminated? Nowadays it would be hard to find legends that did not pass through the labyrinth of multiple means of communication, personal and public. People talk, write letters and memoirs, make phone calls, record on tape and video; but they also listen to professional communicators in print, in audio and visual media, in movies, cartoons, and popular, literary, and scientific writing. The media is a part of folklore and perhaps increasingly becomes the greater part.

Under these conditions, the common knowledge of legendry: belief concepts, stock characters, and situations that force legends to emerge gained gigantic proportions. For example, movie and TV comedies made the 'good' witch character stereotypical, and the jovial demonology of Halloween reinforced the scary figures of innumerable toys, costumes, mumming equipments, greeting cards, and books sold in supermarkets. The vampire Count Dracula is a product composed of elements of a novel and several movie variants, cartoons, toys, costumes, and consumer goods, including the breakfast cereal Count Chocula; very little remains from the original vampire concept. Wolf-Man, hero of many late-night TV movies, modernized the traditional concept of the traditional werewolf and is nearly as popular. These and many others belong to the inventory of modern legend-consumers, who obtain the bulk of their folklore information from the media. In many ways, image and sound replace oral and literary communication. Such familiarity with the stock of legend elements thus secures continuity of the legend in modern American society irrespective of its rural or urban environment.

In more general terms, then, can we differentiate current folklore that circulate in the city and in the countryside? Is there any theoretical or practical gain if we try to identify painstakingly obvious adjustments to the two physical environments? Adjustment – acclimatization is maybe a better word – is a technical necessity to update universal messages. It is not the urban or rural location that characterizes folklore or accounts for its viability or demise. Folklore is as unstable as other cultural expressions, subject to ideological transformation through the ages. Some genres succumb, some barely change or change radically, and others bear new fruits within its traditional conventions assisted by modern technical reportability.

PROCESSES OF LEGEND FORMATION

Legend research has become more active in recent years, and European scholars have tried to attain mutual understanding in developing an international catalogue.[1] The difficulties in constructing categories, groups and subgroups into which international legend materials would be ordered induces me to reconsider the definition question as posed by Carl-Herman Tillhagen at the Budapest conference, October 1963: "Was ist eine Sage?" (Tillhagen 1964.) We do not lack definitions. They are numerous, taken from different viewpoints and different scientific considerations. But since none of them yet answers the needs of a common platform, allow me to add another point of view – that of the fieldworker, approaching the question from the functional perspective.

What is a legend, what kind of basic human attitude is expressed by it, what is its content and what is its form, structure and style? These questions have been dealt with many times. Most students of folk legend began by comparing it to the most elaborate, artistic genre of all folk narratives, the Märchen, to demonstrate what the folk legend is not. Though the contributions of all those who have tried to formulate the legend genre have been helpful in the progress of legend scholarship, none of them – with the exception of Max Lüthi perhaps – have tried to investigate the intricate interrelationships of the form, content, and expression of the legend.

In recent years, the International Society for Folk Narrative Research placed the indexing of national and international folk legend material on its schedule.[2] The main disagreement between representatives of the many countries involved lay in their different conceptions of what a folk legend is, and the kinds of topics and verbal frames belonging to this genre. Vague categories and groups based on earlier classifications could be proposed, but this exercise would not help much. Until we know what we want to systematize, until we have a common understanding of what a legend is, it will be impossible to establish an international catalogue.

Folk legend materials accumulated up to now are insufficient for definition purposes because the methods of collection do not meet the needs of modern folklore scholarship. The folktale, having a stable, traditionally crystallized and conscious art-form, is accessible for scholarly study even in restylized or fragmentary shape. The remodeled, rewritten, and improperly recorded legend, on the other hand, is of no use at all. The legend's essential characteristics are a looseness of form and content, oscillating around a stable nucleus, and an attachment to real life and belief. Thus, only authentic texts can serve our purpose, i.e., those texts recorded with modern equipment in the places of their natural occurrence. Such legend collections are scarce, assembled chiefly during the past few years. One of the best is *Karcsai Mondák*, by Ivan Balassa (1963). It is an analytical collection containing the whole legend body of a peasant village. Since materials from all major geographic areas are indispensable, the most important and urgent task is proper collecting, using generally accepted principles and methods.

An adequate understanding of the folk legend can be realized by utilizing the functional method of investigation. I should like to deal with this point in some detail. Presumably we are equipped with all the theoretical information concerning terminologies (Wesselski 1934: 216–248; von Sydow 1934: 253–268; K. Ranke 1961a: 5–11) and know the discussions concerning the formal and content elements of the legend genre (Röhrich 1958; Lüthi 1962/1980). Still we must go back to the live folk culture before we can isolate the legend from other narratives and other manifestations of folk life. As long as we possess nothing but texts of legends, extracted from their natural environments, and lack thorough knowledge of their role in society, all explanations remain hypothetical speculations based on largely inauthentic materials. Studying legends in the field, as they interact between tradition, community, and personality, would allow us to understand what the legend means to those who maintain it, in contrast to what the student of legend has extrapolated by exploring variants of individual legend types (Dégh 1962). Many such monographs must be made; and since the legend is one of the primary kinds of oral narratives which survive after peasant society is transformed into the modern industrial community (Dorson 1959a: 244–276; Weber-Kellermann 1955; Bausinger 1958), field collection should be extended to urban communities too.

Not to complicate matters, I want to deal here exclusively with legends formed on the basis of living folk belief. Probably the majority of so-called historical legends fall into this category, and those which do not should be carefully considered for their component elements. Legends of memorable events, based on facts of national history – if they do not fall into the category of anecdote or novella (like those included in the international tale type index and adjusted to national heroes such as Harun al Rashid, Solomon the Wise, Old Fritz, King Mátyás of Hungary, King Joseph II, etc., belonging mostly to the type-family of AaTh 921–927) – are less likely to arise than legends about belief. National history creates no daily need and no function in peasant society. Occasionally the history may be brought up by some visible object or a chance question, but people are less interested in the past as a whole than in matters affecting their present existence. Historical notions seldom develop into long stories with an intricate structure but rather remain as brief data of a historic nature. Historical events certainly leave their marks at the places affected by them as was shown in the case of a nationwide collection concerning the Hungarian War of Independence in 1848–1849 (*Ethnographia* 48 [1947]: 230–235), and similar attempts in the European field displayed the same results. Historical memoirs, handed down in local oral tradition, are likely to fade away and be replaced by a new happening of vital importance before they could undergo poetical transformation. The possibility of historical legend-formation greatly depends on the situation of the people. Peoples, living under oppression or occupation, are more active in forming legends out of their historical experience throughout generations. Narratives about folk heroes are the only ones which we definitely consider as historical legends. Legendary folk heroes belong mostly into two categories: (1) national heroes and (2) folk heroes including outlaw heroes and all kinds of personalities of humble origin who gained general appreciation by some outstanding deed (Klapp 1949; Dorson 1959a, 1973). While belief legends are continually fed by the network of actual belief and practical needs, folk history is strongly influenced by school education and political propaganda, and it offers therefore a less significant basis for legends.

In its natural existence, the so-called local or belief legend is inseparably interwoven with other manifestations of live folk belief. This is why they must be jointly investigated. Even isolating the folk legend for the purpose of study is impossible without analyzing the whole complex.

How do we acquire information about a belief? Usually by two means: (1) by observation of some kind of magical act, and (2) by oral communication. It might be by both means, and both might be of diverse character.

The oral communication might contain just a simple notion in the form of a *statement*, without any kind of explanation and illustration: "It is not good to give away fire from the house after sunset." Such information is rare and occurs mostly as a result of direct questioning by the folklorist or any outsider not familiar with local beliefs. It is part of the education of the young in the ways of the culture (enculturation in Melville Herskovits's term). The communication might be an *account* of a notion, or of an experience: "I (my father) gave away fire and I was warned not to do so because . . ." It might be a piece of *advice*, containing the actual happening with an additional *explanation*: "N. N. gave away fire and all his luck went with it." It might be an *elaborate story* to illustrate the belief and to warn against its neglect. Speaking in the terms of folk-narrative genres, the belief might be told in the form of a *simple story*, a *Memorat*, an *Ich-Erzählung*, an *experience story*, or a *Fabulat*.

The same belief, on the other hand, might be expressed by magical action. The protection of the family hearth after sunset might be ensured simply by refusing to loan fire when asked, or, in cases where one is forced to give fire away, by feeding the hearth with magic herbs, by an incantation, or by gestures in a prescribed ritual form to prevent harm in consequence of violating the taboo. Finally, protection might be secured by a communal *dramatic performance* at St. John's Eve by jumping over the fire and throwing wreaths of flowers into it.

All these oral or dramatic phenomena have a common nucleus in folk-belief, and they all depend on each other, expressing the same thing in different forms. Hence the coexisting belief ritual and narrative must be analyzed together, as they occur, in the same culture in the same ethnic group.[3]

The example of the well-known European legend about the milk-stealing witch will show that a single, skillfully performed variant – told for edification, for warning, and at the same time for entertainment of the audience – contains all the components shown above. This is the outline of the story as told in the first person by the narrator as his own experience:

(1) Cow becomes dry after having a calf. Because of carelessness, an unidentified witch appeared and took the milk by magic.

(2) The owner consults a shepherd who has supernatural knowledge and power.

(3) Advice is given and taken: Bring one liter of water from the well of the pasture before sunrise. While coming and going, don't talk to anybody. This done, the shepherd comes to the house with special healing plants. Boiling them in the "stolen water," he smears the back of the cow with the medicine and pours the rest under her for the complete cure. In order to identify the witch next morning, the cow is milked by the housewife before sunrise, according to the shepherd's instructions. The milk is boiled and continuously stabbed with a large knife while she calls aloud: "I invite you to salted bread."

(4) The neighbor woman appears bleeding from many cuts and asks for forgiveness.

(5) The cow is healed.

The story, no doubt, meets all the criteria of a legend, though the essence of it is the careful *account of a magic cure*. It is one of the countless variants of a definite legend-type which varies greatly in the ways of bewitching and in magical cures.

Belief legends fall generally into two categories. They are either stories about sickness caused and cured by magic, or stories of encounters with agencies of the supernatural world. In the first category, we find the dramatic element more comprehensive than in the second where the magical act might be hinted at or more or less concealed or possibly missing. But apart from structural differences in legend types, the proportion of belief and of ritual elements, and the distribution of the dramatic and epic traits in the variants, depend on the actual raconteur. But even in cases when the narrator aims at spinning a good story and limits the magic action and belief element to a minimum, these remain the most stable and important components of the legends. They are the cause of the existence of the legend, the excuse for the story; they are in fact the foundation on which the *form* is built.

The form, style, and structure of the legend genre present other difficulties in identifying the legend. Its elements and preliminary forms exist side by side in the same culture. Taking the belief and the related action as the legend-nucleus, we might try to find out what structure and style its inner meaning allows. The problem is not only that of separation of the legend from its skeleton-forms or from other genres with the same plots, but also establishing what the form of the legend is. The only thing that seems to be stable is the expression of a message (here I agree with Kurt Ranke's opinion as expressed in his "Einfache Formen" [Ranke 1961]); the contents do occur in other genres. Due to the function of the legend, its form is extremely variable, since its primary aim is not to offer poetic entertainment. The story is thus inconsistent and completely in the hands of the actual narrator. Unfortunately, even today we know little of the personality of the legend teller, but one thing is certain: the legend teller is no artist – he or she has no artistic aspirations, and claims only to tell a story that takes place in the real world. He or she is a little bit more attracted by the supernatural world than the person who narrates tales. Some legend tellers are more inclined to hallucinations, and their imaginings are colored by their lived-through subjective experiences. But more importantly, legend tradition is not maintained in a culture only by outstanding personalities as in the case of tales; anybody can be a spreader of legends. Some people know many legends and are thrilled by their themes more than others, but usually the average member of a peasant society (or even of an urban society) can tell a couple of legends he or she has heard or experienced. (A model example of the transcription of casual legend-telling is O. Brinkmann's small book, *Das Erzählen in einer Dorfgemeinschaft* (1933). The construction and performance of the legend is much more *collective* than that of the tale. Nevertheless, the formulation of a legend from raw material of scattered belief concepts depends on the actual narrator.

Returning to the story of the bewitched cow, we might consider it as one of many interrelated episodes about the local witch, or as part of a legend cycle. It is affiliated with other stories of the witch acquiring magic power, learning at the crossroads, stealing milk in animal shape, leading persons astray, collecting dew on St. George's night, getting rid of magic power, dying a torturous death, and so on. Most variants emphasize one episode and only hint at the others, assuming familiarity with the topic, or are sketchy because just one episode was actually experienced. These episodes (or types?) are completely independent; the affiliation of two or more occurs often, but the episode may also stand by itself. Because most stories – like the cow-bewitching – belong to a cycle about a character or a phenomenon, it would be useful to determine the distribution of the type or of the interlinked types. I believe a comparative analysis of all variants within cultural units would serve this purpose.

Text analyses, collected and observed carefully in the field, have led me to discern some important features of the legend form. I have studied legend-telling communities since 1961. As a passive listener and with the help of a tape recorder, I have gained insights into the natural conditions of legend-telling in rural communities. In addition to the texts and the comments of the audience, and as the result of subsequent careful questioning, I have collected data concerning the values, meanings and uses of folk legends and the attitudes of society towards the legends. I want to present here what I learned about the form, style and structure of the legend with the example of a more or less clearly established legend type (as shown by some 92 variants collected in the Hungarian ethnic territory). This is the outline of the legend based on the variants:

(1) Man or woman, living alone, longing for the absent (working elsewhere, or in war) or dead sweetheart or spouse.

(2) A demon spirit, flying in the air like a long burning shaft or a star, assumes the shape of the desired beloved and substitutes for him (her).

(3) The spirit comes regularly and sleeps with the man (woman) causing paleness which arouses the suspicion of friends or a wise woman.

(4) A test (touching left foot with left hand when in bed, or spreading ashes in the yard for footmarks) reveals the spirit's identity. The left foot is that of a goose.

(5) The spirit is caught by means of a string taken from linen trousers and smeared with garlic or a one-year-old onion tied to the window and door. To get rid of it, the alternatives are: (a) its boots are hidden, (b) the sign of the cross is made over its gifts (wine, cake turn into horse's excrement), (c) it is beaten with a birch-twig cut at St. George's night of the same year while counting one, three, five, seven, etc., (d) it is beaten with a burning twig while calling "fire into his bottom, horseshoe-nail into his ear," (e) it is beaten with a seven-year-old pipe-stem, (f) a dummy smeared with human excrement is substituted in the bed for the victim.

(6) The spirit spreads sparks all over the room and yard in anger at being caught and escapes through the chimney, fills the yard full of dirt and sparks, and flies away after resuming the shape of a burning shaft.

(7) To keep the spirit away, the house must be painted again, mixing into the paint onions planted on the day of St. Benedict.

This legend type, as is shown, includes again all the previously described components, though the story is quite different from that of the milk-stealing witch. It is a well-rounded epic, with a complex structure in which the belief and the magical action, though accurately described in detail, are not as prominent as in the other story cited earlier. Twenty-nine variants are complete and follow this outline, although not all of them are long and logically constructed stories. They range in length from three lines to six pages. They might be claimed to be a personal experience of the teller, a known other, and as an event with a known or an unidentified person. The sequence of motifs is variable. Thirty-six variants are intertwined with Tale Type 407; that is, the tale begins with the initial episode, the visit of the dead lover at the spinnery, usually as in AaTh 365. The combination of 365 and 407 supports the assumption that this legend assists – as in so many other cases – the acclimatization of the international Märchen type to the local belief system.

The fragmentary variants are even more interesting, exposing the elements and the process of legend composition. Eleven variants contain only a personal experience (of the informant or of a known person), such as seeing the spirit flying in the shape of a burning pole, throwing fire and dirt. Though this story is the simplest, and might be just a statement of having seen the spirit, its form might be well elaborated and detailed, describing accurately and at length the place and exact time of the sighting, the names of the people around, the nature of their occupation, the description of the apparition and its effect on the teller and the others: fear, mental frustration, etc. But even this vision, lacking narrative elements, may be turned into a full, dramatic story by an inspired person. Three variants tell about seeing the spirit flying above and of people killing it by shooting or stopping it and learning about its errands by running a knife into the ground. Three variants explain impersonally the belief in the spirit. Two versions point out the traces (excrements) which the spirit left behind in a yard. In five cases we have only the advice of what to do when a person is left alone in a house with the spirit, and in five cases the story is blended with other legend elements.

The analysis of the legend of the visit of the incubus flying as a star suggests that the complete story or any of its fragments might exist side by side in the well-rounded form of a *Fabulat*, a *Memorat*, a story of one's own experience, a description of a ritual act, information about a belief, and so on. That is: the *form* and *extent* of the legend is *unstable, oscillating around a stable concept of belief*. All these factors must be considered in establishing the nature of the legend.

Another characteristic which strikes the observer of legend-telling is the *participation* of the *audience* in it (I agree here with Röhrich's remark concerning legend-like narratives as parts of exchanges of opinion at family gatherings; Röhrich 1958: 670). I experienced on occasion, for instance at evening get-togethers, that if people are together, engaged in talking and gossiping, one of them might step over almost unaware into the domain of the supernatural. A person starts a story, and suddenly people display their interest (positive or negative) by adding to it or correcting it according to their own information. Two stories might even run parallel; questions and comments accompany the telling. When the story is concluded, another is started immediately by someone who has had a like experience or knowledge. In a lively dialogue among the active speakers, the stories follow in a long row without halt and with comments by all present. The topic is of general interest and is familiar to everyone present. The silent observer can hardly notice who started and who ended the story, and it is even harder to separate the individual legends from each other, determining where one ends and the other begins, since there is no clear dividing line between them, as Friedrich Ranke has suggested (F. Ranke 1935: 12). The transcripts of my tapes containing legends recorded in social gatherings look like dramatic texts, separated into roles.

Additional formal traits of the legend became apparent during my investigation. The legend certainly has an easily recognizable *frame*, an *introduction* and a *conclusion*, but not in the same sense as that of

a tale. These elements serve to strengthen the credit of the coming
story. The importance of the message therein makes the detailed preli-
minaries indispensable. In this genre, which is marked by inconsis-
tency of form, I cannot tell the precise sequence of elements in the
introduction, but I certainly can tell what belongs to it. It contains,
first of all, the *reason* for the telling, the *essence*, the advice, the abstract
or concrete warning. This is to attract attention, and to impress the
listeners. Secondly comes the *identification* of the acting persons, to
make certain that everybody knows them. This part is displayed
mostly in lively dialogues: information and questions are contributed
by many (where the persons in question live, their looks, social standing, their neighbors, relatives, etc.) who add accounts of other events
concerning the persons. Sometimes this conversation makes it difficult
to go on with the story; other stories are interpolated before the original
can be continued. These introductions of the legend may be so detailed
and lengthy that folklorists, interested only in the content of the story
proper, overlook their importance. And after all that, the introductory
part of the legend still is not concluded. Then comes the detailed
account of the witnesses and the evidences (this is why von Sydow
called local legends *Zeugensagen*), who or which confirm the story. It
is all the same whether it is told in first person, which gives the
impression of having experienced the event, or whether it is told in
third person as having happened to a relative or a friend known to
everybody as a trustworthy man. Agreeing here with Lüthi (1962/
1980) and disagreeing with Röhrich (1958: 664), I fail to see differences
between stories believed or disbelieved by the actual teller. Presenting
eyewitnesses is a salient feature of the legend, as are the other evidences preceding the story: the accurate fixing of the time (year, season,
day and hour) and the exact place as well as the co-experiencers'
activities while they observed the phenomenon. The concluding part
of the legend usually repeats briefly the essential admonition of the
story and again names the source.

It is only natural that after the accurate setting of the introduction,
the story itself is also marked by detailed supporting evidence. The
narrator or narrators elaborately and realistically describe the *social
background* of the legend event and its eyewitnesses, and give a detailed
account of the *mental disposition*, that is, the result of the legendary
experience upon the affected people. Legend heroes – as Lüthi has
pointed out – are emotional, for the legend itself is a subjective genre
of folklore. The moment of the scene is ingeniously set; we know all
about the man or woman, and the situation. And we have an equally
graphic account of his or her mental suffering, fear, and the deadly
torments he or she undergoes during and after the event. All these

traits of the style and form of the legend are easily recognizable even in short and fragmentary variants. They depend on the belief-nucleus of the legend. To learn more of the features of the form, further comparative text studies in this line are necessary. At this time it would not be possible to work out an international legend index without establishing legend types, as has been done in the case of tales. This would be no easy task, but on the basis of the method offered here, it is at least feasible.

DOES THE WORD 'DOG' BITE?
OSTENSIVE ACTION: A MEANS OF LEGEND-TELLING

1.

Homo narrans (Ranke 1967b) tells many more stories than he realizes. He also uses more communicative forms than folklore theory has ever recognized. The contemporary storyteller, furthermore, is even more talkative than his predecessors and abides less and less by a law that folkloristics has still not clearly invalidated: folklore necessarily must be told by word of mouth. To fully understand the message, it is time for folklorists to concede that telling, even in folklore, need not always be identical with talking. Thirteen of the twenty-one definitions quoted in *Funk & Wagnalls Standard Dictionary of Folklore, Mythology and Legend* (Leach 1949: 398–403) state that folklore is transmitted orally. Terms such as "verbal art," "oral transmission," and "tradition through speech" are seldom missing from characterizations of folklore (Pentikäinen 1970c: 90–91). The sociolinguistic influence on some American folklorists offers a new interpretation of "spoken," that is, "verbal art as a way of speaking" (Bauman 1977). There are other forms of communication suitable for folklore materials, some of which seem to achieve particular prominence in our times for reasons related to the spread and increasing influence of mass media, extension of contact by telephone, car and plane travel, and, more generally, the accelerated pace of life.

In this essay we will examine the roles played by communicative means in the dissemination and shaping of folklore in our time. For this examination, we chose the legend as the most appropriate genre for two reasons. First, unlike most classical genres of folklore that seem to decline and lose their former appeal in a world of radically different social conditions, legends proliferate and disseminate with increasing speed and over wider space, exercising more direct influence on the society that called them into existence. Second, legends appear most frequently in non-oral dissemination. The content, style, context, exterior shape, and way of transmission and reception of the legend sometimes suggest that not only can facts become narratives, but narratives can turn into facts as well. For this reason we will pay special attention to communication through *ostension*, a term we borrow from semiotics which originally adapted it from Wittgenstein and Russell. "Ostension can be defined as a type of communication where the reality itself, the thing, the situation or event itself functions in the role of message" (Osolsobe 1971: 35), a perspective so far neglected by folklore theorists. In addition to our own in the earlier 1978 version of this essay, the only other attempt known to us is John H. McDowell's paper "Beyond Iconicity: The Texture of Kamsá Oral Narrative," delivered at the meeting of the American Folklore Society in San Antonio, Texas in 1981 (McDowell 1982). Semiotic literature has not dealt with it in great depth either, and attempts at conceptualization appear to be diverse. This situation motivates us to indicate how we intend to use this term and why we believe it has an important place in the vocabulary of folklore.

Ostension, that is, presentation as contrasted to representation (showing the reality itself instead of using any kind of signification), is "the basic form of human communication" (Osolsobe 1979: 63) and, at the same time, "a distinctively human form of communication utilizing parts of the world as messages about themselves" (Osolsobe 1979: 66). According to a strict particularistic concept, ostension is the only communicative means that, by its very essence, does not use the sign. "A Sign, or representamen, is something which stands to somebody by something," says Charles Sanders Peirce. "The Sign stands for something, its object" (Peirce 1960–1966, Vol. 2: 135). For our purposes, the more elaborate description of sign given by Mieczyslaw Wallis is useful: ". . . a sensibly perceptible *object*, made or used by a certain 'sender' in order that, owing to its peculiar properties, it might evoke in a certain 'receiver' a thought about an object other than itself" (Wallis 1975: 1). Reality thus displayed cannot substitute for anything because nothing can represent itself. In other words, nothing can be its own sign, its own object.

Remember Gulliver's not infrequently quoted visit to the Grand Academy of Lagado where the scholars in the School of Language elaborated "a scheme for entirely abolishing all words whatsoever." They learned how to express themselves by things which they carry about with them in bundles so as to be available "to express the particular business they are to discourse on." Sages, whose business was great and who could afford it, hired strong servants to carry more bundles from which appropriate things were pulled out, all nouns, to be sure, "because in reality all things imaginable are but *nouns*." Jonathan Swift quite accurately described in his satire, without the technical terms of current academe, what is today known as ostension (Swift 1977: 181–183).

Despite the semblance, the members of the Lagado Academy could not be particularists. Although they were showing things actually present as required by particularism, the domain of ostensive discussion would have extremely narrowed the strict application of the method. Since they aspired to make practical communicative use of ostension, they had to ease theoretical rigidity and accept what is today known as the *realistic* standpoint. This standpoint "stipulates that what we are showing are rather properties than things." If so, "there is no need to show them with help of the original thing; equally well, but much more easily, they can be shown by means of miniatures, models, pictures, photographs, reproductions, reconstructions, etc." (Osolsobe 1979: 64–65.)

According to Umberto Eco's formulation, "A given object . . . is . . . *shown* as the expression of the class of which it is a member" (Eco 1979: 224–225). In this sense, Eco also regards ostension as "the most elementary act of active signification." Among his examples, he describes a situation where someone shows a cigarette to an acquaintance standing at some distance. In this case it is not that someone has shown *that* cigarette but, more generally, *a cigarette* "as a member of its class." In the given context, this act indicated to the other person a request to bring a box of cigarettes (Eco 1979: 225). One cigarette signified others as members of the identical class in this instance. Differences might be disregarded because the major pertinent features are virtually retained. Hence, the cigarette to which Eco refers physically presents but one piece; nevertheless, it also represents other members of its identical class. How many? This question is raised by us, not by Eco, but probably is in agreement with his conception. Assumably it represents twenty, because the receiver of the message has most likely understood that his companion ran out of cigarettes and wanted to have another pack as usual. Had this not been the case, the receiver would have indicated it; and the sender would have reacted appropriately, by, let us say, verbally repeating the request. The receiver could understand the silent message correctly only by being familiar with the other elements of the context. The receiver had to know, for example, that the bearer of the cigarette is a smoker of such and such a brand. The sender had to know that the receiver of the message would understand the request and be willing to carry it out. Without these elements, the presentation of the cigarette would have obtained some other meaning or no meaning at all. This complexity of communicative means is not pure ostension in the sense of the particularistic pont of view because the thing presented – the cigarette – also plays the role of a representative sign. It is common knowledge, however, that pure ostension exists more in theory than in reality as much as pure signs do not exist in reality. Signs are in a state of constant fusion with each other as well as with the signlessness of ostension. In our discussion we will interpret ostension as "real," not particular, as a communication that consists, if not purely then chiefly and essentially, of showing.

2.

At this point there is yet little said of the role ostension plays in folklore communication. No matter how large the Lagado bundles, it would be hard to communicate legends by showing the things carried in them. Referents are not always material *things* but are, for the most part, also actions. The communication through ostension is, besides the showing of things, essentially the showing of actions. We will identify this kind of ostension as *ostensive action*.

Ostensive action, that is, the showing of an action by showing the action itself or by another action, might be recognized by some people as acting, either in organized (theatrical or other) or casual forms. The difference between acting and ostensive action, nevertheless, is significant even if not always discernible. Actors intend to create illusion, not delusion. They do not strive at making their acts acceptable as real, and the audience normally does not consider them as such. "Stage actors manage to keep audiences continually convinced that the play they are witnessing is a play" (Messinger et al. 1968: 14). Simultaneously, however, actors are capable of making the audience believe that the staged figures can be interpreted as real on another level of consciousness. That is to say, actors use two signs at the same time: the *actor sign* and the *character sign*. When, for example, Lawrence Olivier created his famous Hamlet, he signaled clearly (actor sign) that he was not Hamlet himself but the actor "signifying the character sign 'Hamlet'" (Zyl 1979: 103). The complete system of *theatrical signs* (Eco 1975) maintains this specific duplicity in professional theatre (film, television) and continually reminds the audience that what takes place on the stage is not the showing of reality, not presentation but representation, the imitation of a real or imagined reality. The audience, no matter how realistic the performance seems, understands this except perhaps in rare cases. "Stories about stage actors who carry their 'parts' home, as well as audience members who take 'character' for 'reality' are common" (Messinger et al. 1968: 9). After attending a German Passion Play, for example, the crowd wanted to stone the actor who played Judas. Actors appearing regularly in bad-guy roles, particularly on TV, often complain of being inundated by hate mail from the public.

In our own field experience, we often encountered poorly educated viewers who confused fiction with reality on the TV screen. With the conviction of an eyewitness, an informant narrated a lengthy crime story to us, culminating in a bomb blast that destroyed an airplane. Nevertheless, all she did was retell a TV program she had seen the previous evening. Such confusion can easily occur because of the exploitation of photo tricks, stunts, and simulations used in the movie on TV. The audience of 'Ta'ziyeh', an Iranian ritual drama, generally believes the events observed on stage, and there is evidence that nineteenth-century showboat voyagers also often took stage plays for real.[1] A nineteenth-century Hungarian comedy pokes fun at probably frequent incidents in its staging of an ignorant country bumpkin's first visit to the city; watching *Othello* at the theatre, he dashes up on the stage to rescue Desdemona. It might well be because of the actor, the audience, or some other unaccountable fact that the actor sign does not always function reliably.

No matter how much it resembles reality, stage acting is still not reality. Acting is not identical with ostensive action. Imitated action (in terms of Arianism) can be at best *homoiousios*, that is, similar to the original in its substance but not identical (*homoousios*). We must remember that ostension is not a sign; it does not stand for anything else but itself either in the strict particularistic sense or in the broader realistic sense. Acting, true to life or not, is a series of signs and stands for the objects (actions) it signifies. Neither is the delusion of the magician ostension but at the most *pseudo-ostension*, imitation of ostension. Through a whole series of signs, the magician strives to create the illusion that the lady in the show really levitates although she does not, as at the same time it is made plausible for the audience through a series of theatrical signs.

The various modes of legend dissemination can be well isolated, observed, and evaluated during specific ritual celebrations. Halloween is a striking example because it is based on legends, communicates legends, and creates legends.[2] Not only does October 31st, the time of institutionalized supernatural and horrible encounters, itself breed legends, but the whole period of transition (the preceding weeks of expectation and preparation and the subsequent weeks of return to everyday normalcy) contributes to the significance of the culminating night. During the entire period, in keeping with other traditionally observed seasonal rituals anywhere in the world. Halloween not only allows but also inspires, demands, and enforces deviation from every-day norms; it is the time when disorder becomes the order through "symbolic inversion" (Babcock 1978). Under the extraordinary conditions of Halloween, like cars at rush hour, the communicative vehicles of the legend create a traffic jam, thus making them all the more conspicuous. As Victor Turner suggests: "Nothing underlines regularity so well as absurdity or paradox" (Turner 1969: 176). Halloween also offers a unique opportunity to show how partly traditional, partly updated, and partly new legends are told and retold, produced and reproduced, presented and represented through mixed, interchanging, overlapping, and multifaceted forms of communication.

3.

The visit of Halloween trick-or-treaters to American homes is a well-established custom. Neighborhood children traditionally dress up as witches, ghosts, skeletons, monsters, and other stock characters commonly known as "scary," with the addition of annually changing popular media figures, for the door-to-door parade. A member of the team of little goblins sometimes carries a plastic pumpkin with a candle inside, while the others have plastic bags bearing brightly colored Halloween symbols for the treats they expect to collect. True to tradition, the mild form of vandalism known as tricking or playing pranks is indulgently acknowledged by the adult world on this one day of the year. Indeed, Halloween is the time when a part of a "status reversal" (Turner 1969: 172) – the children's right to demand, or rather, to extort – is deemed acceptable behavior. In the trick-or-treat ritual, a host of monstrous, mostly supernatural beings, symbolically assault and plunder defenseless homes. They must be rendered harmless by a special ritual act. Such is the message of the simple legend chanted and mimed by the nocturnal visitors knocking on the doors of private homes. Dealing more specifically with the play and games of children, Brian Sutton-Smith's interpretation of children's challenge and reversal of the social order is useful for the observation of children's Halloween behavior (Sutton-Smith 1972; Schwartzmann 1978).

Turner discovers "the traces of rites of age- and sex-role reversal" in Halloween (Turner 1969: 172). According to his interpretation, in addition to securing anonymity and thus escaping the consequences of committing aggression, children's masks and costumes mostly feature monstrous beings and attack the "authority-holding generation of householders" with "tricks similar to those once believed to be the work of earth spirits . . . They often wear the masks of burglars and executioners, . . . criminal autochthonous and supernatural beings" (Turner 1969: 172). In his argument, Turner quotes Anna Freud's observation that children often pretend to be fierce animals and threatening monsters, the objects of their own fear. "What is being given animal guise in child fantasy is the aggressive and punitive power of the parents, particularly the father . . . Small children are quite irrationally terrified of animals, . . . normal fears . . . overdetermined by unconscious fear of the menacing aspect of the parents, particularly father." Identification with the terrifying object thus becomes an effective protection from it (Turner 1969: 174). Austrian psychoanalyst Richard Sterba sees another kind of inversion in child-adult encounters at Halloween. Americans suppress the idea of death and forget to commemorate the day of the dead which "the dead themselves have not forgotten . . . It is our children who take upon themselves to be the executors of our conscience, and who punish us for our neglect. Masqueraded as witches, fierce animals, and other dangerous and grotesque figures, they represent the spirits of the dead who come and haunt our houses" (Sterba 1948: 217).

The role-reversal of children seems evident and happens with the consent of society. Youngsters assume rights normally enjoyed by adults, at least symbolically, by means normally in the hands of the power-holding adults. The status reversal does not take place without some qualms of conscience. Quite a few of our young informants admitted to being afraid while masquerading in scary outfits and uttering scary sounds. On their house-to-house visit in the dark of the night, Halloween mummers often fear the figure they assume as much as they fear members of their own group and that of rival groups they encounter. The expression of fear of evil spirits is manifested in the international legend of sacrilegious dancers who are joined by Death or the Devil (Müller and Röhrich 1967: 353).

Over the last decade, ritual trick-or-treating as a favorite form of panhandling by children dramatically lost its popularity. Year by year fewer groups participated, and most of the treats, thoughtfully prepared by caring adults, remained unclaimed. Last year, no one came to our house. There was perhaps a good reason why. For some time the story had been afloat that the tables had turned and adults were reciprocating the relatively mild tricks of children with full-fledged brutality, thus representing as it were, society's violence. The popular saying: "As American as cherry pie" was extended by H. Rap Brown in his widely acknowledged slogan: "Violence is as American as cherry pie." The drop in the number of Halloween mummers and the discontinuation of the practice by 1982 evidently were caused by the consistently growing, and later officially confirmed, rumors that adults hide pins, razor blades, and glass splinters in apples or inject drugs or poison into candies and other handouts. Year after year, police departments, the press, food markets, and school authorities appealed to adults to take care of children, as they simultaneously pleaded with the children to watch out for adult malevolence. The warning was so frequently and systematically repeated that it became a part of the ritual, undergoing modification. Older people nostalgically recalled that Halloween was once "genuine fun . . . Each group of goblins was invited in. There ensued a guessing game with each and then after 'we give up, who are you?' there was an unmasking. The little ritual was all part of the deal, and they had so much fun out of it" (*Bloomington Herald Telephone*, 31 October, 1969). The joyous, playful act of children becomingly concealed the status reversal, the role change on this modern Saturnalia, and was reciprocated by the warm welcome and generous treats of adults. At that time, Halloween was "as American as cherry pie."

Today Halloween is surrounded by suspicion and fear. Several of our informants told us that they would not open their doors to masked visitors, and even more children admitted that they would not dare to knock on the doors of people they did not know. In the last couple of years a special story type has emerged about Halloweeners experiencing horror in a house located in a strange neighborhood that they accidentally visited. It seems that both adults and children are now appropriately scared into giving up trick-or-treating, the characteristic episode of the ritual cycle of Halloween.

What has actually happened? As far as we can determine, the news about booby-trapped foodstuffs emerged about twenty to twenty-five years ago. First, it seemed to be – and well might have been – a vague rumor of little substance, just like stories about fried rats, ground worms, human ashes, and spider legs fed to people as edibles (Brunvand 1981: 81–90). It does, in fact, frequently happen that a rumor precedes the action to which it pertains as if a certain "incubation period" were required before unfounded stories achieved a factual foundation. This phenomenon has nothing to do with clairvoyance or other occult circumstances but is rather a result of alternate usage of communicative means. Our examination will show that not only can facts be turned into narratives but narratives can also be turned into facts.

Regardless how the story of Halloween atrocities developed, categorical disclaimers appeared in the papers. Since Halloween is not only the season of ghosts and witches but also of a candy boom, the National Confectioner's Association emphatically denied all rumors. As "self-sealing" statements, rumors gained as much validity by this refutation as by proof. Newspapers and other media continued to report unspecified murder attempts at unnamed places. The *New York Times*, on the other hand, publicized proven cases from as early as 1948. Since about 1964, there has not been a Halloween without news, presumably part-real and part-imaginary, about tainted treats. From time to time news-papers also reported incidents of children's vandalism – corning and egging cars, breaking windows, destroying mailboxes, opening fire hydrants, littering patios, soaping door screens, turning off main switch boxes – all accomplished in the guise of "imps and ghouls." Similar pranks by adolescents in other situations were discussed by James Leary (1979: 55–64). To stop the tricksters, police departments nationwide responded with tact. For example, in Reno, Nevada, candy was dispensed from police stations, and cruising police cars carried the sign: "Don't trick, we'll treat" (*UPI report* of 27 October 1969). The picture began to resemble a bizarre and malign generational struggle fought with unequal arms: childish tricks on one side, deadly treats on the other.

As a matter of record, Kay Tolson, a five-year-old Detroit girl, died from eating candies laced with heroin in 1970; and eight-year-old Timothy Marc O'Bryan of Deer Park, Texas, died in 1974 from cyanide poisoning contained in a pixie stick given to him by his father. The father might have found Halloween a suitable context for hideous murders of this sort inasmuch as he could hope to get away with his crime. He was found guilty and sentenced to death. Eight years have passed, and he has been alternately informed – veritably in the spirit of Halloween – that he will be or that he will not be executed.[3] In early October 1982, State District Judge Michael McSpadlen informed O'Bryan he would be executed on Halloween: "I picked it myself, especially for you," the judge told him at the sentencing.[4] But the execution was delayed again, maybe until next Halloween, as the scariest of scary stories may be turned into fact, only to be turned again into story on some future occasion.

On Halloween 1982, the fear stimulated by factual or pseudofactual stories was underscored by the unrelated but coincidental Tylenol cyanide-poisoning case of 29 September. The case contribute to new variants of the razor-blade-in-the-apple and the poison-laced candy stories in nationwide distribution. "Halloween night climaxed a bizarre week during which more that 175 incidents of sabotaged fruits and candies were reported in more than 100 cities in 24 states," accord-ing to the AP report in the *Louisville Courier-Journal* of 1 November. Most of the cases were later exposed as hoaxes. In Columbus, Ohio, a police spokesperson said the attacks did not amount to "more than usual." Nevertheless, as a consequence of the general outrage, many cities banned trick-or-treating in anticipation of "a rash of imitations of Chicago's Tylenol killings" (*Bloomington Herald-Telephone*, 1 November, 1982). The reports that suggested actual tamperings with Halloween treats prompted Police Chief Bill Smith of Atmore, Alabama to say, as cited in a 31 October *UPI report:* "I think what they are doing is killing the holiday." As it happened, fewer children went mumming, while more horror stories than ever before enriched the legend body of Halloween. In other words, although the number of Halloween hoaxes may not have increased, under the influence of the proliferating legends about acts of irrational violence, the general public's expectation of increased irrational violence affected the activity of the imitators.

Deviance also has its logic, its conventions, its fashions, and even its ethic. Frivolous as it may sound, as a consequence of the mere repetition of such criminal acts (as well as of pertinent rumors, reports, warnings, and public discussions), murderous assaults against children on All-Hallows Eve seem to have become almost customary, pardonable, justifiable, and, so to say, fashionable to some people. These people, possibly suffering form some sort of mental disorder, might never have committed murderous assaults or other deviations, despite their inclinations, without the exposure to recurrent actual or imaginary precedents, without actual or imaginary models.

People who imitate others and commit rationally unjustifiable and deviant deeds are known as copycats. The expression "copycat" (or perhaps "copycat-like behavior") occurs more frequently nowadays than ever before. As a lexical item, copycat is "one who slavishly imitates or adopts the behavior or practice of another," and it recently became a household term with news reporters and even with small-town sheriff deputies. When criminal acts are repeated (as, for example, in the case of the infamous Atlanta child murders, the Los Angeles Black Dahlia and Hillside murders, the Skidrow Slasher, the Zodiac killings, or the Boston stranglings), police authorities often assume that the serial acts were not committed by one single individual but, as if obeying some kind of fashion, by copycats independently of each other. Killings which follow the set pattern of the legend of Jack the Ripper are always cited with reference to the original of 1888. In other particularly conspicuous cases (such as the murderous attempts against statesmen, famous people, etc.), police fear that a killer might inspire copycats to imitate the model, making the deed fashionable and attractive also to others. For this reason, in 1979 West Yorkshire police denied information on the murder technique of a ripper.

In general, only famous copycat activities are noted, whereas everyday copycats escape observation. Copycats are present throughout society and in greater numbers than one might believe; their influence on others is substantial. People who imitate, regardless of reason, the behavior of someone (perhaps, indeed, of a significant part of society) cannot be classified into a species other than that of the copycat. Most of the people who follow some "prevailing, usually short-lived, custom, usage, or style" as one can read in the dictionary under "fashion," are copycats whether it means following the fashion of wearing high boots, designer jeans, throwing bombs, highjacking planes, or other "cultural vogues" (Eliade 1976: 3). The surface design of an epoch is determined by the retroaction of copycats of different temperament, ambitions, and intent.

Fashion acts not only as stimulant but also as simultaneous permission and absolution. Contagious violence, for example, in many cases (Berkowitz 1972: 95) may be connected with "inhibition reduction," which means that the model's aggression weakens the observer's inhibition against aggression (Wheeler 1966: 179–192) – a very important phenomenon, valid also in other behaviors. When deeds sink to the level of banality, when a kind of "behavioral indifference" (Bandura 1978: 16) sets in, a moment of danger has indeed been reached. Frequency in itself may persuade occasional or habitual copycats. "Many people take this path; you too can take it!" Conversely, infrequency or the complete lack of occurrence – a sort of zero sign – in social terms means: "No one takes this path; you shouldn't either!" This zero sign is a prohibitory marker, whereas frequency is a green traffic light (a rule discovered and utilized long since by the advertising industry). Thus, Kay and Timmy are not only victims of a single atrocity committed against them individually, but also the vicitims of all previous similar crimes, whether actual or fictitious.

For this reason, violence on TV is of special concern. It might well be true that TV not only depicts violence, but that it also instructs the viewer on how to carry out that violence. But this is only one of its dangers. The other is more serious; through mere frequency, TV creates an impression that violence is a dominant social behavior. Experiments show that those who spend four hours a day watching TV see life as ten times more violent that it really is. TV violence amounts to a tacit moral absolution.

Most of these crimes are not rational. Nevertheless, their perpetrators are usually capable of rationalizing their acts and constructing a philosophy to justify their behavior. In the case of aggressive countertricks by adults at Halloween, it seems as if an unorganized, nameless "vigilance group" exists, a group united by the fact that its members are able to attribute a similar ideology and moral excuse for child murder and the commission of what is called "expressive crime" (Weinstein and Weinstein 1974: 16). What does this crime express? It seems to us that these adults do not mean to play their deadly tricks against only the children but also to conduct a disproportionately vigorous crusade against the mystical forces the children represent on this evening of horrors: to re-reverse the ritual. They protect their homes – their medieval castles – both from naughty neighborhood kids who try to reverse their status and from the supernatural beings the children impersonate. They not only exercise the civil liberty of dignified citizens, combined with the *ius gladii* (the right of sword of feudal lords – two rights not always as far from each other as one would imagine), but they also exorcise, with symbolic though admittedly harsh measures, the supernatural trespassers who nowadays intrude into their venerable homes. They practice a ritual of mass-exorcism (Turner 1976: 19), an unofficial one among the many official Halloween rituals. Their actions must express a belief that whirls shapelessly and confusedly in the impenetrable depths of some minds – a belief, based on one of the many legends not formulated into words, made manifest only in the context of Halloween. The nature of the belief and the content of the legend told through the action itself is not known in detail. But the legend is certainly about Halloween, the climactic night of "Hell Week," when one must be alert, clever, and valiant to fend off the dangers, to kill (as it is customary) with poison and pins, the lurking enemy, both the earthly and the supernatural. The essence of the story is that ritual Halloween killings abound. We have already attempted to describe what consequences frequent repetition of such stories might bring.[5] People retell the story. Some folklore bearers, for example, retell it by word of mouth; some newsmen, for example, through the media; and others: mad killers, by a means of communication reminiscent of, but to be distinguished from, imitation – ostensive action.

4.

The spirit of Halloween penetrates everyday life long before, and makes its presence felt long after, the climactic night itself. With little reference to its supposed original meaning – the transition from a joyous harvest season to the dead stillness of winter – Halloween preparations begin in the early days of September when stores set up displays to exploit the sales potential of the feast of the dead. Business and the supernatural often go hand in hand (Dégh and Vázsonyi 1979: 47–68), particularly at Halloween. If nothing else, the props and paraphernalia offered for sale convincingly indicate this.

The supplies in the local stores fill all the needs of ritual events within the Halloween cycle: trick-or-treat accessories, symbols to decorate homes and public buildings, party supplies, and above all, masks and make-up for costumes of stock characters. There were close to one hundred costumes on the market in the last few years: guises of supernatural beings, monsters, and heroes taken from both the old and the more recent traditions. Model characters created or idealized by successful movies, TV shows, science fiction or comic books, or games and toys are popular: Spiderman, Hulk, Frankenstein's creature, Grim Reaper, Batman, Superman, Superwoman, outer-space creatures, friendly and hostile apes, and, of course, Dracula. Dracula, and Dracula again. Dracula, the undead, has proved to live forever, not only in legendry but also in the Halloween marketplace.

All these figures are familiar to parents and even more so to most children. Each one evokes a legend, sometimes a whole legend cluster; each one serves as an *icon* – a pseudo-icon to be more accurate – of nonexistent, though nevertheless well-known, figures. Each item bought from this collection or made at home is almost tantamount to a told and heard legend. One hundred costumes: one hundred legends. Contemporary *homo narrans* is very communicative and uses a great variety of means for the dissemination of his messages.

The ritual performed in the Haunted House, or Spookhouse (set up specifically, as it were, for this particular epiphany of various communicative forces), is the *piece de resistance* of Halloween, the fulfillment of its essential goals: to scare small children and to wake the memory of childhood fright in adolescents and adults. Most people refer to that which the haunted house has to offer as simply "a good scare." Others theorize that the scare provided by the Haunted House serves as prudent preparation for the real shocks of a dangerous life; while yet others, using the more sophisticated language of an unidentifiable vulgar-Freudianism, like to speak of the stimulation of a "wholesome catharsis." Perhaps there are also people who remember Turner's "anti-authoritarian figures" and the almost manifest, grotesque, minor generational struggle which at this time occurs symbolically although may take cruel turns in reality. Within the confines of the Haunted House, adults seem to grab the opportunity to frighten as a means necessary to exorcise authority from their usurping children.

The activities surrounding the creation of Haunted Houses involve numerous social organizations. The sponsors – Jaycees, PTAs, Chambers of Commerce, Red Crosses, Girls' Clubs, Youths for Christ, and other honorable institutions – regard the setup not only as an entertaining and educational show but also as a money-making or charitable enterprise.[6] The membership appoints a committee, elects a president, and distributes responsibilities. Volunteers make elaborate alterations of the chosen buildings, "painting, constructing false partitions and mazes, and installing black lights to add to the eeriness," informs the AP from Chicago. It is well worth the effort. As the coordinator of a suburban Chicago enterprise stated with considerable pride in an interview: "We have a spider man, a pendulum swinging over a victim, a funeral room, and all kinds of monsters. It is all live performance, with forty club members in various kinds of scary make-up taking part."

The building of spookhouses and participation in live performance is considered an enjoyable duty of adults who also assert that the involvement of children is a felicitous pedagogical means "designed to provide teenagers with a positive off-the-street activity for the holiday . . . The idea is to give the kids something to do at a rough time of the year, something positive for them to do," states an educator. During the preparations for the "live performance," participants learn the parts, rehearse gestures, and prepare costumes and make-up. These preparations already approximate a form of communication used later at the Haunted House: *acting.*

The closer we get to October 31st, the clearer the social significance of the American calendar custom becomes.[7] Its effect on people is profound as Halloween dominates different spheres of life during the whole of the fall season. The lingual formulas, references, jokes, and puns employed in commercial advertisement ("terrorific values," "spooktacular savings," "spirited specials," "bewitching dresses," "we witch you come"), in sports events ("top high school football halfbacks scared opponents Halloween night," "Tricky Jeff treats self to victory over Shelby," "Galloping Ghosts would have been proud of them"), and even in politics ("Trick or Treating for the candidates was only two days away and Jones still didn't have a disguise"), make sense only within the context of Halloween. Likewise, graphic symbols of broom-riding witches, black cats, ghosts, Jack-o-Lanterns and skeletons depicted in cardboard or plastic on public buildings as well as on porches and windows of private homes indicate the magnitude and durability of this common frame of reference. The Halloween slogans and symbols launched by expert salesmanship, intending as it were subliminal exploitation of Halloween, serve as stimulants, excuses, and occasions for recalling and retelling legends. The symbols provoke questions, activate latent materials, and create opportunities for the indoctrination of the youngest, the least informed, and the most innocent members of society. Along with Halloween costumes on display in the stores, they are part of legend-telling events. All are symbols of legends. All are legends.

5.

Halloween, however, is also the high season of traditional oral storytelling. Young people between twelve and twenty-two exchange scary legends at scout meetings, slumber parties, in campus dormitories and fraternities, and at get-togethers or parties. Getting in the mood by sitting around a table in a dark room with only a single candlestick in the middle, they tell horror stories one after the other (Grider 1980: 147–178). The themes do not necessarily deal with Halloween but with anything horrible enough to stimulate the mood of Halloween. Across America, Halloween is the prime time for nocturnal visits to a haunted place well-known in the community – house, bridge, tunnel or cemetery – where ghost stories related to it are recited (Dégh 1973: 341–351; Grider 1976: 451–546). Many young people insist that ghosts, the restless victims of violent death, do dutifully appear as expected on Halloween night if the visitors properly perform the ritual necessary to force them to reenact their past tragedy. A Halloween questionnaire we distributed throughout the United States identified a conspicuously large number of haunted sites as favorite spots for Halloween night visits. Out of more than one thousand respondents, almost 100 percent admitted to having visited "scary places"; 67 percent declared themselves believers in supernatural phenomena; while 18 percent stated that their beliefs were confirmed by what they experienced during their visits. This means that 18 percent admitted to having witnessed a supernatural encounter.

These encounters represent a veritable sampler of the various modes of ostensive folklore communication. Theoretically, four possibilities exist: (1) the apparitions were real; (2) someone, playing a trick, deceived the observer; (3) the apparitions resulted from some sort of error on the part of the observer; (4) the person giving an account of the apparition willfully lied, or more politely and folkloristically expressed, presented an invented story as a memorate based on personal experience.

In the first case, the observer saw something which was really there, just like the wise men of Lagado who saw the objects pulled out from the bundles. Here it is the apparition (a narrator not yet taken into account by folklorists) who tells the story about its existence by ostension. In this situation, the teller (the supernatural figure), the story and the related implications ("there is a ghost, myself, signaling that supernatural beings, at least one, myself, exist"), and the means of communication (the act of the ghost showing itself) blend and create an indivisible trinity. Nevertheless, the observer would not have recognized the ghost if not already familiar with the necessary ingredients from legends, legend fragments, or the information of other people. The observer would not have been able to construct a conception of a supernatural apparition distinct form other (non-supernatural) apparitions. The observer requires a model with which to compare the just-sighted supernatural apparition to ascertain if it was indeed a supernatural apparition. Thus, the communication of the Lagadoans would have been a failure if, for instance, they had no previous knowledge of pens and spoons and if they had not been able to determine that the displayed pen and spoon were pen and spoon. Influenced by the sighting of the apparition, these notions and hearsays – numerous floating, blurred, awkward protomemorates (Dégh and Vázsonyi 1974: 225–239) – contributed the necessary data for its identification and its implications. No matter how real an apparition, it is not the primary phase of the birth of a legend.

In the second case we face another complex situation. This time, the apparition is not real but is the result of a hoax in which the observer does not recognize the deception. Suppose that the perpetrator of the hoax (the actor of a ghost story) puts on white sheets and pretends to be a real spirit. How do both the pretender and the intended victim know how a "real spirit" behaves? Evidently their knowledge is situated in a common frame of reference. Their information stems from the same source, very likely unknown by both the hoaxer and the dupe. Everything to be found within the frame is composed of legends, legend-particles, motifs, and hints, so that the unknown contributors to some extent can be regarded as coauthors of the hoax. The person who follows a collective script supported by society and presents a quasi-collectively constructed figure is also playing a role, is also acting. This acting, however, deviates radically from stage-acting. While the stage actor keeps character sign and actor sign in balance, the hoaxer, in the interest of deceit, strives to conceal as much as possible of the actor sign and simultaneously make the character sign more complete and convincing. That is, someone playing a ghost in the cemetery on Halloween to scare people will try to be as faithful to the commonly acknowledged ghost-stereotype as possible and will avoid any hint that the act is a hoax. Acting in a hoax is not acting in the theatrical sense. From the viewpoint of the unconvinced viewer, only the unsuccessful hoaxer, clad in sheets, exists. From the viewpoint of the believer, on the other hand, it is the actor who succeeds in disappearing behind the ghost and who is given credence by the gullible viewer. Nevertheless, while the "real" ghost of the previous example has shown itself by pure ostension, this ghost is featured by *pseudo-ostension* in front of the misled audience.

In the third case no real ghost nor imitator appears. It is the narrator who experiences the supernatural encounter (Virtanen 1976: 338–347) due to a variety of possible reasons: personal, psychological, or physiological conditions, or an excited imagination. Visualizing apparitions in the shadows of windblown trees or hearing them in the sound of cracking old furniture, this narrator relates personal experience with such sincere conviction that it might launch a legend-chain immediately. Here, too, folklore communication begins in the boundless past, stemming from the uninterrupted current of legend-elements that sometimes coagulates (as mentioned in relation to the first example). The stories are fragile, brittle, and without constant boundaries. They fall apart into tiny particles, continue their journey in hardly discernible formulations, only to reassemble and reinstate old variables and to create new variables. The otherwise normal, but visionary and perhaps slightly neurotic, person creates stories from unconsciously preserved memories. The teller is supported by coauthors – the legend-bearers of society help to form the stereotype the teller visualizes as vividly as if it were really there. Yet, there is no one and nothing on the "stage" where the imagined apparition is reported. For the visionary, the subjectively authentic witness of the legend event, this makes no difference; the nonexistent apparition will be seen in any case. The visionary projects the apparition as both the sender and the receiver of the message. The means of this communication ("autocommunication") cannot be regarded as anything other that ostension. Nevertheless, in this case the subject of ostension is only imaginary, not real, and thus the term *quasi-ostension* is appropriate.

Our fourth case, particularly appropriate for a Halloween primer, is more common than one would believe. Someone knowingly tells a story about an ostensively exhibited action that was, in truth, unwitnessed. It is known that carloads of young people, in order to experience a "good scare" or to carry out a pranking, mischief-making expedition, drive to noted regional "haunted" locations. Popular haunted sites exist in or on the outskirts of any community in the United States. (The *Chicago Sun-Times* published a map of haunted sites accessible to expressway drivers around Chicago for Halloween visitors; Charleston, South Carolina's Chamber of Commerce popularized its famous haunted antebellum mansions in a pamphlet for tourists. The questionnaires we sent to Indiana residents listed 140 locations in the state to be visited at Halloween.) As described in more detail elsewhere (Dégh 1971: 55–68), young men and women from the Bloomington area usually visit one of the regional "spooky places," such as the Avon Bridge, on Halloween night. As the clock strikes twelve, the seekers of a "good scare" shine their lights on the bridge and honk their horns to induce the reenactment of the tragic event from the past. Some of them then experienced the appearance of the headless woman and her baby who were run over by the train or the scream of the worker who fell into the soft concrete when the bridge was built in 1904. These stories are told by many informants who insist that they saw the woman with the child and heard the scream of the dying worker (Dégh 1969b: 54–89). Some male informants asserted that, in addition to the thrill of fear, they hoped to scare their girlfriends enough to make them seek protection in their arms. Is this ostension? If not, it at least stands for ostension and might deserve to be named *false ostension*.

We recognize yet another case where the storyteller draws from material outside of the immediate first-person experience. Instead of preserving its less credible and abstract prior form, a teller, claiming experience, transforms a more distant story (a fabulate) into an apparently verifiable first-person account (a memorate). Legends, as we have stated elsewhere, sometimes regain their credibility and appeal by reverting to their memorate-form (Dégh and Vázsonyi 1974), only to later return to their third-person version. We have also discussed the role of witness deposition in folklore and the quality of proofs, drawing the conclusion that each legend is necessarily preceded by known or assumed memorate, an immediate or almost immediate experience. For the assumed memorate we assigned the term "proto-memorate." The real or assumed regeneration of the third-person legend, known also as fabulate (Honko 1979/1980: 12), is one step back to the original witness-deposition stage where nothing more can be inferred than that someone bore witness to an ostensive action. With some hesitation and with the conscious mixture of viewpoints and nomenclature of two disciplines, we decided to qualify this case as *proto-ostension*.

6.

During the Halloween season, old and new horror movies are shown; newspapers and TV stations routinely revive ghost stories and interview clairvoyants, coven-leading modern witches, and psychics. Viewed as authorities, professors in local colleges are interviewed for newspaper feature stories on the origin of Halloween. With unquestionable certainty, these experts invariably trace Halloween to the Celts and their pagan new year celebration, the Samhain, when the souls of the dead returned. They also mention the Christianization of the feast by linking it to All Saints' Day and All Souls' Day, which excommunicated Halloween completely from Roman Catholic countries. With only skimpy sources to rely on, these scholars are probably correct in tracing the historic antecedents. Their depiction of old secrets, of Druidism, of a world of goblins, evil fairies, mystic rituals, and ceremonies can only enhance the awesome mood of Halloweeners. Even so, Celts and Druids have nothing in common with today's Halloween, a completely profane and secular American holiday.

Halloween is also the time when news circulates of horrible prophecies fulfilled, of unresolved secrets, of never-before-heard-of bloody deeds, along with renewed rumors about sensational outer-space visits, witchcraft cases, and monster sightings. It is as if, at this season, people had nothing better to do than reactivate everything horrible. Halloween is also a party season for adults as well as children – in the Halloween spirit, naturally. At nearly every children's library, zealous librarians dress up in black witches' garb and tell blood-curdling stories as they sit around a boiling cauldron of witch's brew.[8]

As the night of October 31st approaches, the preparatory episodes (acts of fore-pleasure, anticipatory of the impending fulfillment) draw to their end; at long last, we stand at the gate of the Haunted House. Adults and adolescents, who long ago graduated form their indoctrination into ritual behavior, have recaptured their lessons during weeks of preparation and are ready to assist with the indoctrination of the uninitiated. These experienced adults and adolescents reach out for the hands of the children who, even though they have already obtained the basics in scare-propaedeutics, might need assistance going through the Haunted House. In the dimly-lit passages, most of the visitors will immediately recognize the popular character of the *commedia dell'arte* of horror.

The Haunted House is set up in a vacated "spooky-looking" house or in the basement or attic of a public building such as a school or library.[9] Silent ghosts, witches, or sometimes simply signs guide visitors through the passages. Moans, screams, and groans abound; flashing lights illuminate the uninterrupted action of the spookhouse creatures. Witches, devils, spirits, vampires, and monsters charge at the passers-by, now and then symbolically grabbing or chasing children while snickering at their anguish. Except for the youngsters, this frightening scene is familiar to most visitors. The appearance of beings in the spookhouse is an obvious theatrical performance: *representation*.

In addition to the traditional and somewhat faded stock characters of Halloween, customers also will meet more updated horror-personifiers, those created and re-created by TV, movies, and comic strips. These new figures are also stereotypes but more current and viable ones, more aggressive and effective. Originating in the bumpy borderland between the human and the superhuman world and forced by their creators to intrude into everyday life, these more recent creatures are intended to suggest *presentation* – a more naturalistic imitation of figures recognized as real. Characters considered to be horrible, extra-normal, deranged, cruel, disfigured, and disgusting appear in the situation contexts described in up-to-date legends: the escapee from the lunatic asylum, the crazy killer with the hatchet, the mad scientist with his creature, the hunchback with the lantern and shotgun, the executioner in the torture chamber inviting you to try the electric chair, the patient on the operating table with his belly cut open and his bloody entrails to be touched by visitors, the dead on the bier with bereaved wife asking for sympathy, the chained and screaming criminal behind bars, and of course, the ageless Jack the Ripper (or one of his recent followers) dissecting a woman's body. A portion of the audience might actually acknowledge some of these characters as physically present, for at this point we no longer face a totally fictitious story, a story not meant to be believed. We experience, instead, the air of a legend vibratingly active and powerfully persuasive in achieving its inherent goal: to make the story believable. What the viewer obtains is not mere "enchantment" (Bettelheim 1976), but at least partly, deception. "Stage actors . . . provide the audience with a sense of 'play' as distinguished from 'reality'" (Messinger et al. 1968: 7–18). On the contrary, the actors in the Haunted House make an effort to provide the visitors with a false sense of "reality" as distinct from "play." If the spookhouse can be called "theatre," it must be considered a very idiosyncratic, multilayered theatre.

As a rule, theatrical production serves a fairly homogeneous audience in terms of intelligence, educational level, and taste, as well as of the ability to decode the messages addressed to it. Above all, the audience has to understand the first and most fundamental message: "What you will encounter in this place is not reality." In contrast, the heterogeneous spookhouse audience does not share such understanding. Although most of the adults attend on the pretext of entertaining the children, a good many actually believe in witches, spirits, and cosmic monsters. They might forget that they are essentially in a theater and consequently decode the messages of the witches, spirits, and monsters in the Haunted House differently from the nonbelievers who are at best willing to suspend their disbelief temporarily. Among children the diversity of age plays a major role in accentuating differences in interpretation. In their early years, children live in a world of magic (Piaget 1976; Fraiberg 1959). As they grow older, their experience of the Haunted House stimuli will differ, depending on successive stages of development.

Each dramatic performance within the spookhouse includes a set of signs intended to guide visitors and help them interpret the other signs in the set (Honzl 1976: 74). Some members of the heterogeneous audience will inevitably lose or misinterpret such signs; they might miss the *signe Theatrale* and, as a consequence, perceive the behavior of the Haunted House actors as presentation, ostensive action. These visitors will not realize that what they confront is acting, modeling, only a semblance of reality, but they will instead accept the scene as reality.

With his single appearance, each Haunted House actor plays at least four synchronic roles (which, for obvious reasons, partly coincide with the examples given above to illustrate supernatural encounters). Let us assume that the actor plays the role of Dracula.

(1) For the youngest visitors or those unfamiliar with the legendry of Halloween from which the scary figures emerged, the monster-like actor does not represent anyone but himself. To the uninitiated then, the actor tells only this much with his act: "I am a scary figure." The observer recognizes this reality communicated by "ostension."

(2) In his second role, the actor addresses himself to those people whose ceiling of awareness is somewhat higher, people who possess the referential framework necessary at least for a limited understanding. These audience members – older children and perhaps also naive adults – might have come with a previous belief in the existence of Dracula or might have been convinced by the Haunted House experience. (Attitudes toward belief range from absolute acceptance through many intermediary stages to absolute rejection [Dégh and Vázsonyi 1976: 116–118].) Such persons will probably identify the actor with the character he personifies.[10] In other words, these viewers do not notice the "actor sign" and misinterpret the "character sign." For them, the Haunted House Dracula does not seem to be imitation but the genuine Dracula declaring, "I am Dracula." As in one of the above examples, the audience makes an error by incorrectly decoding the signs. Instead of being the victims of a hoax, here they err because they accept role-playing as reality. This action also belongs to the category of "pseudo-ostension."

(3) Another role is offered to those who understand that what they see is not reality but rather a sort of stage performance. Even so, these individuals believe that the originals of the imitated characters actually do exist. (We should once more remember the delicate oscillation of "belief" and the persistent uncertainty this oscillation causes.) Hence, this group of viewers interprets the Dracula impersonator as: "I am a person who imitates the real Dracula." Because the real Dracula, however, does not exist, the actor can imitate only an imaginary Dracula. This behavior may deserve to be called "pseudo-imitation."

(4) The more sophisticated audience members are clear about what is to be taken for granted: the essentials of theatrical performance and the imaginary nature of Dracula. For these people, the actor appearing in the costume of Dracula summarizes his behavior with these words: "I am an actor who plays the role of Dracula, regardless whether it is real or imaginary."

Both the figures we encounter in the Haunted House as well as those less elaborately acted and masqueraded whom we meet trick-or-treating make reference to commonly known legends. They activate these legends without embroidering the condensed forms into standard narratives. As we noted in our discussion of the significance of masks and costumes, these legends are stored in the preconscious mind of most people and need not enter consciousness in their entirety. Thus, the legend-stock of tellers and listeners contains a large quantity of *latent legends* that carry out their folklore function in this state of matter.

What happens, though, if a person does not know the story of the character presented? Even the uninformed will be sure that there is such a story; there must be, otherwise the presence of the character in the given context would not be justified. People mixed in with monsters also must be monsters. And if the stories of their fellow monsters are scary, their stories must likewise be scary. Given this state of mind, the outlines of the legend begin to take shape in front of the trained eyes of adepts. In 1975 at the Indianapolis Children's Museum's Haunted House, we were allowed to stand, in normal street dress, in a quiet corner of the hallway to take some snapshots of actor-audience interaction. Because of the situational context, the children reacted to our presence among the ogres with screams, as if we too were monsters. In the same treasury with latent legends, innumerable *presumed legends* are also stored, some of them because (perhaps by mere accident) they fit in some appropriate contexts. Such legends might be best characterized as *contextual legends*.

Paradoxical as it sounds, there are also legends which do not exist but still have a similar effect as the existing ones. Dracula, the most popular among all monsters, has no real folklore. There is only the single, brief, trivialized story, taken in many cases directly from Bram Stoker's novel and its multifarious media adaptions, containing not much more than the fact that the Transylvanian count was a vampire. The public seems convinced, nonetheless, of the existence of a lush legend realm. The term *fictitious legend* best describes the case of Dracula. Fictitious, not because the story is untrue and the hero of the legend nonexistent, but because the legend itself does not exist.

"A story can be danced or played on the stage or on the screen; it can be communicated my mime, by drawing and recounted without losing any of its essential attributes" (Crépeau 1978: ix). In addition, there are numerous other means of communication. One can transmit using words or other signs (or even without signs) with ostension, by showing reality as it is – or even without ostension, with no reality to show. (One is not sure whether oral transmission has lost its significance in our time or whether it ever carried the weight now attributed to it.)[11] This is what we have learned from the Haunted House spooks.

7.

We leave the Haunted House at the fall of the day. As the exit door closes behind us, the piercing, vicious peels of laughter from vampires, witches, and wolfmen accompany us, intermingled with screams of genuine fear from terrified children. But we have not yet left the legend world of Halloween. Miniature monsters are out on the streets offering to exchange trick for treat, unless warnings about adult counter-tricks have spoiled their fun. Trick-or-treating is the time when the modelings of the adult's pseudo-modelings and pseudo-ostensions appear at people's front doors to communicate the condensed legends which the audience is expected to understand and recall as much as necessary or, in some cases, even more than necessary.

Even this does not exhaust the telling of legends. Remember, the rumors concerning cyanide and sewing needles began to circulate and become familiar many years before the first documented assault took place. If it is acceptable to say that the legend is a "solidified rumor" (Allport and Postman 1947: 162), within a few years the solidification process becomes complete and the rumor earns its promotion to legend. After a certain time, however, the "solidified rumor" might turn into "solidified legend"; that is, it may turn into action. More specifically, a legend communicated by signs might switch into a legend communicated by ostensive action, only to be turned eventually into a legend again, transmitted orally, in writing, on the screen, on the stage, or otherwise. Afterwards it might continue its journey via intermittent communicative means, thus again and again turning itself into self-exhibiting ostension: fact. Copycats operate in this way as well.

Another example, which concerns a Halloween prank perhaps not as brutal as the trick of adults but not very innocent either, illustrates this point. We have repeatedly heard a story from informants in a small Canadian Prairie town about local youngsters who, a few years earlier on All Hallows Eve, removed an outhouse from the backyard of an old farmer. On his nightly visit to the outhouse, this farmer did not notice the uncovered cesspool and fell into it. "He had to wash himself for weeks and weeks and was still smelling," one of the tellers laughingly remembered. We were still in town when someone brought news that the previous evening this same trick had actually been played on another resident.

This event suggests a likely scheme for the spread of stories. Theoretically, someone somewhere performed this practical joke for the first time. Next, people began to reenact the funny legend[12] through the vehicle of oral transmission. The local paper might have given publicity to the event, attracting more publicity as other papers adapted the hilarious story. It probably spread in several directions until, at one point by accident (or possibly because of our presence), right in this particular town it was brought to life again. The legend had entered another communicative form, the form which directly presents reality: ostension.

We will try to complete the scheme. The story transformed into ostensive action during our presence then soon switched back into an orally mediated story. There were only a few who knew about it at first: the injured party, the neighbors, and, later on, more and more people, including ourselves. At some point within the context of the communication chain – maybe at next year's Halloween – someone will get the idea that the trick, not the story should be repeated. The initiator probably will not know the term "ostensive action" but will know its practice. Under the cover of night and in the company of cohorts, the initiator will sneak into the backyard, lift the outhouse, and put it down elsewhere, neatly presenting the action previously heard in the story. Once the trick is carried out, one link in the chain is completed. Afterward, transmission and multiplication may continue until the occasion for ostension arrives again.

8.

Cases known as "helter-skelter vandalism," or sometimes even as "helter-skelter killings," are only loosely connected with Halloween. But these cases are quite closely related to the general questions we raise in this discussion. In the early 1970s it became customary (the fashion has begun to slacken only in the last few years) for young pranksters to vandalize their schools. Students broke into the schools at night and destroyed everything they could lay their hands on: benches, tables, and audio-visual equipment. Entering the natural history laboratory, they emptied the fish tank and killed the caged rabbits, mice, and hamsters. With the blood drawn from the butchered animals, or with red ink, they inscribed "helter-skelter" on the white walls. This often happened on Hallows Eve but also during nights of no particular significance. After a break-in at a Chicago grade school, we saw the bodies of dead gerbils and a canary among uprooted tropical plants. We also saw the customary slogan in child-handwriting on the wall. School authorities never caught the culprits who had climbed in through the window, nor did they learn why this destructive act had been committed.[13]

Young men and women barely past the age of trick-or-treating exhibit the same kind of irrational behavior, not however by symbolic but by real murder. The motivation of the children and young adults was the same: senseless devastation which seemed to express a worldview that identified with the slogan "helter-skelter." Roger C. Drollinger and his four pals picked Valentine's night in 1977 to enter the modest trailer of a family in Hollandsburg, Indiana to shoot to death four teenagers without reason. Drollinger admitted imitating the Manson murders. Remarkably, the mystic term "helter-skelter," written in blood on the refrigerator of the LaBianca couple who were targeted by the second killing spree of the Manson family, inspired in the Drollingers some kind of obligatory ritual performance.

The Manson murders were extensively covered by the press and most impressively by television. Due to publicity during the lengthy court trial, the number of helter-skelter vandals grew out of proportion. The climax was reached with the publication of the book *Helter-Skelter*, authored by the prosecutor Vincent Bugliosi. Between 1974 and 1976 the book was reprinted twenty-seven times – small wonder that the bestseller was converted into a TV show that aired repeatedly. After this consistent flow of information, it would be difficult to find people in the country unfamiliar with the details of the Manson case, including the words "helter-skelter." (According to Bugliosi, even Manson could not explain its meaning.) The words became the unifying umbrella for an invisible fraternal order of those prompted to commit more or less serious, more or less bloody but always senseless, tricks. Aided by this slogan, the tricksters reached the necessary threshold of inhibition restraint. Helter-skelter not only became the rallying cry of an ideology, not understood even by its bearers, but it also became the Manson-substitute, the personification of a hero for young people seeking a "good scare" and the remedy for their conflict with the adult world. Elizabeth Tucker described how preadolescent girls at a scout camp participate in a seance in which the trance subject told the story of the Manson murders and ended with the threat, "Helter Skelter is coming to getcha!" (Tucker 1977: 418–420.) The interpretation of a participant – "People never pay attention to young teenagers . . . that's the reason they killed those seven people" – makes clear the identification with the young Manson family killers and expectation that the Helter-Skelter will mete out justice in a manner analogous to western bandit heroes.

In the Drollinger case, it is clearly not a mere assumption that the young men committed mass murder under the influence of the TV movie. They themselves admitted it. In general, movies (particularly those shown on television) launch stories that instantly enter the folklore circuit. As we have stated already, there are viewers who take the show for real just as there are viewers who take real reportage for invention. The first discernible station for many folklore sequences is the film or the television. Drollinger was deeply influenced by the film version of the Manson case, and his attraction was probably supplemented by information obtained from a variety of earlier sources. This influence was so strong that he felt the urge to communicate the story through an available means of folklore transmission. Had he been a narrator by nature, he perhaps would have recounted it orally to one of his neighbors; had he been a folk poet, he would have composed a ballad; had he had the talent of mime, he would have played it with gestures; had he had the skill of writing, he would have written it down in a short story, a letter, or a diary, and so on. He had a variety of communicative vehicles from which to choose. Drollinger, however, for some reason which only a psychiatrist could explain, chose *ostensive action*. He recruited friends of similar inclinations, and together they faithfully presented the Manson case – in fact, the Manson legend – producing a new and striking prototype of the *action gratuite*, a senseless act. For verification, they put on it the seal of "helter-skelter."

We have followed roughly the trail of the Manson legend through alternative communicative vehicles, thus, perhaps giving the impression that the first murder event, the first ostensive occurrence of the theme, was the Manson case. Nevertheless, no one can ascertain this. Manson, of course, had many precedents – all the earlier perpetrators of irrational murders (more broadly, of irrational acts). As a result, the ostensive actions in Los Angeles showed the cumulative history of irrational actions. The murderous assault, itself, the crystallization of loose elements preceding the act, however, can lead only to admittedly debatable speculation. But for the current stage of the story, reached only after passing through alternating vehicles until finally, with the influence of a TV movie, transforming it into live ostension, we may claim a less hypothetical conclusion. We have to accept that fact can become narrative and narrative can become fact. In this case the narrative, as the last phase which precedes and helps the fact to existence, could be regarded and named "proto-fact."

Ostensive and nonostensive communication – or in the familiar terms, fact and narrative – continue an ongoing process of retroaction, the strengthening of each other's viability in this paradoxical situation of coexistence. The study of the interplay between legend and pertinent reality will reveal rules about the recent enhancement of the role of folklore in society. It might help to investigate, if not the reason why, then at least the process whereby the border traffic between the two regions of talking about something and actually doing it becomes so lively – why people are inclined and able to transmit legends so often by ostensive, and, in many cases, deviant actions.

We should be careful. William James once said that the word 'dog' does not bite. Was he right?

WHAT DID THE GRIMM BROTHERS
GIVE TO AND TAKE FROM THE FOLK?

Are oral and literary tradition two separate entities which can be studied independently from each other, or must their interdependence be taken into consideration when looking at a folklore genre, the *Märchen* in particular, as it evolved and developed through the ages?

This question touches upon essentials about the nature of folklore and its study. In view of a chronological process of interaction between folk and elite, oral and written sources, we may look at the folk-product and its managers: scholars, artists, educators, politicians, and marketers who shape the product in service to their diverse goals. I will try to evaluate the influence of the Grimm tale corpus on oral tale production from the viewpoint of the folklorist.

At the beginning of folklore study, the subject of interest consisted of materials edited and formulated in the service of nationalistic ambitions from both literary and oral sources. Later, at a more emancipated stage of ethnic consciousness, folklore theory developed the notion of authenticity and the criterion of genuineness, striving after the elicitation of exclusively oral texts, from the illiterate tradition of the "folk," that is, the peasant untouched by literary intrusion. It was assumed that the "folk," as a primitive human contingent, unwittingly preserved elements of a forgotten, superior, national poetic heritage. Thus, for a long time individual contributors of folklore were only marginally recognized as reservoirs and retellers, not inspired artists. Schools were established to trace unilinear avenues of the anonymous oral tradition and determine the role of collective and personal memory in its survival or erosion. Field collectors looked for archaisms, "pure" items, free of what they judged to be folk-alien urban pollutants.

Following World War II, however, folklorists had to realize that the designated "folk" in the isolation of the rural countryside could not be the exclusive target of a discipline. Technological advancement invaded most remote areas of the world. Diverse strings of traditions obtained through print contained orally learned and performed folk lore. The celebrated and promoted folklore genres, whose identification, classification, and analysis was the main routine of scholarly practitioners, dwindled under the pressures of industrialization. Changed lifestyle and worldview of peasants did not allow time for the singing of archaic ballads or the telling of magic tales for recreation as before. There was no other choice but either to declare that folkloristics had reached the limits of its inquiry and had to resort to the study of the past, preserved in manuscripts, or to realize that the meaning of the "folk" and its "lore" must be extended beyond the narrow confines of preindustrial, preliterate peasantries. Folklorists chose to lift the old boundaries of their trade. Instead of the continued search for relics of the past "anachronistically still living in vestigial forms," scholars switched to living folklore in the here and now (Schenda 1970: 124–154). The new folklore was discovered as an integral, inseparable constituent of culture striving in contemporaneous social groups to serve as meaningful and creative expressions of relevant ideas. This new conception of folklore not only revealed the naiveté of purist fixation on a hypothetical, untained, self-perpetuating oral tradition, it also opened new perspectives for tracing folklore as a product of social reality in continual processes of change.

If, at the outset, folklore was defined as a fading, perilous oral tradition of national significance which must be saved, restored, and preserved by the literati in order to maintian cultural disctinctiveness, it is now defined as the product of people taking advantage of a variety of available auditive and visual media in order to bring oral and literary tradition into synthesis in communicating relevant messages.

All this seems clear and obvious.[1] Nevertheless, it might seem outrageous to some folklorists who are divided according to their interests in diverse developmental stages and do not recognize the logic of the inevitable process of change. Marxist theorists still maintain that folklore is an art of the exploited classes and succumbs only when social oppression ceases to exist (Voigt 1972), whereas modern European theorists do not trust their own judgment. They tend to see mass society as producing only normalized and secondhand, instead of "real," folklore (Bausinger 1976: 1–3), and some mention the term "folklorism" disparagingly as something inferior to folklore (Voigt 1986). Those who are not ready to deal with the problem of adjustment in folklore theory resort to the study of marginal groups where no disturbing questions concerning the nature of folklore must be raised.

Any folklorist who wishes to define the *Märchen* in its historic development and current existence will somehow relate it to the *Kinder- und Hausmärchen* of the Grimm brothers. This collection is a landmark, deeply rooted in sociocultural conditions of nineteenth-century Germany. But, at the same time, it is also a source for the scrutiny of previous history of the European folktale, and a point of departure for the study of its worlwide dissemination. The *KHM* was the most complete, representative collection of miscellaneous narratives, chosen from literary and oral tradition in and outside of diverse social contexts (Berendsohn 1921/1968; Bolte and Polívka 1918–1932: 467–475). It is an irony that the documents from which folklorists infer the primacy of an oral tradition come from fixed literary and artistic versions. The themes can be traced back to literary documents of early simple narration, and there is little unanimity concerning when the oral genre *Märchen* emerged. Wesselski cautiously marks the beginning of the *Märchen* as a distinct genre with Straparola's *Nights*, or even later with Basille and Perrault (Wesselski 1931: 196), whereas Schenda points out that the *Märchen*, earlier far less popular than jokes, horror, or personal experience accounts, became the literary fashion of high society only as late as the eighteenth century (Schenda 1983: 28–30).

It was within the nineteenth-century romantic milieu that a new "folk" tone was attributed to the *Märchen*, that its rustic simplicity was highlighted and viewed as a survival of ancient poetry preserved by the lower classes. The Grimm brothers earned recognition for their "rescue mission" to save "these innocent household tales" (*diese unschuldigen Hausmärchen*, the introduction to the 1819 edition) from oblivion. Their activities were taken as models by the early schools of folklore and harshly criticized by later schools, which did not take into account that they worked before the discipline was established. In celebrating the two-hundredth birthday of the Grimm brothers in 1985 and 1986, new research efforts contributed to our better understanding of their work technique and philosophy of tale collection and edition and their influence on folk narrative scholarship. Special studies also threw new light on the most popular pieces of the *KHM*, their meaning, continued social relevance, modification, and travesties in modern urban society. My discussion will focus on a rather neglected area which concerns the fieldwork-based folk narrative: the complex relationship of oral and written folk tradition in the light of our recognition that orality is just one of the means of tale transmission. The question I will raise concerns the influence of the Grimm tales on oral folk tradition.

As is well known, the Grimms created the artistic form of the *Märchen* by gradual improvement of their text, until it reached perfection in the 1857 version. During the process of variation, a distinctive short narrative genre emerged which contained a characteristic episodic structure, style, and tone. Once set in print, the whole collection and its individual pieces became models for both scholarly and literary authors – a source for both told and written *Märchen*, influential in reinvigorating fading oral tradition, in creating regional variables, and in the general adaptation and spread of the genre in the modern world.

The Grimms never made a secret of their data-compiling method, which exploited both literary and oral sources. The collectors – the Grimms and their friends and acquaintances – retold and rewrote what they had remembered from childhood or obtained through questioning. The new variants, taken as raw data, were shared with the members of the circle the Grimms called the "Märchen-Gesellschaft," by definition a folklore communicating group in itself, and those variants were subjected to continuous polishing. In his recent book, Heinz Rölleke lists the members of this cooperative team and also appends Jacob Grimm's appeal to others he hoped to include from the whole German-speaking territory (Rölleke 1985: 63–69). However, as Ranke observed, time was not yet ripe for such an undertaking: no one joined the Grimms. The Austrians and the Swiss wanted to work on their own (Ranke 1978: 87–91).

Grimm philologists and folklorists have criticized the brothers for merging oral and literary traditions indiscriminately. From Berendsohn's cautionary note that the collection is far removed from living oral telling and may be used only for the study of content (Berendsohn 1921/1968: 11), to Ellis's recent attack on the honesty of the brothers (Ellis 1983; Rölleke 1984: 330–332), many comments have been made. Critics who stated their belief in an oral tradition free from book influence, however, were not so far from the Grimmian principle in their own work. They did not record total storytelling events as social acts, as modern ethnographers do (Schenda 1983: 31–32). We cannot speak of authenticity in our sense before the 1940s. The general public did not distinguish between oral narrator and tale writer and regarded published stories as common property free for anyone to change (Kovács 1961). Scholarly recording of oral tales from the folk, at the same time, meant notation of a skeleton content of stories judged to be genuine. Style editing along the lines of existing models then embellished the tales to reflect more the style of the collector than that of the raconteur. Texts the scholars regarded as folk-alien, nonauthentic, corrupt, or retold from a book were omitted. Small wonder that most published collections reflect the wishful thinking of folklorists, not the real folk repertoire: an oral tradition of miscellaneous provenience.

The influence of the Grimms' work on subsequent generations of folk narrative scholars, in spite of repeated criticisms, was decisive and determinant. National and regional collections assembled, revised, and published in the Grimmian manner appeared one after the other in Europe. Since the Grimm model was disseminated early through diverse print media in many countries (Hand 1963b: 525–544), partial or full adaptation of texts was common. Early collectors sub-scribed to the editorial principles summarized in the 1840s by the Hungarian classical poet, János Arany (1817–1882): "The good collector must have the genius of a perfect storyteller. Being there, at the fireside, the spinnery, he must know the language, expression, and the style of narrating. He must have the imagination and the knowledge of how the folk-mind works. He must be as gifted and as inspired as the native folk and become as good as the best narrator of the region." (Kovács 1961: 435.)

While the Grimm corpus was always regarded as literary, it soon became a standard for comparative tale philology. Since Köhler and Bolte–Polívka's type listings and annotations (Thompson 1960: 49–57), the titles of the tales appear as type names to which oral variants are compared. Several Grimm titles and type descriptions were adapted by the Aarne–Thompson index, such as Hansel and Gretel (327A), Godfather Death (332), Jorinde and Joringel (405), Snow White (709), Ferdinand the True and Ferdinand the False (531), and so on.

Furthermore, German folklorists in their tale studies often still depend on the Grimm texts and cite the KHM instead of the Aarne–Thompson index numbers in referring to international tales. Scholars to this day often analyze the Grimm version as representative of its kind, in complete disregard of the limitless number of oral variants. In his analysis of Snow White, N. J. Girardot uses the Grimm version with reference to Max Lüthi. Admitting that cultural and individual variations may be important, he felt that, since "every single fairy tale has a particular message," in the case of Snow White, the Grimm text particularly controlled oral variables: "Its basic frame of formulaic form, main events, and episodic sequence remains generally constant" (Girardot 1977: 279–280). In the same vein, Steven Jones follows the Grimm outline in his Snow White study. More than one hundred versions he examined "eschew most of the 'traditional' motifs taken from the Grimms" (Jones 1983: 56–71).

Robert Darnton convincingly criticized Bettelheim's reading of the Grimm variant of Little Red Riding Hood as "flattened out, like pati-ents on a couch, in a timeless contemporaneity," irrespective of other versions of the type (Darnton 1984: 13). He calls for "rigorous docu-mentation – the occasion of the telling, the background of the teller, and the degree of contamination from written sources" (Darnton 1984: 16). One can agree with such a demand, but Darnton, a cultural historian, commits similar mistakes, using the Grimm tale to illustrate

German mentality in contrast to the prerevolutionary French mentality he deduces by analyzing two late-nineteenth-century notations from oral informants (Darnton 1984: 50–51).

Separation of oral and written forms in considering the life history or the just-performed variant of oral art, particularly the *Märchen*, is and always was problematic. "Folkloristics lives in literature," observed Schenda. "Oral literature is a paradox; it freezes when fixed in writing" (Schenda 1981b: 489–530). Obviously, the two can live only in interdependence, influencing content, composition technique, style, situational details, and the rules of performance. "Whoever sees folklore communication intact only where it involves clearly illiterate tradition bearers," writes Bausinger, "is as mistaken as those who believe forms and contents of oral folklore communication are in all cases offshoots of literary production" (Bausinger 1981: 14).

Nothing is really new about this. In 1931, Wesselski had already taken issue with adherents of the Finnish school for claiming the existence of an independent oral channel which would account for the extraordinary stability of tales. The scholar of medieval *Märchen* argued that Walter Anderson's hypothetical "magic tale village" (*Märchendorf*), in which tales are common pastime, cannot exist because "*Märchen* in folk-telling can survive only if bearers and preservers of tales (*Märchenträger* and *Märchenpfleger*) appear at brief intervals" (Wesselski 1931: 127–131, 156–157, 197). According to Wesselski, these bearers can be gifted raconteurs as well as literary authors like the Grimms. Wesselski claims that "without the crutches of a book," the *Märchen* would not have blossomed in modern Europe.

It seems the complex and untraceable relationship between oral and literary traditions accounts for the stabilization of tales into story units and types. The agents within the transmission process together perform conventional creative acts, producing myriads of variants by repeatedly telling, retelling, reading, editing, printing, illustrating, translating, and thereby adapting and disseminating seeds of the folktales around the world. In their utilization of sources that were partly "literary art form" and partly "popular oral tradition" (Berendsohn 1921/1968: 24), the Grimms met the criteria according to which folklore creation is being defined today (Dundes 1980: 1–19).

In the course of 130 years since the final form of the *KHM* left the press, the processes of selection, variation, and spread, corrosion and restoration, innovative formulations, translation, and reinterpretations according to innumerable conduits and microconduits (Dégh and Vázsonyi 1975: 207–254) took their course not only through telling and print, but also through the more effective electronic media of mass communication. While tales travel from medium to medium and meet the expectations of diverse population groups in the world, one feature remains constant. It is in the nature of the tale that at a certain stage of its life it is told orally, or read aloud, in face-to-face proximity. Modern society established its institutional storytelling services through professional and amateur performers, in addition to the traditional and natural narrators, whose primary repertoires have been sanctioned by the Grimm Collection (Wehse 1983; *The National Storytelling Journal* 1984–; Dégh 1985). This collection presents the *KHM* as a stabilized version of a genuine folktale repertoire, a sourcebook for adaptation and a link in the continuing chain of tradition. In essence the *KHM* does not differ from the repertoire of any illiterate master storyteller whose performance in front of his village listeners is also the product of previous literary and folk manipulations and whose artistry reasserts fading traditions and determines future ramifications. The "genuine" tale is the one told and listened to irrespective of its literary antecedents.

My long-term fieldwork in a village community in Hungary – where traditional storytelling maintained its popularity after World War II as a socially important act with regular performances by prominent illiterate and semiliterate narrators – gave me a representative example of the nature of standard literary influence. The folktale corpus I collected from major, minor, and occasional tellers consisted of some 450 items. Most were complete stories in active use; others were fragments, faintly remembered or in the process of formation. On the basis of information from the narrators, as well as my own examination of the texts, I found 40 percent of the total body directly or indirectly related to booktales (Dégh 1969/1989: 146–158). Narrators were actively seeking to expand their repertoires by listening to the reading of stories, which they then kept retelling and gradually shaping. In addition to classic literary themes mediated through chapbooks and pious exemplum collections, storybooks constituted the major sources. In 1894, Elek Benedek compiled a five-volume book whose influence on oral tales was comparable to that of the Grimms. Benedek, himself a member of the first team of fieldworkers, stylized the stories, intended for juvenile and uneducated popular audiences, written down by himself and others. Many of the folktales were originally adapted from the Grimms, but Benedek did not hesitate to add direct translations of his own (Kovács 1961: 430–443). His books became the most influential source for Hungarian village narration in the twentieth century. His style-editing and acceptance of the Grimmian principles helped homogenize rules of narration through innumerable editions of selected tales. There are eighteen tales in Mrs. Palkó's repertoire (Dégh 1969/1989: 153–154) from the Benedek collection and

eleven Grimm tales among the current favorites of Mrs. Fábián (Sebestyén 1979; 1981).

The impossibility and futility of separating oral and literary phases
in folktale transmission is obvious. Considering the crucial impact of
the *KHM* on live narration in the twentieth century, folktale research
needs to take another direction. It needs to recognize that the comparative study of direct or indirect literary influences and processual stages
of retroaction between written and oral variants can offer new insights
into the nature of creative processes in storytelling. As a matter of
fact, examples at our disposal indicate that most folklorists have mini-
mized the influence of the booktale and that only very few experimented with comparing oral tales to the literary models.

As early as 1912, Elizabeth Róna-Sklarek discussed the striking similarity of five tales in the Berze–Nagy collection from North Hungary
with five from the Grimms' collection (the Grimms' nos. 4, 21, 47, 80,
and 129).[2] She found that the verses in the tales are identifical with
those of a specific translation from 1889. In an article on acclimatization
of foreign tales, S. Solymossy identifies other Grimm tales mediated
indirectly through chapbooks to literate peasants, despite structural
and compositional modifications. Referring to these, Ortutay observed:
"It would be fruitful even today to follow the avenues of Hungarian
peasant adaptation of the Grimm tales" (Ortutay 1963a: 181).

Wesselski reported how the "retelling" of "Little Red-Cap" (Red
Riding Hood) in his experiment with thirty-eight schoolgirls resulted
in a variety of versions (Wesselski 1931: 127–131). Twenty years later
Max Lüthi convincingly demonstrated that "the substance of a literary
form changes according to specific tendencies." In the case of Rapunzel, writes Lüthi, the basic folk stratum provides the driving power
to sustain the story. It is no accident that the additions of the ladies
of the French court and German upper class could not survive. Once
returned to the folk, tales gradually lose the traces of literary revisions.
Lüthi regards the work of Jacob Grimm as a link in this transaction:
"He created what he assumed would have been created 'by itself'
among the folk, consciously developing the story in a new direction
for the retellers. His version, even if scholarly and scanty, selects
essential images and trends, erases arbitrary embroidery inherent in
literary narration" (Lüthi 1959: 112–113). In his comparison, Lüthi
shows how two oral narrators – one from Danzig, another from Hajós,
a German-Hungarian village – dropped banalities in folklorizing the
Grimm tale.

Working with narrator Egbert Gerrits, Gottfried Henssen examined
the retelling of four Grimm tales which Gerrits had learned in his
early youth from his grandmother in the Netherlands. "Contrary to

the literary archetype," writes Henssen, "the tales were brought closer to the real world made more reasonable and logical, while maintaining the outlook of the Märchen. Formulas are also more genuinely folkloric than those of the Grimms" (Henssen 1951: 16).

Vladimir Propp reports two kinds of adaptation by master storytellers. They either internalize whole tales from the Grimms, or adapt single motifs and ingredients learned from storybooks. He illustrates both, citing young narrators (Propp 1963: 104–112).

Felix Karlinger found two versions of the Grimms' no. 161 ("Schneeweisschen und Rosenrot") directly adapted by Sardinian storytellers who drastically removed most of the artificiality of the original (Karlinger 1973a: 585–593).

In a monograph description of the Danish redaction of AaTh 1640 (The Brave Tailor), Laurits Bødker asserts that Grimm no. 20 has been read since 1821, and has exerted its influence on the oral form of every subsequent generation (Bødker 1957: 21–22).

These examples of willingness to consider possible literary origin or influence are not free of bias and depart from the convictions that (1) the folk has an independent oral tale tradition free of literary intervention, and (2) the folk rejects and corrects artificial elements of booktales and restores the canon of hereditary types. This rigidity of scholars led also to the narrow view that real folktales are transmitted by illiterate peasants in isolated communities, and texts suspect of literary reminiscences need to be omitted from scholarly collections. The book influence, however, was not determined by rigorous comparative analysis of materials but on the basis of the folklorist's sensitivity as to what is and what is not a real folktale.

An interesting case in point is that of American tale collectors. They ignored Dorson's verdict that no American group corresponds to what is denoted by the term "folk" in Europe: "a deeply rooted, traditionally minded community, with a direct ancient past with its accumulated heritage" (Dorson 1945: 207). They also ignored the fact that for the American folk "Masses of popular narrative became accessible in print, in almanacs and magazines, especially for example, after the Civil War" (Christiansen 1962: 58). Following the example of Cecil Sharp, who journeyed to the southern Appalachian mountains in search of British ballads preserved by emigrants in their primitive retreat (Karpeles 1967: 140–171), folklorists visited the mountaineers to find the residues of the European oral *Märchen*. What they found was, to a considerable extent, retelling of the most popular, often reprinted pieces of the *KHM*. Two prominent Kentucky fieldworkers, Marie Campbell (1958) and Leonard Roberts (1969, 1974), depicted in compassionate colors the traditional life and wisdom of the settlers, giving the impression that the tales in "oral tradition" "are all from 'across the ocean waters' brought to Kentucky 'by our foreparents way back in time'" (Campbell 1958: 9). In the introduction to their collection, neither Campbell nor Roberts gave accounts of the personality and educational level of their informants or the sources of their folklore. Many of the tales were privately, so to speak discreetly, told by very old people upon the insistence of the inquisitive outsider (Campbell 1958: 24–25) or written down by the informant and sent to the folklorist by mail (Roberts 1969). It is quite remarkable that while the collectors provided type and motif numbers for each item and made reference to international variants including the Grimm collection, they never raised a question concerning the conspicuous closeness of the texts to the Grimm tales. One cannot tell whether the brevity, lack of coherence, yet almost slavish retention of Grimmian features was due to fading memory or inability of the narrators to integrate storybook materials into local oral tradition. The retold Grimm texts from Kentucky are nevertheless valuable documents worthy of source-critical analysis.

Prejudice weakens considerably Kurt Ranke's surprising statement that the Grimm tales influencing narrative tradition throughout Europe had little or no effect at all on the living German tale tradition (K. Ranke 1955: 126–135, esp. 132). In his rebuttal of von der Leyen's observation that "Das Folk hat den Brüdern für ihre Märchen in seiner Weise gedankt. Es hat sie aufgenommen und weiter erzählt und neu verschlungen und durch die ganze Welt geschickt." (The folk in its own way thanked the brothers for their tales. It has accepted them, continued to tell them, newly absorbed them, and sent them through the whole world.) (Ranke 1955: 127.) Ranke examined one hundred post-Grimmian collections from marginal peasant villages and concluded that the Grimms' modifications were alien to tradition and therefore unacceptable to the folk, which continued its mouth-to-mouth transmission undisturbedly. His findings were based on variant comparison, not on the microanalytical measurement of cultural revision by individuals and their supporting communities. The examples – that out of thirty-one variants of AT 451, only two have seven ravens like the Grimms' no. 25, while all other retained the original number three; that out of sixteen versions of The Girl Without Hands, only one accepted Wilhelm Grimm's contamination of this type with the introductory episode of another; that out of thirty-six variants of Godfather Death, only four follow the Grimms' conclusion (extinction of the candle of life of the doctor) – do not even prove that the few identical elements came from the Grimms. The subjectivity of the argument is obvious and justifies the question: Is there a more dependable way to observe processes of narrative development than in a book-to-teller and teller-to-book relationship?

It sounds almost a commonplace to repeat that the *KHM* is "still the most often reprinted and translated German book, next to the Bible" (Röhrich 1976a: 21). Yet perhaps this fact is the strongest evidence of its efficacy in keeping the world of the *Märchen* alive. Although it has been stated that the tales were translated into 140 languages and reached thirty million editions, we have no accurate figures to show how many modern language translations have been made; how many are in current circulation; what tale selections were made for abridged editions or for miscellaneous storybooks; and which individual tales have appeared separately for educational or other purposes. The limited number of available bibliographies, mostly from Europe, reveals little (Kozocsa 1963: 559–574; Voigt 1972: 336–338).[3] We may gather impressions from the multitude of reprints and paraphernalia that appear annually on the European Christmas market. Evidently, the popularity and applicability of the tales to diverse needs in diverse types of societies keeps the *KHM* viable and exportable.

We sometimes tend to consider oral tales moribund on the basis of our own experience: modern urban society cannot accommodate traditional village-style narration and has replaced it with other kinds. It must be remembered, though, that the rest of the world continues oral narration the way non-urbanized cultural styles require. According to a UNESCO estimate, there are 900 million adult illiterates, and the number is increasing. To give folklorists the opportunity to study live, emergent, variable oral tradition (Ortutay 1974a: 18), UNESCO's Sector on Culture delegated a subcommission to protect and safeguard the natural flow of folklore (Honko 1985: 3–11). Here again, folk, folklorist, and cultural managers join forces to redefine and mark out the boundaries of folklore for future generations.

With this prospect of manipulation for the future in mind, I would like to illustrate the adaptation of Grimm tales by master storytellers in their radically diverse cultural settings. This will show the continued viability of the *KHM* beyond our world. It seems the messages these stories convey are of general validity and cross the narrow confines of ideological systems. Because we lack systematic research materials, the examples are drawn from accidental and impressionistic observation that serves only to indicate the possibilities of research in folk narrative adaptation, choice, and rejection. Much must be done before we can attempt anything more.

(1) Storyteller Minya Kurcsi spent his life in the Transylvanian mountains working as a lumberman. For half a century he traveled on foot to work sites and entertained fellow workers with his tales at

night around the campfire. He had a sixth-grade education and loved to read storybooks. Although as a youth he had listened to many narrators, he never retold any of their tales. József Faragó, who recorded thirty-seven of Kurcsi's tales, discovered that these were Elek Benedek's versions of Grimm tales. "Old Minya is living witness to the folklorizing process of which not only the tales but also the Grimm translation of 'Grandpa Elek' ultimately became a part" (Faragó 1978: 559–618). Kurcsi chose thirty of the forty items from the book he had read. Faragó's exploration revealed that Kurcsi, at the age of sixty-four, now retired from the lumberyards but performing in schools for children and clubs for adults, did not remember the source of the tales after so many years. His adaptation of the best-known pieces – Snow White, Hansel and Gretel, Little Goose Girl, Frau Holle, Godfather Death, Learn What Fear Is, The Twelve Brothers, Seven Ravens, Cinderella, The Clever Peasant Girl, among them – consists of stylistic embroidery, the addition of dramatic dialogues between the main characters, change of episodic construction, and the introduction of elements from everyday life.

For a well-liked migrant narrator of his type, Kurcsi's dependence on the *KHM* as the source of his total repertoire is quite unique. It is unusual that he did not care to learn from the storytelling of other lumbermen at the alpine log shelter – one of the classic places for story exchange among adult men (Dégh 1969/1989: 74–76; Faragó 1969). Perhaps Benedek's book decisively influenced him to become a storyteller, and he wanted to be different from the others? But was he different? Were others also learning from books without telling the collector? Were folklorists naive enough to believe in exclusive orality even if the classic "liars" often referred to book sources in their playful introductory formulas? Or were folklorists disposed to accept the run that stated: "Once upon a time in the world there was a large tree. On the top of this tree there was a smaller tree. On the top of the little tree there were three hundred and sixty-six ravens and tied around its trunk, three hundred and sixty-six stallions. Whoever doesn't listen to my tale, may the three hundred and sixty-six ravens pick out their eyes and may the three hundred and sixty-six stallions scatter their bodies . . . in the hut underneath there was a big book whose three hundred and sixty-six pages I read through. I read this tale from it." This introductory cadence to a complex *Märchen* I recorded from fisherman János Nagy is typical (Ortutay, Dégh, and Kovács 1960, Vol. 2: 110). Is this common formula not a bantering reference to a book source? Be that as it may, over the years Kurcsi's choice of tale, variation, and stabilization through retelling, and his influence on others, is what counts. Unfortunately, the collector did not ask the pertinent questions.

(2) In his doctoral dissertation, Robert Adams gave an account of a Japanese woman's change in social identity from a story listener to a storyteller. At age forty-seven, Mrs. Tzune Watanabe, owner of a tea shop and grandmother to her son's eight children, began to lose her hearing. Isolated by deafness, this former farm girl who had once enjoyed listening to and telling folktales decided to teach herself how to read because, in Adams's words, "her deafness had deprived her of the mental stimulation she demanded form social contact in an intensely oral community. As soon as she began reading, she was able to use the stories in the books, not only for her own enjoyment but as additions to her repertoire of tales. With this new material, she renewed her activity as village raconteur insofar as societal conditions allowed, and was able to completely integrate the tales into her storytelling style and into the Japanese milieu" (Adams 1972). All this took place while she was operating the tea shop.

The first storybook she was able to read contained seven European *Märchen*, among them Snow White, Snow-White and Rose-Red, Rapunzel, and Hansel and Gretel. Mrs. Watanabe continued to tell stories, despite illness, and acclimatized Grimm tales to her repertoire. Her mastery of traditional narration enabled her to carry on and develop her style within a speedily changing urbanized milieu. Not essential episodic substitution but rather intricate elaboration of small details characterizes her skill. Seven years after reading Rapunzel, she had expanded the Grimm sentence describing what the prince overhears the girl singing into a lengthy account and a song. Mrs. Watanabe "appropriated the tale as an expression of her own personal experience when she detailed the subject of the song which Rapunzel sang, and related it to the objects which she supposed constituted the totality of Rapunzel's world" (Adams 1972: 154). Furthermore, the raconteur did not omit elements of the Grimm tale, except those which did not fit her cultural and personal biases. For example, she dropped the cruel torture of the stepmother in the Snow White story. Her restructuring of tales "to conform to a pattern established by her versions of tales heard from her mother and grandfather reflect the influence of the internalized pattern which governs all her tales" (Adams 1972: 147). The modifications give insight into techniques of cultural, communal, local, and personal acclimatization. Adams's penetrating comparative analysis of tale passages – repetitive exchanges of dialogue in the Grimm version compared to Watanabe's version of several tales – is revealing and suggestive.

(3) In the Philippine Islands, the Ilianen Monobo represent an ethnic minority culture without a written language. Although their Moslem

neighbors, the Magindanao, enslaved them for a while, in the 1970s the Monobo fled from Islamic unrest to safer valleys where they made contact with more recent immigrant groups who have had a history of four hundred years of Western influence. The team of linguists who wrote down the Monobo language recorded forms of oral art and discovered a blooming storytelling tradition maintained by a number of master storytellers and supported by community acclaim. Hazel Wrigglesworth, a member of the team, wrote her dissertation on the tale repertoire of two prominent Monobo storytellers as an expression of native rhetoric within a system of exclusively oral culture (Wrigglesworth 1975).

How is it possible that the repertoire of these Monobo narrators (Mrs. Ampalid told sixteen, Mrs. Mengsenggild twenty-three stories) consists of a majority of European-type *Märchen*? Although the tales are set in a mythological context with culture heroes as actors and contain genealogical episodes and references, the European influence in story content and structure cannot be mistaken. The presence of AaTh 300 (Dragonslayer), AaTh 400 (Swan Maidens), and AaTh 425 (Cupid and Psyche) may be attributed to an oral tradition, but can this also be the case with AaTh 566 (Fortunatus, widespread through chapbook reprints), AaTh 314 (Goldener), AaTh 130 (Bremen City Musicians), and above all AaTh 480 (Frau Holle)? There are chances of monogenetic transmission, of course, and such triviality as the recent telling by a visiting missionary is always possible. Mrs. Ampalid's grade-school education in a regional compound cannot be overlooked either. But hearing an unusual foreign story does not account for its reception and integration, as happened in this case. We have seen many examples of how long it takes for an imported popular literary story to lose its exotic features.

The Grimm version of Frau Holle was recorded twice from Mrs. Megsenggild. She learned it from an aunt, and it seems to be one of the community's favorites. It is also known under the title of "Good Character Girl – Bad Character Girl." Since Monobo culture and language have been influenced mainly by Malaysian and Indonesian sources via contact with Islamized tribes, Wrigglesworth compares the basic elements of Mrs. Mengsenggild's tale with a Javanese and an Indonesian version and Grimm's "Frau Holle." Examination of the amount of elaboration shows that the Grimm and the Javan texts consist of 1,100 words each, the Indonesian has 3,000, and the Monobo contains more than 7,000. The embroidery and modification of the Grimm story is considerable in all Asian versions, resulting mainly from cultural dissimilarities, but the Monobo text displays quite a bit of personal creativity. The chief means by which the Monobo variant is amplified is a fourfold repeated encounter for each of the two girls in which a new set of *dramatis personae* and events appears. Unlike the three other versions, the two girls are not identified in the Monobo version as the real daughter and the stepsister; the journey is not taken for the acquistion of wealth but for a more basic commodity, food. In both the Indonesian and Monobo texts, the girls encounter an alligator or crocodile who asks them to care for her child in return for granting their request. Also, the lullabies sung first by the kind and then by the unkind girl to the alligator's baby bear strong resemblance in the Indonesian and the Monobo texts. The old woman's tasks are relevant only to the German and Javanese versions, while the cock's song assumes the form of a lullaby in both the Indonesian and the Monobo versions and is sung by the girls themselves, thus retaining the contrast between the golden and the filthy appearance. Finally, the reward of wealth in the other three versions becomes a "reward of both food and beauty" in the Monobo. Additionally, in the Monobo story, the Bad Character Girl does not limit herself to one journey, but repeats her attempt to succeed four times (Wrigglesworth 1975: 197–204). Considering lasting historical contacts, Wrigglesworth believes there is a likelihood that European folktales were introduced to the Philippines via Malaysian immigrants (Wrigglesworth 1975: 203).

(4) Péter Pandur was a transient between worlds; a man of many trades, a dreamer, and an accomplished storyteller. Born in Transylvania in 1881, the son of estate servants, he began his career as a hired hand at twelve. After domestic service at the home of local nobility, he entered military service. Following his discharge, he traveled to Budapest and worked at construction sites. He married a girl he met at work, settled in her home village thirty miles from the city, and continued to accept odd jobs at diverse locations. He spent four years on the Eastern front during World War I. In 1938, an injury took his eyesight.

I met Pandur and his wife in their village on my first field trip and recorded his total repertoire of 108 tales (Dégh 1943). I recorded his life history twice in fifteen years, the second time shortly before he died at seventy-nine. The couple lived in the "poor quarter" of a well-to-do peasant village. As an in-migrant poor man, Pandur remained a misfit, never accepted by the villagers. His days of glory, of storytelling in migrant workers' camps, were over; occasional drunks in the pub, Gypsies, and children were his listeners.

Pandur's education, following his four years in school, was unlike that of the classic type of narrator. Most tradition-minded folklorists would have judged him uprooted and urbanized; and indeed his exposure to a great variety of social groups through employment had influenced to a great extent the stylistic shaping of his tale repertoire.

Yet in content, this repertoire reveals stronger roots in oral tradition than the convoluted style indicates. Seventy percent of his narratives are classic *Märchen*, twenty percent show haphazard, forced accumulation of episodes lacking a consistent frame, and ten percent originate in the Grimm collection.

In Pandur's case, certainty about the origins of his stories would be hard to establish. Unlike most narrators who name their sources, he emphatically denied that he had learned his stories from someone else and claimed he made them up himself. He demonstrated this to me by changing episodes or conclusions whenever I commented on an unusual turn. He saw himself as an author and planned to dictate a book to me. We would be joint authors and make much money.

The stories borrowed from the Grimms include The White and the Black Bride (AaTh 403), Sleeping Beauty (410), Kind and Unkind Girls (480), Snow White (709), and A Child of St. Mary (710). Pandur's version of each shows close proximity to the Grimm version, but each in different ways. The White and the Black Bride and the Kind and Unkind Girls are abbreviated retellings of the contents, lacking a personal touch. Sleeping Beauty is somewhat longer, with dialogues typical of the storyteller's featuring of formal conversations in the parlors of high society, as he overheard tea-party chats as the butler of a country gentleman. In A Child of St. Mary, on the other hand, after the girl's expulsion from heaven, the life story of the prince from AaTh 450 (Little Brother and Little Sister) is inserted, only to make the two meet and prepare for the usual happy end. The most remarkable is the composition of Snow White, blending AaTh 709 and 883 quite innovatively. The evil stepmother is replaced by a Roman Catholic priest in whose care the father leaves the girl while he travels overseas on business. Also, twelve robbers replace the seven dwarves who are deeply moved by the fate of the innocent girl. When she dies, they commit suicide next to her glass coffin in repentance.

I see here two kinds of influences by the Grimm tales. The close and succinct variants may have come from the schoolbook of Pandur's only daughter, a source too close and recent for creative manipulation. The other two stem from an earlier Grimm influence by way of popular chapbook prints, bearing all the marks of the narrator's usual way of internalization. In both cases, I suspect secondhand literary influence rather than reading.

These examples may give an idea of the continued viability of the *KHM* even beyond Germany and the rest of the Western world. It seems the messages these stories convey are of general validity, cutting across ideological systems. Lacking more focused research concerning the interaction of oral and literary tradition, storytellers and their repertoires are the best sources to consider. Once scholars record the total corpus of narrators, without ignoring, rejecting, or only grudgingly acknowledging materials their own sense of style would regard as inappropriate, the nature of folk narrative processes will be better understood. The four examples show diverse relationships to the booktales of the Grimms. Some are more direct, coming from first-hand reading; others show secondhand oral adaptation. Depending on personality, cultural context, temporal distance, and experience, there are many other possible variables. The literary influence, in a subtle way, may not only be discerned from single tales but from personal and communal repertoires, revealing the stylistic rules of narration in general.

It should be made clear that modern, particularly Western, urban society's profound involvement with the Grimm tales as "folktales" is not limited to the telling of, or listening to, formal narration. The presence of the tales may not even have to be manifested by passive knowledge of story plots. The spirit, philosophy, ideology, and behavioral patterns of the tales appeal to a much larger audience, beyond the telling context. The metaphoric uses of tale characters, images, sayings, situations, dialogues, miracles, transformations, and figurative speech formulas are generally known and appear as useful and meaningful tools in everyday life. The acts and even the total careers of tale heroes appear to be models for men and women to follow (Dégh 1983: 122–126; Stone 1983: 78–98). Thanks to the *KHM* and its new version, comprised of a selected set of tales normalized and "adapted" (*umfunktioniert*) by child psychologists, educators, writers (Bausinger 1971: 145), and professional narrators, Sleeping Beauty, Rapunzel, Frog Prince, and Cinderella became assumed or ascribed personality types in the Western world. This might well be the case; and, as Bausinger claims, the new rational worldview drove primary tale communication from adult society into the nursery. But how could the booktales of the Grimms eclipse storytelling tradition when the earlier practice of booktale retelling did not? Bausinger stresses here the passing of face-to-face storytelling as an adult pastime, not the abandonment of oral tradition, which already in the eighteenth and nineteenth centuries was strongly influenced by tales read from storybooks (Bausinger 1971: 146).

The strongest impact the Grimm tales made on modern civilization – and I would not want to distinguish here the adult world from the world of children – is outside formal storytelling in the traditional sense. Modern society is aware of the power of tales and their symbolism. For that reason, educators and psychologists keep debating whether tales are helpful or harmful to mental health. Currently, in addition to Bettelheim's book (Bettelheim 1976), the books of Jungian interpreters fill the shelves of German bookstores, analyzing the Grimm tales' meaning and appeal to modern audiences.

In modern society, tale particles divorced from the book assume a life of their own. They become symbols for reference, capable of describing feelings, arguing for right and wrong, and summarizing conditions in delicate situations. Tale motifs have become commonly understood signifiers, formulas to cite, metaphors to substitute for lengthy explanations. The capability of tales to break into meaningful units accounts for their practical exploitation in today's consumer-oriented world. Commercial advertisements in print, in radio broadcasts, and on television screens depend heavily on the magic tale's promise of happiness to sell products and lure tourists. Political cartoons feature topical events displaced in a satirical never-never land; toys, games, costumes, and other paraphernalia of the *Märchen* help indoctrinate children into the modern Grimm-*Märchen* subculture. In Germany, storybooks are accompanied by audio cassettes or even videotapes. The method of merchandizing Grimm resembles the selling of popular American movie characters and events as toys and games. This type of adaptation may be characteristic of the further ramification of the tale tradition and continued fascination with its implications. After all, the objectified artistic land of the tale offers fulfillment of hopes and desires to those who can daydream and assume the roles of heroes and heroines, taking a guided tour through the "fairy-tale woods" (*Märchenwald*)[4] and its clearings, the avenues of danger and adventure, between good and evil. As Kurt Ranke said, the tale hero is a wanderer between the worlds (Ranke 1958: 656). Indeed, there is no better expression of hope in terms of human creativity than the tale told, read, played, or gestured, and the tale normalized and standardized by the current edition of the *KHM*.

Transformations of some popular Grimm tales and their adaptations for drama, ballet, opera, puppet play, for stage, movie, radio, and television presentation, and for poetry, novel, short story, joke, and political cartoons, are innumerable (Hand 1963; Röhrich 1979, 1983; Dégh 1983; Rogge 1983; Mieder 1979; Horn 1983). It would seem worthwhile to explore the literary fairy tale in its development as related to the Grimm collection from the mid-nineteenth century to our day, especially during the last decade, which has witnessed a growing interest among writers and artists in developing satires, travesties, fantasy tales, and even science fiction movies exploiting Grimmian formulas. Their success attests that the popular audience has internalized these formulas. But since the authors depart sharply from traditional folklore patterns, little if any return influence on folktale may be expected from them. For this reason, their work is beyond the scope of folkloristic consideration.

In the country of the Grimms, founding fathers of folklore and discoverers of the genre *Märchen*, the telling of *Märchen* seems to go far beyond any expectation. The Grimm corpus has become a shared national property, representative of what average people know as folktales which are to be studied, performed, enjoyed in multiple forms, peddled, and sold in manifold packaging. The attitudes toward the tales change, but neither hostility nor support can alter the fact that they are alive and well in the crossfire of controversies. Opinions about the *Märchen* are expressed by everyone in the intellectual marketplace, and no one is neutral or indifferent. It is unlikely that the tales will cease to exist or be replaced; they permeate the landscape of the country wherever the Autobahn takes the traveler. The German ADAC (a motor club) provides drivers with a map to guide them through the world of the magic tale, the sites where Grimm heroes resided – from the modest night quarter of the Bremen City Musicians to Sababurg, the hunting castle of the Landgraf of Hessen, and the residence of Dornröschen. There are some two hundred "fairy-tale woods" (*Märchenwälder*), parks or lands in Germany to enculturate children and adults seeking family recreation. These feature a repertoire primarily of Grimm tales, in this order of popularity: Hansel and Gretel, Cinderella, Snow White, Little Red Riding Hood, Sleeping Beauty, Brother and Sister, Frog King, Lucky Hans, Frau Holle, Tischlein Deck Dich, Rapunzel, and The Brave Little Tailor. Helga Stein (1979) asks: Is this a new form of tradition or transmission of folktales? The question is timely, but an answer may be expected only after the function and influence of the fairy-tale gardens (*Märchengärten*) have been adequately explored.

In the festive atmosphere of the Grimm anniversary, Frau Dorothea Viehmann, the *Märchenfrau* from Kassel, narrates again. This charming old lady, in her traditional costume and bonnet and with her Niederzwehrn dialect, was reborn as if stepping out of the familiar pictures drawn by Ludwig Grimm. But there is one slight difference between Mrs. Viehmann and her current representative in Niederzwehrn. The latter, unlike her predecessor, has a book in front of her from which she reads her tales – a selection of Grimm *Märchen*. The present *Märchenfrau* is Anni Keye, who is in her seventies; she is so impressed by her act that even her husband, who drives her to storytelling appointments, is not sure if she is Dorothea or the Anni he married long ago.

The costumed *Märchenfrau* and her numerous counterparts in Germany, and elsewhere in Western Europe, and maybe in the world, become, so to speak, the symbols of folklore transmission. With the printed book in their hands, they communicate their messages by word of mouth. Perhaps they also appear on the film screen. The *Märchenfrau* is a conscious cultivator of tradition. Ever since a public appeal for an official "German fairy-tale road" (*deutsche Märchenstrasse*) was made, she has been active in contributing to the program of the Kassel station. Anni is regarded as an important contributor to the Kassel club and group travel programs (as witnessed by the tourist guide for 1985). The length of her tales ranges from three to fifteen minutes: she goes on as long as the customers want to listen. And they do, indeed! The enchantment of the *Märchen* is as much in demand as before. As reported in *Heim und Welt* (Jan. 15, 1985), "today's fairy-tale tellers have become fully integrated into mass tourism." Even more important, according to a poll of the Sample-Institute, 94 percent of West Germans are familiar with the adventures of Hansel and Gretel, 93 percent with Snow White, 91 percent with Little Red Riding Hood, and 90 percent with the Grimm version of Sleeping Beauty (*Abendpost*, Mar. 28, 1985).

Since the time of the Grimms, folklore has been regarded as the treasury of the past, which must be rescued and preserved. Although traditional folklorists have kept tolling the bell over the demise of the folktale, its techniques of transmission and spread may speed up and change, the formats of the stories may multiply with the introduction of modern media, but the folklorization of the Grimm tales appears as strong evidence of the persistence of the folktale. Tradition may live only because – not despite the fact that – it is carried and supported by modern means of communication.

Part Four

CASE STUDIES FROM THE MODERN INDUSTRIAL WORLD

SYMBIOSIS OF JOKE AND LEGEND:
A CASE OF CONVERSATIONAL FOLKLORE

> The culture of Gary-East Chicago is largely an
> oral culture, in the sense that talk flows
> freely. Television has not displaced
> conversation. (Dorson 1970: 209.)

1.

It was December of 1964 when I first met Steve Boda and his wife Ida. This was on my second field trip to the Calumet Region, where I was collecting materials on Hungarian immigrant culture (Dégh 1968–1969: 97–107; Dorson 1968–1969: 65–69). I visited the Boda couple following the advice of several community members. Still somewhat unclear about the ways, goals and potentials of research among ethnics in a complex, urban-industrial area, I was looking for tellers of stories in the way traditional folklorists had for the past century and a half. Entering the neat home of the Bodas, I found not only the storytellers I wanted, but also the direction I needed in researching Hungarian-American ethnic life. They turned out to be the most authentic and versatile guides to ethnicity, interethnic relations, the sustenance of traditions of adaptation, as well as the ensuing formulation of new folklore. I also learned from them the importance of carefully observing the story-performance that flowed naturally in their home. The Bodas led me to some theoretical conclusions concerning the specific nature of the folk legend (Dégh and Vázsonyi 1971: 289–294; 1973: 29–30).

The situation I encountered on this first visit remained similar to those visits I made for eight subsequent years. The only difference was seasonal change. The first visit came during an unusually cold winter. The lawn that in the summer months displayed the plastic statue of a sitting deer and a grazing fawn was frozen gray in front of the fenced yard. The precious flower garden and the vegetable patch so characteristic of Hungarian peasant immigrant homes (Dégh 1968–1969: 140) was reduced to dry twigs and empty shells. The plastic wrappings on the rosebushes and the barren fruit trees rattled in the icy wind under the leaden sky, forcing me to hasten towards the glass door on the side of the house which was coated with the vapor of kitchen steam, cigarette smoke and warm air from the oil furnace. The main entrance of the spacious red brick house was permanently blocked from the inside by a large buffet, the centerpiece of the front room used only on extraordinary festive occasions, such as receiving guests after family weddings or funerals.

The side door yielded immediately to my knocking, and our host opened it, revealing the entire living space of the residents. This was the kitchen in which guests were received with warm hospitality and treated to food and drinks spiced with entertaining stories. But even on the rare occasions when the Bodas expected no visitors, the kitchen would be their living quarter until the late hours, when they would retire to their bedroom, overcrowded with two large beds, two bed-stands, a sofa and a vanity. The bedroom wall was covered with landscape paintings and rustic Old Country scenes by an artist who was a relative of Aunt Ida who also had "made it" in America.

Entering the kitchen, the visitor can see two other doors. One leads to the bathroom, conveniently located between the kitchen range and a large refrigerator; the other leads through a small passage to the living room, the bedroom, and a staircase to the basement. The pantry is the only room in the finished basement that is in active use. Two other rooms had been leased to two working men. The pantry has a prominent role in food provisions as well as in the manifestation of loyalty to the old country and the reinforcement of intergroup rela-tions. The products of the garden are lined up on the shelves, canned or dried by Aunt Ida, awaiting consumption. The seeds of special flowers and herbs are carefully stored for the next season and for exchange. There is a ring of procurement and exchange of the cher-ished *Székely* spices that are proudly distinguished from the common Hungarian kinds. The Bodas are prominent artists of the *Székely* cui-sine, one of the symbols of ethnic solidarity in the Old Country as well as in America. The Székely-land is located in Southwest Transyl-vania (Dégh 1969/1989: 3–4). Whoever visits the homeland, the *Székelyföld* allotted to Romania after World War I, must bring replen-ishment for the transplanted stock of savory, penny royal, tarragon, sweet basil, dill, or anise. Seeds are also sent by mail, enclosed in ordinary letters, and the *Székely* clan within the Calumet Hungarian enclave keeps up a lively network of barter and mutual food sampling, in order to check out the best kinds for cultivation. Uncle Steve is as active in ethnic cookery as his wife. A former butcher, he still is the foremost authority in sausage-making, and his masterpieces – home-smoked bacon, ham and sausage – are hung from the pantry ceiling in an orderly row.

The kitchen is large, with sparkling white walls, ruffled curtains, furniture and cabinets, and stainless steel pots and pans. There is not much room to move around. A large oblong table occupies the main space in the center of the room, surrounded by chairs. The main chair is occupied by Uncle Steve at the head of the table, opposite the entrance door, with a white cupboard behind him and the bathroom door at his right. A chain smoker, Uncle Steve has a large ashtray in front of him and several packs of Lucky Strike cigarettes. Aunt Ida's place is before the refrigerator, the electric range and the sink, so that she can perform her kitchen duties with ease while participating in the conversation. She is a virtuoso in fixing delicacies quickly. If old friends arrive, it is her habit to start cooking. "I'm sure you are hungry," she says, "how about a nice pancake?" and without waiting for the answer she sets to work.

At the time of my first visit, the couple was alone. The small stout bald man behind the table started to talk without being asked. Joke-telling was a natural pastime for him. He was known to the neighborhood and among his peer group as a funny man who never missed an opportunity to crack a joke or to make jocular remarks about anything that came to his attention. He introduced himself to me as a jokester as soon as I took off my coat and sat down.

Mr. B.: I bet you haven't heard about that man here . . . he started to drink, got into real bad ways. His wife divorced him . . .[1]
Mrs. B.: That made bad worse, indeed, for him.
Mr. B.: Two years later he went to see the *Reverend: "Father,"* he says, "You know what? I want to come back to the Church. I want to join in again." "How come? I haven't seen you for two years . . . you drank." "Yes, I did. But now I am good, I don't drink anymore." So the Reverend tells him: "*All right.* I take you back. But go home first and come back again in a week. I will examine you from the Bible and I will see if you haven't forgotten your religion. If you can answer my questions, I will take you back." So it happened. The man goes back to the Father, back to the minister, and the minister tells him: "Where was Jesus Christ born?" And he says: "In Pittsburgh." "In Pittsburgh?" "Oh," he says, "hold it, I know! He was born in Bethlehem, *yes*," he says, "*sorry*, I knew he was born someplace in Pennsylvania, Pittsburgh, or Bethlehem, I mixed up the two cities. I wanted to say Bethlehem." He says, "Go home, get out of here, go home, you do not belong here." But the man insisted, "I tell ya, I knew he was born in Pennsylvania, I just mixed up Pittsburgh with Bethlehem."

[He gives a big laugh and Mrs. B. heartily seconds.] But the Reverend did not take it, *no*. [Chuckle.] "Go home. Pittsburgh, not Bethelehem, you fool!" "Sorry, I said I thought it was Pittsburgh but I knew it was in Pennsylvania." [The couple laugh together.] *Yeah*. The Reverend did not take him back, *no*. The fool! This really has happened. The man was a Hungarian.

This brief anecdote had a tremendous effect on Aunt Ida. She could not stop laughing and could hardly catch her breath. She finally rose to her feet and reached out to tear a paper towel from the roll on the wall and wiped her eyes, and Uncle Steve was ready for some more. This time he did not continue with his favorite stories of local numskulls he had known, but picked one of his set of anticlerical jests. By staying with the topic of church and clergymen, he wanted to introduce himself as a critic of bigotry and hypocrisy. He went on with a direct question:

> Mr. B.: Do you go to *church* every Sunday? [pointing at his wife] 'Cause she does.

This was an unnecessary question. He knew that I had met his wife through the minister of the Hungarian Presbyterian Church in Indiana Harbor, the most durable ethnic institution in the region. But Uncle Steve did not really expect an answer. He turned immediately to his view on churchmen. In later years I heard his argument many times, addressed to his church-going wife and her female friends of different denominations, as garnishing to his jokes about religious orders. These jokes, usually emphasizing the mercenariness, greed, adulterous sex life, and unbecoming behavior of clergymen, expressed his reasons for anticlericalism. This time, he wanted to tell me why he does not attend the services with his wife:

> Mr. B.: I am an honest man. I never took what did not belong to me. I believe in God, but I do not believe in going to church.[2] Still I have got as much *chance* to go to heaven as my wife. That's what I told this old *Reverend* who is now retired. And guess what did he say? "*Listen*," so he says, "Uncle Steve, you won't be admitted to heaven if you don't pay your dues to the Church." Hey, that's the pastor, hey? Wise guy, *see*? Main thing I pay my dues to the church. *No sir*.

This was more than Aunt Ida could bear.

> Mrs. B.: You know what? Go and get a piece of sausage. We'll talk while you are gone, *okay*? Bring a piece of sausage so that I can roast it. Yes, because we have real good smoked sausage. Real, homemade, nothing you can buy in Bloomington groceries. We make it. I want to make a little lunch . . .

But Uncle Steve was hard to stop, once he was talking. In view of Aunt Ida's interjected comments and big belly laughs, I did not get the impression that she really wanted to stop him. I realized much later that her embarrassment was a pretense, a part she played in supporting his joke-telling. This time she had to go get the sausage from the pantry herself.

> Mr. B.: This is a good *business*. The church, I mean. They want to grab everything they can. And they sure can as long as you are concerned with the thereafter. When I was in the hospital, the nurse asked me right away, *"Are you Catholic?" "No,"* says I, *"I am retired."* The Catholic Heaven isn't any better than the other.
> Mrs. B.: [pointing to the tape recorder] Stop that, will you? Every word you say is recorded. Take care.
> Mr. B.: Why should I? I don't mind. This doesn't kill me.

With a shrug he began to tell about a compatriot who became a Pentecostal minister:

> Mr. B.: Smart man, I tell ya. He came to America long ago, he still was a child. They took him to Ohio. Now, he has an *office*, you know, they send him letters, lined with twenty dollars, ten dollars. Yeah. Joe, my buddy told him, "Look. You are a smart guy, that I can see. Do you really believe what you preach? You don't really believe, do you?" You know, this man was speaking in tongues. He can speak all tongues of the world – oh hell. He is just talking, talking, talking and the folks just listening, listening, listening. "And do you really believe what you tell them?" my buddy, Joe asked him. "I bet you don't." But he makes big money. His son is a *foot doctor, a specialist*. And he's got a home worth forty thousand dollars, a new home. He is a millionaire, *sure*. Needn't work. He only talks. He can talk German too and these guys listen to him. They give him one percent of what they make. Those rich people in Akron, Ohio, there are those rich *tire companies*. Fifty, sixty thousand people work there; they make fifty, sixty thousand dollars on them. They all give to the church, yeah. Because he is a smart guy, you know, he knows how to talk to people and he milks them. The fools. All he does is, he preaches in church once a week, on Sunday, and then talks for half an hour on the *radio*. That's all he does. *You see?* Smart man.

By this time, Aunt Ida had fixed the sausage and we ate. But there was one more story to put down churchmen and exhaust the topic. This time it was Aunt Ida who reminded her husband:

> Mrs. B.: Why don't you tell how it was when you went to Heaven?
> Mr. B.: Ah, what?
> Mrs. B.: How did you bow to St. Peter?
> Mr. B.: Oh, that? The one *Reverend* said? Shall I tell it all?

Mrs. B.: *Why, sure.*

Mr. B.: *Okay.* Well, you know *Reverend* M. was from Transylvania. You know? We met at the *courthouse*, we had some *business* to settle and then we had a drink. There was another man there and we were drinking with the minister, you know. And he said: "Now I'll leave you, but I'll tell you something before I go, *Mr. Boda.* You will never go to Heaven." "I won't? Why not?" "Why not? Do you want to know why not? *Listen.* When your spirit goes up there, you go and you knock on the door of St. Peter [he knocks on the table three times], you say: 'I am here, István Boda from earth, please, let me in.' But," he says, "we cannot go there like this, holding up our head high and proud and with a cigar in our mouth. Now, we must bow there, like this: 'I wish you a good day, Sir, St. Peter.' And when St. Peter will see you there, will see your bald head, he will believe that you went with your arse first. He will kick you so hard that you fall down to hell." So. The minister said that. Just him, don't forget it.

Mrs. B.: Well, you did not make an obeisance in greetings. [Chuckles]

Mr. B.: Oh yes, I did, didn't I greet him? And he told me not to forget to go to church on Sunday. I said: "Sure, I'll go. You don't believe yourself. Why should I believe if you don't? What are you talking about?"

At this point the telephone interrupted the conversation. It did not take a minute, and Aunt Ida excitedly hastened to the bedroom to turn on the television. The caller was Lizzie, a young neighbor woman who said that a pilot who talked to Martians was on the screen, telling about his experience. Unfortunately, the show was over by the time Ida turned the TV on, and we could never learn what the planet-men said when their space ship made a crash landing near the Little Calumet River. However, this incident diverted the trail of our talk.

Mrs. B.: I wish she had called sooner.
   [I wanted to know what language the pilot could communicate with the Martians.]

Mrs. B.: This is no problem at all. They had been in touch for so long through signaling that they can make themselves understood in English. Why couldn't Liz call earlier? She was too excited. What bothers me is that swampy place at the river . . . why, all strange things happen there?
   [I ventured a question here, being ignorant of strange happenings in the area.]

Mr. B.: [airily] No strange things ever happened there. There are some liars who try to scare others, and she falls for that sort of thing. I've been on the road night after night but never saw a ghost. You and your friends!

Mrs. B.: Don't say that. How about the house that burned down with the woman inside? Didn't Mr. Kiss the coalman see her in white, rocking her baby on the *porch*? And didn't your godson (a *police officer*) tell you about the woman who was killed by her husband right there? Wasn't it just seven years this *Halloween*? Don't you remember how many people waited out there to see her appear on the anniversary of the murder? The *policeman* saw her.[3]

Mr. B.: They are all crazy like you and your lady friends.

Mrs. B.: Here we go again! Look. You never believed us when we heard my *sister* cry . . . [Here she seemed to address herself entirely to me.] The only daughter of my sister died. And when she died, she was laid out at McGuan's[4] . . . there were four of us here in the kitchen. We fixed *lunch*. That the guests come, the relatives, so . . . everything was here. We ran to this door. There were four of us. We ran to that door; nobody there, nobody. *Well,* my *sister* came back later and we told her how much she was crying, it was her voice, we all recognized it . . . One was her daughter-in-law, the other was my daughter, my other sister and myself. There were four of us. We ran from one door to the other and nobody was there. When she came back: "No," she said, "I wasn't here, I was at the *undertaker*, we had *pictures* taken." Well, it was the spirit that cried just like my *sister*.

Mr. B.: Well, I can't believe this. No, I can't . . .

Mrs. B.: Don't say that because there were four of us. We are four who say it, all four of us ran to the door. If it would be only for me, they could call me a fool, or that I am raving, but all four of us ran; my daughter, my *sister*, we all heard her crying. And she was nowhere. This is something, a wonder . . .

Mr. B.: Nothing . . . [gesture of dismissal]

Mrs. B.: We should have written somewere, to someone who understand this, who looks into such matters.

Mr. B.: Cheaters!

Mrs. B.: And I tell you another thing. When this girl died, it was so sudden. We celebrated March fifteenth in *church*.[5] While the program was on, they wanted me on the telephone. We didn't realize she was that sick. It came as a shock to me. The *Reverend* asked me if I wanted to make the announcement now or after the program? *"No,"* I said, "we should not make such an *excitement*, please, announce it after it's over." Later we all went to the home of my *sister* to pay our respects. As we all were there, suddenly the door quietly opens and then nicely closes again. We go to the door, maybe someone is there? *Nobody*. No one . . .

Mr. B.: It was imagination.

Mrs. B.: *No, no, no, no!* It opened and closed.

Mr. B.: I don't believe in this.

Mrs. B.: *Now, wait a minute!* And before Betty died, some two weeks before, she was still at home, there was a sudden clattering sound in the house at night. My sister believed that the pastry board fell off the wall. But next morning the board was still on the wall, only that loud sound . . . Betty too . . . *"Mother, what was it, mother?* What was it?" And she said, *"I don't know,* maybe the pastry board fell down!" And this clattering sound occurred two weeks before Betty died. All this . . . then . . . was related . . . I mean, this is really true. This is all true, everything I said . . .

Mr. B.: *Baloney*. They were dreaming.

Mrs. B.: There must be something. Really, this spirit thing. There is such a thing. We heard her cry, scream, she cried so much. Where and who did it? It must have been her ghost. I don't know how it can appear in body, in shape that I haven't seen. But in sound . . . Yes, I can prove it, we heard the voice clearly . . .

Mr. B.: How can somebody cry without having a body?

Mrs. B.: Come now. My sister can also prove it. Yes. We knew that *medium* in Hammond. She called the spirit: "Come, my dear spirit, come, my dear spirit," she said; she talked nicely to the spirit, and everything. Well, once it really came. We were seven around the table and our hands had to touch. Once then, the table started to rise . . .

Mr. B.: Someone was pushing, right?

Mrs. B.: Oh *no, no, no-no-no*, nobody was there. We touched the edge of the table. We wanted to prove that it is true, but a man didn't believe. She said then: "Dear Spirit, if you are here, show us whom you don't like and press him against the wall." Well, once the table moved right against the wall pushing the man to the wall. He was so scared that he ran away. I jumped up on the bed, didn't know how to flee, we were all scared, because the table was dancing. It was of fine wood; my grandpa made it. I'm telling you, this was true. Where is the spirit then? It must be somewhere. It must live some place. My *sister* cried, you see, who else could it be once she was not here?

Mr. B.: This is just a joke. Someone tried to trick you like it was with those two in our home town. Remember? One told the other: "You know what? I bet you would not dare to go to the cemetery" . . . The *jackass* believed in ghosts.

Mrs. B.: Ya, midnight, twelve o'clock. *"Yeah,"* he said, *"Sure* I dare." And he took off and went to the cemetery when the clock struck twelve. And the other followed him and stuck the tail of his jacket with his knife to a grave so he could not move from there. He thought the ghost had caught him.[6]

Mr. B.: See, and he died of the scare. This was true.

Mrs. B.: Yeah. But his friend did it as a practical joke to . . .

Mr. B.: Look, I don't believe in ghosts and the likes but I would not go to the cemetery at midnight. Not that I would be afraid . . . *No*, I wouldn't go.

Mrs. B.: The devil wouldn't take you [chuckles].

Mr. B.: Sure. You heard of the devil carrying the man on his back to hell? And the devil carries him and they are on their way. And there they meet the neighbor of this *Székely góbé*.[7] The neighbor tells him: "How are you, friend, neighbor?" And he says: "I could be worse than that." And he says: "How on earth could you be worse than that? Isn't it that the devil takes you to Hell?" "Oh, I would be much worse if I had to carry the devil on my back to Hell. [laughs] I would be much worse!"

With this story Uncle Steve managed to engineer the conversation back to his humorous favorites while Aunt Ida modestly withdrew and switched from her role as active legend teller back to that of member of the anecdote-audience.

This small sample from the first tape recorded by the Bodas is representative of their performance and interaction, and it displays their distinctive repertoires. During subsequent years I had many occasions to observe the Boda couple in different performance situations. I watched them at this first encounter, as they introduced themselves to me, heard them later perform for diverse audiences, and could observe them as their houseguest when no one was around and they recounted only to each other. I have re-recorded the stories several times under different *ad hoc*, contrived conditions and could determine the permanent and transient pieces of their repertoire, the new acquisitions as well as the rejections. No matter what the actual conditions were, there was a conspicuous interdependence in the conversational performance between the husband and wife. They seemed to be engaged in an everlasting, never-to-be-resolved debate, caused by two conflicting ideologies manifested by a rationalistic joke teller and a mystic-transcendentalist legend teller. Each time narration was cooperative; they gave cues to each other like actors in a theatrical play; they reacted with rebuttal or with supportive comments to each other's statements. Jokes and legends were alternately and interdependently told and it was seldom that one spoke up while the other was absent. This relationship can be called *symbiotic*. By this I do not mean only that jokes and legends get on well together under the same roof but also that they provide the necessary living conditions for each other.

2.

Usually Uncle Steve started to tell some stories – generally a string of anecdotes of some sort – until the opportunity came for Aunt Ida to take the lead. His telling aimed at entertaining, hers at stimulating discussion of extranormal events (Dégh and Vázsonyi 1973). He liked to laugh and make other people laugh at comic situations not necessarily topical; she liked to report on supernatural incidents that captured her attention in normal daily life, made her wonder and eventually led to the legends she told. Steve and Ida Boda have been married for more than fifty years, and narration has always been part of their life together. No matter how different their personalities and interests, they could always reconcile conflicting ideas through discussing their differences in terms of stories. Uncle Steve was a carefree, happy-go-lucky man who liked his work, his food and his booze, and resolved

his problems in life by a strong sense of humor. Whatever happened
to him, no matter how disadvantageous it looked, he made it appear
funny. It was not always others who played the dupe in his stories;
he did not spare himself from ridicule. One of his funniest stories is
about how his driver's license was suspended because of drunken
driving on the wrong side of the highway. Even his arrest sounded
like a hilarious experience. If one can believe relatives, friends and
neighbors, Uncle Steve's easygoing way caused him much trouble;
and his wife, spoiling him immensely, often came to his rescue. She,
on the other hand, was always the one who cared and worried, who
saw the dark shades and the drama behind the facts of life. The loyal
belief in traditional superstitions which she inherited from her beloved
mother and grandmother obtained reinforcement through her friends
with whom she talked of supernatural encounters, ominous predictions, dreams, signs and the horrors of violent death. Uncle Steve did
not need to search for inspiration or assurance from others. He rather
needed a stage on which he could play his role. People came to hear
him and offered him raw materials on which he elaborated. Aunt Ida,
on the other hand, went out of her way to find those who shared her
interest, who told her new stories that she could add to her corpus,
to take home and tell. The couple compared notes on new acquisitions,
providing the necessary reactions: objection, rebuttal, banter, mockery
on his part; embarrassment, astonishment, forgiveness, alleviation,
hearty laughter on her part. This set a well-rehearsed pattern to be
staged for their audience. If one can say that Steve Boda was the
member of a joke-conduit and Ida Boda was the member of a legend-
conduit (Dégh and Vázsonyi 1975: 211–214), one can also say that
both acquired their materials in the specific way jokes and legends
are learned in their cultural setting: the Székely ethnicity was their
donor culture, just as its Calumet-colony became its current base. Each
repertoire shows the chronology of its bearer's life history.

This life history is simple. It is the success story of modest working
men who made the transition from a rural-peasant to an urban-industrial way of life, while accommodating their ethnic loyalties to a multiethnic environment. Steve and Ida Boda were born and raised in
Udvarhely County, the very heart of Protestant *Székelyföld*. They were
married in their home village and came to the United States with their
small duaghter in 1924. They were twenty-six and twenty-one at the
time. For them, America was not a new adventure. Steve came first
in 1921, to "look around" and then returned for his bride, and together
they joined a colony of compatriots who had arrived earlier. The
Székelys, born entrepreneurs whose mass emigrations have been
known to historians since the sixteenth century, were also among the

earliest Hungarians who made the trip to America in search of labor (Dégh 1969/1989: 30). Aunt Ida's grandfather tried his luck in the oilfields in the 1880s; her father Lajos Frencz worked from 1905 to 1910 at Pullman. He became a successful farmer in his homeland, adding more acres to his estate after three consecutive work periods in the South Chicago mills. Of his seven children, only two remained home; the others settled in the Gary-Chicago area and raised their children and grandchildren to become prosperous Székely-Americans with strong loyalties to both the original and the adopted country. This double loyalty remains unchanged in the upcoming generation despite gradual loss of competence in the old cultural values. Kinship ties persist as a cohesive force in the ethnic community and lend respectability to the Boda couple.

In 1963, Uncle Steve retired from Inland Steel after twenty-nine years of labor. By this time his home was paid for in full, and he could also buy a lot for a family home for their daughter, Julie, and help build it. His income from pension, social security, and four rented rooms totaled $500 per month, enough for a comfortable life. The household budget allowed the luxurious cookery, feasting and generous treatment of guests – essential to the concept of the good life for the Boda couple. It also included obligations: sending packages to relatives in the Old Country, gift-giving to relatives and friends here at birthdays, namedays, Christmas or other occasions, and charities channeled through the ethnic church. Even extra hobbies for Mrs. Boda, playing bingo once a week and going to sales, could not exhaust the monthly income.

The Boda home, the permanent stage of story-performance, was located on the main street of the original Hungarian ethnic enclave of Indiana Harbor. The audience of the storytelling was variable with a solid-core membership consisting of visitors who can be classified according to the frequency of their visits: (1) neighbors, (2) relatives, (3) friends within the local ethnic community, (4) old friends outside the local community.

(1) The primary audience. At the time of my fieldwork, there were just a few Hungarian families living within walking distance: two old Székely couples, a half-blind widow, a young woman married to a Slovak, and a Slovak woman who spoke fluent Hungarian. Only two blocks away there was also a Hungarian couple, owners of a grocery store that catered to the needs of Mexican customers. But these were not the only steady neighborhood visitors, who could drop in any time of the day. There were Polish, Croatian, German, and also two Italian neighbors who regularly came by, in addition to the Mexican friends of the Bodas living further down the street. It did not make

much difference who was what; the ethnic residents spoke the same broken English slang learned and homogenized in the Calumet mills, stores and streets. The immigrant generation retained its lifestyle; the multiethnic neighborhood of the Bodas shared their experience and worldview, even if their American-born children and grandchildren departed from it. The Boda home was an ideal place to exchange common experiences. The favorites, however, were the Mexicans, the latest arrivals. They looked with respect at the Bodas who had started their American career as they had – forty years ago. The old couple had a weakness for the Mexicans, and they admired their cleanliness, modesty and hard work, which corresponded to their own inherited ethos. If there were no Hungarian refugees in need, they rented rooms to Mexican newcomers for a nominal fee. Uncle Steve used his old connections to get them jobs; Aunt Ida cooked for them; and when they decided to settle for good, bring wife and children from Mexico, the Bodas babysat for them. Thus, neighbors were the most frequent casual visitors and listeners to legends and jokes. Women brought a sample of a new pastry recipe or a cut from a meat dish to taste, borrowed cooking ingredients or kitchen utensils, asked for some advice, or just stayed to chat. Men more often came to listen and sit silently. The neighborhood relationship of the Boda couple was very similar to that of Old World peasant narrators.

(2) The second class of visitors consisted of members of the family. For Székelys the degree of respectability still depends on the size and strength of a clan. The Boda–Ferencz kinship has a large American branch including blood and affiliated kins in different degrees, several of whom eventually came by for a visit on Sunday, holidays or after the working hours. Drawing up a family tree of Aunt Ida's lineage, I noted forty out of seventy-one contemporaries who kept in touch, depending on their time and the driving distance.

(3) Friends within the local ethnic community were largely identical with the members of the ethnic church and the different action-groups, composed mostly of Aunt Ida's women-friends, who shared her fascination with the supernatural. These women were active in helping the church with bake sales. During noodle- or sausage-making in the church basement, they liked to exchange extranormal experiences. If they came for a visit to the home in connection with some project, legends were passed on in the atmosphere of an enjoyable controversy stimulated by Uncle Steve's disparaging remarks accompanied by seconding husbands.

(4) Old friends who moved away from the Calumet Region were occasional guests: former cronies of Uncle Steve and former roomers, protégés, and refugees of the Hungarian revolution of 1956 whom the

couple sponsored and helped through the first critical years. Such people usually paid their visits during vacation time, accompanied by their families. It was an emotional journey for them. I understood how they felt when once Aunt Ida bade farewell to Andrew and me with these words: "Come back *home* soon, don't wait until next Christmas."

Evidently, the audience fluctuated from morning to evening. The actors were always ready to perform.

3.

Uncle Steve became a real homebody after his retirement. Seated at the kitchen table, as I found him for the first time, he was always available for receiving guests and telling stories to them. He hated to leave home, and if he had to pay a visit – for a grandchild's birthday, the annual picnic, or other community affairs – he kept nervously looking at his watch and soon found someone to drive him home. Since his arrest twenty-five years ago, he had not driven a car, and he was satisfied to learn about the outside world through those who brought him the news. He never watched TV, but glanced through the daily paper for headlines and through the Hungarian weekly for obituaries. He depended altogether on oral communication. It was his wife who read the paper, watched the news on TV and used the telephone, meeting social obligations, attending weddings, baptisms and funerals. Funerals annoyed Uncle Steve in particular; he said:

> At the funeral of my brother-in-law, Uncle Takács started to wail, and to cry, "O my Lord, this is the second this year, o my Lord! Who's going to be the next to go, Steve?" "Are you looking at me? You're old enough. Who will be next? Don't look at me."

He often said his purpose in telling stories was "to have a good time," "to make people laugh" and "to frisk about." A real anecdote-teller, Steve Boda's style did not follow the strict rules of specific humorous narrative genres. He spoke rather liberally in a free conversation manner, setting his stories into realistic contexts. In this way, his anecdote style was similar to that of legends. (Bausinger 1967: 118–136; Neumann 1967b: 137–148.)

He often related his stories to situations with which he was familiar. They all took place in the *Székelyföld*, in the Calumet Region or in generally known cities like Budapest, New York, Cleveland or South Bend. His characters were Székely tricksters, Gypsies, Blacks, Irish, Scotch, or Jews, in addition to the general run of fools and tricksters. He often went so far with localization that he diluted the punchline of his stories by repeating incredibly stupid acts and utterances – as in the story quoted above of Jesus's birth in Pennsylvania. The responsive audience, with his wife as choir leader, encouraged him to involve himself in the tales. He would even go so far as to add his own judgments and personal opinions, giving the impression that the account was based on a real experience. In one of his "madhouse" jokes, localized in Logansport, Indiana, for example, a doctor went to see the patients:

> "Come with me," said the director. So they walked. There is a young man behind bars, shaking the bars. "What's the matter with this, do you know?" the doctor asked. "Poor man got married, he was married hardly a week . . . well, a *roomer* eloped with his wife. And he went crazy, because he loved her very much. The fool!" They walk, and walk. *Well*, there is another young man behind bars and . . . and he said: "What?" He said, "What is this?" "This is, this is the one who eloped with his wife. He also went mad." [Laughs. General laughter: six people are present.] *Yeah*. He went crazy. The fool. He deserved it, sure. Why did he have to bother? *What?*

Obviously, the success of this joke was enhanced by the audience's familiarity with earlier boarding house love-affairs within the ethnic group. Another comes still closer:

> The man goes to the *bartender*: "Hey, Joe, give me a *pint* beer!" "Man, you're drunk. Sorry, no beer." "No? You don't serve me?" "No. Now look. I tell you, you are drunk, I tell you. You're drunk." Well, you know, it was summer and the swinging door, you know, was open in the *saloon*. And he said, "You know what? I am not drunk." Well, um, a cat went out from the *saloon*. And its tail was up high and went out. And the man said to the *bartender*: "You know what? I am not drunk," he says, "I can even tell you that I can see that a one-eyed cat just came in, it has only one eye." And the cat went out, not in, his tail was raised, see, he only saw this. The dupe. "Get out of here you fool." *Yeah*. I knew this man. This happened here, in Indiana Harbor. *Honest to God*!

The popularity of Steve Boda as a "funny guy" was not earned only by his repertoire of one hundred and fifty-eight humorous stories. In addition to these, he liked to clown and make people laugh by citing grotesque situations, people's strange and funny sayings, word-games, puns, tricks and puzzles. He also liked to play practical jokes on his visitors. He often quizzed his guests: "How can you take a broom from a room with closed door and windows?" (By taking it to pieces and pushing the broom straws one by one through the keyhole.) He always had some funny experience that had happened to him "just the other day." Once a public opinion agency asked him to watch a "gangster picture" on TV and polled him over the tele-phone. Uncle Steve hated the telephone and did not pick it up if his wife was around, but this time he did, and improvised a hilarious story around the conversation he had with the girl over the gangster picture. He poked fun at such everyday events; however, this kind of improvised humor did not enter the standard repertoire but remained short-lived and was easily replaced by another topical story.

The pieces of this standard repertoire, that could be ascertained by more than one recording and by repeated hearings during the period of our acquaintance, fall into the following categories:

(1) Anecdotes which were localized in the ethnically mixed Calumet Region or in the Hungarian ethnic community, within or outside of the Calumet; these deal with common concerns of the ethnic and non-ethnic population in the area. Many fall into the "dialect story" cate-gory (Dorson 1948: 113–50).

(2) Traditional anecdotes (Schwänke) classified in the Type index; these were mostly numbskull and trickster stories. All of these origin-ated in *Székelyföld* and were learned in childhood and imported by the Bodas or their friends and relatives. New additions to the old stock were acquired from newcomers or from those who had visited back home.

(3) Short, punchline jokes of diverse nature and origin: obscene (mostly in Hungarian or Székely urban or rural setting), political (related to topical events both in Hungary and in America), ethnic and racial (partly fashionable, widespread American, and partly local banters from the Calumet Region).

When the couple was alone, they always spoke in Hungarian, although the language of the stories varied according to their origin. Even if a pure Hungarian audience was present, stories were told in a characteristic mixture of English and Hungarian, depending on the setting and the actors. If actors in a story were English speakers, they were cited in English and then repeated in Hungarian translation, mixed with distorted loanwords. A part of a story told at an evening get-together after two neighbor women mentioned something about the ignorance of hillbillies will illustrate Uncle Steve's English style.

This lengthy story is about a simpleton who came from Kentucky to work for Inland Steel but who worked at Youngstown unwittingly because he could not read the sign and caught the wrong bus every morning:

'Yeah, listen," he said, "you are good people," see? "Come, and," he says, "look me up." And I say, "How should I look you up? Where do I find you?" *"You know what?" "What?" "You know where*

Louisville, Kentucky?" You know, Louisville is a big city. I say: *"I been there." "You know, when you come to Louisville, Kentucky?"* so should I stop like this. *"This was a jackass, see?"* "When you get there," he says, "that we go to the *country, reach four corners, you know, four corners?"* I say: *"Me know me side."* "Ok. *Here a drugstore, right-hand side, there a drugstore. And on the left side, left, that's a left-hand, see, there are saloon. There's a stockhouse and you turn that way, left at the saloon. You don't go straight, don't go left, you just turn right and you go, aaa – let's see, about two or three miles and then about two or three miles just go fast and don't go right, go left again. Turn left and about a mile and a half and then you stop. And you look. See, my wife she has lived there but we have no gas, we burn wood and you see the smoke above my chimney: that's my house."* "Well, if I go, I'll never find it. Well, there are other places too with *smoke in the chimney.* Oh no," I say. *"I never catch you that way!"* He says: "Just come, where the smoke comes that's my house." Well, I say "Where is your house, in what street?" "Oh," he said, "No name, no street, no number, nothing, nothing. Where you see smoke, that is my house."

At this point Aunt Ida could not keep silent. She did not like her husband to put down a former buddy who stayed with them for a while and felt that she had to say something nice about Southern migrants. Actually, she felt bad also because an Appalachian family rented their basement rooms.

Mrs. B.: These here are no such ignorants. Their *brothers* and *sisters* are all *teachers*, and one is in *college.* And the other is a very rich man in Florida. He is the poorest among them. But they are very fine people. And they love to be with us so much because he can save much of his good earnings. They are used to us and the little girl is always here in the kitchen. She loves my cooking very much, better than that of her mother, she says her mother cannot cook so well. If I make some stuffed cabbage, I have to give her some. She just loves it. Baked sausage, too . . .

4.

If Uncle Steve is the entertainer in the husband-and-wife team, Aunt Ida is a firm believer and the possessor of mystic knowledge. Unlike her rationalist husband, she is driven by an insatiable hunger to seek the secret powers that govern human life and death, destiny and continual contact with the dead. Her curiosity is inexhaustible, she is always looking for people to share her interest, people who can tell her about similar observations. Her primary inspiration, however, came from within, from the extranormal experiences she has had since early childhood. She has a large stock of stories on second sight, precognitive dreams, sighting of ghosts in various shapes, encounters with evil spirits and witches, evil eye, sickness and healing by magic.

As a legend teller, Aunt Ida, always persuasive, is heated by her own conviction. She calls for response, stimulates the skeptic to argue and the believer to testify. Her style is captivating, dramatic; her language is more artistic than that of the average legendteller. The essential story in Mrs. Boda's legends is usually preceded or followed by her reflections concerning its truth. "What makes that you think of someone and then he will come to you?" "How would this be possible if there would be no way for a ghost to return?" "How would you explain my dream of three rivers of blood that warned me of the car accident of my three relatives next day, but at different places?" "If you say charms do not help, how could my mother cure the sick horse the vet gave up, just by commanding the disease to get out of its body?" All her life Aunt Ida had been in touch with professional healers, seers, palmists and clairvoyants in whom she had great confidence. A "knowing woman" told her from a book a week before her wedding was to take place, with an unwanted young man, that her family would not go through with their plan to force the marriage. She liked to visit magic practitioners in need. When she worked in a canning plant in Kansas City during the Great Depression, a seer predicted her near-fatal sickness and surgery. She consulted a Negro clairvoyant in Gary after her sister died. The woman lit a candle, prayed and started to talk Hungarian, without knowing what she was saying, because the dead sister spoke through her. Aunt Ida knew a Croatian, a Gypsy and a Mexican clairvoyant in the Calumet Region, but there was also several among her friends and relatives who had ESP, could read from cards and had precognitive experience of some kind. She knew all the legends that had currency in the Region.

Ida Boda's legend repertoire and knowledge of related beliefs and activities can be traced to the archaic system of folk religion characteristic of the culture in which she was born. Some of her stories occurred in the environment of her native village. They happened to people she knew, or people she had heard of, who had died before she was born. Some of the stories came from the personal experience of close or distant relatives, but most of them came from her mother and grandmother, who must have been as much attracted to supernatural belief as she is. The wrongdoers and the victims of these legends were known as local villagers. Certain topics were the main concerns of the peasant women: the milk witch, the changeling, bewitching of babies and domestic animals, horseshoeing the witch, witches' Sabbath, demon as lover, treasure hunt. Mrs. Boda also has a number of stories about local healers who miraculously cured people whom doctors could not help. She could recite magic prayers that were several centuries old (Hampp 1961). One which she claims her mother learned from a Catholic priest gave her goosepimples. In spite of the strong ties of these legends to the Székely land, they have not faded from memory, but were kept within the standard repertoire because of the constant company of women who had a similar Old World peasant indoctrination. Apart from the classic European legend themes, she inherited a sensitivity that is not necessarily and narrowly culture-bound but can exist in changing social situations. It is the interest in second sight, precognition, spiritualism and dream visions that have continually kept its topicality in the modern industrial environment. Aunt Ida had many prophetic visions and tragic dreams. One particularly impressed her: she saw her mother's funeral at the same time that her mother died in the old country.

Mrs. Boda had three overwhelming experiences that she never could forget. She repeated these whenever she could grab the floor from her husband. All three are characteristic of her personality as a legend teller and revealing of the consistency of folk belief patterns despite the change of cultural values. One is about the death of her first-born child by the effect of Evil Eye in the Old Country. The other is about her miraculous rescue from suspicion of theft by a Kansas City clairvoyant who told her where to find the missing money. The third is about the already quoted spirit crying at the door. The legends formulated from these experiences were of general interest for the audience that reacted in accordance with the rules of legend communication. For Aunt Ida, the most effective and lasting was the memory of the crying dead imitating her mother's voice at the door. In addition to this, she recounted several other ominous death signs related to the premature death of her young niece. I have heard these separate stories quite often and recorded them three times, always in the presence of a different audience. The supportive behavior of the listeners, countering Uncle Steve's negative attitude, was interesting. This situation illustrated the merger of Old World tradition with modern American supernaturalism.

Nothing can better demonstrate legend performance in its proper context of controversy than to quote here two brief sections from a tape-recorded session. In this particular case, Mrs. Boda was joined by a close friend, Mrs. Ethel Deme, as co-proponent of legends and their belief ingredients, while Uncle Steve acted as the usual *advocatus diaboli*. Mrs. Deme is also from the *Székelyföld* but from a different district; the Bodas did not know her in the Old Country. She lost her husband twenty years ago and now lives with her daughter's family. Like Aunt Ida, she is active in church work, and the two women meet regularly. After Sunday services, she sometimes lunched with the Bodas. The following sample was taken from an all-afternoon conversation and is representative of the communication of legends anywhere where they are alive.

Mrs. D.: Why do we have always to think of the person of whom we will hear news? Even my daughter believes this is so.

Mrs. B.: Me, too. Last night I went to bed and my poor dead niece came to my mind because I laid on my side. Poor Betty could not turn around, she was always on her back. The middle board immediately fell from my bed. It never did. With a big noise it fell under the bed. I got such a scare, I shuddered. It made a big clack under the bed.

Mrs. D.: There are no board beds today . . .

Mrs. B.: *No-no*, not the board, there is a board under the *spring* that supports the *spring*. But it clapped so strong and I was so frightened. Wasn't it that her spirit came back and sat on the spring?

Mrs. D.: Sure thing, one never knows.

Mrs. B.: It made such a terrible noise. Poor Betty, she could never lay on her side . . .

Mrs. D.: And the board fell.

Mrs. B.: And I had that horrible feeling . . .

Mrs. D.: Hm. These are true . . . these noises.

Mrs. B.: This was true.

Mrs. D.: Even my grandchildren believe in this, Lyn, the daughter of my daughter. If there is some clap in the house, she knows this is a danger sign. If a mirror or a picture falls from the wall, it is no good. . .[8]

Mrs. B.: *Yes, Mrs.* Davis told me . . .

Mrs. D.: I heard it in the radio. It was also in a book.

Here the conversation is interrupted by Uncle Steve who enters with a glass of goat's milk that was ordered for him because it has less fat than cow's milk. With disgust he occasionally utters a "ba-a" to express his opinion on the topic of the two women.

Mrs. B.: Well, my mother went to town, to Udvarhely with her godmother and as they are on the way back, the town was so about fourteen kilometres from us, it was far for a walk and she asked my mother: "Well, how do you want to go home, in a sieve or on foot?" And my mother said, "*No*, I won't go in the sieve."[9] So they went on foot. But it was rumored that when it was the coldest winter and women were spinning, these have just disappeared somewhere and soon they brought back ripe red cherries. They put them on the table for the spinning women, the ripe red cherries, in winter. In winter. And they were witches. They speedily went to Turkey,[10] brought the cherries and placed them on the table. Yes. My mother said this and she never told a lie, she always used to tell this to us.

Mr. B.: In what did they go? In a sieve?

Mrs. B.: *Yes*. She asked: "Do you want to go in the sieve?" Somehow they turned themselves into spirit shape . . .

Mrs. D.: Broom . . . broom?

Mrs. B.: They flew somehow. And she said: "Hoopla, I be where I want to be" with the broom.

Mr. B.: The English says: *bullshit* . . .

Mrs. D.: They said broom-riding old witch . . .

Mr. B.: The American calls what you are talking about *bullshit*.

Mrs. B.: Well, *I don't know* . . .

Mr. B.: Aaaah, there is no such thing.

Mrs. B.: You see that the big . . .

Mr. B.: An American, tell this to an intelligent American, he will call it *bullshit*.

Mrs. B.: Listen, scientists are looking into this, isn't that so? You hear me? They directly look after such things to find out . . . well.

Mrs. D.: We went to do our work in the fields. My father got up early and my mother went to milk the cow. And it came out from a big dark cloud. Its tail stayed outside. But it was huge. That snake-dragon.

Mr. B.: Dragon!?

Mrs. D.: My father was not a liar.

Mr. B.: Seven-headed dragon? What?

Mrs. D.: My father saw it, it was very early, it hardly dawned, the clouds laid on the mountains.

Mr. B.: Did it have two heads in front? [jokingly]

Mrs. D.: My father did not see its head only when its waist slid from one cloud into the other. And there was a horrible rain that morning. My grandmother predicted of this – she still lived then. "Dear son," she said, "Rain will stop." Because it rained for six weeks and they could not do any work in the fields. Because he saw the snake-dragon.[11] My father said that. And he did not like superstition, he did not want to listen to such talks, no. But he saw the snake-dragon.

Mrs. B.: They toll the bells so that the clouds dissolve . . .[12]

Mrs. D.: In Erzsébetváros the great Armenian, no the Greek church, was dedicated that if the bad weather comes . . .

Mrs. B.: They always tolled the bells when the storm came . . .

Mrs. D.: The bells are consecrated for that, otherwise it would not help. I was a young woman, o my God, as I remember, poor hens were all flooded in the pen . . . it was hoeing time . . .

Mrs. B.: My dear mother stood on the porch and when the storm came, she crossed the sky and prayed the prayer she learned from the priest whom I told you about and I remember . . .

Mr. B.: But you still know how the prayer went?

Mrs. B.: Oh yes. "They set out . . . be off, be off to Venice, take three drops of the milk, three drops of the Virgin Mary, take it to faraway snow-covered mountains where you could not harm anybody, anything . . .!" But there was more to it and then she crossed herself in the name of the Father, the Son and the Holy Ghost, Amen. And then the cloud dissolved nicely. I really know this.

Mrs. D.: Ida! Ida, listen.

Mrs. B.: *No*, he does not believe anything.

Mr. B.: Now, wait a minute. If there were so many smart people in the world, you hear me: in the whole world that it comes . . . when the radio warns ahead that the tornado is coming, take care, if there would be such a man who could stop it . . .

Mrs. D.: No, man could not do that . . .

Mr. B.: Noooo, naaa, you can pray as much as you want, once it comes, it takes everything.

Mrs. D.: Oh, but it avoids many places.

Mr. B.: Oh well, but not because you say all this hocus-pocus. To hell.

Mrs. B.: This is a prayer.

Mr. B.: Prayer is *all right* but not to take away the storm.

Mrs. D.: But the prayer can help.

Mr. B.: It would not. The English say: *bullshit* of this kind of talk. Ah. Pray or curse is all the same.

Mrs. D.: I don't like this kind of talk . . .

Leaving the home of the Boda couple, one becomes suddenly aware of the enormous distance that separates the surrounding inscrutable, noisy, polluted industrial town from this profoundly harmonious haven within it. There are many good reasons for the perfect harmony between Ida and Steve Boda: mutual love and respect for each other, warm relationship within the peer group, and, of course, the feeling of being well provided for. But the folklorist can see a significant dimension of the couple's union: the capability of turning their happy, successful marriage also into the creative, successful symbiosis of their narrative art.

TWO OLD WORLD NARRATORS ON THE TELEPHONE

Gary, Indiana, situated on Lake Michigan southeast of Chicago, is one of the giant industrial cities in the United States (Moore 1959). Gary and vicinity accommodate the world's largest steel mills, and almost all the residents of Gary work in the plants or cater to the needs of their employees. Besides the majority black population, there are about twenty sizable and another thirty smaller nationalities residing in Gary. Huge freighters and tankers ply the lake, thousands of trucks and automobiles congest the superhighways cutting across the city, and the network of tracks within the city runs freight trains day and night. The wind blowing perpetually above the Great Lakes whirls black smoke and mixes yellow and purplish-pink poisonous steam into the air. It is an unlikely scene for peaceful traditional storytelling.

But "Aunt" Marge and "Aunt" Katie, both residents of Gary, are born village storytellers. What can they do, how can they make use of their talents, their fantasy, sense of humor, pleasure of narration, in this most unlikely spot of the world?

It was in the fall of 1964 when I first met them. I had ample opportunity to study the anachronistic manifestation of their many-sided gift within the limits of the industrial city. I was able to observe them as their houseguest and also as a participant in the communal life of the Hungarian ethnic enclave to which they belong. It was easy to explore their way of life on both workdays and holidays, and to follow their contacts with the outside world as means of expressing themselves. Nevertheless, evaluating their oral folklore and their personalities required comprehension of their cultural environment, so I had to familiarize myself with the worldview, value system, and aesthetic standards of the ethnic community. The dominant Hungarian peasant tradition I knew had gone through considerable modification. Hence, the function and quality of the actual oral literature would have been difficult to understand without knowledge of the ambiguous, uneven, and variable processes of this modification.

Sociologists dealing with immigration to the United State have come to an agreement concerning the sequence of the stages of acculturation, assimilation, and integration. When immigrants, attracted to this country by economic opportunity, decided to stay for good, they settled in ethnic communities, but within these communities there have been unlimited variables due to ethnic, situational, and positional differences (Hough 1920: 18–19; Moore 1959: 356–357; Dégh 1966: 551–556).

The history of the steel industry in Gary and in the neighboring steel cities belonging to the larger Calumet Region can be traced in the life history of the Hungarians and the other ethnic communities in the area. The pioneer group that transformed the marshland around the Little and the Grand Calumet rivers and on the sand dunes on the banks of the lake was composed of the masses of Southeastern and Central European peasantry (Handlin 1951: 7–36; 1959: 26–29). They were the builders of the industrial plants in which they acquired jobs, and they were the builders of the cities in which their dreams of comfortable living came true. Among the cities in the area, Gary was the last to be built, following the construction of the plants of the U. S. Steel Corporation in 1906. The company settled its employees close to the workshops and named the new city after Judge Elbert H. Gary, chairman of the board of directors (Moore 1959: 254). Because the ethnic settlements were established on uninhabited land and could therefore develop more or less by themselves, they were able to retain their ethnic character.

> The Calumet Region became a mixing bowl, rather than a melting pot, of races and nationalities. Melting pot suggests a oneness of features and characteristics produced by a simultaneous amalgamation of different elements. This did not occur in the Calumet area. Instead, the movement of the population groups into the region during the first fifty years was such that each had the opportunity to make its presence felt. . . . The presence of so many nationalities and races produced a variety of flavors almost unique. (Moore 1959: 244.)

Both our storytellers were "charter members" of the Hungarian ethnic colony of Gary that has been dissolved now for some time. Both remember the initial hardships in the barren land and can tell when and in what succession the main buildings were constructed. The fate of the Hungarian community and other ethnic communities was shaped by the fluctuation of economic conditions. Depression, war boom, the importation of new workers, and other factors transformed the ethnic composition of the city. Broadway, the fifteen-mile-long main street and business district of Gary, is today inhabited almost exclusively by blacks. The folklorist who wants to visit more than one of his informants of European extraction during the day has to travel some fifty to eighty miles from house to house within the limits of the city.

Gradually, new cultural features accumulated in different layers of the dominant peasant heritage. In spite of outward appearance, the immigrant generation did not change its essentially peasant world-view and behavior. The commonly acknowledged attributes of the initial phase of immigrant readjustment, such as language learning, adoption of different food and dress habits, and acquisition of new technical skills (Willems 1955: 225–226; Park 1950: 138–151), remain imperfect up to this day and have not affected important cultural traits. The process of assimilation followed an uneven course, depending largely on the need for individual adjustment. At the time of their retirement, even those who were exposed to the impact of the dominant culture returned to the old world lifestyle abandoned in early youth.[1] We can speak only of attitudinal changes, which affect mostly the material life of the immigrant generation. Yet these changes are extremely meaningful, since they react on the essential values of the subculture itself. Assimilation generally occurs with the first American-born generation, whereas integration becomes complete with the second.

The acculturation of the Gary settlers is the result of two parallel processes: the substitution of the urban-industrial way of life for that of the rural-peasant, and the accommodation of national minority groups to a multiethnic environment. Consequently, the form, role, and function of folklore underwent a basic transformation from its peasant model.

Mrs. Katie Kis and Mrs. Marge Kovács today live quite a distance from each other in neighborhoods to the east and west of Broadway. Mrs. Kis is eighty-six, and Mrs. Kovács is seventy-five. They came from the same Hungarian ethnic region and brought the same linguistic and cultural backgrounds to the United States. Like many other peasant immigrants prior to World War I, neither Mrs. Kis's husband nor Mrs. Kovács's father saw New York except for the landing port, Ellis Island. Typically, immigrants traveled by train directly to one of the industrial cities on the East Coast, where earlier immigrants helped them find places to live and work. Their jobs were in factories and mines. Meanwhile, the dream of making enough money to return and buy land in the Old Country faded because of the war and the Depression (Lengyel 1948: 127). Our informants, Mrs. Kis and Mrs. Kovács, followed their elders and settled with their families in the Hungarian ethnic neighborhood of the newly erected midwestern industrial metropolis. Neither of them has ever seen any of the big cities, the skyscrapers, and the various technological wonders that are characteristic of urban America.[2] Having left the familiar environment of their home village, they sought protection in a neighborhood similar to what they knew. Mrs. Kis and Mrs. Kovács were next-door neighbors in the Hungarian community of Gary and were related by marriage. They belonged to the same Hungarian Protestant church, the Church of Christ, that acted as the protector of the national identity and became the center of social activities for the group (Handlin 1951: 117–143; 1959: 77–84; Fishman 1966: 15–16, 20–22).

As long as the Hungarian community did not exceed its original four-block area in downtown Gary, its population was not forced to learn English or to adjust to an urban way of life.[3] When the steelworker's earnings became steady and the typical Hungarian peasant frugality and hard work bore fruit, the families prospered and the old community began to disperse. One by one, families moved to a healthier location in the "green belt" within the city limits, away from the congested, polluted streets. They built their comfortable homes according to the standard of respectable American workingmen: the three-bedroom type with a roomy basement, one bathroom, a screened or open porch, and a handsome garden. The homes were well equipped with modern conveniences. In such homes the "front room" has wall-to-wall carpet, and the kitchen is large and bright with big windows, built-in cabinets, a freezer, and other household appliances. Who would ever compare this home to that of a Hungarian peasant family? Yet this house represents the fulfillment of a peasant dream. It is roomier and certainly more luxurious than the house of the biggest farmer in the Old Country, but its interior arrangement and decoration and its functions are very much the same.

Taking the homes of Mrs. Kis and Mrs. Kovács as models, we find similarities to their Old Country homes. As in the Hungarian peasant's home, the center is the kitchen, not only as a place where food is prepared and consumed but also as a place of relaxation for the members of the household and a favorite gathering spot for neighbors, relatives, and intimate friends. The heavy decoration of the kitchen walls is remarkable. Colorful ceramic plaques, plastic fruit, flying birds, framed articificial flowers, and other ornaments from the supermarket replace the earthenware plates of the peasant kitchen. The embroidered prayers, the "house blessings" made by the lady of the house, are as popular as in the Old Country. The function of the living room is the same as that of the "clean room" of old. It is crammed with the most cherished knickknacks but is not used much. American in-laws, acquaintances, and other callers are seated here. Mrs. Kis still has the traditional chest of drawers full of trinkets on the top and surrounded by family photographs. Mrs. Kovács, on the other hand, has replaced the chest with a vanity that gives more room for family snapshots and keepsakes. Besides the objects in this "sacred corner," the walls of the living room are decorated with pictures of her parents on their wedding day and of her father in his military attire, framed certificates of citizenship, and a faded wreath from her father's grave. It is also interesting to note that the porch, like its Hungarian equivalent the "tornác," served as the farewell place where visitors are shown out and kept for a while, to emphasize hospitality.[4] Outside the home is the garden, not the spotless smooth lawn of suburban American homes but the colorful carpet of flowers in front of the windows. It is a source of pride to grow a Hungarian flower garden, and the women are eager to get the seeds of the favorite geranium, petunia, mignonette, rosemary, rose mallow, and gillyflower. They order the seeds from the Old Country, and they exchange breeds with friends. The backyard, on the other hand, displays a touching holdover of the peasant vegetable patch, evidence of the tenacity of the traditional ethnic diet. The care of vegetables is normally in the hands of the master of the house. Since both the informants are widows, they tend and renew faithfully year after year the plant stocks on the patch built by their husbands, giving away the excess of herbs and vegetables.

Mrs. Kis and Mrs. Kovács reside today in their comfortable homes completely alone. They have no financial difficulties, since their pensions and Social Security benefits cover their immediate needs. All the extras are well taken care of by their children and grandchildren. However, their lives are marked by isolation and solitude, largely because of the dissolution of the old ethnic community, the dissemination of the neighbor families, and their inability to adjust to this new environment. Those above the age of sixty who lived through their active years within the ethnic ghetto found themselves in a strange neighborhood at old age. The lively system of kinship and neighborhood contacts had been replaced by an environment in which there are neighbors whose customs and language they do not understand. At the same time, their old family ties had fallen apart. Their children prefer to speak English with their American-born spouses of diverse origin, and their grandchildren, as a rule, do not speak Hungarian at all. Meanwhile, the most prominent cause of isolation is the enormous distances within the city. It is difficult for relatives to spend their little spare time after working hours on the busy rush-hour highways in order to pay a short visit. The relatives of Mrs. Kis and Mrs. Kovács are more devoted than the average, but their visits are still usually limited to Sunday afternoons, except for occasional calls to deliver essential foods or medicine or to do some urgent repair.

Both the elderly women remain by themselves almost every day of the week and almost every hour of the day. Aunt Marge told me once: "Sometimes I do not talk to anyone for a whole week, only to myself." The size of the city condemns them to solitude and to boredom. They do not own cars, as women of the immigrants generation; they never even learned how to drive a car. They are too old for long hikes, and even if they were able to walk, there would be no place to go in the big noisy city full of unknown people. The ethnic church still stands in the old neighborhood, but the neighborhood itself is no longer Hungarian. Church services would still be available to them if there were someone to drive them there. Occasionally the minister does gather the senior members for the Hungarian language services, since their relatives participate in the English service – if they have not relinquished membership in the ethnic church entirely in order to increase their status by joining a more attractive suburban church.

All these facts suggest a hopelessly bleak and useless existence, almost like being in a prison. Nevertheless, the lives of Mrs. Kis and Mrs. Kovács are anything but bleak. Their solitude does not mean apathy or desperation or merely waiting for the years to pass. Loneliness shows itself when they warmly welcome even occasional visitors, such as a repairman, the mailman, the deliveryman, or the insurance agent. Once in the kitchen, visitors are overwhelmed by funny stories, which can be enjoyed despite the language deficiency. But except for the rare pleasure of telling stories for a live audience, what makes life bearable, even pleasant, for these women of cheerful disposition? In other words, how do they spend their time?

The telephone plays the predominant role in maintaining and transmitting folklore, as well as in keeping Mrs. Kis and Mrs. Kovács in touch with the outside world and passing on news. Their children call them daily, and they may talk more than once a day if a problem arises. In such cases, the telephone substitutes for personal visits, but a call lasts only for minutes.

The telephone is also almost the exclusive communication link between members of the immigrant generation. Our storytellers discuss with their friends, who are as isolated as themselves in their own homes, the social rites in which they participated or of which they have learned. They exchange opinions on weddings, birthday parties, meetings of the ladies' aid association, and bingo parties. They enjoy gossiping, and the telephone is an excellent outlet for discussing the behavior of the others. Unusual events affecting the life of the ethnic community are passed around in minutes through the telephone. Following a report about a sudden illness or death, female members of the community call all their acquaintances and stay up all night to enjoy the pleasure of passing on the sensational event embellished by naturalistic details. The telephone spreads personal news on health and everyday trifles and is a means of comparing notes on events from the outside world as understood, or more often misunderstood, through television.

Besides the usual exchange of opinions, our informants use the telephone for telling stories, although they limit their talk with busy younger people to the minimum. Experience has taught them telephone etiquette prescribing who can call whom and when, and how to refuse an unwanted call.[5] But Mrs. Kovács and Mrs. Kis converse for hours and never exhaust their pleasure in narration.

As is proper, it is usually Mrs. Kovács, the younger, who greets her older partner each morning with: "Good morning, Godmother, how did you sleep?" "All right. And how about you?" Thus, storytelling is usually launched. These telephone narratives almost without exception begin with an actual experience: a dream, a strange feeling bring up old memories, something seen on television or heard on the radio, a funny spectacle observed through the window. This is usually linked to an anecdote formalized as real event. Mrs. Kovács, for example, mentioned that an old fool bragged about his readiness to wed her. "Just like the gypsy who talked about marrying the princess. . . ." On another occasion, Mrs. Kis told me about the latest visit of the minister. Giving a lively presentation of their talk, Mrs. Kis reproduced her answer to the minister's question about whether young girls in her hometown used to wear short skirts like girls do nowadays. The short skirt reminded her of a well-known obscene joke concerning the short skirt of the lady teacher and the view of the little boy, and she reshaped the story as a truthful event involving her own grandson. In this fashion, the two narrators exchange folk narratives in long succession over the phone. Obscene anecdotes alternate with jokes and witch stories in turn.

Mrs. Kis and Mrs. Kovács love to laugh, and they laugh freely, totally relaxed by their phone stories. One can hardly wait for the other to finish a story, having an even better story to tell. They do not hesitate to ridicule their acquaintances, and they do not spare themselves either, once they begin to joke. They know very well that it does not fit their age to laugh loudly. Their daughters are quite critical of their long phone conversations. Mrs. Kis's daughter does not like phone gossips. "You two understand each other!" remarks Mrs. Kovács's daughter-in-law. A good source of laughter is one of Mrs. Kovács's neighbors, Mrs. Nagy, a nosy old woman, a real paragon of virtue. Because of her barbed words directed against the hilarity of Mrs. Kovács and Mrs. Kis and their "laughing with their mouth open," Mrs. Kovács compares Mrs. Nagy to the woman in one tale who fixed her mouth in front of the mirror before going to a wedding party, then had to talk to someone on her way, so she returned home to fix her mouth again.

I have observed and recorded telephone narration sessions with Mrs. Kis and in turn with Mrs. Kovács. Although I always questioned the caller about the responses at the other end of the line, this one-sided recording did not give me a total picture of the joint performance of the two informants. The only way to find out about their cooperative storytelling was to bring them together at the home of one or the other. During the period of observation, I found the standard repertoire of the two narrators to be variable and continuously renewed by actual experiences.

While the telephone functions as a means of acquisition and transmission of knowledge and also as a means of keeping up communication with the ethnic group, television opens a window into the unknown world in the intimate surroundings of their comfortable homes. The set is on almost all day, and its presence is felt even unconsciously through its little noises. It is on while the women perform daily chores and receive guests; even if they relax in the lounge chair in front of the set, it does not matter what is on the screen. They are not at all disturbed that they do not fully understand what is happening there. Both Mrs. Kis and Mrs. Kovács were able to list the shows they favor, but they were unable to describe the contents. Colorful action, spectacular scene, dancing and singing and buffoonery entertain them well enough without dialogue. Misconceptions arise because of their inability to distinguish fiction from reality. The traditional realm of folk belief is reaffirmed through science fiction, modern ghost stories, and supernatural mysteries. Mrs. Kis is especially sensitive to TV witch stories. When watching the serial "Bewitched," she immediately responded: "As I saw this witch last night, you know the witches of our village came to my mind. Oh my God, I left the village because I was so scared of them. . ." Here she tuned in a well-shaped belief legend about the witch who was caught and shod with horseshoes when she pursued young people in the shape of a yellow filly.

Information about the outside world transmitted by television in the United States is hardly stranger and less intelligible than the language of the newspapers, the sermon of the minister, or the speech of the intelligentsia, even in the Hungarian village where Mrs. Kis and Mrs. Kovács were born. The attitude of peasant immigrants in the New World is very similar to that of Old Country villagers, who were content with only a partial understanding of the world beyond their own, taking it for granted that the affairs of the masters are none of their business.

Neighborhood relationships of our two narrators are quite different from those in the Old Country or in the original ethnic community of Gary. Friendship and kinship affiliations formed in the old neighborhood proved to be tenacious when people set up houses in different places, while new ties in the new locations had to remain superficial because of the diversity of ethnic origins among the new neighbors. Mrs. Kovács has two Hungarian neighbors, both of them Catholics and therefore members of another ethnic nucleus. One of the families is second generation and speaks only English. Except for the senile 90-year-old grandfather, there is no one worth talking to. With the other aged couple, however, Mrs. Kovács is in a continual village squabble. Mrs. Nagy, a 79-year-old "fussbudget" with a snappy tongue, has been mentioned already. She never stops scrubbing floors, polishing doorknobs, or repainting kitchen walls. Whenever she takes a break in her self-imposed work, she keenly watches the window of her neighbor and usually finds what she is looking for: something she disapproves of.

Mrs. Nagy has lived for sixty years in the United States and never learned to speak English. Still, only the oldest three of her nine children speak Hungarian, and only a broken Hungarian at that. She still lives by the norms of Veszprém County,[6] according to which Mrs. Kovács does not behave as she should. As already noted with regard to telephone narration, Mrs. Nagy objects to Mrs. Kovács's loud laughter and bad conduct. Mrs. Nagy even objects to Mrs. Kovács's guests, her way of treating them, her way of cleaning house. Mrs. Kovács is both annoyed and amused by all this. She never stops talking about it, and as a born entertainer, she imitates Mrs. Nagy, makes fun of her criticism, and incorporates her sayings into racy anecdotes. Listening to Mrs. Kovács, one would believe that the two women see each other often. In truth, they usually observe each other through closed windows, and except for accidental encounters, meet only once or twice a year.

Mrs. Kovács's closest relationship in the neighborhood is with a Rumanian couple. She knew them before they moved out here, and she learned from them most of the charms, magic prayers, and home cures she shows. The husband understands some Hungarian, and they converse in the scanty English they both possess. Other neighbors – a "hillbilly" family, a Polish couple, an Irish couple, and a Croatian-German couple – are the topics of conversation rather than acquaintances. Mrs. Kovács is well aware of ethnic differences and collects every little bit of information about the neighbors, whatever she overhears from behind the closed doors and what she can conclude from the behavior of household members.

There are no Hungarians in the neighborhood of Mrs. Kis. She must content herself with what goes on in the home of the "hillbilly" across the alley, what the many children of the Croatian family across the street do, and how the love affair stands between the boy and the girl in the two American households down the street. She takes notice of unusual sounds and motions, and shapes exciting, horrible, or funny stories out of the meager facts. Contrary to the Hungarian peasant attitude, compulsory for elderly women, neither Mrs. Kis nor Mrs. Kovács breaks her back with housework. They consider themselves entertainers, and thus differ from those retired people who cook and wash and clean all day with an almost fanatic sense of duty in order to justify the usefulness of their own lives. Our informants find other pleasures. This does not mean that they are sloppy and neglect their homes. They take particular care to prepare traditional ethnic dishes for themselves and their visitors. For example, it is most repulsive to them to buy noodles in the store instead of making their own.

Under the circumstances, it is small wonder that the arrival of a guest is welcomed by these village raconteurs who are forced to limit their natural talents to telephone conversation. When relatives announce their intent to stay longer than usual, or if the visitor is in no hurry, like the minister, a church elder, or myself, both storytellers return to the long-abandoned style and tempo of village narration. Once again they live in the environs of their happy youth in the ethnic community where they played leading parts in entertaining at social occasions.[7] Nowadays, if there is a chance, they give generously of the rich store of the folk narratives accumulated in their memories. They incorporate both old and new and retain at the same time the body of their traditional narratives. On these rare occasions, traditional food is always offered with the proverbial Hungarian hospitality. One can visualize the past glory of these two born entertainers in the happier days of the Hungarian community in Gary.

Occasionally Mrs. Kis and Mrs. Kovács leave their homes, usually to attend church and meet old friends in the congregation. Besides attending church services now and then, they occasionally meet their contemporaries in the church hall at benefit bingo parties, baby showers,[8] birthday parties, wedding dinners, and more often at funerals. Women of the immigrant generation contribute their ethnic cooking to the get-togethers. Mrs. Kis is especially popular for her sausage- and noodle-making. The communal preparation of well-liked ethnic specialties is a favorite pastime in the Hungarian churches of the area. The women of the church sell the delicacies in order to increase the meager parish budget. At the same time, the communal work of twenty to thirty women is a unique survival of customary social work of women in the Old Country. While the dull manual work is being performed, the women sing songs; tell tales, jokes and legends; gossip and trade home remedies and ethnic kitchen recipes.

Visits to the doctor for checkups also yield experiences with which our storytellers enrich their narrative stock. They love to talk to doctors and nurses about the condition of their health, and they enjoy medical attention, especially since Medicare is free for them. Receiving "shots," taking medication, undressing in the doctor's office, and watching other patients all generate countless humorous stories with both women. They also like to talk about diseases and cures. In spite of their frequent visits to doctors and nurses, Mrs. Kis and Mrs. Kovács are profoundly interested in traditional home remedies and occasionally resort to them in addition to modern health care.

Traditional entertainers of a diminishing immigrant generation, Mrs. Kis and Mrs. Kovács live happily and enjoy every minute of their limited possibilities to display their talents. They prepare themselves with special enthusiasm for their last public appearance. They look forward to the day when they will receive beloved friends and relatives. They will then be dressed up in their Sunday best, with new hairdos and scarlet nail polish; beautifully rejuvenated by the expert hand of the embalmer, surrounded by flowers, they will be awaiting their guests in the reception room of the funeral home. As in the Old Country village, the farewell reception of the acculturated Hungarian-American in the funeral chapel is of extreme importance. No one regrets saving for the funeral what they would never spend on doctors' bills. Mrs. Kovács, for example, has two thousand dollars in her bank account, but her sons have a hard time making her accept money for her medicine.

When I helped the two narrators to visit each other in person, they were thoroughly delighted. They did not run out of wordplay, jokes, and witty quibbling. Verbal sparring continued for hours until they were quite out of breath. They were grateful for the afternoon full of laughter. They recalled storytelling in the Old Country and in the Gary of their youth. "It isn't worth bringing us together," said Mrs. Kis in a brief pause of laughter. "Once we start cracking jokes, nice and ugly come one after the other," upon which Mrs. Kovács poured out a load of dirty jokes which she allegedly had told to people in the church hall during a bingo party break. "You are a hell of a woman, Mrs. Kovács!" said the men, and the minister avoided looking in her eyes because of embarrassment. Both Mrs. Kis and Mrs. Kovács are typical village jokesters. Their style of narration is similar in many respect, but it also differs.

Mrs. Kis was born in 1882 in a village in southern Hungary. "Born on New Year's Eve," she says with emphasis, "I was the thirteenth child of my mother." She likes to stress the peculiarities of her childhood. The father, an old widower, married the young midwife of the community, who seemed to be the target of village gossip because of her profession, which caused her to be away mostly at night. "People told me, I do not belong to my father. My real father was a big millionaire." Telling about her mother, Aunt Katie pictures an outgoing young woman who liked to dance and sing. She has told the episodes of her mother's life so many times that each has become a refined, well-rounded narrative. She indicates her mother's voice modulation, sings her favorite songs, and shows how she danced. Because her mother did not love her, Mrs. Kis was brought up by her father's sister, an unwed mother whose tragic fate is one of Mrs. Kis's fine epics. Mrs. Kis finished two years in grade school and took up work as a kitchen helper at the estate of the local squire. She was seventeen when the young coachman married her. "Not because of the property," she explained. "Father owned four acres – he was too proud to become a slave of the earth as peasants are."

Her husband left Mrs. Kis with two girls when he went to the United States in 1909. She joined him in Gary in 1913. Her disappointment at beholding the barren land for which she had abandoned house and property is the source of another dramatic story. The daughters did not recognize their father waiting at the depot. There were only shacks on the barren sand hills, and stakes marked the line of the future Broadway. Had she come here to live in misery? Mrs. Kis raised her hands above her head, wringing them with emotion, and said, "I will not stay here. I will go back home." But there was no place to go, because the war broke out. The Kis family shared two rooms with another Hungarian family. Mr. Kis worked in the foundry; Katie went to do housework in American homes. She tells a whole cycle of dialect jokes about the troubles of Hungarian women not knowing English, including many familiar ones, as if they had happened to her. But, in fact, neither she nor her husband needed to learn English, because all their contacts at the factory and in the neighborhood were with Hungarians. They bought the lot and built the house in which Mrs. Kis now lives. Everything was paid for by the time Mr. Kis planned to retire, he was not to enjoy the fruits of hard labor. He was sixty when a mishap in the foundry caused his death. Two years later a good friend of Mrs. Kis, a widower, proposed to the widow. Their adherence to different faiths, however, caused trouble. The husband-to-be, a Catholic, did not want to give up his religion, nor did Mrs. Kis. The Hungarian Catholic congregation denounced them because they had set up house together without getting married, whereas the Hungarian Church of Christ accepted them as they were. Mrs. Kis relates the story of her second marriage in funny and exciting episodes. She never even acknowledged her mate of ten years as a real husband, but consistently talked about "my Kis" with whom she spent the happiest years of her life.

This sketchy life history shows how Mrs. Kis usually formulates her narratives as episodes of her own life. This does not mean that her stories are not in traditional folklore form. On the contrary, Mrs. Kis's stories, as shown in repeated recordings, are well-shaped traditional and variable folk narratives rooted in actual facts. The wealthiest body of her stories seems to come from the old home village and is based on childhood memories. She reshapes them over and over again, describing village life with an almost ethnographic authenticity. She often inserts her stories into the frame of a ceremony, visualizing a baptism, a wedding party, a pig-killing dinner, or a dance she once attended. Getting involved with her narration, she brings the typical village characters to life. She plays the parts of each, imitating the tipsy, the haughty, the bashful, and the braggart.

As for anecdotes, Mrs. Kis prefers the spicy and the lewd, if not the definitely obscene. However, she is most at home in the realm of the supernatural. She firmly believes in magic healing, the curative power of herbs, the evil eye, and the wisdom of seers and fortunetellers. She also believes in witchcraft. Her favorite stories are genuine folk legends, and in telling them she pictures the village community where she was born as a place plagued by malicious witches. She has known the witches who used to sit on the street corners around midnight spinning hemp and beating up young people who dared to be outside in the late hours. She herself was chased once by a witch who turned herself into a dog. Another time, a young woman fooled her husband by changing into a rooster, and another witch tortured a young fellow who preferred another girl instead of her own daughter. Mrs. Kis's father also had firsthand experiences with the supernatural. He attempted to learn superhuman skills at the crossroads, and the fairy folk later made him dance with his own boat.[9]

The stories that originated in the United States differ from the earlier themes, and the scene and sources of inspiration have changed. These narratives reflect the experiences of immigrant and urban life. A group of stories in Mrs. Kis's repertoire focuses on hardship in adjusting to the unknown environment. Another group of stories is less homogeneous. It gives an idea of how and to what extent mass media replace folk tradition as a source of material for new folklore forms. The latest sensations from newspapers, magazines, radio, and television are passed on from mouth to mouth to create well-rounded oral narratives about the crimes, love affairs, and mysteries of the metropolis. The newer anecdotes of Mrs. Kis are partly old forms set in modern context and put in the first person. They tend to be more concerned with sexuality than are the older stories.

Mrs. Kis is a verbose narrator; she expands even brief jokes with a lengthy introduction. She meticulously prepares the comical situations to make the punch line more effective. Her manner of rendition is not only epic but dramatic. She acts out her stories, accompanying them with body and facial motions characterizing the actors. She involves herself in the narrative both as a spectator and as a participant in the event. In other words, she claims credence for her realistic narratives that shift between legend and anecdote. She easily improvises stories upon suggestion. It occasionally happened that she did not know a story I asked for, though she did not admit it. As an accomplished raconteur, in order to gain time until she could find something, she would begin: "It was long ago, to be sure, my lady . . . I was a little girl when this happened . . . isn't that strange? Believe me, this really happened . . . " and so on. Then if she remembered something, often half-heard and half-improvised scraps, she happily recited it instead of what I asked for. Once I asked her whether she had heard of "Diana of the Dune," the mystery woman who, according to historical sources, used to live on the sand dunes.[10] The story Mrs. Kis immediately started had nothing to do with this subject. On another occasion she gave the girl a different name; and the third time she told me the story, the heroine was a close acquaintance of hers who occasionally sought her advice. My interest inspired Mrs. Kis to spin a handsome sentimental story.

Mrs. Kis's narratives are characterized by her personal involvement. All of them stem from a direct experience. As already noted, she has an extremely lively imagination, which carries her far from everyday reality, from solitude and silence. At night or in the early morning, when she lingers between sleep and wakefulness, the moving shadows and the cracking of old furniture acquire meaning. Her dreams and hallucinations are of great importance to her. She remembers the happy and the sorrowful days of the past and lives them again in her memories, and she tells about the colorful play of her fantasy if there is anyone around to listen. Even if she is alone during the day, she might recite a wordplay or a rhyme, sing an old song, or tell a story aloud and laugh or cry at its outcome. Things going on in the neighborhood also stimulate her imagination. Even one example demonstrates her ability to build up a story around mere observations. Mrs. Kis in this case tells about the death of a neighbor with whom she was never actually on speaking terms. The story begins at noon, with the neighbor walking his dog around his grape arbor. Mrs. Kis yells at him jokingly from her porch, "Hi, neighbor! When can I come to the grape harvest?" "You just wait," came the answer, "we will have a dance, you and me!" This jolly conversation was shaped by our narrator only to sharpen the contrasting gloom of the second part of the story. The sound of an unusual vehicle makes her look out some time later, and who is there but the undertaker with a hearse. He is a familiar person, a prominent character in Gary; everyone knows him. Mrs. Kis converses with him, and the surprise turn ends on a tragic note: the same neighbor she had joked with earlier had died.

Mrs. Kovács was born in 1894, not far from the hometown of Mrs. Kis. Her father came to the United States in 1906, and a year later her mother and the children followed. Margie, the oldest, went to work in a cigar factory at thirteen because the family, with four small children, needed the money. Worried about the young girl living as a roomer in a big city, her parents gave her in marriage at fifteen. Her short girlhood was the happiest season of her life. She bought nice dresses for herself and went to dances with other girls. She was reluctant to accept her parent's decision, but had learned to obey. The 31-year-old factory foreman of Hungarian background meant security and well-being. A family picture made at the wedding shows her silent revolt: she has obscured the face of her husband and that of herself with the bridal veil.

As soon as the construction work in the Gary region had started, the family moved there. The father worked for U. S. Steel, the husband for Inland Steel Company. All the brothers and sisters of Mrs. Kovács stayed in Gary, and soon an extended family grew up around her. Six children were born to her, and today she has twenty grandchildren. Most of them are hardworking skilled laborers, respected in the community. Some of the grandchildren attend colleges and universities. They all want to help "Grandma," to make her life happy. But she does not want modern luxuries and the gadgets they bring her. She was definitely angry when her youngest daughter "wasted her money" on a bathroom scale. The elegant dresses, shoes, and hats they give her rest among mothballs in the closet. She does not need them, and maybe sometime her grandchildren might like to have them. She ardently opposes the wastefulness so typical among young Americans. Her house is full of odds and ends that she refuses to throw away.

Mr. Kovács, an obstinate carouser and a boozer, was not easy to live with. Often on paydays he came home from the tavern, beat his wife, and chased his children from the house. However, Mrs. Kovács overcame hard times because of her happy disposition and her strong inclination to humor. One tragedy overshadowed her life: her youngest son was accidentally shot to death at fourteen by a school-mate. She still cannot speak of it without tears, remembering the fatal afternoon. Even if it was difficult for her to cope with her husband's whims, she treated him with the care and reverence required in the traditional peasant family. Fortunately, her husband's love for convivial evenings sometimes gave her the opportunity to attend parties and have a good time in the Hungarian community. Mr. Kovács was an outstanding singer, and his wife learned all the songs he knew and has sung at the Hungarian festivals in Gary. She does not have a musical ear but she insisted on singing some two hundred folk songs into the tape recorder as they came back to her while she was telling stories. Some of the wives of Mr. Kovács's drinking partners became lifetime friends with Mrs. Kovács because of their common lot. The couple spent much time with the Tóths, for example, and their relationship was based mainly on their mutual interest in joke-telling.[11] In the old system it was not becoming for women to leave their homes without their husbands. Mrs. Kovács and her friends, however, always found an excuse to have fun. Whenever they wanted to see a movie or a show, or play cards, they would stop briefly at the get-togethers of the church ladies and then take off. They were always eager to assist with food preparation for the festive occasions of the community.

The social life and the rituals of the Hungarian community were the framework within which the personality of Mrs. Kovács could find its expression. She is much more a social entertainer than Mrs. Kis, the epic narrator with a vivid imagination and a deep feeling for the supernatural. Mrs. Kovács, in contrast, does not lose herself in lengthy dreams; she likes action. She loves company, and the more people around the better she performs. To make fun, even to play practical jokes, is natural for her, even if the audience can be reached today only by telephone. As soon as she thinks of something worth telling, she calls her acquaintances and tells it.

Mrs. Kovács has been a widow for fourteen years. The first few years brought her the freedom and relief she dreamed of, and she quickly became an enthusiastic organizer of social activities and an accomplished performer in the Hungarian community. She recited poems at national celebrations, wrote verses and greetings for name-days, and taught Hungarian dances to the girls. The schoolchildren learned from her how to greet their teacher in traditional verse. She joined the carol singers at Christmas from house to house. Mrs. Kovács likes to masquerade above all and seizes every opportunity to dress

up and act. As other informants tell us, she was always ready to put
on her husband's suit, hat, and boots, paint a mustache with soot,
and fool around at Halloween, at pig-killing dinners, and at wedding
parties. Many people still laugh at the fun they had when she appeared
at a wedding with a carrot fastened to the zipper of her pants and
danced in the traditional bridal dance. However, she did not need a
special occasion to put on an act. Another time, for example, she
visited a neighbor who complained that the tinker did not come to
fix her pots and pans. Masquerading as the tinker, she hammered flat
all the useless pots beyond repair. When the neighbor complained to
her about the clumsy tinker, she gave her some of her own pots. She
would do such things even today is she had the opportunity.

Mrs. Kovács is an intelligent woman, still interested in increasing
her knowledge. She is especially concerned with medical terms and
with the "secrets" of the English language. She learned from the
schoolbooks of the children, but her speech is poor and she tries to
widen her vocabulary by noting words and idioms not heard before.
She keeps a diary, she writes poems, and she learned how to write
letters from a popular book of correspondence. She likes to watch TV
shows, especially the comedies ("The Red Skelton Hour") and the
spectacles ("The Ball-Dance"). She avoids anything violent, exciting,
or horrible.

Cracking jokes is Mrs. Kovács's favorite pastime. Her humorous
skills range from the descriptions of comical situations to the well-
developed anecdote. All genres are represented in her repertoire. Life
is full of funny turns for her, and whether she experienced these
herself or heard them from others, she tells the stories with much
pleasure. The older part of her repertoire contains traditional jokes
and anecdotes that she brought along from her home village, or heard
from older immigrants in Gary, or bartered from joke-telling partners.
Beside a valuable body of gypsy anecdotes, numbskull stories (Kovács
and Maróti 1966), and "slippery" parson jokes, she has a fine set of
dialect stories on words mistaken for something else and oddities of
the different ethnic groups. She does not hesitate to make fun of her
own ignorance, and tells a "true story" about how she allowed her
children to stay away from school by not knowing what it meant to
"play hookey."[12]

The great majority of Mrs. Kovács's stories are pithy jokes, however,
sometimes even reduced to the minimum explanation of a proverbial
saying. These color her conversation, as do her anecdotes. As already
noted, it is her technique to insert jokes into everyday speech, to
illustrate how she or someone else fared. When she could not open
a door that was stuck, for example, and I offered a knife to force it

open, she was immediately ready with a saying, leading to a joke: "Let's try, as the man in the tale said," and then came an obscene joke. Her improvised jokes are as innumerable as her sources – most often everyday events and her talks with and observations of whoever happens to come by.

Mrs. Kovács does not have too many biographical stories. Her memories of the Old Country are fading, so she does not have more than a couple of episodes of her childhood. The stories formulated on her experiences in the United States are also quite weak. She has some stories about her girlhood in the cigar factory, about the life of the family during the Depression when they tried farming and went bankrupt, about the horrible ordeal of the family when gangsters tried to force her oldest son to enter their gang. There are also some horror stories from neighborhood gossip, radio, television, and newspapers. But as we have seen already, Mrs. Kovács does not like to see the tragic aspect of life. She is extremely sensitive; she laughs easily but also sheds her tears easily.

In spite of her rational worldview, she has told me many legends and items of folk medicine. She does not believe in them but she has heard them from relatives, friends, and neighbors all her life. She does not pass them on voluntarily; she told them only at my request. However, she believes that dreams come true and that experiences of pregnant women can result in markings on their unborn children. She has tried magic formulas for getting rid of styes and warts on herself and on her children. "I do not believe in it, but it cannot do harm," she explained to me.

We conclude from this survey that the two storytellers remain as two traditional types mainly because of their constant contact with each other (Dégh 1969/1989). Both of them are community narrators who draw inspiration from and depend heavily on the immediate response of an audience. In their present situation, however, they do not have an actual audience. Resorting to the only means to overcome isolation and the loss of storytelling opportunities caused by the distances in the city, they use the telephone as the vehicle for exchanging stories. Mrs. Kis is a very imaginative raconteur. Her style is rich and abundant; she improvises easily and switches skillfully from the epic to the dramatic presentation. Mrs. Kovács, on the other hand, is a high-spirited performer and jester, with a strong feeling for the humorous. Uprooted from their original setting, both narrators were compelled to avail themselves of whatever materials they could find in an environment hostile to traditional folklore. The composition of their repertoire thus became a mixture of old and new elements, each of them

choosing whatever suited her personality best. Autobiographical
stories usually become particularly important with migrating workers
who enter a new community, because newcomers can always tell
something interesting and different from the usual.[13] This is also true
of Mrs. Kis, whose old memories were polished by the many retellings
into magnificent prose narratives, as refined as her most archaic belief
legends.

The common ground between Mrs. Kis and Mrs. Kovács is mainly
their preference for dialect jokes, their keen sense of the comical in
human errors and frailties. Their abilities to observe people, others
as well as themselves, and to express themselves in jokes and jocular
wordplays are based on common experiences. Both women also have
a remarkable interest in erotic themes. They surpass the usual amount
of obscenity that occurs in the jokes and talk of old peasant women.
Both of them favor discussing sexual affairs, and above all they love
to tell about their own past erotic experiences and project them to the
present. Jocular remarks about a "boyfriend," an old fool, real and
imaginary marriage proposals, and indecent passes are often the topic
of phone talks, winding up in sensual laughter.

Our Gary phone narrators raise a question that was not a problem
when storytelling was observed exclusively in traditional communities. We took it for granted that tradition, performer, and a participating audience had an equal share in the creation of oral narratives
(Dégh 1969). It was difficult to imagine how the quality of the narrative
would be affected by the dominance of one of the three. However,
assuming that the tale audience strongly influences the creative personality of the narrator, the case of Mrs. Kis and Mrs. Kovács demonstrates that the creative individual can overcome unfavorable conditions, can survive, and find her means of expression. It is definitely
worthwhile to investigate storytelling situations in modern urban
life.[14]

THE JOKES OF AN IRISHMAN
IN AN MULTIETHNIC URBAN ENVIRONMENT

Von der Seite der Volkskunde gibt es zwei sehr unterschiedliche,
aber doch gleichwertige Aufgaben der Witzforschung: die eine
Aufgabe besteht darin, den Witz als Erzählform zu erfassen; die
zweite Aufgabe liegt darin, den Witz in seiner Rolle als Kommunika-
tionsmittel zu untersuchen. In einer Zeit, in der sich die Volkskunde
in zunehmenden Masse als Sozialwissenschaft versteht, ist diese
zweite Aufgabe, den Witz in seiner sozialen Funktion innerhalb der
Gesellschaft zu untersuchen, besonders vordringlich und wichtig.
  Es gehört eine psychische Disposition dazu, einen Witz zu erzähl-
en, und es bedarf auch einer gleichgerichteten Bereitschaft, um
einen Witz lustig zu finden und ihn überhaupt anzuhören. In diesem
Sinne ist die Erzählsituation und die Persönlichkeit des Witzerzähl-
ers und -hörers von ebenso grosser Bedeutung wie der Text des
Witzes und Kontextanalysen, d.h. wir wissen noch viel zu wenig
darüber, aus welcher Situation heraus, wann, wie, von wem Witze
erzählt werden. (Röhrich 1977: 31, 32–33.)

As a modest contribution to knowledge concerning joke-telling situations and the role of personality and audience interaction, which
Röhrich rightfully finds almost completely lacking, I am presenting
the transcript of a genuine occasion. For most of my professional life,
I have been primarily interested in the performance of prose narratives
and only secondarily in the texts. This interest prompted me to observe
the processes of telling personal experience stories, legends, tales, and
anecdotes, as they were routinely and spontaneously told in everyday
situations. I tried to avoid the kind of manipulation most folklorists
do by inteviewing and cross-examining narrators privately in a sterile,
face-to-face encounter of their two distinctive cultures. I never
"hunted" or "elicited" folklore but painstakingly tried to minimize
the effects of my intrusion in communities where stories were told. I
was an observer to learn about life and the significance of narration
in society. This is the aim of the collection, description and analysis
of the joking occasion that follows.
  In recent years, much has been written about performance of folklore, but most of the "innovative" ideas and theories did not take

their departure from existing folklore trends (Dégh 1977: 386–406) but were rather adaptations of models from related fields, linguistics in particular, without an attempt at validation regarding the nature of folklore field data. While theorists rightfully encouraged practitioners of folkloristics to divert their attention from the text to the context, from the lore to the folk – to gather folk commentaries, oral literary criticisms; to emphasize "events," communication, the artistic action, and the feedback – the results, so far, have been modest, if not disappointing. While microanalyses of lesser genres in their situational contexts have been successfully carried out, the proponents of the method seemed to be little interested in society – the social context, as well as the personality of the performer. In the domain of folk narrative research, speculation has been little tested on rigorously recorded and described field materials. Rather, texts, resulting from interviews, have been scrutinized for their story and non-story contents in order to document hypotheses (Georges 1969; 1979: 104–110; 1981: 245–252).

Background. Over a period of six years, between 1965 and 1971, I collected ethnic folklore in the Calumet Region of Northwest Indiana bordering on Lake Michigan. This fortress of the American Steel Industry is surrounded by a densely populated area where several – according to some authors, as many as sixty nationalities – settled beginning in the late 19th century. The flow continues till this day; so does the move of ethnic neighborhoods gradually upward from poor tenements to affluent suburbs. This was the place where I first became acquainted with the specific folklore of urban-industrial life in America, the change from Old World peasant to New World industrial lifestyle and worldview through passage from immigrant to ethnic stages of accommodation in a multicultural environment (Dégh 1968–1969: 97–107; Dégh 1969d: 71–86; Dorson 1970: 185–222; 1981). Although I focused on the Hungarian ethnic group, it was necessary to become familiar with the whole fabric of the interethnic network in the region, in order to learn and understand specific features of that group.

It was during the fall of 1971 that Andrew Vázsonyi and I paid a visit to our old friend and treasure-trove of information, Mrs. Arthur Green, the owner and operator of the Baltimore Hotel, right across the entrance of Inland Steel Company. A native Hungarian, born Elizabeth Préda in 1898, she was reunited with her immigrant parents in 1902, and became a lifelong resident of the East Chicago Hungarian neighborhood. Baltimore Hotel is a soot-covered, gloomy tenement, showing industrial filth at its worst; when the wind blows from the Lake, poisonous brown vapor inundates bed linen hung on the clothesline in the yard. But the $9 weekly rate hotel is also a haven. Many immigrants and in-migrants, newly hired workmen, bachelors, widowers and divorcees begin their new career here. Mrs. Green, a perfect bilingual, accepts tenants through the Hungarian Protestant Relief and helps refugees settle and find work. The Welfare Department often places runaway children and rehabilitated alcoholics with her. During the day, the restaurant is the meeting place of people of different racial and ethnic origin; they drink coffee, munch corn chips, and talk. Mrs. Green listens while serving the customers. After five, she opens the bar for customers; she closes early. She does not like to leave the business to others, not even to her daughter. Mrs. Green is a wealthy and shrewd businesswoman who also operates a bowling alley, sells hot sandwiches and Cokes at ballgames and owns valuable real estate. Mrs. Green does not trust anyone. Her Hungarian peasant rules of life conflict with that of her American-born children, grandchildren, and British-born third husband. When she is not too tired after nine o'clock, she closes the business and walks over to the Depot for relaxation. The railroad station is only one block away, and if George McCanky is on the nightshift, there will be entertainment. At least, this is what she promised us when we agreed to join her at George's that evening.

Situation. It was pitch dark when we entered the small room, except for the dim light of a small lamp at the shabby desk next to the telephone. Mrs. Green introduced us to George, the recognized joke-teller in the area. Born in Gary 56 years ago, he was the son of a second-generation Irishman who worked on the railroads in South Chicago and Valparaiso. A lifelong resident of Indiana Harbor, George followed his father's trade because "this was where the Irish were accepted."

Three other men were in the room when we came in. Pete Jacobs identified himself as a Polack ("I go by an assumed name; mine was a mile-long; no one could repeat it") without knowing any Polish or the origin of his family. Young Steve Conti claimed Italian ancestry; he attended night classes at Indiana University's Northwest Campus and majored in sociology. Both men worked at Inland Steel and resided at the Baltimore Hotel. The third man, the neighborhood letter carrier, never said anything while the others spoke, but his bubbly laughter contributed greatly to the merriment of the evening. As it turned out, the three men and Mrs. Green, sometimes accompanied by her daughter Betty, were regular guests at the Depot when George was on night duty. Often, especially on winter weekends, more people came, most single middle-aged workingmen from the hotel or nearby streets. The oldtimers of Indiana Harbor dropped in sometimes to reminisce and exchange jokes. It seems George's repertoire was intended for an audience of men in the same social rank.

The presence of Mrs. Green was not conspicuous. As the patron of hotel guests and an old-time neighbor, she was well-liked by all. Also, because of her seniority, men felt comfortable sharing risque jokes with her. Being so much above the age, personal allusion, like the teasing response of George – "You want his address?" – to her guffaw on No. 18, do not sound provocative. She was appreciative of wit and she honored George's humor with big belly-laughs; her contralto peels of laughter rose above the choir of men's giggles.

We were seated in the background with our tape recorder. George did not mind the instrusion; he trusted Mrs. Green that we were "okay." I was careful not to interrupt the flow of conversation, keeping questions to the minimum. In fact, questions were raised only at the beginning, during general talk about ethnic relations and social conditions in the past. I stopped talking as soon as storytelling began. Yet two times explanations were directed toward the visitors without request, anticipating ignorance concerning the puns in Nos. 26 and 27. Despite this sign of awareness of outsiders' presence, the joke-telling session with George's leading role and lively response from his regular audience can show some features otherwise hard to stimulate.

As usual, George was visited by his friends while he was on duty till the morning hours. The friends came with the anticipation that, as always, George would tell jokes and they would have a good time together. In the barren, poorly furnished room, there was nothing to offer the guests – no booze, not even a pack of beer or soft drink or other treat, and it was uncomfortable to sit on the plain chairs for long. Still, conversation precipitated jokes; jokes provoked laughter, teasing repartees, commentaries, and discussions, which, in turn, led to other jokes. The interruption came when George had to perform his duty. From time to time the phone rang, and he picked up the receiver to learn which freight train was approaching. He then took the appropriate parcels and letter bunches fastened to a loop and walked out to the tracks. The train slowed down and the man in the caboose held out his arm to catch the package. After an interval of five to ten minutes needed for the job, George routinely continued the joke where he left off. He never asked, "Where was I?"; the interruption came naturally to him and to the audience. Narration was built around the expected breaks, as TV shows are interrupted for commercial ads.

The sequence of conversation and joke-telling. When I introduced myself, I did not ask for jokes. I said I was a teacher interested in the history of the town and the people of different national origins. This was the reason that our conversation, which took about two hours, including the breaks, began with general observations on ethnicity, experiences of past discrimination against the "poor people" (non-Anglo-Saxon immigrants).

Like most people in the Calumet, this group of speakers also showed concern with ethnicity on the basis of personal experience. In the recollections of an Irishman, Polishman, a Hungarian, and an Italian, the memory of past discrimination and that of the once-vigorous life of their own ethnic groups intertwined. The rather repetitious talk was interrupted by our question (following Pete's statement that he was a Polack), "How do you feel about Polack jokes?" and led directly into the initial joke-proposition by George. The nonjocular conversation on ethnic experiences was picked up again when triggered by No. 20, possibly because of the participants' identification with the Civil Rights movement. Discrimination against the Irish was discussed, but then the whole theme of ethnicity was dropped for a new, rather philosophical joke (No. 21). It is interesting to note that No. 22, essentially a sex joke, characterizes the Jewishness of the actors through their way of talking to each other and their habit of playing poker. The skillful ethnic portrayal by George, however, did not appear insulting; the punchline was metaphoric speech concerning the sex act. "The slurs are told and enjoyed by members of the group concerned," Dundes says; they are "part of ethnic identity" (Dundes 1971b: 202). In this case, however, talking about self as ethnic in terms of experience and in terms of joking characterization, or about other ethnics in terms of observation and jocular caricature, was carefully distinguished by the speakers. The serious statement was compassionate and thoughtful; the joke was teasing without the venom of hate.

When the joking sessions opened with my question, it was not Pete but George who told two jokes in a row about Irishmen. Both jokes belong to the category Dorson calls dialect joke (Dorson 1948) featuring the greenhorn's ignorance. George continued with two Negro jokes,[1] but soon Pete grabbed the word, initiating a string of playful Polack riddle-jokes in which both George and Steve participated.[2] Soon, however, George got tired of the silly sequence and introduced a longer traditional "horse and buggy" dirty story. Encouraged, Pete's response was another sex joke, but afterwards he continued the farm scene with a clean but "very funny" joke, a "homely one." In the same vein, George told two sex jokes from "the old days of the horse and buggy." Here the chain was broken by Pete, who suddenly remembered a venereal disease joke heard some time ago from George. Pete gave him the cue: the scene from farm moves to the doctor's office. After the joke was finished, Mrs. Green commented on doctors abusing

ignorant female patients, drawing on "real life" information; this
brought up another joke in the doctor's office (No. 19).

There was no clear indication what made George switch back to
the ethnic theme once again, after a little silence and breath-catching.
Pete, Steve, and Mrs. Green commented on ignorance about the word
"intercourse" and then Pete reminded George again about one of his
"choice" stories, leading to the recital of No. 20. The Negro/Polack/
German banker comparative slurring draws real hilarity at this point.
George boasted about his skill in joke application and referred to a
higher status man (a banker) in his neighborhood who loved his jokes.
This one had particular appeal because of the *ad hominem* reference,
"The man laughed until the tears rolled down his eyes." In the discourse, George initiated discussion of ethnic hardships through his
humorous statement of ethnocentrism: "I don't care what nationality
a man is as long as he is Irish." The conversation was silenced by a
phone call.

When George returned, he tried the metamorphosis joke on the
company. It was only Mrs. Green who laughed. Then he challenged
all of us to see if we knew the terms of poker playing. We all knowingly
nodded, so he went ahead, but at the end, to make sure, reasserted
that "You've got to know poker terms" to understand the joke. Before
further jokes, the phone rang again and George, out at the tracks,
away from his audience, remembered again this time an unusual
nonsense joke. He seemed to play a trick on us. He laughed and then
others joined in hesitatingly, whereupon George repeated the punchline, suggesting we try the story on others to experience its effect.

Immediately, George now told a joke which seemed a modernized
version of the Schwank around AaTh 1833**. He made sure that we
all knew what alum was, then explained his imitation of defective
speech. "That's a visual joke." Being rewarded by appropriate laughter, George continued with that which he felt most comfortable – farm
stories. The connective that led from No. 24 to 25 was the minister,
if not entirely in the same role. To prepare his audience, he began
with reference to a recent previous telling: "I just tole a fella this,
today; I told my neighbor." And finally, after appreciating our laughter, he openly made the connection to the two bull jokes by telling
us: "So, that leads to another farm joke, right?"

The phone cut him short here and we left with Mrs. Green shortly
after 11 o'clock.

The Repertoire. Out of twenty-seven jokes communicated during the
evening, George told twenty, Pete three, George and Pete two together,
and Steve two. It became clear during the exchange that George was
a recognized master of jokes whom others identified as such and who

can look back to a long career of entertaining. Except for two incidents, when Pete suggested to George what he wanted to hear, it was George who chose the pieces he wanted to tell, as the conversation themes dictated, or as the participants' comments, questions, demeanor, laughter, gesture, and mimic signaled to him. Detached or unrelated jokes like Nos. 21 and 23 were less common; they mostly occurred after interruption when he walked to the approaching train, temporarily separated from his audience. He seemed to take pride in his joke telling, by making reference to his success and appreciation by others, elsewhere. Clearly, neither Pete nor Steve are storytellers. Pete initiated two and participated with George in two other question-answer riddle jokes during the rapid exchange of the Polack-cycle to which Steve also contributed with two. The performance of riddle-joking (Nos. 5–12) with the participation of three men in equal measure stood apart from the rest and seemed to be accidentally built into George's one-man show. It was in sharp contrast with his well-polished narrational act, more on the side of reporting than entertaining. That the Polack joke cycle was given room after George's initial narrative jokes (Nos. 1–4) may be attributed to the ethnic reference. In other words, jokes about Irishmen and Negroes induced Pete to propose the first Polack joke that caused the interruption of George's usual telling.

From then on, except for Pete's one venture (No. 14), George obeyed his audience's expectation. Audience contribution to George's performance certainly was significant in that it directed and controlled the flow of jokes. Verbal and gestural acts of the listeners, preceding, following, and connecting the stories were advisory, evaluative, and stimulative. Maybe Mrs. Green was the most vocal commentator, but Pete was more suggestive. All participants together reacted regularly with laughter. The length and intensity of laughing was the most telling qualifier of the jokes. From mild smile to giggle and big "ha-ha-ha," interrupted only because the participants ran out of breath, there were fine transitional stages and individual variables. In the midst of the merriment, George never laughed, except when he wanted to tease the listeners or when the punchline did not produce enough satisfaction (Nos. 21, 23). Most of the time he remained stern in his facial expression, making the jokes all the more hilarious.

Beyond performance, the texts of George exhibited a colorful narrative style, well-balanced dialogues, scenery description and characterization. He staged his actors through conversation featuring ethnics (Irish, Negro, Jewish), occupations (traveling salesman, farmer, farmhand, minister), male and female fools. The narrator had a good sense of proportion; his stories were never overextended, and the punchlines

were appropriately delayed. At least half of his repertoire pieces in
this performance were taken from a traditional "old-fashioned,"
"horse-and-buggy days" category, and none of the fashionable urban
joke categories were included. All pieces were punchline-oriented
jokes, yet descriptions of situations and characters reminded one of
the traditional Schwank-style. Eleven of George's stories dealt with
sex, and (not counting his participation in the Polack cycle), five concerned ethnicity; only three were of different orientations. In his choice
of themes for an evening performance, George was faithful to his
multiethnic setting in Indiana Harbor and also to the traditional narrative style of his generation of immigrants with peasant background.
This small sample of his repertoire might be comparable to that of
Steve Boda, the jester of the Hungarian community in the same town
(Dégh 1976: 101–122).

> George: . . . during the Depression . . . everybody was friendly,
> nobody was jealous of each other . . . that's right, everybody talked
> to each other, got along together, but now since these good times
> came, everybody's gettin' independent, everybody seems to be
> better than the other, 'cause they make a little more money . . .
> Interviewer: So you liked it then?
> George: Oh, Depression time, oh sure, you could go to anybody's
> house to . . ., and you'd been welcome.[3] Sure. They had any food,
> they had any extra food, they shared it with you.
> Mrs. Green: They had no money.
> George: That's right. But only thing I can say about this Civil Rights
> business[4] and all this stuff like this here, it's the white people
> that did it. Years ago did it to themselves. Years, years back.
> 'Cause I know certain nationality use' to kick on other nationalities
> and it be certain nationalities livin' in a certain part of town. And
> if certain nationalities comin' to that part of the town, they run
> them out, or called police and put'm in jail or do sumthin' . . .[5]
> Mrs. Green: That was them nationalities before . . .
> George: Yeh, I tell you what. It still works to a certain degree.
> Mrs. Green: Oh no!
> George: It does. I remember a . . . just like here . . . your . . . that's
> right. 'Cause the Irish wouldn't have . . . for the Polacks. That's
> right. 'Cause the Irish used to live away from Grand Boulevard,
> Sunny Side, Indiana Harbor. And the Polish people used to live
> on that side 'cause if they did the police had them . . . the neigh-
> bors do sumthin' to them.
> Interviewer: What?
> George: Uh, ya, it was really so. No, it just . . . it just seemed to be
> that in Sunny Side and Grand Boulevard and First Street and so
> forth, it used to be what you call the superintendents, these vice
> presidents of these mills or politicians, they were better people
> than the rest. And the other people were poor people, and they
> had no use for them. I remember lot of times, I got on Grand
> Boulevard, as soon as I go down Grand Boulevard . . .

Interviewer: Where the Hungarians lived?

Pete: Well, they lived all over Carey Street in Indiana Harbor, they were Hungarian people, Polish people, Slovak people, colored people. They all live there, they all get along good, no trouble. Irish people . . . some . . .

Interviewer: What are you?

Pete: I'm Polack, Polish . . .

George: Tell'm sumthin'.

Pete: I'm tellin' that during the Depression, Gran' Boulevard and Sunny Side used to be where all the vice presidents and all the big shots used to live. And those people, the poor class of people from Carey Street or Drummond Street or so, did not dare to go down that street . . . 'cause they're right put in jail right quick.

Interviewer: How do you feel about Polack jokes?

Pete: Well, they do not bother me. But it seems to me like every joke that comes up, it's got to be about a Polack.

Interviewer: Oh really?

Pete: Yeah, that's right. But you can always change nationalities.[6] It all depends on who you're talking to. See? If you're talking to a Hungarian you can say, well, you know about the Hungarian, or sumthin' like that.

George: That's right! You can change it around.

Mrs. Green: They want something, they want something . . .

George: (1) Okay, this is a nice joke. There was an Irishman, a young Irishman was goin' to leave the Old Country and come to America. This was years, a few years ago. And as he was leaving, why, everybody was down . . . to see him off at the train and . . . he was goin' to go to the seaport to get the boat. And, just as the train was about ready to pull out, an old lady came up, and she said to him, "Oh Tom, would you like a . . . would you, you see, if you could find out where my boy Pat is over in New York? He hasn't written to me in for five years." He says, "Mrs. Dunn, – her name was Dunn – "ah, I look him up and tell him to write to you right away. So, where does he live?" She says, the last she heard he lived in a little white house in Connecticut. So, ah . . . when he got to this country, his relations showed him around, they took him to, to Massachusetts and New Jersey and that. And one Sunday they told him: "You're now in the state of Connecticut." And, ah, he thought of Mrs. Dunn's boy, Pat. So they stopped for gasoline, and he asked the gas station attendant, he says, "I'm looking for a little white house in Connecticut." And the gas station fella says, "Well, go behind the gas station and you'll find it." So he went around behind the gas station . . . There was a little bitty place, so he went over and he was just about to knock on the door. And the door swung open and there's a man, just pulling his pants up. And he says to him, he says: "Are you Dunn?" And the guy says, "Any of your business? Yes, I'm done!" He says, "Well, why don't you write to your poor old mother?"[7] (laughter) That's right, right! They're trying to make out the Irish are so dumb, you know. Well, they know more of backhouses, ye know . . .

Mrs. Green: Oh well, there's a lot of jokes about all nationalities . . .
George: Uh, ya . . .
Mrs. Green: Them Hungarians, and . . . and . . .
George: (2) There was two Irishmen, Pat and Mike,[8] worked in a
    brickyard. And . . . , one day, a whole load of bricks fell on Mike
    and killed him. And the foreman said to Pat, he said: "Pat, I want
    you to go down and tell Mike's widow what happened." So Pat,
    on his way home, he stopped and he knocked on the door, and
    Mike's wife was taking a bath. And she hollered, "Who is it?"
    And he says, "It's Pat." And she says, "I'm in the bathtub." Well,
    he says, "I've gotta talk to you right away." So she got out of the
    bathtub, as she went to the front door, she held a big towel up
    in front of her. And, she opened the door and she says: "What
    is it?" He says, "I've got some bad news for you. Mike was killed
    today at the plant." And she threw her arms up in the air, and
    the towel fell to the floor, and she says, "Pat, did you ever see
    anything like it?" And he says: "Yes, once on a cow"[9] (laughter).
George: (3) A . . . this colored family, they had a little baby. And
    the baby was, six months old. And one day the father was holding
    it, and the baby says, "Mother." And the father says: "Six months
    old and he can say a-half a-word already!" (laughter) You get it?
Mrs. Green: No, I can't get it.
Pete: We have to have the explanation (laughs).
George: What? It's pretty bad. Why not? Oh, all right, you said you
    wanted to know. One of their favorite things that they say is, is
    "motherfucker."[10] You ever hear that? Yeah, you hear that
    (laughs). So this baby said, "mother," and that a half a word to
    them, see?
Pete: (4) Tell'm about one, George, about them guys, the guys, these
    colored guys with these white Cadillacs going to Texas and all
    that stuff. You remember that one?
George: Oh gee, I almost forgot that.
Pete: You remember, you use to tell it?
George: Let's see, I haven't told that for a long time.
Pete: You said it so many times though. I couldn't repeat it. About
    these three colored guys meeting on the bridge, talking about: "I
    wish I had this, I wish I had that . . ."
George: Oh, yeah.
Pete: About this Cad . . .
George: Let's see. Oh yeah. This colored guy won a lot of money.
    Wasn't that it?
Pete: Oh ya.
George: He won a lot of money. And he said that . . . they asked
    him, what he was gon' to do with the money. And he says: "I'm
    gonna get me a white suit, and a white hat, and white shoes, and
    I'm gonna get me a big blonde woman and a big white Cadillac
    and I'm goin' down to Texas and I'm gonna show them Texans
    how us northern niggers live." And the other guy, he had won
    the money too, see? He said, "What are you gonna do?" He said,
    "I'm gonna get me a black suit, a black hat and black shoes. I'm
    gonna get me a black prostitute and a big black Cadillac, and I'm

goin' down to Texas and watch them hang your ass!"[11] (laughter)

Mrs. Green: That's about the fact too, ha-ha, well, ha-ha-ha.

Pete: (5) Ah-hah . . . Why did the Germans beat the Polacks over in Poland during the war? Because every time the Polacks blew up a bridge they ran back to pick up the scrap iron, remember that one?[12]

George: Yeah.

Pete: And what . . . what is the . . .

George: (6) What is the most dangerous job in this country today? Riding shotgun on a load of scrap iron through a Polish neighborhood (laughter). You know in the old days of the stage coach, they had a guy up on there, ridin' with a shotgun in case the mail robbers were gonna rob them, see? So the roughest job today is riding shotgun on a load of scrap iron through a Polish neighborhood[13] (laughter).

Pete: We had a whole list of Polish jokes, didn't we?

Interviewer: Why do you need? . . .

Pete: (7) Why they needed five persons . . . Five persons? One guy paints and the other four turn the ladder.[14]

George: (8) That's the same as puttin' in a light bulb. How many are puttin' in a light bulb? One to hold the bulb, and the other four to turn the ladder[15] (laughter). (9) Let's see . . . why do they have food in a Polish wedding? Why do they?

Mrs. Green: Don't know.

Pete: (10) To keep the flies away from the bride![16] (laughter) And how can you tell the bride at a Polish wedding? You see the one in the new tennis shoes[17] (laughter).

George: Bowling shirt.

Steve: (11) Bridegroom in the bowling shirt. You can tell the bridegroom at a Polish wedding if he's got the new bowling shirt on (laughter), says "Joe's Bar" or something like that?[18] (12) An' what do they put on the bottom of Coke bottles in Poland. On the bottom of Coke bottles? . . . "Open other end."[19]

George: (13) Never heard that one, did you? (laughs) Wanna hear an old story? Back in the days of the horse and buggy, this fellow and his eighteen-year-old daughter were riding along in their buggy, horse and wagon. And a highwayman jumped out and stopped them. And he says, "My gosh, I'm gonna lose everything!" And the daughter quick grabbed his watch out of his pocket. And the highwayman took all his money. He made him get out of the buggy, and then he drove off with the horse and buggy. And the father, he felt very bad about it and he said, "Boy, I lost my gold watch that was given to me by my grandfather." And his daughter said, "No, here it is." He says, "Well, where did you have it? The man searched you." She says, "I stuck it up between my legs." He said, "Boy, if your mother had been here we wouldn't have lost the horse and buggy"[20] (laughter).

Pete: (14) A, a little boy was playing marbles and a marble went under his mother's chair. You heard that one didn't you, George? And the boy asked his mother, "Mother, can I get the marble from under the chair?" She said, "Yes, but don't look up." So the boy went underneath the chair to get the marble and he looked up. He said, "Mama, what's that over there?" She said, "That's a brush, when Papa comes home he'll put the handle in it."[21]

George: (15) Well, there was a . . . (phone rings). Shut it (the tape recorder) off, that's for me. (Pause until George returns) . . . Two fellas were riding along the highway, in their car, and they passed a farm, and in a pen by the road was a big beautiful-looking pig. And, the driver stopped, he said, "Boy, did you see that pig? Let's steal it, there's nobody around." So they backed up, and they opened the gate, the pig was kinda tame, they were driving along, they had the radio on and then they heard a report, that a prized pig had been stolen. And, the police were setting up roadblocks. So the one fella said, "Let's get rid of it, we don't want to get punched." The guy says: "I'll think of sumthin!" So they're goin' along and they see a roadblock. So he pulled over to the side, and he went and got the pig out and he put the pig on the front seat between them. And he put his coat on the pig, and his hat, and . . . they drove on, up to the roadblock. And two state policemen were there, and, they wanted to look in his trunk. And they looked in his trunk, and they looked in the car, and they said to the driver, "What's your name?" And he says, "My name is Tom Green." And he said to the other guy, "What's your name?" And he says, "Joe Green." And he says, "All right. You, in the middle, what's your name?" The pig didn't make a sound so the guy poked it with his elbow and the pig says, "Oink." And the cop says, "OK, go on." And they drove away, and the one cop turned to the other one and he says, "Boy, that Oink Green was sure a homely son-of-a-bitch (extended time of laughter), turned around and gave him a name, Oink, kind of a cute joke, isn't it?[22]

Mrs. Green: That's a good joke . . . homely one.

George: (16) There was a . . . long time ago there was a farmer, and his wife and eighteen-year-old daughter, and a hired man, all lived together. And every night when they got through supper, they had a big argument who would wash the dishes. The woman claimed the men should help. So this one night, the hired man hadn't got back from the field, and . . . they got through supper and they started the argument about the dishes. So they agreed, everybody lay on the floor and the first one that talked, washed the dishes. So they're laying on the floor, and the hired man come in, and he says, "Supper ready?" Nobody says a word. The daughter was laying there and her dress was up a little bit. And all of a sudden, he jumped on . . . and took a ride. And he went back outside and he came back again. And he said, "Well, how about some supper for me?" And the old lady there, she got a little excited, you know, by golly, he done the same thing to her. And he went back outside, and he put the horses in the barn. And one of'm had a little sore on his shoulder. So he was gonna get some vaseline and put on it. And he came back in and he says, "Where do you keep the vaseline?" And the old man jumped up and he said, "I'll wash the goddam' dishes!"[23] (laughter).

Mrs. Green: He was afraid he was gonna be next.

George: (17) He was gonna be next, catch it? Yeah. There was a traveling salesman in the old days of the horse and buggy . . .

Steve: That must be old, talking about horses and buggies.

George: . . . and, he was in this town, and, he had written a big order up for the storekeeper. And, when they got through he had missed the train out of town. And so he wondered what he'd do. So the storekeeper says, "You can stay at my house tonight and you get the morning train." So that evening this storekeeper's daughter, a nice young girl, she asked him if he'd like to go for a buggy ride. And so they took the horse and buggy and went for a ride in the country. And this fella left the next day. And a couple of weeks later he got a letter from the storekeeper and the letter read like this:

> This is just a token,
> of a buggy whip that's broken,
> and the footprints on the dashboard upside down.
> I know that you were pushin'
> 'cause there's grease spot in the cushion
> and my daughter Venus hasn't come around! (laughter)

So, the salesman wrote back to him and said:

> I'll admit that I was pushin'
> and there's grease spots on the cushion,
> and there's footprints on the dashboard upside down.
> But since I met your daughter Venus
> I've had trouble with my penis
> And I wish I hadn't been in your damn old town.[24]

Mrs. Green: That's a good one. That really rhymes.

George: And you know, and now, . . . what is you doing now, what is you doing now, you know right along.

Pete: Oh yeah.

George: And that she says now, now what I'm doing is . . . that's a good one . . .

Pete: And she said, now what I'm doing?

George: I remember.

Pete: That's a good one.

George: (18) This beautiful blonde went up to the doctor and she wanted an examination. And he had her take off her clothes and lay on the table. And, he, took off his clothes. And he kissed her, he says, "What am I doing now?" She says, "You're kissing me." And then, he started feeling her breast, and he says, "What am I doing now?" She says, "You are feeling my breasts." And he climbed up on top of her, and started in. And he says, "What am I doing now?" She's gettin', she says, "You're getting the worst damndest dose of gonorrhea you ever had"[25] (laughter).

Mrs. Green: Oh, that's a really good one (laughs). That's some examination, ain't it?

George: You want his address?

Mrs. Green: Whose address?

George: The doctor's address.

Mrs. Green: I've read in the paper about such cases. Not about gonorrhea, but I mean, where a woman went for examination and the woman sued. Of course, he said he was treating her but I don't believe that any woman is that dumb that she didn't know that that was no treatment. So she claimed she didn't know that that was a treatment. Aaah, no. She just woke up and thought, by golly, he's . . .

George: (19) Well, this young fella, he was kinda dumb. He took his wife to the doctor, and, . . . She was nervous and everything. And the doctor examined her. And he said, "Well, the only thing," he says, "your wife needs intercourse, three times a week." And he said, "Well," he said, "I tell you what. If that's necessary, it's OK," he says, "I've got to go down the street here for a few minutes, " he said, "You wanna give her the first treatment, OK." So, he came back, and he opened up the door and here the doctor was up on the table. And he said, "What in the hell are you doing, man?" He says, "Well, why I'm giving your wife intercourse." "Oh," he says, "I thought for a minute you were screwing her"[26] (general merriment, laughter).

Pete: He didn't know that . . .

Steve: He didn't know what intercourse was, did he?

Mrs. Green: He didn't know the word.

Pete: Remember that one? (whispers in his ear).

George: Oh yeah. That is a gag . . . that's a choice one. (20) There was a big beautiful blonde woman. She called in the television repair man to repair her set. And, she said to him, she said, "My husband will come up from the basement and he'll tell what's wrong with the set." So, in a little bit the basement door opened and a big Negro came up and he told him what was wrong with the set. The guy fixed the set, and the colored fella went down in the basement. And this blonde came in from the kitchen and she said, "Well, how much do I owe you for fixing the set?" He says, "Wait a minute – you told me your husband was gonna tell me." She says, "Well, that was my husband." He said, "You mean to say that you're married to a Negro?" She says, "That's nothing. I've got a sister married to a Polack (big, long-lasting laughter).[27]

Mrs. Green: It was worse than a Negro . . . a, a Polack.

George: I told that to a German banker. Out where I live. Uh, he has, an' old people coming in there about their interest and their mortgages, and all that, ye know. And he loves it when I go in, I give'm a few jokes I've heard, you know. And that man, I told him, she had a sister married to a German banker see, you know. That man laughed until the tears rolled down his eyes. He really enjoyed that (laughs).

Mrs. Green: This is a good one.

George: I don't care what nationality a man is as long as he is Irish (laughs).

Pete: It's, he's the same way, right?

Mrs. Green: Well, they said that the Irish had an awful hard time in the beginning and what's-they-call on the TV just a few days ago says that when the Irish first started immigrating – in Chicago, they even had signs: 'If you're Irish don't ask for a job.' They didn't want them at all. Oh, they was tellin' the Irish says, that the Irish had just the harder in the beginning as the Negro is having or have had.

Steve: At one time . . .

Pete: It was the Irish, then, the Italian, then the Poles. Now . . . and the Negro . . .

Mrs. Green: Yeah, each nationality. They wasn't accepted at all, only in their own community.

George: Well, at one time, on the section gang laying the railroad was all Irish, at one time.

Mrs. Green: Were they really?

George: Then the Italians. Now is the Mexicans and Niggers.

Mrs. Green: Yeah, it changes. You know that this town, North Avenue down here was the purtiest street when I was a little girl? That was the finest street. The first platform was on the lake. All the richest lived there. And the other down here was the mediocre families. And then Punchion Bar . . . that was the poor. Oh well, OK, we'll leave you then, heh? (Phone rings, long pause.)

George: (21) When a man dies, they bury him in the ground, and his body turns to fertilizer. And it makes the grass grow, and the horse comes along and eats the grass, the grass goes through his body, and comes out the back end. And the moral of the story is: never kick horse manure – it might be your uncle![28]

Mrs. Green: That's really good (laughs).

George: You know the terms about poker? Playing poker?

Interviewer: Ya.

George: (22) Straight flushes and all that. Well, this Jewish couple, they always played poker, and the husband was very tough-talking, very uncouth. Whenever he wanted any sexual relations he's always say, "Well, mama, let's screw." And she said, "Papa, why don't you say it nice?" He says, "How do you want me to say it?" She says, "Well, we play poker," she says, "use poker terms. When we go to bed, and you feel like it, you say'n', "How many cards?" If I don't feel like it, I say: "Pass." He says, "OK, anyway at all, so we get a little screw." So that night they went to bed, and he says, "Mama, how many cards?" She says: "Pass." The next night they went to bed he says, "Mama, how many cards?" She says, "Pass." And he's laying there. Boy oh boy, I'll fix her some of these nights! So the next night he turned over and he sighed, don't say nothing. And she says, "Papa, how many cards?" He says, "Pass!" She threw the covers down and she says, "What? You passing with a big straight like that?"[29] (long laughter) You've to know poker terms, you know.

Mrs. Green: Yeah. (Phone rings. Pause.)

George: (23) This is very corny. But there was a farmer. He planted a whole acre of carrots. And the carrots grew up real nice. And one night, a rabbit came along and pulled up a carrot and ate it and it was delicious. And he ate two or three more. Then he went home and he told the mother and father rabbits about the delicious carrots and they took the rest of the baby rabbits and they went over and they all ate some carrots. And they were delicious. And they told their aunts and uncles about them, and they went over and ate carrots. And every night they went there and they ate the carrots, and ate the carrots. And pretty soon, there wasn't even one single carrot left in that garden. And do you know, to this day, that farmer doesn't know what happened to his carrots. But we do, don't we? (Laughs, others join.) Tell that to some guy and he'll say you're crazy, 'cause it's corny, you know. But we do, don't we?"[30]

(24) Well, there was an elderly woman that always played the organ at church. And she had a big bosom. And every Sunday when she played the organ she used to pinch herself in the keys. And it got very provoking. So she went to the doctor. And he says, "Well, I don't know," he says, "the only thing I can think of, Sunday morning before you go to church, make a solution of alum and water. You know what alum is? Very shrinking, you know, . . . rub them. And on your breast and perhaps that might do the trick." So, she did that, Sunday morning, and, she played the organ, all morning and she never pinched herself once. And after she got through playing the organ, the minister got up and he said, "They'll be no sermon this morning" – with burned mouth – (imitating speech difficulty because shrunk mouth) (big laughter). That's a visual joke, visual joke.[31]

(25) I just told a fella this, today, I told my neighbor. This farmer and his wife had invited the minister for dinner. And, after they were through with the dinner they were having a cup of tea, and the little boy run in, and he said, "Pa, the bull just screwed the black cow!" The father took the boy outside and he said: "Never say things like that when the minister is here," he said, "say the bull fooled the black cow, that'll sound nice, see?" So, in a little while came in and he said, "Dad, the bull fooled the black cow, he screwed the white one"[32] (everyone laughs). So, that leads to another farm joke, right?

Pete: Yeah.

Mrs. Green: Yeah.

George: (26–27). There were two bulls in the barn loft, in the winter time. It was bitter cold. And the one bull says, "I'm gonna jump the fence, and get out of here and go down south where it's warm." And the other bull said, "I'm gonna stay here for heifer and heifer and heifer (explains for interviewer who does not laugh with the others:) A young cow before it has a calf is called a heifer. So he's gonna stay there for heifer and heifer and heifer."[33] Another: Two bulls were there together, and, one of'm says, "I think I'll go up in the barnloft and slip into a Jersey." (Explains again:) A Jersey is a type of cow. He's gonna go to the barnloft and slip into a Jersey. Also it's a what? It's also a sweater too, but it's a cow (phone).

THE LEGEND CONDUIT

A conversation in Hungarian occurred in Kakasd, County Tolna, Hungary, on July 17, 1986, at the home of Mátyás ("Matyi") Szentes, 67 years old, grandson of János, son of József, nephew of János and Mrs. Zsuzsanna (Palkó) Zaicz, all venerated community storytellers.[1] Present were his wife Mári, 65, and three guests: Mr. Ambrus Ágoston, 76, a tailor specializing in traditional costume (he now makes costumes for the Kakasd Székely Folk Ensemble); Mrs. István (Anna) Kerekes, 69, a neighbor; and Mr. Ádám Sebestyén, 61, church singer, bank director, founder and head of the Folklore Ensemble, native folklorist, author of several collections and a book of local history. As he usually did when socializing or seeing clients in his office, Ádám carried his tape recorder to fulfill his mission "to save the Székely culture." The sixth participant was Emma, 59, Ádám's wife and partner in ensemble work, a self-consciously active bearer of tradition.[2]

It was Sunday afternoon, time for a relaxed get-together for old-timers who preferred a chat – gossip and remembrance about olden times to a ballgame on TV. As had been my custom since 1980, I was staying with the Sebestyéns, whose hospitality is unsurpassable and whose cultural knowledge is inexhaustible. Living in their home gave me a fairly complete picture of their views, politics, likes and dislikes, as well as their relationships with other villagers, but at the same time it deprived me of hearing other voices. Like all communities, Kakasd had its factions and rivalries, and the Sebestyéns are too prominent and powerful not to antagonize some members of the community. The Sebestyéns influenced friends to take their view of community affairs and to form opinions on the basis of their version of information about people and their acts. Once the family had to leave town for a week while I stayed alone in the house. Before they left, Emma told me, "Well, I'm sorry for you because now that we will be gone, people will not talk to you. It is because of us that folks are so friendly. Remember the woman who turned around when she saw you coming? She did not want to meet you." As soon as they left and I walked

across the street to take a picture, the woman in question came forward
to the fence. "You are avoiding us? How could you forget us?" she
reproached me. Indeed, the situation was the reverse of what Emma
had led me to believe would happen. I saw many others during their
absence with whom I could not have renewed our friendships had
they been there. For years Ádám never succeeded in tape-recording
Mrs. Palkó's cousin's tales – the 86-year-old illiterate woman always
was busy when he visited. Yet, this woman told me two long, elaborate
magic tales without any persuasion when she dropped in at her daughter's house where I happened to be.

People knew me and were open with me because I published the
tales of their beloved storyteller, Zsuzsanna Palkó. Her book (Dégh
1955–1960) went hand to hand in the community, and her printed
stories became the source of new variants. I was an old friend they
remembered from Kakasd. They recalled that I was there during the
miserable years of hunger, deprivation, and humiliation; they told
little anecdotes about how they saw me back then and what they
thought of other folklorists and students who came with me. People
in Kakasd thought that by my publishing Aunt Zsuzsa's book, I had
a role in their ethnic survival. Rozália Kóka, a native grade-school
teacher turned professional folklore performer, found my address in
Bloomington, Indiana, and sent a letter to me thanking me for "saving
the precious Székely folk tradition."

The people of Kakasd met many other folklorists during the years
and came to understand what they were doing. They themselves
became active collectors, preservers, popularizers, and propagandists
of their own culture. The modern bearers of this culture – archaic and
modern at the same time – view themselves as insiders but are able
to distance themselves and take the outsider's position to create a
new ethnic identity (Dégh 1969/1989: 290–295).

That Sunday afternoon my presence was no handicap to the formation of a "legend-conduit."[3] I have used this term to draw attention
to the way legends are transmitted through a conduit composed of
people of shared interest, distinct from those for other kinds of folklore
expressions. As I conceived it, the line of transmission of legends
which is created by affinities between certain people forms a legend
conduit: by this term it is understood that contact is established
between individuals who qualify as legend receivers or transmitters.
But this definition also assumes that there are persons who qualify
neither as receivers nor transmitters of legends. These individuals
may be the "passive bearers" of legends, or else they simply may not
choose to communicate legends. The same persons, however, might
prefer to narrate other genres and participate as "active bearers" in

different communicative sequences. The forms of oral transmission are extremely diverse, and the eventualities of affinity between people and folklore are just as multifarious (Dégh and Vázsonyi 1975: 211).

The six people who gathered for this chat were all old-timers. All were born in the Bucovinian village of Andrásfalva and remembered the traumatic flight and relocation to Hungary; they were neighbors and relatives by blood, kinship or godparentship. They shared a common worldview that includes devout Catholicism, trust in God's providence, and belief in evil supernatural forces. Nevertheless, new experiences made them adapt to the modern world and question the persistence of traditional knowledge about consequences of misconduct and the reciprocity of crime and punishment. As elderly people, they also shared a concern about proper behavior to win God's mercy at the time of death.

With everyone participating, the conversation was lively and solidified at points into thirteen legends. Typically, the stories – some told by one person, some by two co-proponents, most supported by additional information or questions from the others – were well known and probably often repeated in the community. The numerous referents mentioned by name also show that speakers brought well-established experiences into the conversation, although not all the experiences were developed into legends.

Small talk preceded the telling of legends. The participants discussed Matyi's health; he was treated for ulcers and had just returned from the hospital. Then the discussion shifted to eternal themes: young people do not listen to their elders, boys date the wrong girls. . . . Emma's youngest son just did. This brought up the first story by Mári. Then, after two legends were recited, a break came. Fulfilling an old promise to Ádám, Mrs. Szentes told three tales she had learned from her father-in-law. Another shift in the conversation occurred after the third story. It was a spin-off from the story of a jealous husband who became possessed by an incubus, reminding participants of a local scandal ending in tragedy, the death of a wife beater and the wife's descent into lunacy. It was then easy to return to the previous theme, picking up the thread of accounts regarding wise women and luminous evil spirits. The legend exchange ended when the last string of stories about the controversial church-oriented ritual of fasting, praying, and confessing to destroy a human being led into talks about people who achieved a "good death" without suffering because of constant fasting and praying with the rosary.

Under the given conditions, the presence of a folklorist known as culturally distant did not prevent the airing of embarrassing social conflicts or practices of magic and countermagic in the context of devout Catholicism. My translation from the recording of the Hungarian conversation follows.

The Conversation

1. Playing Ghost[4]

Mári: The Fábiáns, the old fox and his boys. All gigantic, big men. So tall. It was the second son. The first was Pál, then came Andy, and the others after. Well, this András dated Anna Kalinka – I really don't know what their other name was. . . .[5]
Matyi: That's how they called them, okay?
Mári: I know them by this name. No . . . it was not Kalinka, it was Kocziba. Mrs. Miska Kocziba. Miska Kocziba was the father.
Matyi: It was Miska, ya.
Mári: He was so much into this dating that he went to see her early in the evening and it was midnight when he came home. Old Fábián did not want to let him, he was against his son's dating. But this went on for long. He did not listen no matter what they said. He left early in the evening and who knows when he came back? "Well," said his father, "I'll scare him good." "Oh, no," said the woman, "you can't. It's not possible." They had a stable with a roof that was high in front but low in the back so that the cart could haul up the hay. And the old man took a white sheet and wrapped it around himself. It got dark, there was no moon. He waited until András showed up at the end of the street. He came as far as the gate but did not dare to come in. He ran back from the gate. And his mother called after him: "What's the matter? Why are you standing there? What is the matter?" "Well," he said, "there is a big ghost on the roof of the stable," he said, "it may be two meters tall." "Gee," she said, "we haven't seen it, we were asleep." All right. She brought a lamp. He never dared again to stay out that long. He went home early. "Yes, yes," said Uncle Miska, "after eleven the ghosts walk. From eleven till midnight, one o'clock, this is their time," he said, "that's when they walk." They did not tell him that he did it, he was the ghost. They laughed at him; after he got married, they told him. "That's how the ghosts are." Uncle Fábián was some character.

2. Towel Mistaken for Ghost[6]

Matyi: Oh, our neighbor is also something. He said they went to bed – he was still with his first wife, not this Márta who is now his wife. Well, he says, they went to bed. They weren't paying attention, he said, there was a full moon. Once they see that at the corner of the door, there is a man standing. I was looking, but I didn't dare to get out of bed, not for the mercy of the Lord. It's a ghost on the door. There was a candleholder, he said, and he threw it that direction to have the ghost leave, to scare it away. But, he said, it just stayed there. Until morning, he said, "we did not dare sleep or get up, we just stayed under the comforter. Then," he said, "in the morning, the cocks began to crow," he said, "thank God, it's morning." It still did not leave. "This must be something . . . I got out of bed, took one of the candles and lit it – what is it? Oh Lord, Creator," he said, "it was a towel on a nail, folded halfway down [laughs]. I didn't sleep all night." The old man could tell some stories.

(There followed three tales by Mári.)

3. The Lüdércburján[7]

Matyi: In the war of [19]14 they dug trenches. There were many. There was a man among them, had a beautiful wife. He wasn't ugly either, but his wife was a beautiful woman. And his friends constantly teased him [about this and that]. Because they could not go home, they had to work at the trenches, dig. My father was also there. They said to him: "Your wife is sleeping with a soldier." He took it so much to his heart that they joked with him; he ultimately imagined that they are right, that it is true. Then, when he went home, he believed that while he was away his wife slept with another man; he visits her . . . this was her . . . whatever. The war came to its end, but this was still constantly on his mind. Finally what happened was that the *lüdérc* began to haunt him. So that at night, during the day they did not bother him, but when evening came the *lüdérc* was always there. Others did not see it, but he did. Wherever he went, he went with him, this spirit. They called it *lüdérc*. Well, time passed, much time. They told him to put a rosary to his neck and pray. It was all in vain, the *lüdérc* was always with him. No matter what he did, he could not get rid of it. So, there was an old woman, well, she was already 80 years old and she had learned from one even older. They used to collect herbs in the fields before, how to say it, they picked all sorts of crabgrasses and leaves and made medicine of them.

Emma: They do it still.

Matyi: So she went there, this old woman, she said she will find the *lüdércburján*. She picked half a sack full and took the *lüdércburján* home: "Don't worry my son, this will chase the spirit away; it will never come again." So, she put it into a big cauldron, she cooked it for so long that it could have been eaten as a salad. They took it off the fire to cool, not to . . . to cool it. When it cooled down she put it into a vat and poured it on the young man. She washed him. Once the *lüdérc* comes to the window he screams and groans through the window so that he almost fell into despair.[8] They drove him away from the man, because they bathed him in the *lüdércburján*. It could not get to him because it had been washed off from him; this *lüdércburján* washed the spirit off him. So the *lüdérc* split. But when they did not treat him with the *lüdércburján*, did not give him the bath, the spirit came every night, he could not rest. The man had it always on his mind.

Ádám: It followed him everywhere?

Matyi: Yes, every evening . . . true or not? But he saw him all the time.

Emma: What did it look like?

Matyi: I don't know because I have only heard about it, I did not see it.

Emma: What did this *lüdércburján* look like?

Matyi: I don't know because I have only heard about it, I did not see it. I asked Mrs. Barabás. She said that it was true. What it looked like she didn't know either. Aunt Erzsi, she only heard about it. This is how they chase the *lüdérc* away, with picking the *lüdércburján* and having the victim bathe in it.

Anna: And there are things like this, just the same.

Ádám: Not in Kakasd; that is I haven't heard about it. But for sure, there are in County Tolna.

Mári: Very likely there are.

Matyi: There are those who believe in this and there are those who can heal it. In County Tolna, they did not say which village. I heard that there is a man or a woman who does this and can heal it.

Emma: The daughter of Péter Ráfi was it . . .

Ádám: Near Kalocsa . . . or where? The same place where this folklorist lives.

4. The Woman Who Can Talk to the Dead[9]

Emma: They talk to the dead. They still do it. Zsuzsika, the daughter of Mári Lengyel, told me, her son hanged himself, the brother of Tera. On a tree. And this hurt his mother so much, so much that she heard it in Szekszárd, from whomever I don't know, that this woman can talk to the dead. The mother went to see her with Mári, oh, she told where it was . . .

Anna: I know where she was. I heard about her, they mentioned her on TV. And what did she say?

Emma: Well, and then they got there, they didn't let him in. That she is busy . . .

Anna: This was the mother-in-law of Zsuzsika . . .

Emma: Well, and then, he hung himself. And she said she will go because she suffers so much from the pain. She had three sons, all died, one by one. And she became mentally sick . . .

Mári: This Zsuzsi remarried . . .

Ádám: Her husband died. One of the sons had lung cancer. The other son had colon cancer, and the third hung himself.

Mári: Oh, oh . . . what pain a mother has to endure!

Emma: So then she went there and she said there were so many people in front of the house – there aren't so many at a funeral. But, she said, the police were already there.

Anna: We saw it on TV, long ago . . .

Ambrus: She is a seer.

Emma: I know where she lives. I saw her address.

Anna: And she had the guts to go and speak to her.

Emma: Zsuzsika told me that her mother-in-law will accompany her. They did go but they weren't let in.

Ádám: This seer, she made lots of money.

Emma: There were two women who went to see her, one took her daughter along. And one of the two did not believe. And when they got there, "Don't come in, you don't believe." And then, the other woman was allowed in. And she started to talk, and as she talked, it was recorded on a tape. And the flower came out from the vase, and the dead appeared and they conversed. The woman cried terribly on the tape, we just listened.

Ádám: They play these at national conventions.[10]

Emma: Oh dear!

[Long conversation about family violence. Heated discussion about sex life and the decline of decency and morality in the community.]

Emma: Listen, pardon me for saying this, but there is much dirt around the church. Once this, then that, first it was the trouble with Jóska

Ferenc, then with Mrs. Márton, with Laci, with Jóska Kák . . .
Mári: Whew, really too much . . .
Emma: I am telling you, this neighborhood is damned; all drunks, cocks, and whores.

5. Fishing Adventure[11]

Matyi: My grandfather . . .
Mári: No, I didn't know him. He was my godfather. I didn't know him, only heard of him.
Matyi: He went fishing, the old Zaicz. And I don't know, maybe you remember . . . here in the . . . there were some houses, there was an old straw-roofed house, and an old woman lived there. Well, they found this old woman dead. She had nothing but a cat and the cat was found there dead. Of course nobody went there for long before they found her. Well, she had no relatives and they buried her. Then they tore the house down. And this smokey reed that covered the roof was there, in a heap. Old Kozma and my grandfather, they were fishing there. They put the net down. They fished all night, they stayed out there. They made fire, they burned this . . . smoked their Miska-pipe. I remember, this was a pipe made of clay, burned black. They took out a little tobacco, spit into it, squeezed it into the pipe, and placed it into the fire to bake it a little. This was so strongly baked that it became one hard lump. It was so strong that if a fly came by, it fell into it. And they sat there, smoking. But then the fire needed more fuel. And my grandfather told him: "I am getting some of this reed, pal." He took his jacket, walked to the heap, and picked up as much as he could cover with his jacket and threw it on the fire. This smoky reed was better than dry straw; it burned slow and kept the amber glowing. They sat down and talked. He said that the flame was gone, only the amber glowed. Once my father said to the old man that the amber was rising up. Old Kozma was staring at it. He said, "Pal, what is lifting off the ashes?" and he backed up, "What is it?" And, he said, suddenly a big frog came out from the ashes. But he, he said, they were already jumping up and started to run toward the hill. (The women laugh.) And he said, "I took this fishing axe. I said, 'I'll get this frog.' And when I wanted to hit it," he said, "It jumped and turned into some kind of black bird. It flew towards Kostich. Because there Kostich was not far." (The women groan.) "It flew away high and threw sparks, fire," he said. "Well, it was a *lüdérc*," he said. This is what they told, these old men. But this was true. "Then, my pal came back. The other night," he said, "I went again.

But when I reached the hill, there was a balloon there, like the ball of an ox," in front of him, as he walked on the road. And he said, he had this fishermen's axe with him to scare animals away from him. "Well, he said, "I grabbed the axe and threw it toward the ball. The ball transformed into a bird and threw sparks after him – it was a *lüdérc*." Well that's what they said. How come they were then and they aren't now?

Ambrus: I can't understand why don't they exist now?

6. The Candle[12]

Mári: They were brothers.

Emma: Sure?

Mári: With the brother of my father, this thin old man.

Emma: Yes, yes. I knew him. And then he died. Then Gizi came to my mother in the evening – Sunday evening, I'll never forget – to ask for a sheet.

Mári: Wasn't this the father of Jóska Daradics?

Emma: They wanted to make a wake and they did not have enough bedsheets. Then my mother took an embroidered sheet[13] out of the trunk – we still have it – and gave it to Gizi. And when my mother walked with her to the door, she said: "Look Aunt Mári, up there, there is a candle." But then we also dashed out, because . . . we went to see it . . . and it was a little light that floated. Our János was already gone . . .

Matyi: He died earlier.

Emma: No, he died in '42, your grandfather, the year we got married.

Mári: I was still a little girl.

Ádám: It was in '43, the year I was drafted.

Emma: He was almost 100 years old.

Matyi: Yes, yes, I remember him, he was 98 years old.

Ádám: He served twelve years and two months.

Matyi: I also saw the candle, and told it to Péter Benda; he didn't say it is not true. I saw it at the Ágoston's [house], you know where it is.

Emma: Yes, sure, I know.

7. Another Candle[14]

Ádám: Buriáns were their neighbors, behind them there was a . . .

Emma: Big empty house.

Ádám: And we talked there in the gate, a few houses below, us young people. And suddenly it came down behind the house nicely, down the window of the shed. There it stopped for a while, then it flared up and went down into the shed. That is, it disappeared. It was there for about 10 to 15 minutes. And we watched: Now, what next? Then, after a while it got tired of it and left the same route it came. But it was around midnight. Then – not a grain of oat could be put into my ass as I walked home.[15] I did not dare to go places.

Matyi: There is no such thing now?

Ádám: Yes. They also call it a firebug but that's different.

8. White Woman Ghost[16]

Mári: He, our Márton, used to date a girl in the big village. And it always took him late to come home. It struck midnight when he reached the rectory. "And as I walked home," he said, "there is a white clothed woman coming across. But her dress rustled loudly, but it was pure white. And then, I even greeted her 'good evening' but she did not call back. Neither did she speak, she just walked on." And he said: "When I went further, it occurred to me that this is a dead woman who came out of the grave, that's what it is." And he said, "It may be the spirit, because the dead cannot come out of the body," he said. "And I went home so . . . I never stayed out until twelve, never."

9. The Bouncing Frog[17]

Mári: And once, they started a fight at Mátyás Begyi's on a Sunday. I was a little girl then. But I could pay attention to everything. They sat down to talk but the talk ended in a squabble. Then, when he was leaving, on the way home he noticed that a frog is leaping in front of him. He said that he kicked the frog and the frog disappeared. He fell into despair and started to scream from fear: "Uncle Mátyás, Uncle Mátyás, please help." They were already in bed. "What is it, what do you want?" "Please come because I am falling into despair." And my godfather didn't see anything, but he had to take him home to save him from desperation. And he also made peace between the two.

Ádám: That was the good side of it (laughs).

Mári: Yes. Well, the world is full of these things.

10. Frog That Turns into a Dog[18]

Matyi: István Barna told me that he went home from Jóska Gyurkacs-ka's and as he was on his way, he dated Erzsi. And they talked until midnight, and he said that when he went home, a big frog jumped on the side of the street. It was brown, frog-shaped, it jumped. When he reached home, it turned itself into a big dog at the gate, it accompanied him all the way. But he didn't dare to stay out after midnight after that. I think he also kicked it. I think the man would tell about this anytime.

11. Fasting on Rózsi Diszke[19]

Emma: And then, they fasted on the mother of Jani Fábián.
Mári: Who? Who fasted on her?
Emma: You know who it was.
Mári: Her aunt.
Emma: Yes, her aunt.
Mári: I know that. 'Cause Rózsi Diszke was an old maid. And she lived across grandmother's.
Emma: Yes.
Mári: I heard it from Mommy.
Anna: Yes, I heard it too.
Mári: And then, she, the first wife of Gergely Fábián . . .
Anna: Yes, yes.
Mári: Her aunt. Someone was dead and there was the funeral. In the rear side of the house there was a little window and she knew the way, because she used to go there, and took those many bedsheets, the decorative woven ones, and I don't know what else.
Emma: She stole . . .
Mári: I don't know what, but a lot. But no one knew who was doing this. And she pledged a fast on Rózsi Diszke. And before the fasting was completed, the woman . . .
Emma: She was well, only she began to have headaches, but suddenly she dropped down and died.
Mári: Kicked the bucket.
Emma: And then they made a wake and many people went.
Anna: I heard it, we were neighbors.
Emma: But Mrs. Dobondi also came as she heard the news that Rózsi . . . they told that they caught that woman who stole. They told her that Rózsi died, she had no sickness, she was a big, fat, healthy pretty blonde, young, and she died all of a sudden. And all the women came. They bathed her and made a vigil. Once, she said, they were about

to go home. Mrs. Dobondi told me this. Yes. She said that they did not gather enough courage to go home. "Wait, Boris, I'll see you home if you are afraid." 'Cause she said that she is terrified. Because she knew that she was involved (laughs), not lily white. Red. She did not want to go and Manyi went with her. And she says that at a big meadow, all along the way, a frog leaped after them. But she did not see it, only Aunt Bori saw it. Then she spelled it out. "Bori, say it after me, say it: If God is with me, nobody is against me." And Bori said it, but, she said, "I did not dare enter her house." "Come in Aunt Erzsók, please, come, sleep here with me." Well, she went in and Bori made a bed for her. And they closed doors and windows. And a big black . . . I don't know what went on the window. Aunt Bori saw it but Erzsók didn't. And it made her fall into despair. "Oh my, I'm dying, I'm falling into despair" – she kept wailing. Mrs. Dobondi told me all this, she said: "Had your mother not been with me I would have died of fright." Then, she said, she prayed there with her. They prayed and prayed until they both fell asleep. Nothing happened then. "I stayed until daylight with her," she said. "Oh my," she said, "if András comes home he will spank me if he finds out that I got home at dawn." So Boriné took her home. She was a little guilty. She bought the stolen goods from Rózsi, she knew well, why this woman had died. That's why she was scared.

Mári: I heard it from Mom because we were neighbors . . .

Ádám: They said Rózsi Diszke was an old maid, or a widow?

Matyi: An old maid. She picked up much stuff.

12. Pledge on Mrs. Fazakas[20]

Emma: You know what? There is such a thing in Kakasd still. I just heard it. That's what this Anna Sebestyén told me. It's Mrs. Lajos Fazakas, the thief, that's why she cannot die.

Mári: Why?

Emma: Because Anna's goose down was lost. And the police were after it. They investigated, and she was charged. And it came to nothing. And then she, Mrs. Sebestyén, pledged a fast. Aunt Anna told me that herself when I went to see her. A very quiet woman. She did not learn the truth until she did not do it. She is a regular church-goer, she, I am sure, confessed it to the priest.

Ádám: Really?

Emma: The priest would not tell what someone confessed. But Anna told us that she told the priest that she did the pledge. Since that time she does not attend services.

Ádám: She hasn't been in church for long.

Mári: I heard it from Kicsi András Jóskáné, from Erzsi.

Emma: I heard it from the mouth of Aunt Anna herself. But God beware, one does not pass on such a thing. I would not tempt the Lord. I was so shocked when I heard about it. Half of her head was gone, half of her skull; it is a miracle that she still lives. Oh, you haven't seen her?

Mári: No, I haven't.

Anna: It's a wonder that she still lives.

Emma: You see, because she cannot die.

Mári: No.

Emma: And this whole thing came up that you told us how sick Mrs. Lajos Fazakas is, that she was gone. Because Anna Sebestyén asked whether she had died. And she cannot die because she is cursed. Because Mrs. Sebestyén put a curse on her.

Matyi: Is it true or not?

Emma: It is true. Aunt Anna told me. She told where she went and how she did it, that she committed herself to the pledge that God enlightens. But she did not tell me more. That God enlightens. And the police caught her.

Ádám: And the pledge she did for God to enlighten her first, but that she resisted and did not confess, it made her suffer.

Emma: And you know what? She went around to borrow, or to buy feathers. And Teri Kovács, who she asked, told her: "Máriné, do you hear me? What kind of an idea is this? I saved my down for so many years, for myself, for my grandchildren, how should I give it away?" She wanted much, for a whole bed, as a load. And she said: "No, I won't give, neither will I sell it; there are people to whom to give." She would never return it to me, never. Well then, soon enough, a few weeks or a month later, she took sick. She was cursed. Her whole body was covered with wounds. And she told everybody that it was because she did not give her feathers. And then, Máriné's (Aunt Mári's) daughter wanted to get rid of the feathers. She offered it to me. I needed them badly, for the girls, you know, I could have also used some to renew my bed, but I wouldn't buy this. It was cheap and beautiful, incredibly clean, swan-white but . . .

Mári: I wouldn't have touched it, no matter what.

Emma: They took it to the market and the Gypsies bought if for an incredible low price. God beware . . . who wants that stuff with the curse on it? They got a good bargain but I wouldn't have anything to do with it. Ten kilos, 800 forints the whole stuff.

Mári: Oh my!

Emma: I needed it, but . . . no, no, that someone should put a curse on me? This was tampered with, who knows what token was among the feathers? Not for money, let alone for free, she wanted to give it to me. Then Laci (her son) told me: "Mother, why didn't you buy it, we also need new filling." Then Erzsi came, she wanted to take it too. No-no-no! Then, she wanted me to store it for her, in the attic. But I didn't want to have anything to do with it. Somebody would have accused me of taking something out of it. You understand? She brought a huge sack and asked if I can keep it for her. "What is in there?" I asked. "Sheets, some pillowcases, stuff." "Take it away, don't leave it here, get out of here as fast as you can walk! Go!" I didn't want to be suspected and cursed. Am I right?

13. Son Cursed by Father for Stealing[21]

Ambrus: Yea, they really put curses on people. It's dangerous. This man's eye flowed out . . .
Emma: Sure, because he stole from his father.
Ádám: It was the Berkóci boy.
Emma: Right.
Ambrus: I knew the son and the old man. I know where they lived.
Ádám: Then you know how it happened.
Ambrus: Yea. The son took something from him and the old man fasted him out. As I heard it, he confessed it to the priest and he had to do penitence. He had to pray at the grave of his father every night at twelve o'clock. If it was true or not, I don't know. I tell you sincerely, as far as I'm concerned, I don't believe in this fasting.
Mári: But the fasting is true. And the good Lord answers to the prayer.
Ádám: In desperate situations. I don't know, I can't answer the question.

* * *

At this point I threw in the question: how does one do the fasting? All five answered and the response was so intense that the tape recorder could not make it intelligible. Only Ádám's voice came through.

* * *

Ádám: They have their animals fast with them. Once a week you do it for six but mostly seven weeks, each time, on the following day. You take a candle to the church and pray that God enlightens you about who did the ill to you. When this person is identified – in vision or dream – he can be confronted and if he doesn't repent, the curse takes full effect.

* * *

From there the conversation took a new direction, picking up the idea of praying and fasting. The group felt it was important for God to bless them with a "good death." Participants mentioned people who prayed every day with the rosary and fasted once a week at least, or in general, fasted every day by refraining from eating meat and rich delicacies. They commented that these people were deeply religious and never suffered from torturous sicknesses but died by falling asleep in old age.

The Conduit and Its Content

The conversation of six people in the presence of a mostly listening seventh on this summer afternoon had the potential to form a legend conduit. They were talking about general concerns, not "folklore." As folklore informants, they were accustomed to being interviewed on diverse genres and topics. This time, however, it was only Aunt Mári who offered tales (as folklore) to Ádám's tape recorder. Otherwise, the discourse addressed not folklore, as they knew it, but problems that excited them in the past and continue to create social conflicts in the present. They were concerned about the decline of morality, particularly in the neighborhood of the church (the center of the community, where the most prominent families live), marital distrust, adultery, family violence, disobedience of children, thievery, magical manipulation, and misuse of religious rituals. The legends were based on a deep religiosity and on a profound belief in witchcraft, evil spirits, and the return of the dead that constitute the pillars of the folk religion of the Bucovina Székelys.

Not all stories were rounded out and polished: several remained brief, sometimes merely a statement, a question, or an unfinished sentence, as they deal with familiar matters known to everyone in the village. The immediate relevance provides a common frame of reference which keeps the statement intelligible. Therefore, I would not feel comfortable forcing the finished and unfinished stories into the artificial categories we create to distinguish the ways they are narrated. The folklorist's knowledge of "more complete" variants – memorates, fabulates – should not interfere with the native sense of story. More importantly in this conversation, the broader social and cultural and the closer intertextual contexts along with the speakers' personalities and relationships to one another reveal how legends emerge as the conduit is activated.

The participants were not telling legends *qua* legends (folklorists did not teach them what a legend is). They talked, gossiped, and created an atmosphere that accommodated the climate of the legend. The exchange was lively: many people were named – those who knew about the occurrence, saw something, were involved closely or distantly, or just talked about the occurrence; and perpetrators and victims were also identified. Through introductory, connective, and conclusive dialogues, speakers revealed community affairs, personal relationships, worldview, and formal and informal religiosity. All were well educated in supernatural belief by experience and by knowledge of tradition. All were articulate, intelligent, and interested in formulating speech when it comes to reciting folklore, yet none of the stories seemed to be artistically polished. Speakers retold communally known "events" about diverse kinds of hauntings, first to prevent young people from staying away from home at night and second to show that misconduct results in haunting by evil spirits. This legend exchange showed that legends that are so relevant to reality, as in the case of the Kakasd people, cannot become polished and standardized texts distanced from actual concerns.

The sequence of stories displayed smooth logical connections. The first, Mári's negative legend, was based on positive belief, that is, firm knowledge of ghosts or evil spirits that follow, haunt, and cause people to fall into "despair," as is shown in numbers 3, 4, 7, 8, 9, 10, and 11. Playing ghost reminded Matyi of a laughable incident (no. 2) a couple experienced when they realized that their ghost was imaginary. In no. 3, following Mári's three tales, Matyi brought up a story about the expulsion of the *lüdérc*, the most feared incubus figure of the Bucovina Székely folk religion. This figure is usually described as a male or female demon who sleeps with and tortures people who have lost their marriage partner. The figure appears as a chicken, turns itself into human shape, but travels as a candle, a ball of fire, or a burning shaft, trailing sparks as it flies (Hoppál 1969: 402–417; Dégh 1965a: 83–85). It was the first time that I heard about the *lüdércburján* and the administration of a bath by a wise woman. The story provoked questions that Matyi could not answer. He had no firsthand knowledge but rather had heard it from others. The theme stimulated interest in wise women, and the conversation switched to the healer-seer, in connection with a Kakasd suicide case and the quest of the bereaved mother who wanted to talk to the dead son.

In no. 4, a visit to the nationally known, media-propagated seer, commonly known as the *putnoki asszony* (woman from Putnok), was related in the conversation that continues the theme of family violence and community morality with reference back to no. 3, also a story of jealousy. With no. 5, the incubus theme continued with Matyi's version of an incident told to me by Mrs. Palkó in 1949 and again in 1954, and by György Andrásfalvi in 1948. This version, more than 30 years later, was a faint reflection of the earlier ones by two master storytellers who happened to be daughter and grandson of the experienced old József Zaicz. If names were missing and the real cause of the *lüdérc*'s appearance – the woman was a witch with a spook-cat – was not mentioned, the story in this skeleton form still raised interest and was worth retelling. In no. 6, Emma mentioned a candle (the incubus flies looking for its victim), and in no. 7 Ádám tells about seeing one. In no. 8 Mári told about a white woman revenant scaring her brother; in no. 9 Mári again brought up the ghost-frog's stalking as punishment for fighting, and in no. 10, told by Matyi, the frog turns into a dog as scarer of the late dater.

Here the talk shifted to another emphasis: "pledging" for divine revenge. Spooks continue to appear, this time as punishment for the pledge. Emma and Mári were the proponents of the first fasting story (no. 11), which Emma had referred to when mentioning in no. 6 that she loaned a sheet for the wake because the thief took the woman's linen. Emma (with involved comments from the others) continued with the case of Mrs. Lajos Fazakas (whom I knew personally, and visited during her nine-year-long sickness). The great complexity of fasting was also shown in the final brief story by Ambrus. I should add that the practice (or talk about it) continues to this day in Kakasd. According to local gossip, untimely death is never accidental but someone's "secret pledge." Victims of fasting plague the faster as ghosts (or *lüdérc*) and return to complete unfinished business.

The conduit presented here illustrates an approach to folklore from the viewpoint of human creativity. It was developed in field ethnography, based on the study of individual performers, their audiences, communities, and encompassing traditions. "Creativity and tradition, individual and community, together produce vital variability, thus keeping alive the very items that their integrated forces help to shape," writes Bill Nicolaisen (1990: 45). The participants in this conduit, members of the last Bucovina-born generation of Kakasd settlers, as an integrated force, demonstrate the power of tradition in their emergent conversation about current social concerns in the symbolic speech of legend and belief.

SATANIC CHILD ABUSE IN A BLUE HOUSE

Since the 1980s, average Americans have become progressively educated in Satanism. Simply by reading their daily paper and weekly magazines, and watching television, they learned about Satan's attempts to seduce the innocent and destroy the power of God. Satanic seduction was blamed for any ills, immorality, or deviance from accepted social norms. In the eyes of ordinary people, the world was transformed into an increasingly unsafe place to live. Women allegedly were impregnated to produce babies for cannibalistic consumption, children were kidnapped, tortured, sexually molested, and inducted into ritual orgies. People were abducted and used for satanic sacrifice. Worship sites were identified on the outskirts of towns, in meadows, woods, and hilltops as well as in basements, abandoned houses, barns, and shacks; human remains mixed with the remains of sacrificial animals, goats, cats, dogs, chickens attested to infernal activities (Mandelsberg 1991). Youthful witnesses came forward and testified about having been born into satanic families and having been victimized by them and by schoolteachers, doctors, lawyers, and parish clergymen to whom they turned for help – in vain, because these responsible adults and authorities were also involved in the plot.

Intelligent average readers of the popular press and watchers of television must have been greatly disturbed by these spine-chilling confessions and revelations. Since 1985, personal testimonial narratives aired by the mass media – particularly on TV by prominent talkshow hosts Geraldo, Phil Donahue, Oprah Winfrey, Sally Jessy Raphael, Barbara Walters and others – have claimed there is a conspiracy among well-to-do, upper-middle-class educated urbanites. The professional elite, so the story goes, have signed their lives over to Satan in order to achieve power and dominance through a blood-consuming sex ritual sacrifice, offered to Satan as codified by Anton Szandor LeVay's *Satanic Bible* (1969), an inverted version of the Christian symbolic union with God, the holy communion. But as the narrative expands, the satanic conspiracy goes beyond affluent child-abusing family units of secret worshipers. The real instigators are the leaders of the business elite, whose success is attributed to pacts with the Devil. These people head and subsidize the invisible satanic church. Ultimately, big business enterpreneurs – Wendy's, MacDonald's, Procter and Gamble – the biggest sellers of consumer goods, are accused of trying to destroy humanity by contaminating basic and popular products (Fine 1985: 63–65). A question in *Parade* magazine's "Personality Parade" (Oct. 13, 1991) asked whether Liz Claiborne gives a large percentage of her income to the Church of Satan; the reader had heard about a confession by Miss Claiborne on the Oprah Winfrey show. No, she never had appeared on the show and has no connection with that church, answered the editor. Rumors related to the fashion queen continued as the 1992 December issue of *Foaftale News* reported (no. 28, p. 11).

The world of electronics operating in the money-empire is also satanic: it brands our consumer products with the sign of the Beast: "666" hidden in complicated computer-codes and charts on credit cards, bank checks, and packaging. The world of secular entertainment – rock music (heavy metal in particular), movies and theaters – shelters other allies of Satan: Ozzie Osborne, Madonna, Alice Cooper of the living, Sammy Davis Jr., Marilyn Monroe, Jayne Mansfield of the dead have also sold their souls to the Devil, the story goes. Capturing more souls for Lord Satan, the reward is power, dominance, and world rule. Clearly, the struggle is between power-holders and the powerless; Evil versus God.

Two evangelical Christians, speaking of "ritual child abuse," warn us:

> Satanists infest every level of society from poor to rich, police, businessmen and women, even government officials. Most attend local Christian churches and are considered 'good citizens' because they are involved in local civic activities. They lead double lives and are experts at it. . . . They practice human sacrifices several times a year and animal sacrifices on a monthly basis. The human sacrifices are most often babies – born out of wedlock to various cult members, cared for by the doctors and nurses within the cult so that the mother is never seen in a hospital; the baby's birth is never registered, neither is its death. Other sacrifices are kidnapped victims, or a cult member who is being disciplined or who volunteers. (Phillips and Robie 1987, 136–137.)

In the scenario of this drama in many acts, or this legend in many episodes, is plenty of room to fantasize. Youngsters play harmless games of deviance to vent generational conflict (Martin and Fine 1991: 107–123). They tell the pertinent stories, following the guidelines of countless horror movies, docu-dramas, tabloids, and books; and they

display their rejection of adult values by wearing shocking and dread-
ful satanic symbols on T-shirts, jewelry, and bumper stickers. Playing
with ouija boards, forming secret societies, masquerading in satanic
garbs, building altars for a mock black mass, etc. (Evans 1991), are
innocent, everyday games, like playing with fire. On the other hand,
apart from the imaginary horror-play of the innocents, it also happens
that psychotics and criminals contextualize and rationalize their violent acts by framing them with the mass-popularized paraphernalia
of the satanic cult-world as justification for ostensive narration: telling
the story by actually doing it (Dégh and Vázsonyi 1983; Ellis 1989b;
Dubois 1990). Criminals as well as psychotics always commit their
anti-social deeds in reaction to the normative rules of social behavior
and the trivia of the day.

   The legend of Satan, built on the solid foundation of ancient nature
religion and Christian demonology, was updated and homogenized
for modern consumption by two authoritative institutions whose goal
is to maintain their control over the social order they have created:
the church and the state. Both these institutions appeal to the sacred
and the profane domains, criminalizing traditional belief and rationalizing (as well as trivializing) legendry. In fact, fundamentalist
churches are the main propagators of satanic legendry, and they are
assisted by law enforcement agencies on all levels (Hicks 1990). Their
education of the public borders on ethnographic reports: tent services,
mass meetings, songfests, and revivals are held by eloquent preachers;
and the messages are further communicated by their own propaganda
machinery – booklets, audiotapes, videos, fliers, slides, T-shirts, but-
tons, posters and pencils, reinforcing consciousness of traditional concepts of black magic. In the long run, a third group of professionals
contributes to the growing belief in satanic child abuse legends. They
are authoritative mental health professionals who, according to Sherill
Mulhern's report, promote legend motifs told by mental patients and
very young children under specific social and mental conditions
(Mulhern 1991: 145). "Shielded by the mental health perspective of
belief, therapists and their patients continue to spread the satanic cult
rumor," she writes. "Together they speak out authoritatively in public
forums, describing the behavior and practices of a network of cults . . .
Medical professionals are part of a cultural elite, presumed to speak
with scientific authority . . . they are using that authority to accredit
the belief that thousands of apparently normal people switch into
satanic alter personalities and meet on a regular basis to commit
wholesale slaughter right under our noses" (Mulhern 1991: 146).

   Sociologists of religion attribute the tremendous success of the Pentecostal movement to the fact that it offers warm, familial-emotional,

anti-intellectual companionship to people living among the alienating conditions of mass society. Living by miracles day by day in expectation of the Second Coming of Christ helps them prepare for Armageddon but also cautions people that the satanic threat is growing as the year 2000 approaches. The fear of Satan is overwhelming and produces hysterical manifestations. All ills, in fact, are attributed to him. Law enforcement agencies fighting drug- and cult-related serial killings they call occult crimes (Hicks 1991: 175–189) have inadvertently contributed to the Devil mythology. At an 1989 Ellettsville, Indiana, community church service addressing high school students, two Pentecostal evangelists testified about their close cooperation with police officers involved in the investigation of satanic rituals, labeling drug-related murder, sorcery, and sexual perversion as "another kind of satanism." Preacher John Baker relates the following story citing a police chief with whom he had worked:

"One afternoon," said the police officer, "this young 24-year-old man came home from work, the day before Thanksgiving. He walked into his apartment – the first thing he noticed was the most horrendous odor that he ever smelled in his life. He ran around the corner and he saw his wife, face down in a puddle of vomit, where she had overdosed on drugs. He ran very quickly back in the bedroom, where his little 3-month-old baby was supposed to be sleeping. And he opened the door, and he looked in the crib, and instead of finding the baby, he found an 18-pound turkey thawed temperature. He ran into the kitchen, and he opened up the broiler – there was his 3-month-old baby, cooked alive . . . Kids, say no to drugs, say yes to Jesus" (transcript from the video recording of the preaching and slide show "Frontline Ministries Exposes the Occult" by Frontline Ministries, November 11, 1989).

This is a skilled adaptation of the legend about the hippie babysitter who, high on drugs, broils the baby instead of the turkey while the parents who hired her attend a party (Brunvand 1981: 65–69; af Klintberg 1990: 141–142; Brednich 1990: 119–120).

The complete merger of traditional Devil legends with factual reports of psychotic and drug-related criminal assaults by the interaction of diverse media of communication reveals to us something of current social conditions. And since this legend has solidified and spread with a basically consistent content throughout the USA, England, and further in Europe, how can we tell more than the obvious and the expectable, the general and the unspecific, if we do not wade into the depth-study of local ethnography? Folklorists studying the spread of legends, accelerated by the participation of alternative media, have a hard time following the fast-breaking process. Remember good old days when folk narratives were passed on from generation to generation and one did not have to keep looking to the next move in the daily news coming through TV, radio, and the press? How terrible if you missed one. Because if you overlooked something, it meant you may have missed a crucial link in the process that is not running smoothly, in developmental stages, from *casus* (Jolles 1930) or *rumor* (Fine and Severance 1987: 1102–1109) to *fabulat* (von Sydow 1934), but appears simultaneously and retroactively in all possible oral, written, signaled, gestured, drafted, played, and acted versions – that is: presented and represented forms. How can we ever keep abreast of legends that take advantage of all existing vehicles of communication? Maybe it is worthwhile to look at a local variant no matter how much it has been influenced by parallel existing variants in other towns in the USA and elsewhere.

The local legend that came my way from Evansville, Indiana, is by no means unique or extraordinary. It is almost commonplace. Concern with satanic child abuse is often expressed in neighborly get-togethers anywhere in the United States. Irrespective of race, religion, educational, or economic status, people ask themselves, "Can this story be true?" (Recently a friend of a friend told me her sister's child in an Ohio small town had witnessed a child sacrifice. This woman, with a college education, was dead serious, in full belief that it had truly happened, and she wanted my advice.)

I will try to give a microscopic account of the Evansville legend of satanism in the hope that a drop from the Ocean may give us an idea about the nature of the Ocean. I will focus on the developmental process of the legend during a brief period of its life during which it was shaped by extraordinary conditions that pushed it into the limelight of national attention. The story is one version of hundreds that have been reported and investigated by police over the last several years, and unknown numbers of others that have remained hidden from the public eye, spreading only in local gossip and keeping families tense.

What is the specific story? Nine children give the same account: they were taken out of school and abused in a blue house. They were forced to participate in the killing of animals; they were cut with knives, and some of them were sexually abused. The children also drew pictures of what they saw on the premises: satanic symbols and the torture of people and animals.

This scenario sounds strikingly similar to one that surfaced after a two-and-a-half-year nightmare existence in Rupert, Idaho, by way of publication in the *Los Angeles Magazine* on May 17, 1992 (Siegel 1992: 16–22, 42).

The Evansville legend has led a subterranean existence over the last eight years. It has spread in whispers, gossips, and rumors, poisoning the air and keeping families with school-age children in fear. Without surfacing, it has driven people to despair. Then, suddenly, nine children's essentially identical but formally diverse stories about the origin of cut marks on their arm were brought to public attention.

The oil on the fire did not come from the inside but from outside pressures. Coinciding satanic blood ritual and child abuse legends nationwide gave the opportunity of formation of interest groups with militant advocates, traveling place to place, reaffirming and homogenizing text variables. According to the report of the *Evansville Courier*, February 14, 1991, Faye Yager, leader of the controversial Atlanta-based Children of the Underground faction, came to town under sponsorship of the local chapter of SLAM (Society's League Against Molestation). She led a workshop and "spouted verbal venom in Evansville . . . labeling the city a cesspool populated with satanists in high places." "We weren't surprised," the reporter writes. "She's done it elsewhere to other communities, a modern-day vigilante riding the talk-show and workshop circuit." The allegations forced city officials to respond. Confrontations of accusers and accused ensued in an attempt to identify victims and perpetrators. In the fact-finding process, five police officers interviewed 150 people to come up with nothing. The prosecutor found all accused innocent – only the legend remained in the local grapevine, feeding on the existing cultural knowledge and rationalized by tabloid news about allegations of satanic ritual child abuse elsewhere (Richardson, Best and Bromley 1991). Then, the story surfaced in a grandiose way and attracted national attention. This was enough for the Fox television program, "A Current Affair," to turn it into a juicy show.

On May 22, this program aired the story of "The Devil's Playground" in Evansville, Indiana. Reporters and cameramen invaded the town and talked to key *dramatis personae* and explored the main premises where the legend events were alleged to have happened. A local affair became a nationwide sensation. Without consideration of latent oral legends, whispered rumors, gossips, and commentaries precipitated by the publicity of the television show, the immediate reaction of the local press alone gives us an idea of the dynamics and dialectics of the legend in flux. It also gives an idea of the value of local reportage that contextualizes the folklore texts for better understanding.

Any small town likes national attention, to be "put on the map" (Langlois 1985: 17–33), but there was a dismal feeling in Evansville (population under 200,000) when its child abuse story was distributed nationwide by a wire service, before it was aired by "A Current Affair," television's version of the supermarket tabloids. The *Chicago Tribune* and the *Evansville Press* featured the story on the same day, May 17. The press release was certainly shocking. "Evansville must be hell on earth," writes the editor of the *Evansville Courier*, "if one judges our community from the rumors of satanic activity being glibly tossed around. Regrettably, some Americans who don't know us may come to some conclusion from the stories . . ."

" . . . How does a community refute such illusory information, such vague unsubstantiated hysteria?" asks the editor further. In light of the fact that neither police nor the prosecutor's office found evidence, he refers to the logic of rumormongering: "For someone to believe the rumors, he or she would have to believe there is a gigantic conspiracy operating here involving police, prosecutors, educators and the media, among others . . . protecting people who hurt children . . ." This, in itself, is the subliminal legend: satanists in local leadership conspire against the little people. This legend was not invented in Evansville; it is a localized variant of nationwide distribution.

The *Evansville Press* reprinted the *Chicago Tribune* story by Michael Tackett, prefacing the reprint with a summary of events. Tackett's article indicated the controversial atmosphere surrounding the children's versions. The police and the public prosecutor found no evidence of any of the accusations, whereas the parents, a practicing child psychologist, and the local representative of a child abuse rescue network gave credence to the children. The controversiality so common to legends was further enhanced by the reporter. Well informed about current criminal child abuse accusations (Nathan 1991: 75–94), he placed the local story into the national/international/historic context, saying criminal cases related to satanic violence do exist but that at the same time, witch-hunt related blood-rituals and blood-libel accusations are age-old myths.

A day after the "Current Affair" show, on May 23, two *Evansville Press* reporters told their readers that "A Current Affair" depicted Evansville as a small town where "children are victims of satanic rituals and officials refuse to act," and that the story had "polarized believers and unbelievers." They added to what had already been reported and increased the ambiguity of the issue. While police and prosecutor reiterated that their fact-finding search had failed to turn up any evidence, and while the school board attorney called the accusation "a complete hogwash," the former prosecutor pointed out that in his time, there were other blue houses at other places in town . . . "That's the beauty of not having been tied to the truth or reality" . . . "you can just change the story as it becomes convenient." The folklorist can best appreciate this insight by a local lawman observing manipulation of folklore.

Meanwhile, the accused school principal, school bus driver, and the implicated teachers turned to the Indiana State Teacher's Association for legal advice and help. "How do you prove you haven't done something?" was the question. The story of negation, by its very nature, is dull and uninteresting, while the accusers in the drama appear more colorful and interesting. The authors introduced controversial child advocate Rick Doninger, on record as supporting continued investigations of satanic child abuse claims. He insisted that police searched the "blue house" after incriminating evidence had been moved: neighbors had seen big packages smuggled out at night, he said. As head of the now defunct local chapter of SLAM, Doninger appeared as the champion of child rescue: he helped a woman hide her child from her estranged husband accused but cleared of satanic molestation in 1989. Another supporter of the satanic abuse claims was Sue Donaldson, a psychology professor at Indiana State University, who inferred from the identical scars on the children's arms that something did indeed happen to them. Maybe abuse of another kind – who knows? But she admitted that the children, ages 6 to 12, came from five "dysfunctional" and low-income families.

On the same day, another reporter of the *Evansville Courier* discussed "The Devil's Playground" show with antagonists and protagonists who also appeared on "A Current Affair." Antagonists (prosecutor, detective, and the owner of the blue house) expressed their displeasure with the show's tendentiousness, whereas Doninger "thought it was the first time that the media actually let the community see a little glimpse of the other side. They let the victims speak for a change." The psychologist felt the children's stories sounded believable, but she expressed reservations that were not aired.

Next day, May 24, the *Evansville Courier* in two articles expressed disgust over the image of Evansville that had been painted by the TV show. Too bad for the city to be on "trash television," it read, and its prosecutor was "offered up as the bad guy." City officials, the chairman of the Visitors Bureau, the mayor, school officials, and an investigative detective were distressed, even outraged by the show's groundless allegations.

On May 25, the *Evansville Courier* featured Andrew and Mildred Hight, "a 74-year-old man with heart problems" and his 64-year-old wife as victims of the Devil's Playground story. They were renters of the vinyl-sided blue house and took legal action for "bizarre false and defamatory statements and publications that were made with reckless disregard for the truth." They filed a petition asking the court to subpoena Doninger and his wife and the producers of the TV show. The hearing was set for June 20. On May 29 the *Courier*'s article – "Our Current Affair" – took another stand to support the victimized residents of the Blue House, pointing an accusatory finger at the aloof reporter of "A Current Affair" and Rick Doninger, the leader of the anti-Satan group and the main promulgator of the legends. How come the stories change? asked the reporter, who raised questions in an attempt to fill gaps in the story which would be the subject of a forthcoming hearing. The questions revealed more legends: "Babies are being murdered in the blue house and the children are forced to drink the blood;" "A school official removes the baby's heart and stores it in the cabinet in school. Then, the baby is buried on a baseball diamond under a tarp." These seem indigenous variables of the ritual child abuse legend.

And finally, Patricia Swanson, staff reporter of the *Evansville Press*, combined the bits and pieces of the story and made it into a coherent whole. The composite story concerns nine children from five families who said they had been ritually abused by school officials. In this text, the official voice is strong, represented by Sgt. Larry Sparks, who reported that five policemen had worked on the case, interviewing 150 people, but had been unable to present a trace of evidence. The place of abuse (the Blue House) had been impossible to locate because none of the claims had been consistent. "Up to six blue houses have been identified by children as the site of ritual abuse, and none of the facts described by children could be verified." The main contenders, Rick and Sue Doninger (claiming that the rituals occurred at several blue houses), appeared at this stage in the debate as the losers, as manipulators of children, whose statements were too elusive to be admissible.

The viewers of the TV show have seen reporter Lydal Marks in front of the light blue vinyl-covered framehouse she identified as the playground of Satan. No wonder that Thomas Massey, attorney of the Hights, filed a motion asking a judge to order that a deposition be taken from the couple and from Rick and Pam Doninger. But court records show no legal action on the matter since July 1, 1991, according to the summary statement on the whole affair by staff writer Ella Johnson (*Courier Journal* Feb. 4, 1993).

Following a visit to Evansville two years later, there is not much to add as a postscript. With the lawsuit dropped, there has been no legal action since July 1991. Some thoughts for speculation, however, may be given in view of the premises. A considerable distance separates the two locations of the legend events, the school and the blue house. The Howard Roosa School is located in the city's crowded poor-working-class neighborhood, several miles from and in extreme opposition to the neatly landscaped, ornate and friendly westside middle-class location where the blue house stands. A funeral home is located across the street, and a Catholic church further in the same block. The neighbors do not see much of the old couple; they moved away, stopping by only occasionally to collect their mail. The house itself is modest and mysterious. Two steps lead to the entrance door with two windows to the right and an upstairs window above. Otherwise, the house is enclosed by a wooden fence and a separate large storage building in back. If there are more windows and doors, they are hidden from the outsider, concealed by the lush bushes and trees behind the fence. For concealment of secrets, the setting seems ideal. Whatever the neighbors think, the continuation of the legend is invisible to strangers, until a new coincidence of contributing factors attracts public interest.

A "blue house" as the scene of satanic ritual seems not to be unique, although the color blue is not related to the devil in Christian demonology. Yet the house in which the Hights resided is one of the several other blue houses of Evansville branded by the local grapevine. In a letter of March 9, 1993, Sherrill Mulhern called my attention to a similar case in Martensville, Saskatchewan. A couple operating a baby-sitting service was accused of being involved in satanic child abuse in their blue bungalow and "in a large blue Quonset machine shed about five miles northwest of town, identified as 'Devil's Church' by a child (Hazelwood 1992). As Mulhern writes to me:

> According to my Canadian informants, the quonset hut only emerged in the case after the children had been in therapy for several months. At the time, an older boy, one of four close friends, said that the accused had taken him and others to a blue house where they performed sexual rituals with the devil. This allegation triggered a massive house hunt during which the father of the boy purportedly rented an airplane and flew over the Martensville area until he spotted the relatively isolated blue quonset hut from the air.

We may note that the distance between the two locations of satanic abuse is geographically and socially as distant as that in the Martensville case.

The color blue furthermore connects the story to another famous Indiana legend. A reader's letter to the editor of the *Evansville Courier* indicates the general public's awareness of so-called urban legends. The author, who requested anonymity, suggested that the story may be a "modern version of an urban legend," the House of Blue Lights, popular in the Indianapolis area (Dégh 1969a). "It's possible that the central motif of the story – the house with blue lights – has been transformed by retelling into the blue house. The weird-scary events told about the house in Indianapolis – glass casket on display with a corpse, dead cats, mysterious deaths, etc., have become satanic rituals practiced by witches in the Evansville version." Although the Blue Lights House legend is not related to our story, the correspondent is right in that the current variants of traditional haunted- and mystery house legends are affected by the great popularity of legends about satanist atrocities.

What happened in Evansville is that a local redaction of a "hot" legend living in oral form in the community was lifted from its intimate environment and exposed to the television-watching public. Authoritative bearers (unbelievers) who professionally dealt with the factual and fictional parts of the legend were ready to help TV publicity benefit their community but were disappointed by the callous, insensitive handling of its statements by the outsiders, mainly the researchers and producers of "A Current Affair." They felt the sensationalizing of the legend resulted in the casting of an unfavorable image of the community. On the other hand, believers enjoyed their day in the limelight and the publicity their claims received, obtaining credibility by approximating the nationwide known archetypal legend. Those caught in-between – the accused, school officials, the blue house patron, children and parents, nameless transmitters of the legend – remained largely unaffected by the national attention and continue to keep the story rolling. Believers and unbelievers express their opinion; the debate continues, and the legend conduit proceeds. We could keep track of the legend in further evolving stages; and it may be useful to examine how the further spreading and changing satanic legend in public knowledge influences its future formulation, its periods of blossoming and decline. We could also explore how television reportage of further local variants assists story enhancement, homogenization, or specification in the future. Even this much, our simple reviewing of newspaper reflections during the week after the television show, allows us a closer look at a segment of the ongoing legend process shaped by interacting oral and non-oral communicators.

NOTES

1. The Creative Practices of Storytellers (pp. 33–46)

This essay is a revised edition of a paper presented in German at the first congress of the International Society for Folk Narrative Research in Kiel and Copenhagen (Dégh 1961: 63–73). An extended version in Hungarian was published in 1960 (Dégh 1960: 28–42). This text is a combination of the two.

[1] These concepts were coined by Walter Anderson (1923: 403 and 1935: 16).

2. Biology of Storytelling (pp. 47–61)

From Volume 7, Number 3, of Folklore Preprint Series, published by the Folklore Publications Group, Indiana University, 1979. A shorter version in German, "Biologie des Erzählguts," appeared in *Enzyklopädie des Märchens* (Dégh 1977, Vol. II: 386–406).

[1] See the monograph studies of Ortutay, Banó, Dégh, Kovács, Béres, Balassa, Dobos, and Erdész listed in the bibliography under *Uj Magyar Népköltési Gyüjtemény*.

[2] Reference is made here to the plenary session on Tradition and Personality and to a session on repertoire study, both at the Helsinki conference. The plenary session included papers by Köngäs Maranda, Pentikäinen, Dégh, and Newall. The session on repertoire study included papers by Jansen, Gwyndaf, Blehr, and Ozawa (Pentikäinen and Juurikka 1976).

3. The Nature of Women's Storytelling (pp. 62–69)

This essay is the original English version of the entry "Frauenmärchen" in the Enzyklopädie des Märchens (Dégh 1985: 211–220).

[1] "'Märchenpflege' bedeutet, der modischen Märchenschwämme die echten Volksmärchen entgegenzusetzen, die Erzählgelegenheiten und Erzählgemeinschaften von heute zu fördern" (Flyer from 1981).

[2] For example, "The Spider's Web" is a national broadcast noncommercial radio program (WCBH from Boston) for family audiences.

[3] For example, the Lexington (Kentucky) Storytelling Weekend (June 22–24, 1984) was widely publicized.

[4] For example, *Swapping Ground* is the newsletter of the Chicago Storyteller's Guild. A quarterly, *National Storytelling Journal*, has been published by the National Association for the Preservation and Perpetuation of Storytelling in Jonesboro, Tennessee, since 1984. Interestingly, *Die Märchen Zeitung, Informationen des Märchen, Folklore, Fantasy* was also instituted in 1984 for the "Friends of the Märchen" by Hans-Christian Kirsch in West Germany.

4. Manipulation of Personal Experience (pp. 70–78)

A shorter version of this essay was presented at the plenary session of the 8th Congress of the ISFNR in Bergen, Norway, on June 12–16, 1984. In 1985 it was published in *New York Folklore* (40: 99–109). The essay has been revised again for this book.

5. The Legend Teller (pp. 79–89)

This essay, originally entitled "What kind of people tell legends?" is a reprint from the festschrift *Folklore Processed*, in Honour of Lauri Honko on his 60th Birthday (Kvideland 1992: 104–13).

[1] The name "Screaming Bridge" denotes several Indiana bridges famous for being haunted as a result of the accidental death of a workman who fell into the concrete, or a car crashing into the river, killing the passengers (Dégh 1969b: 54–89).

[2] The multimedia existence of this classic legend was already recognized by W. H. Jansen. "Who could trace the migration of 'The Vanishing Hitchhiker' through a cinema version, a television show, a country western song, several journalistic articles, and dozens of straight-faced 'news' accounts, particularly when each 'nontraditional' appearance may be sandwiched into the midst of authentic orally performed 'traditional' appearances?" (Jansen 1977: xii.) One would not want to embark on the wild goose chase of tracing the origin and ramifications of this particular legend. (For a partial summary, see Brunvand 1981: 24–46.)

6. The World of European Märchen-Tellers (pp. 93–118)

This chapter is a revised version of the "The Peasant Element in the Hungarian and East European Magic Tale," published in *Cahiers de Litterature Orale* 1981, Vol. 9: 45–78.

7. The Magic Tale and Its Magic (pp. 119–127)

This essay is reprinted from *International Folklore Review* 1981, Vol. 1: 71–76.

[1] The most comprehensive bibliographical compendium of the history of the tale is contained in the last two volumes of Bolte and Polívka 1918–1932. A more up-to-date survey is still lacking.

[2] Folktale studies by anthropologists are represented essentially by the followers of two distinctive trends: the British school of anthropology (Dorson 1968: 196–201), and that of German-born Franz Boas in America (Boas 1940/1966; Benedict 1935; Georges and Jones 1980).

[3] The discipline of folklore in its historic evolvement comprises literary, linguistic, art-historical, and mythological orientations (Cocchiara 1954).

[4] For a concise and representative bibliography of Freudian and Jungian analytical studies of tales, see Lüthi 1979.

[5] On tale occasions and their significance, see Dégh 1969/1989: 63–120.

[6] A more recent example: Clarkson and Cross 1980.

[7] Items from Hans Christian Andersen, *The Arabian Nights*, classical mythology, Perrault and Grimm are treated as equals with oral folktales by Bettelheim (1976).

[8] From the classic work of Max Lüthi (1974) to efforts at genre distinction by Vilmos Voigt (Dégh, Glassie, and Oinas 1976: 485–496), many attempts could be listed.

[9] Location shown on "A Ghostly Guide to Chicago," *Chicago Daily News* (April 7–8, 1973), 15.

[10] The scarcity of knowledge of *Märchen* in America has been noted by Stone 1975b; and Carolyn See reported on an experiment in the classroom in which 61 boys confessed to not remembering any tale (See 1979).

[11] The proliferation of "normalised" tales for children in Germany is reported by Jack Zipes (Zipes 1979/1980: 22–41).

[12] Reassertion of tale materials can be seen in Wolfgang Mieder's edition for school use (Mieder 1979) and in Fetscher 1974.

8. The Approach to Worldview in Folk Narrative Study (pp. 128–136)

This is a revised version of a plenary paper read at the 1992 Congress of the ISNFR at Innsbruck, Austria.

[1] A special issue of Western Folklore (1991) reflects many similar concerns. See particularly Georges 1991: 3–12.

[2] Lauri Honko (FF Network for the Folklore Fellows, No. 5, August 1992) noted that "the trend continues" with the selection of "Folk Narrative in a Changing World" as a general theme for the next ISFNR Congress to meet in Mysore (India) in 1995. "Such a general topic," writes Honko, "may reflect the realisation that whatever the theme, the folklorists will deal with their actual research." Honko, as past president of ISFNR, supported this policy of broad general themes previously. The folklorists constituting the membership are folk narrative specialists who are committed to the study of narration. Joining the advocates of a "paradigm change" – the Geistesbeschäftigung of our days – he asks "whether 'folk narrative' really is the best common denominator for folklorists of the world now that Kurt Ranke, who needed it for his Enzyklopädie, is no more with us and the Encyclopedia is well established." The answer is easy. No, folk narrative is not a common denominator for all folklorists of the world, only for those who specialize in folk narrative, who want to maintain an international association in support of promoting and exchanging ideas and who want to keep their "professional identity" even without "proclamation." This desire has nothing to do with Kurt Ranke's original intentions. And why the feeling of "some frustration" seeing the Society's Innsbruck gathering as a "happy reunion" resembling a "family gathering"? Isn't it true that people who like each other have a better chance to work better together?

[3] Lüthi defined and elaborated this term progressively, reaching its fullest form in the 7th (1980) edition of his Märchen. See also Dégh 1975: 386–406.

9. How Do Storytellers Interpret the Snakeprince Tale? (pp. 137–151)

Reprinted from The Telling of Stories: Approaches to a Traditional Craft, a symposium, edited by Morten Nøjgaard et al. (1990: 47–62).

10. The Crack on the Red Goblet, or Truth in Modern Legend (pp. 152–170)

Written with Andrew Vázsonyi (Dégh and Vázsonyi 1978). Reprinted from Folklore in the Modern World (Dorson 1978: 253–72).

[1] "We have termed the lines of transmission of legends which were created by affinities between certain people legend conduit. By this term we understand the contact that becomes established between individuals who qualify as legend receivers or transmitters" (Dégh and Vázsonyi 1975: 211).

[2] For a summary statement see John M. Vlach 1971: 124–125.

[3] Peuckert also asserts here that the legend is an important device for expressing both mythical and rational worldviews.

[4] This term, adopted from Rudolf Otto (1958), is widely used in the works of Heilfurth, Lüthi, Peuckert, K. Ranke, Röhrich, and many others. Honko linked this concept to the supranormal experience (1962: 88–93), retaining numen for a basic underdeveloped stage of supernatural cognition (1965: 16–17).

[5] This term, introduced by Will-Erich Peuckert (1938: 111), has been in general use since its first application.

[6] "Actually tradition is maintained not by certain individuals, but by social roles" (Honko 1965: 14).

11. The Hypothesis of Multi-Conduit Transmission in Folklore (pp. 173–212)

Written with Andrew Vázsonyi, and reprinted from *Folklore Performance and Communication* (Ben-Amos and Goldstein 1975: 207–254). A part of the study leading to the revision of some theoretical thoughts of folklore and the composition of this paper were performed during Linda Dégh's tenure as a Guggenheim Fellow, 1970–1971. The authors are grateful to Dan Ben-Amos for his criticism of the first draft and for his suggestions that were extremely helpful in the final formulation of this paper.

[1] Kenneth Jackson does not mention Anderson's thesis, but his own is not far from it. "The complex tale as we know it in Europe and Asia has an exceedingly tight-knit plot. It holds itself together almost automatically because of the logic of its interlocking constructions . . . Such a story is not easily forgotten" (Jackson 1961: 56). Furthermore: " . . . the oral tradition of the popular tale has a built-in self defense – these undesirable 'mutations' quickly die out because they are not equipped to live, and it is not Gresham's Law but Darwin's 'Survival of the Fittest' that rules the popular tale" (Jackson 1961: 59).

[2] Goldstein questions the validity of Anderson's experiment; nevertheless, he confirms his "single source principle" as well as Anderson's "Law of Self-Correction." See Goldstein 1967a: 74. Furthermore, an example, selected at random, might show that Anderson's thesis acquired a rather broad meaning and is being utilized also in support of field observation. Henry Glassie describes a case in which the members of a tale audience correct their narrator when he deviates from the text of his own story (Glassie n.d.: 31).

[3] The term was coined and discussed by Max Lüthi (1968: 73–84).

[4] According to Sharp, continuity, variation, and selection are the main forces that act simultaneously on oral transmission; individual suggestions are balanced out by the choice of the community (Sharp 1907).

[5] Although the term *conduit* in its lexical usage refers to a man-made channel for the conveyance of some kind of substance, we propose here its application to denote a spontaneous way of oral transmission. Among the many synonyms, this seemed to be the most convenient because others already had been adopted by social scientists to denote other phenomena. It was especially important to distinguish the transmission sequence described in this article from what is known as *channel* in several disciplines. Similarly, it was important to distinguish our *multi-conduit transmission* from the *multi-channel communication* generally known in information theory. We are indebted to Thomas A. Sebeok for his suggestion in the choice of the term conduit.

12. Is There a Difference Between the Folklore of Urban and Rural Americans? (pp. 213–225)

Translated and revised version of "Stadt-Land Unterschiede in den U.S.A., dargelegt am Beispiel moderner Sagenbildung" in *Stadt-Land Beziehungen* (Kaufmann 1975: 93–108).

13. Processes of Legend Formation (pp. 226–235)

Reprinted from *Laographia* 22: 77–87 in 1965. Paper read at the Fourth Congress of the ISFNR in Athens.

[1] The first plans were laid at the statutory conference of the International Society for Folk-Narrative Research held in 1962 in Antwerp (Peeters 1963). Further steps have been made at a meeting of folklore scholars the following spring in the same city (*Volkskunde* 64 [1963]) and at the Budapest meeting of the Legend Commission. See *Acta Ethnographica* 13 (1964): 1–131.

[2] The first resolution concerning the establishment of legend-groups: *Acta Ethnographica* 13 (1964): 130–31.

[3] Similar ideas have been expressed by others who analyzed legends and their connections to related folklore genres. In this respect, my conversations with Wayland Hand were particularly helpful. See Hand 1961: 105–112; and Dömötör 1965: 88–93.

14. Does the Word 'Dog' Bite? Ostensive Action: A Means of Legend-Telling (pp. 236–262)

With Andrew Vázsonyi; reprinted from *Journal of Folklore Research* 20 (1983): 25–34. A shorter version of this study was one of the papers of the convention "Forme e paratiche della festa" in Montecantini Terme, Italy, 27–29 October 1978. It was published in Italian (Dégh and Vázsonyi 1981) in *Festa antropologia e semiotica* (Bianco and Del Ninno 1981). We would like to express our gratitude to Thomas A. Sebeok who gave us much useful advice in developing the first version of our essay.

[1] Sincere thanks to Walter Meserve for these two examples.

[2] In this essay the term "legend" will be understood as a story (story element, fragment, or reference) that concerns socially important themes not completely clarified and thus provoking controversial dialectically opposed standpoints. We named this phenomenon "Dialectics of the Legend" (Dégh and Vázsonyi 1973).

[3] Sylvia Grider followed up on this case which became the subject of national attention through media coverage. In her paper read at the conference "Perspectives on Contemporary Legend" (12–18 July 1982, Sheffield, England), "The Razor Blades in the Apples Syndrome: The Synergistic Media Treatment of a Halloween Legend," she gave an account of her research and hypotheses resulting from interviews with Ronald Clark O'Bryan (known as the Candyman), a convict on deathrow at the Texas State Penitentiary.

[4] *Houston Chronicle*, 9 October 1982. I am grateful to Sylvia Grider for the newsclip.

[5] There is a report of a case which seems to have worked by a similar mechanism. It was stated that a Palestine organization poisoned oranges from Israel with mercury. The rumor was probably unfounded. Later, however, oranges containing mercury were found, so the "migratory legend" became fact. The author of the paper given at the Seventh Congress of the International Society for Folk Narrative Research (Edinburgh, 1979) believes that the rumor was introduced by sympathizers of a Palestine organization (af Klintberg 1979: 61; Bird 1979: 180–184).

[6] In addition to the great variety of Haunted Houses set up in grade schools, community cultural centers, rented buildings, and museums, private enterprises should also be mentioned. The Lane family of Bloomington, for example, first tried their hand at converting their garage into a Haunted House. For ten years they improved their show with the help of relatives, neighbors, and friends until it became a seventeen-room "succession of fright" in a local elementary school with a cemetery in the backyard (*Bloomington Herald-Telephone*, 30 October 1979).

[7] According to general opinion, Halloween was an import of Irish immigrants and became popular in America during the late nineteenth century. It has become almost a commonplace that the American Halloween is linked to pagan Celtic and Anglo-Scottish solstice celebrations. Regarded as a "survival" with reference to European bearers (the Irish and the Scottish and their expatriot residents in the United States), the essential significance of the American custom remains unexplained (Sterba 1948: 213–224; Glassie 1975: 115–118; Mook 1968: 124–129; Myers 1948: 565–571). For more

background, see the "Halloween" entry in *Encyclopaedia Britannica Micropaedia* (1974: 862).

[8] Examples drawn from our personal experience at the Monroe County Library in Bloomington, Indiana, 1976. That same year, the children's library printed a special list of its ghost and horror story collection catering to Halloween.

[9] This discussion is based on our visit to ten different spookhouses in the following Indiana towns: Clear Creek, Dunkirk, Lebanon, Lafayette, Portage, Madison, Indianapolis, Martinsville, and Bloomington.

[10] "Children under certain ages, for example, cannot retain the sense of play as play" (Messinger et al. 1968: 15).

[11] At an international meeting, the orality of folklore was posited as an essential phenomenon in culture (Voigt 1974). On the other hand, more recent studies admit non-oral formulations into the category of folklore in the technological world (Loukatos 1974; Dundes and Pagter 1975; Dégh and Vázsonyi 1973: 35–38; 1979; Bošković-Stulli 1979: 8–17; Röhrich 1979: 170–192). The special issue of *Narodna Umjetnost* (Bošković-Stulli, 1981) addresses itself to the question, is oral communication an essential criterion of folklore? Deserving particular attention are the articles by Bausinger, Strobach, Sirovátka, and Simonides.

[12] In a seminar paper, graduate student Moira Smith surveys the most prominent Halloween prank stories and makes the following observation: "Halloween pranks, which are the expression of the folk festival's function to invert and so challenge established categories and orders, should be celebrated in a genre of folk narrative which has essentially the same function. It remains only to explain why tipping over outhouses and putting vehicles on rooftops should be the most legendary of all Halloween pranks" (Smith 1982).

[13] Two separate acts of school vandalism with "helter-skelter" signatures committed in Monroe County, Indiana, 4 February and 18 March 1979, were reported in the local press.

15. What Did the Grimm Brothers Give to and Take from the Folk? (pp. 263–282)

Originally presented at the International Bicentenary Symposium on the Brothers at the University of Illinois in Urbana-Champagne in 1976, this essay was published in *The Brothers Grimm and Folktale* (McGlathery 1988: 66–90).

[1] "Wenn wir also hiermit ganz besonders die Märchen der Ammen und Kinder, die Abendgespräche und Spinnstubengeschichten gemeint haben, so wissen wir zweierlei recht wohl, dass es verachtete Namen und bisher unbeachtete Sachen sind, die noch in jedem einfach gebliebenen Menschengemüth von Jugend bis zum Tod gehaftet haben" (from the Grimms' appeal to all friends of German poetry and history, cited by Rölleke 1985: 65).

[2] *KHM* 4: Fürchten lernen; 21: Aschenputtel; 47: Machandelboom; 80: Vom Tode des Hühnchens; 129: Die vier kunstreichen Brüder.

[3] Kozocsa (1963) and Voigt (1972) list seventy-three collections and 220 editions in Hungary between 1861 and 1961. Similar listings are also offered in vol. 54 of the *Hessische Blätter*: "Dem Gedenken der Brüder Grimm am 100. Todestag von Jacob Grimm 20. September 1963" by H. Ikeda from Japan, K. Briggs from Great Britain, Wayland Hand from the United States, and Vladimir Propp from northern Russia.

[4] The fascination of Germans with the forest as the mysterious dwelling of supernatural tale actors is delicately featured in Heine's childhood fantasy poem "Waldeinsamkeit"; see his *Sämtliche Werke* (Heine n.d., vol. 1: 391–395).

16. Symbiosis of Joke and Legend: A Case of Conversational Folklore (pp. 285–305)

Reprinted from *Folklore Today: A Festschrift for Richard M. Dorson* (Dégh, Glassie, and Oinas 1976: 236–259).

[1] This as well as all following narratives and statements were told in Hungarian, interspersed with occasional English words. In my translation, I tried to follow the original as closely as possible and italicized the English words to show the variable degree of adaptation of loanwords in the different texts. The Bodas spoke a very captivating, archaic Székely dialect but used many English terms, as is typical of the industrial regions of the United States. In common speech as well as in folklore texts, their Hungarian was mixed mostly with distorted English loanwords, as is usual within the peer group.

[2] The religious belief of this rational thinker became apparent to me years later. At that time, he was seriously ill and underwent treatment in the hospital for seven weeks. After his recovery, on returning to his home and regular audience, he repeatedly told the story of his miraculous cure, without medicine. When the nurse brought him his regular medicine, God whispered to him, "Don't take the pill." And God healed him in His way. Uncle Steve was as distrustful of doctors as of clergymen. He did not believe in pills or in diets; he preferred traditional home remedies. He refused to eat the hospital food and had his wife bring his meals.

[3] This Vanishing Hitchhiker legend is generally known and localized to this area by residents of the Calumet Region. In 1965, Halloween was the time when the ghost was expected to appear because it was the seventh year of her death. Police had to disperse the cars of experience-hunters who blocked the highway from traffic. See the formulation of the legend by Mexican residents of the region by George (George 1972: 56–91).

[4] The local funeral parlor of Thomas McGuan.

[5] National day of the Hungarian nation, commemorating the declaration of independence from Austria in 1848.

[6] Type 1676B, "Clothing Caught in Graveyard."

[7] According to Hungarian folk concept, Székelys are born tricksters: the *"góbé"* is the hero of many anecdotes.

[8] E 765.4. Life bound up with external event; M 341. Death prophesied.

[9] G 241.4.3. Witch travels in sieve.

[10] D 1531.5. Witch flies with magic aids.

[11] The snake dragon, often associated with the *garabonciás* in Hungarian mythology, raises storms, as in nos. 63 and 64 in Dégh 1965a.

[12] D 2141.1.1. Church bell rings as protection against storm.

17. Two Old World Narrators on the Telephone (pp. 306–324)

This article first appeared in 1969 in *Kontakte und Grenzen: Probleme der Volks-, Kultur-, und Sozialforschung. Festschrift für Gerhard Heilfurth zum 60. Geburtstag* (Göttingen: Verlag Otto Schwartz). It later appeared in *Women's Folklore, Women's Culture* (Jordan and Kalčik 1985: 3–25).

[1] I recently visited one of my most outstanding folklore informants, who had retired and moved with his wife to Florida. Their newly built home, their thrifty economy, their *Weltanschauung*, and their folk medicine were those of the farmer who never left his home village on the Great Hungarian Plains. The couple had entered a community of Hungarians of similar extraction on the west coast of Florida whose members reinforced the old values retrieved after fifty to sixty years.

[2] Mrs. Kis, who had lived in Gary for fifty-four years, has never seen the center of Chicago, just twenty-seven miles away. "I had no relatives or acquaintances there," she explained. Mrs Kovács and her husband used to visit the Hungarian ethnic section

"Burnside" in South Chicago almost every weekend. They had a good time in the settlement created for the workers of the Pullman plant, but they never went downtown. Only recently, when her youngest daughter, the wife of a successful businessman, took her to a good restaurant, has she seen the Loop. She still speaks about this experience, incorporating what she saw into Märchen-like story embellished by traditional motifs.

[3] One example of the unanimous statement of our informants will suffice: "Everybody was Hungarian at that time. The store owner, the saloon keeper, the butcher – and there were no church services in any other language but Hungarian. The mailman was Hungarian and the policeman was Hungarian. Even the bosses, the foremen in the workshop, were Hungarians. When my auntie died at seventy-five, she could not say more than 'good morning' in English, though she had been here for forty-five years."

[4] Mrs. Kovács told me once how she had to teach her American daughter-in-law good manners. The young woman used to open the door for departing guests, which could be understood as an insult – as if she were urging them to go.

[5] Mrs. Kovács once called a woman who apologized and cut her short because she was busy baking a cake. The storyteller was too embarrassed to repeat the call because "she had the same excuse a month ago, so she obviously does not want to talk to me."

[6] Veszprém County in western Hungary. Mrs. Nagy is an excellent informant in folk religion and in folk medicine. She claims to cure by magic. She told us that Americans are not so "well educated" as the folks in her hometown used to be, when she was a girl.

[7] Elderly people usually idealize the life of the old community and blame affluence for its dissolution. Both Mrs. Kis and Mrs. Kovács stated, "We were all brothers and sisters during the Depression. And now? Everyone wants to cut the throat of the other, even if they are related by blood. Men were out of work, and they built their own church together in 1932. Women did the cooking and we talked, played cards, and sang all day long. But today? Everyone is busy making more money than they ever can spend but everyone wants to beat the other. There is no friendship anymore."

[8] Hungarian-Americans have adapted baby showers and bridal showers, according to their standards. The godmother of the bride or the expectant young mother throws a party for female relatives, who donate basic necessities in the form of gifts.

[9] This legend has a wide distribution in Hungary, and Berze Nagy (1957) included it in his tale type classification under No. 814*. More recently, Balassa assessed the unpublished versions (1963: 531).

[10] This eccentric recluse caught the fancy of local news reporters around 1916 (Moore 1959: 601–605).

[11] At a single session the couple told me 120 jokes, most of them traditional Aarne–Thompson types.

[12] To play hookey is to skip school. In the story, Mrs. Kovács's children asked their mother every morning if they could play hookey. Not knowing, she always told them: "All right, dears, you be good boys and take care of yourselves."

[13] The realistic rendition of human experiences has long been known to students of the folk narrative. These were given different names: "Geschichte" (Wesselski), "Memorabile" (Jolles), "Memorat" (von Sydow), "Bylichki" (Sokolov), "Erzählung wirklicher Ereignisse" (Pomeranceva), "Alltagserzählung" (Bausinger), "True stories" (Dobos), and so on. However, the interest in the genre – or rather the mixture of genres, cutting across more recognized and more stable forms – is rather recent, having begun when urban folklore became a major issue (Bausinger 1958, 1968, 1975; Dobos 1964; Neumann 1967a).

[14] This study is based on fieldwork research of the Calumet Hungarians carried out jointly with Andrew Vázsonyi from 1964 to 1967.

18. *The Jokes of an Irishman in a Multiethnic Urban Environment* (pp. 325–340)

Reprinted from *Festschrift für Lutz Röhrich zum 60. Geburtstag* in Jahrbuch für Volkslied-forschung (Brednich and Dittmar 1982: 90–108).

[1] Dundes (1971b) as well as Donald Ward (1976) see the roots of Polack jokes in the transposition of racial hostility against the Negroes to another minority group in a period of explosive political confrontation.

[2] The riddle joke is regarded as a modern American genre (Brunvand 1970); Röhrich also notes that while the Polack joke swept through America during the sixties, there was a cultural delay in its adaptation to European minorities. It became, however, a model for ethnic joking both in content and structure (Röhrich 1977: 273–274).

[3] Common misery during the "dirty thirties" was often referred to in my fieldwork among immigrants and ethnics in the United States and Canada. Older people of the immigrant generation often remembered their hardships when poverty coerced people to join forces and share with what they had, unlike their American-born offspring who never knew what need is. Invariably, critical comparison was made with the current affluence, upward mobility, money-mindedness and consequent loss of community cohesion. The positive evaluation of behavior during hard times exhibits not only an idyllic view of the past: youth, years of struggle that led to the achievement of status and security, but also antagonism with the younger generation, beyond their control (Shannon 1960).

[4] A reference to current concerns of white ethnics of the Calumet Region in the period of rapid growth of the Negro population, the political atmosphere of raising consciousness culminating in the election of black Major Richard Hatcher, in 1967 (Dorson 1970: 188–95).

[5] Reference to the original segregation of ethnic neighborhoods in the Twin Cities (East Chicago and Indiana Harbor) from each other and particularly from the residential areas of the American-born elite: the factory proprietors and bosses. The whole area, essentially populated around the turn of the century, settled the arrival from the outset in neighborhoods according to place of origin. As soon as the groups became established, and people could afford better living, they moved away from the proximity of industrial plants. Building their healthier suburban homes, they turned over their neighborhoods to new immigrant groups. The discussion here concerns the earliest ethnic neighbor-hoods in the area, which have totally disappeared by now and were remembered only by older people. In the speaker's sense, minority means 'poor' and low social status.

[6] Pete, who identifies himself as 'Polack,' seems to agree with the opinion of the participants in this conversation, that nationality is convertible, that the joke can be used as a vehicle of friendly banter, interethnically, rather than as insult (see below George's comment to No. 20). Although past minority discrimination in the area is remembered, personally the speakers seem not to be hurt by being teased with the jokes concerning their own nationality. Indeed, they themselves tell stories ridiculing their own countrymen with gusto. As Lawrence La Fave and Roger Mannell state, "ethnic humor – any communication intended to amuse which makes reference to a particular subculture – not invariably discriminates again the ethnic group" (La Fave and Mannell 1976: 116).

[7, 8] Baughman X 621* jokes about the Irish. Both texts broadly fit into this category. "Silly stories about Pat and Mike became commonplace in American humor following the mid-nineteenth century Irish immigration . . ." writes Dorson (1956: 175). It appears though that Irish dialect jokes as well as Pat and Mike stories in general were recorded mostly from black informants (Levine 1977: 301–304).

[9] Motif J 1499.7. Person attempts to break death news gently (J 1675.2.).

[10] The word "motherfucker" is common in black speech, particularly in jokes and the stereotypical ritual insult game, the dozens (Abrahams 1970).

[11] The affluent, conspicuously dressed northern Negro going south, driving a Cadil-

lac, is often featured in jocular confrontations with whites (Levine 1977: 341; Cross 1973: 651).

[12] Generally fits C 3.3. How to Kill All the Polacks in South Bend: Plant mushrooms on the toll road. No closer variant in Clements 1973.

[13] Clements (1973), C 5.1. The Most Dangerous (Popular) Job in a Polish Neighborhood. Riding shotgun in a garbage truck.

[14, 15] Essentially identical jokes. Clements E 7.6. The Number of Polacks Needed to Screw in a Light Bulb.

[16] Clements K 1.5.2. A Large Amount of Food at a Polish Wedding. In order to keep the flies off the bride.

[17] Clements K 1.2. New Tennis Shoes.

[18] Clements K 1.2.1. New Bowling Shirt.

[19] Clements E 8.4. Open Other End.

[20] Motif F 547.5.2. Enormous Vagina (Legman 1968: 378–379).

[21] From the large category of metaphoric response to child voyeurism jokes (Legman 1968: 52, 55–57).

[22] Motif K 406. Stolen animal disguised as person so that thief may escape detection; AaTh 1525 H* The theft of a sheep; Motif K 406.1. The sheep sits at the helm of the boat dressed in coat. Remarkably, American versions occur primarily in Negro folklore collections such as Dorson 1956: 82; Dance 1978: 199–200.

[23] Motif J 2511. The silence wager; K 1354. Seduction by bearing false order from husband or father.

[24, 25] Legman (1975) dedicates a whole chapter to jokes about venereal disease but mentions only two (313, 316) which vaguely resemble our two stories. It seems a whole string of jokes fit the frame of 30: traveller bemoans effects of sexual intercourse in distant town after returning home. The letters in verse form (a limerick) impress as belonging to older tradition. In addition to the identical punchline, 31 bears more situational than content similarity to 30 depending on the foreplay dialogue concluding with the double meaning of "getting at" in the sense of "reaching;" "arrive to a point" and "getting" in the sense of "obtaining," "coming into possession."

[26] Motif 1315.2. Seduction by posing as doctor; K 1315.2.3. Seduction by sham process of repairing vagina. One version appears in Legman (1968: 131) three from black informants in Dance 1978: 94–96. The previous story is close to this one, both could be entitled: Doctor takes advantage of patient.

[27] Clements M 1.13, Why Dean Rusk Committed Suicide? His other daughter married a Polack. Telling that Polacks are inferior to Negroes, technically this is a double-insult joke. Dundes comments on comparative slurring of Negroes, Jews, and Polacks (Dundes 1971b: 202). In our case the informant himself indicates that the ethnic group is replaceable according to whom the joke is told (see also Pete's comment).

[28] Motif D 223. Transformation: man to grass; D 451.5. Transformation: grass to object. The word "fertilizer" for manure is noted by Legman (1975: 683).

[29] This joke is identical with the one in which the word for sexual intercourse is substituted by "doing the wash" (Burns 1976). With the switching from washing machine to poker playing and with the changing of the tone and the style of delivery, this joke approximates criteria known as Jewish in America.

[30] This joke is a teaser: "corny" as George puts it. One might speculate of the possible sexual implication of rabbit jokes, as noted by Legman (1968: 193–194).

[31] Identical story reported by Legman 1968: 573.

[32] Resembles children stories concerning four-letter terms used in front of others but placed into a farming family context (Legman 1968: 63 and 1975: 685).

[33] The two bull jokes come close to the widely popular one, featuring conversation of an old and a young bull in the pasture (Legman 1968: 208). Two distinct jokes are created by concluding with different punning: heifer = ever; jersey type of knitwear and jersey type of cow.

19. The Legend Conduit (pp. 341–357)

Originally printed (Dégh 1992) in *Creativity and Tradition in Folklore: New Directions* (Bronner 1992: 105–126).

[1] Szentes is an assumed name Matyi chose to replace the German-sounding family name Zaicz. As a gesture of loyalty, others with foreign names also Magyarized their names: another Zaicz, the storyteller Andrásfalvi, memorialized the name of his beloved native village, Lajos Rancz became Lajos Rózsa (Rose); and Károly Daradics became Károly Derék (honest, brave).

[2] For details on the Sebestyén family see Dégh 1969/1989: 302–303.

[3] Although the term "conduit" in it lexical usage refers to a man-made channel for the conveyance of a substance, I proposed its application to denote a spontaneous way of oral transmission. It was especially important to distinguish the transmission sequence from what is known as "channel" in several disciplines. (See Dégh and Vázsonyi 1975, 1976; Dégh 1979a.) I have also pointed out that if the legend is transmitted by members of the legend conduit, we might as well assume that jokes, for example, are dispensed through the joke conduit by a sequence of witty people: riddles pass through the riddle conduit made up of riddle fans; and tales progress through the tale conduit shaped by different types of storytellers, and so forth. This assumption is logically plausible and may be supported by careful observation of the social transmission of folklore. Furthermore, within a single genre – as the tale, for example – different types, type clusters, episodes, minor incidents, and even motifs and formulas have their own conduits, as they are all subject to transmission (Dégh and Vázsonyi 1975: 212).

[4] Playing Ghost (Mrs. Szentes). For easier reading and reference, I have given titles to each narrative. I call this a negative legend because it negates the belief in revenants but is told in a legend climate. An anti-legend, with its rational emphasis, intends to attack and destroy the legend as a whole; the negative legend substitutes one belief for another (see Dégh and Vázsonyi 1978: 254–257). This particular negative legend is based on a belief in revenants. The father assumed the role of the ghost as a disciplinary measure to make his son give up his date. The father's effective imitation of a ghost must mean that he conformed to the community's belief in ghosts; his masquerading did not preclude the possibility that at other places and on other occasions ghosts may appear.

[5] The frequent reference to names in this transcribed text reflects the cultural practice of name-giving among these people: use of nicknames and informal names showing descent and both maternal and paternal lineage to identify individuals. There is also a ritual and supernatural aspect to replacing a name earned at baptism (Lörincze 1948).

[6] Towel Mistaken for Ghost (Mrs. Szentes). This story is an addition to other innumerable scares people had at night, on the road, on the village street, near mills and cemeteries, or at home in bed, mistakenly identifying shadows and sounds as supernatural agencies culturally known to them. Realizing that the vision was not a ghost is a relief, indeed, and a contributing factor to a tellable story for amusement, without undermining the belief in the existence of revenants.

[7] The *Lüdércburján* (Mr. Szentes). An unusual version of the widespread legend complex prominent in the Hungarian language territory about the incubus figure (MI F 491, Bihari 1980: 135–139). The male or female demon who sleeps with and tortures people who have lost their marriage partners appears as a chicken, turns itself into human shape, and travels as a candle, a ball of fire, or a burning shaft, shooting sparks as it flies. For the semantic model of the legend, see Hoppál 1969: 402–417; for the developmental process, see Dégh 1965b: 83–85.

[8] *Kétségbeesés* ("desperation, to fall into despair") is equivalent to "his heart broke" and appears as a general concept in the sense of causing sudden, unexpected collapse and death by a scare or shock from an evil spirit through magic manipulation.

[9] The Woman Who Can Talk to the Dead (Mrs. Sebestyén). (Bihar 1980: 96–98.) The

famous fortune-teller and seer was fined several times for her quackery and fraudulent dealing with gullible clients. She also became the subject of folklore research: the story of her life and activities was made into a film documentary and published in a book by Domokos Moldován (1982).

[10] Reference to the annual convention of the Hungarian Ethnographic Society that Ádám attended.

[11] Fishing Adventure (Mr. Szentes.) (Bihari 1980: 138). This is a late variant of an adventure Mrs. Palkó's father had in 1927, fishing in the Suceava river with his buddy, Orbán Kozma. Mrs. Berétyi, the Romanian widow who lived alone with her cat beyond village boundaries, was a witch who was buried by a charitable Romanian peasant. The appearance of evil spirits (frog, bird, burning shaft, or a fiery ball: *lüdérc*) was caused by the disturbance and the use of the witch's remains. Mrs. Palkó's two texts (Dégh 1955–1960, 1969/1989: 135–137) and Andrásfalvi's version (Dégh 1960, 1969/1989, no. 75) in which he included himself as a participant, are elaborate, masterful accounts of skilled narrators.

[12] The Candle (Mrs. Emma Sebestyén). (Bihari 1980: 139.) A widespread concept known as foxfire is referred to here as the *lüdérc* that travels in the air (Dégh 1965b: 84).

[13] Called *ablakos lepedö*, made particularly for the bier.

[14] Another Candle (Ádám Sebestyén). (Bihari 1980: 139.) This is also a *lüdérc* story: young people spot it traveling to someone's place. Even the innocent bystanders are scared out of their wits.

[15] A common Hungarian proverbial expression for being scared.

[16] White Woman Ghost (Mrs. Szentes). (Bihari 1980: 28,32.) [MI E 425.1., 424.1.3.].

[17] The Bouncing Frog (Mrs. Szentes). Frog pursues quarrelers [MI 211.13.].

[18] Frog That Turns into a Dog (Mrs. Szentes). (Bihari 1980: 25.)

[19] Fasting on Rózsi Diszke (Mrs. Szentes and Mrs. Sebestyén). See Mrs. Palkó's story and comments about current practices (Dégh 1969/1989: 13, 300). According to belief, the dead are rendered restless because the survivors force them to return by fasting. A narrative collected in 1954 bears this belief out. "The woman began fasting so as to harm her husband. The man had beaten the woman badly and she was very bitter about it and then started to fast, and then he had to stay in bed for twenty years" (Dégh 1989: 300).

[20] Pledge on Mrs. Fazakas (Mrs. Sebestyén). This story's personalization is remarkable. The homemaker's treasury, particularly the highly valued goose down, is at stake. The whole household, the domain of women, may be destroyed by such tampering.

[21] Son Cursed by Father for Stealing (Mr. Ágoston) [MI E 415].

20. Satanic Child Abuse in a Blue House (pp. 358–368)

I want to express my gratitude to Marilyn Jones, instructor of Anthropology at the Evansville campus of Indiana State University; she called my attention to the Current Affair program and sent me a set of clippings from the local press.

BIBLIOGRAPHY

Aarne, Antti 1913: *Leitfaden der vergleichenden Märchenforschung.* FF Communications 13. Helsinki: Academia Scientiarum Fennica.

Aarne, Antti & Stith Thompson 1962: *The Types of the Folktale.* FF Communications 184. Helsinki: Academia Scientiarum Fennica.

Abdelsalam, E. Sharafeldin 1983: Sudanese Muslim Saints' Legends in View of the Contemporary Sociocultural Institutions. Ph.D. dissertation. Indiana University, Bloomington.

Abendpost 1985, March 28.

Abrahams, Roger D. 1970: *Deep Down in the Jungle: Negro Narrative Folklore from the Streets of Philadelphia.* Rev. ed. Chicago: Aldine.

Abrahams, Roger D. 1976a: Genre Theory and Folkloristics. See Pentikäinen & Juurikka 1976, 13–19.

– 1976b: The Complex Relations of Simple Forms. See Ben-Amos 1976d, 193–214.

Adams, Robert J. 1972: Social Identity of a Japanese Storyteller. Ph.D. dissertation. Indiana University, Bloomington.

Allport, Gordon W. & Leo Postman 1947: *The Psychology of Rumor.* New York: Holt, Rinehart & Winston.

Anderson, Walter 1923: *Kaiser und Abt: Die Geschichte eines Schwanks.* FF Communications 42. Helsinki: Academia Scientiarum Fennica.

– 1935: *Zu Albert Wesselski's Angriffen auf die finnische folkloristische Forschungsmethode.* Tartu: K. Mattiesens Buchdv.

– 1951: *Ein volkskundliches Experiment.* FF Communications 141. Helsinki: Academia Scientiarum Fennica.

– 1955: Eine neue Monographie über Amor und Psyche. *Hessische Blätter für Volkskunde* 46, 118–130.

– 1956: *Eine neue Arbeit zur experimentellen Volkskunde.* FF Communications 168. Helsinki: Academia Scientiarum Fennica.

Arensberg, Conrad & Solon T. Kimball 1965: *Culture and Community.* New York: Harcourt, Brace & World.

Asadowskij, Mark 1926: *Eine sibirische Märchenerzählerin.* FF Communications 68. Helsinki: Academia Scientiarum Fennica.

– 1932: *Russkaja skazka: Izbrannie mastera.* Leningrad: Izdatelstvo Akademia.

– 1960: *Russkie skazočniki: Stat'i o literature i fol'klore.* Moscow.

Austerlitz, Robert 1976: Commentaries to papers by R. D. Abrahams and L. Honko. See Pentikäinen & Juurikka 1976, 26–29.

Babcock, Barbara A. 1978: *The Reversible World: Symbolic Inversion in Art and Society.* Ithaca, NY: Cornell.

Bächtold-Stäubli, Hanns & Eduard Hoffmann-Krayer 1927–1942: *Handwörterbuch des deutschen Aberglaubens,* Vols. 1–10. Berlin: Walter de Gruyter.

Baker, August & Ellin Greene 1977: *Storytelling: Art and Technique.* New York: Bowker.

Baker, Ronald L. 1970: Legends about Spook Hill. *Indiana Folklore* 3, 163–189.

Balassa, Iván 1963: *Karcsai mondák* [Legends from Karcsa]. Uj Magyar Népköltési Gyüjtemény 11. Budapest: Akadémiai Kiadó.
– 1966: Die Sagen eines Dorfes. *Acta Ethnographica* 15, 233–291.
Bandura, Albert 1978: Social Learning Theory of Aggression. *Journal of Communication*
28, 16.
Banó, István 1939: Két szëm magyaró. *Ethnographia* 50, 159–161.
– 1941: *Baranyai népmesék* [Folktales of Baranya]. Uj Magyar Népköltési Gyüjtemény
2. Budapest: Franklin.
– 1944: Egyéniség és közösség szerepe a népmese életben [The role of the individual
and the community in the life of the folktale]. *Ethnographia* 55, 26–33.
Bartlett, Frederic C. 1920: Some Experiments on the Reproduction of Folk Stories. *Folklore*
31, 30–47.
– 1932: *Remembering: A Study in Experimental and Social Psychology.* Cambridge, MA:
Cambridge University Press.
Bascom, William R. 1953: Folklore and Anthropology. *Journal of American Folklore* 66,
283–290.
– 1954: Four Functions of Folklore. *American Anthropologist* 67, 333–349.
Basgöz, Ilhan 1986: Digression in Oral Narrative. A Case Study of Individual Remarks by
Turkish Romance Tellers. *Journal of American Folklore* 99, 5–23.
Bauman, Richard 1977: *Verbal Art as Performance.* Rowley, MA: Newbury House Publishers.
– 1983: The Field Study of Folklore in Context. Richard M. Dorson (ed.), *Handbook of
American Folklore.* Bloomington: Indiana University Press, 362–368.
– 1986: *Story, Performance and Event.* Cambridge, MA: Cambridge University Press.
– 1992: Performance. Richard Bauman (ed.), *Folklore, Cultural Performances, and Popular
Entertainments.* New York: Oxford University Press.
Bauman, Richard & Americo Paredes (eds.) 1972: *Toward New Perspectives in Folklore.*
Austin: University of Texas Press.
Bauman, Richard & Joel Sherzer (eds.) 1974: *Explorations in the Ethnography of Speaking.*
New York: Cambridge University Press.
Bausinger, Hermann 1958: Struktures des alltäglichen Erzählens. *Fabula* 1, 239–254.
– 1967: Bemerkungen zum Schwank und seinen Formtypen. *Fabula* 9, 118–136.
– 1968: *Formen der "Volkspoesie".* Berlin: Erich Schmidt.
– 1971: *Volkskunde. Von der Altertumsforschung zur Kulturanalyse.* Darmstadt.
– 1975: Alltägliches Erzählen. *Enzyklopädie des Märchens* 1. Berlin: Walter de Gruyter,
323–330.
– 1976: Kinder und Jugendliche im Spannungsfeld der Massenmedien: Die Wiederkehr
des Märchens. *AJS Informationen* Sept.–Oct., 1–3.
– 1980: On Contexts. See Burlakoff & Lindahl 1980, 273–279.
– 1981: Mündlich. See Bošković-Stulli 1981.
Bausinger, Hermann & Wolfgang Brückner (eds.) 1969: *Kontinuität? Geschichtlichkeit
und Dauer als volkskundliches Problem.* Berlin: Erich Schmidt.
Beauvoir, Simone de 1953: *The Second Sex.* (Translated by H. M. Parshley.) New York:
Knopf.
Beit, Hedvig von 1952–1957: *Symbolik des Märchens.* Vols. 1–3. Bern: Francke.
Ben-Amos, Dan 1971: Toward a Definition of Folklore in Context. *Journal of American
Folklore* 84, 3–15.
– 1975: *Sweet Words. Storytelling Events in Benin.* Philadelphia: Institute for the Study
of Human Issues.
– 1976a: The Concepts of Genre in Folklore. See Pentikäinen & Juurikka 1976, 30–43.
– 1976b: Introduction. See Ben-Amos 1976d, ix–xiv.
– 1976c: Analytical Categories and Ethnic Genres. See Ben-Amos 1976d, 214–242.
– (ed.) 1976d: *Folklore Genres.* Austin: University of Texas Press.
– 1992: Do We Need Ideal Types (in Folklore)? An Address to Lauri Honko. *NIF
Papers* 2.

Ben-Amos, Dan & Kenneth S. Goldstein (eds.) 1975: *Folklore, Performance and Communication*. The Hague: Mouton.

Benedict, Ruth 1935: *Zuni Mythology*. Vols. 1–2. New York: Columbia University Press.

Bennett, Gillian 1985: Heavenly Protection and Family Unity: The Concept of Revenant among Elderly Urban Women. *Folklore* 96, 87–97.

Berendsohn, Walter A. 1921: *Grundformen volkstümlicher Erzählkunst in den Kinder- und Hausmärchen der Brüder Grimm. Ein Stilkritischer Versuch*. Wiesbaden: Dr. Martin Sändig.

Béres, András 1967: *Rozsályi népmesék* [Folktales of Rozsály]. Uj Magyar Népköltési Gyüjtemény 12. Budapest: Akadémiai Könyvkiadó.

Berkovitz, Leonard 1972: *Social Psychology*. Glenview, IL: Scott, Foresman & Co.

Berne, Eric 1973: *What Do You Say after You Say Hello?* New York: Grove Press.

Berze Nagy, János 1957: *Magyar Népmesetipusok*. Vols. 1–2. (Edited by István Báno.) Pécs: Council of County Baranya.

Bettelheim, Bruno 1976: *The Uses of Enchantment. The Meaning and Importance of Fairy Tales*. New York: Knopf.

Betz, Felicitas 1983: Der Märchenerzähler nach dem Ende der mündlichen Überlieferung. See Wehse 1983, 113–125.

Bianco, Carla & Maurizio Del Ninno (eds.) 1981: *Festa antropologia e semiotica*. Firenze: Nuova Gueraldi Editrice.

Bihari, Anna 1980: *Magyar Népmonda Katalógus* [A catalogue of Hungarian folk belief legends]. Budapest: MTA Néprajzi Kutatócsoport.

Bird, Donald Allport 1979: Rumor as Folklore. An Interpretation and Inventory. Ph.D. dissertation. Indiana University, Bloomington.

Bîrlea, Ovidiu 1973: Über das Sammel volkstümlichen Prosaerzählgutes in Rumänien. See Karlinger 1973b, 445–446.

Bloomington Herald Telephone 1969, October 31.

Boas, Franz 1927/1955: *Primitive Art*. New York: Dover Publications.

– 1940/1966: *Race, Language and Culture*. New York: Free Press.

Boberg, Inger Margaret 1938: The Tale of Cupid and Psyche. *Classica et mediaevalie: Revue danoise de philologie et d'histoire* 1, 177–216.

Böckel, Otto 1913: *Psychologie der Volksdichtung*. Leipzig: B. G. Teubner.

Bødker, Laurits 1957: The Brave Tailor in Danish Tradition. See Richmond 1957, 1–23.

– 1965: *Folk Literature*. Copenhagen: Rosenkilde & Bagger.

Bogatyrev, Pjotr (ed.) 1954: *Russkoe narodnoe poetičeskoe tvortshestvo*. Moscow: Academy of Sciences.

Bogatyrev, Pjotr & Roman Jakobson 1929: Die Folklore als eine besondere Form des Schaffens. *Donum Natalicum Schrijnen*. Nijmegen, Utrecht: Dekker & van de Vegt, 900–913.

Bolte, Johannes 1921: *Zeugnisse zur Geschichte der Märchen*. FF Communications 39. Helsinki: Academia Scientiarum Fennica.

Bolte, Johannes & Georg Polívka 1918–1932: *Anmerkungen zu den Kinder- und Hausmärchen der Brüder Grimm*. Vols. 1–5. 2nd ed. 1963. Hildesheim: Georg Olms.

Bošković-Stulli, Maja 1959: Neka metodoloska pitanja u proucavanju folklore granicnih i etnicki mjesovitih podrucja. *Papers from the Yugoslavian Folklore Congress in Varazdin*. Varazdin.

– 1979: Zeitungen, Fernsehen, mündliches Erzählen in der Stadt Zagreb. *Fabula* 20, 8–17.

– (ed.) 1981: *Folklore and Oral Communication*. Narodna Umjetnost. Vol. 19. Zagreb: Zavod za istrazivanje folklore Instituta za Filologiju i Folkloristiku.

Bowra, C. M. 1964: *Heroic Poetry*. London: McMillan & Co.

Brachetti, Machtilda Agnes 1930: Das Volksmärchen als Gemeinschaftdichtung. *Norddeutsche Zeitschrift für Volkskunde* 9, 197–212.

Brandes, Stanley H. 1975: Family Misfortune Stories in American Folklore. *Journal of the Folklore Institute* 12, 5–18.

Brednich, Rolf Wilhelm 1990: *Die Spinne in der Yucca-Palme. Sagenhafte Geschichten von heute.* München: Beck.

Brednich Rolf Wh. & Jürgen Dittmar (eds.) 1982: *Festschrift für Lutz Röhrich. Jahrbuch für Volksliedforschung* 27–28.

Briggs, Charles L. 1988: *Competence in Performance. The Creativity of Tradition in Mexicano Verbal Art.* Philadelphia: University of Pennsylvania Press.

– 1993: Metadiscursive Practices and Scholarly Authority in Folkloristics. *Journal of American Folklore* 106, 387–434.

Briggs, Charles L. & Richard Bauman 1992: Genre, Intertextuality, and Social Power. *Journal of Linguistic Anthropology* 2, 131–172.

Briggs, Katharine 1963: Grimm Tales in Britain. *Hässische Blätter für Volkskunde* 54, 511–524.

Brinkmann, O. 1933: *Das Erzählen in einer Dorfgemeinschaft.* Münster: Aschendorff.

Brittle, Gerald 1980: *The Demonologist. The Extraordinary Career of Ed and Lorraine Warren.* New York: Berkeley Books.

Bronner, Simon J. (ed.) 1992: *Creativity and Tradition in Folklore. New Directions.* Logan: Utah State University Press.

Brunvand, Jan 1970: Some Thoughts on the Ethnic-Regional Riddle Jokes. *Indiana Folklore* 3, 128–142.

– 1981: *The Vanishing Hitchhiker. American Urban Legends and Their Meaning.* New York: Norton.

Bühler, Charlotte and Josephine Bilz 1961: *Das Märchen und die Phantasie des Kindes.* München: Johann Ambrosius Barth.

Bünker, Reinhold 1906: *Schwänke, Sagen und Märchen heanzischer Mundart.* Leipzig.

Burgess, Ernest & Donald J. Bogue 1967: *Urban Sociology.* Chicago: University of Chicago Press.

Burlakoff, N. & Carl Lindahl (eds.) 1980: *Folklore on Two Continents.* Bloomington: Trickster Press.

Burns, Thomas A. 1976: *Doing the Wash: an Expressive Culture and Personality Study of a Joke and its Tellers.* Pennsylvania: Norwood.

Cammann, Alfred 1961: *Westpreussische Märchen.* Berlin: de Gruyter.

– 1967: *Deutsche Volksmärchen aus Russland und Rumänien.* Göttingen: Schwartz.

– 1973: *Märchenwelt der Preussenländes.* Schloss Bleckede, Elbe: O. Meissner.

Campbell, John Francis (of Islay) 1860–1862: *Popular Tales of the West Highlands.* Vols. 1–4. Edinburgh.

Campbell, Marie 1958: *Tales from the Cloud Walking Country.* Bloomington: Indiana University Press.

Caplow, Theodore 1948: Rumors in War. *Social Forces* 25, 298–302.

Carr, David 1986: *Time, Narrative and History.* Bloomington: Indiana University Press.

Cattell, Raymond B. 1966: *The Scientific Analysis of Personality.* Chicago: University of Chicago Press.

Chicago Daily News 1973: A Ghostly Guide to Chicago. April 15, 7–8.

Christiansen, Reidar Th. 1962: *European Folklore in America.* Studia Norvegica 12. Oslo: Universitetsforlaget.

Čičerov, I. V. 1946: Traditsija i avtorskoe načalo v folklore. *Sovjetskaja Etnografija* 2, 29–40.

Clark, Kenneth B. 1940: Some Factors Influencing the Remembering of Prose Material. *Archives of Psychology* 253, 61.

Clarkson, Atelia & Gilbert B. Cross 1980: *World Folktales: A Scribner Resource Collection.* New York: Scribner.

Clements, William M. 1973: The Types of the Polack Joke. *Folklore Forum Bibliographic and Special Series* 3. Bloomington: Folklore Publications Group.

Cocchiara, Giuseppe 1954: *Storia del folklore in Europa.* Torino: Einaudi.

Cockrum, William Monroe 1907: *Pioneer History of Indiana Including Stories, Incidents and Customs of the Early Settlers.* Oakland City, IN: Press of Oakland City Journal.

Cord, Xenia E. 1969a: Department Store Snakes. *Indiana Folklore* 2, 110–114.

– 1969b: Further Notes on "The Assilant in the Back Seat." *Indiana Folklore* 2, 47–54.

Courier Journal 1993, February 4.

Crépeau, Pierre 1978: *Voyage au pays des merveilles: Quatre autobiographies d'immigrants.* Ottawa: The National Museum of Canada.

Cross, Paulette 1973: Jokes and Black Consciousness. See Dundes 1973, 651.

Crowley, Daniel J. 1966: *I Could Talk Old–Story Good. Creativity in Bahamian Folklore.* Berkeley and Los Angeles: California University Press.

Dance, Daryl Cumber 1978: *Shuckin' and Jivin'. Folklore from Contemporary Black Americans.* Bloomington: Indiana University Press.

Darnton, Robert 1984: *The Great Cat Massacre and Other Episodes in French Cultural History.* New York: Basic Books.

Dégh, Linda 1940: *Pandur Péter hét bagi meséje* [Seven tales from Bag by Péter Pandur]. Budapest: Officina.

– 1943: *Pandur Péter meséi* [Tales of Péter Pandur]. Vols. 1–2. Uj Magyar Népköltési Gyüjtemény 3–4. Budapest: Franklin.

– 1944: Adatok a mesekeret jelentöségéhez [The importance of the tale-frame]. *Ethnographia* 55, 130–139.

– 1955–1960: *Kakasdi Népmesék* [Folktales of Kakasd]. Vols. 1–2. Uj Magyar Népköltési Gyüjtemény 8–9. Budapest: Akadémiai Kiadó.

– 1957: Some Questions of the Social Function of Storytelling. *Acta Ethnographica* 6, 91–147.

– 1959: Latenz und Aufleben des Märchenguts einer Gemeinschaft. *Rheinisches Jahrbuch für Volkskunde* 10, 23–39.

– 1960: Az egyéniségvizgálat perspektivái [Perspectives of personality study]. *Ethnographia* 71, 28–43.

– 1961: Die Schöpferische Tätigkeit des Erzählers. See Ranke 1961b, 63–73.

– 1962: *Märchen, Erzähler und Erzählgemeinschaft dargestellt an der ungarischen Volksüberlieferung.* Berlin: Deutsche Akademie der Wissenschaften.

– 1965a: *Folktales of Hungary.* Chicago: University of Chicago Press.

– 1965b: Processes of Legend Formation. *Laographia* 23, 77–87.

– 1966: Approaches to Folklore Research among Immigrant Groups. *Journal of American Folklore* 79, 551–556.

– 1968a: The Runaway Grandmother. *Indiana Folklore* 1, 68–77.

– 1968b: The Hook. *Indiana Folklore* 1, 92–106.

– 1968–1969: Survival and Revival of European Folk Cultures in America. *Ethnologia Europaea* 2–3, 97–107.

– 1969/1989: *Folktales and Society. Story-Telling in a Hungarian Peasant Community.* (Translated by Emily M. Schossberger.) Bloomington: Indiana University Press.

– 1969a: The House of Blue Lights Revisited. *Indiana Folklore* 2, 11–28.

– 1969b: The Haunted Bridges Near Avon and Danville and Their Role in Legend Formation. *Indiana Folkore* 2:1, 54–89.

– 1969c: The Roommate's Death and Related Dormitory Stories in Formation. *Indiana Folklore* 2:2, 55–74.

– 1969d: Two Old World Narrators in Urban Setting. *Kontakte und Grenzen: Probleme der Volks-, Kultur-, und Sozialforschung. Festschrift für Gerhard Heilfurth zum 60. Geburtstag.* Göttingen: Schwartz, 71–86.

– 1970: Narratives from Early Indiana. *Indiana Folklore* 3, 229–241.

– 1971: The Belief Legend in Modern Society: Form, Function, and Relationship to Other Genres. See Hand 1971, 55–68.

– 1972: Folk Narrative. See Dorson 1972, 53–84.

– 1973: Neue Sagenerscheinungen in der industriellen Umwelt der USA. Lutz Röhrich (ed.), *Probleme der Sagenbildung.* Freiburg: Deutsche Forschungsgemeinschaft, 34–51.

- 1975a: Stadt-Land-Unterschiede in den USA, dargelegt am Beispiel moderner Sagenbildung. See Kaufmann 1975, 93–108.
- 1975b: *People in the Tobacco Belt: Four Lives*. Ottawa: National Museum of Canada.
- 1976: Symbiosis of Joke and Legend. A Case of Conversational Folklore. See Dégh, Glassie & Oinas 1976, 101–102.
- 1977: Biologie des Erzählguts. *Enzyklopädie des Märchens* 2. Berlin: Walter de Gruyter, 386–406.
- 1978a: The Tree That Reached up to the Sky. See Dégh 1978b, 263–318.
- (ed.) 1978b: *Studies in East European Folk Narrative*. American Folk Society Bibliographical and Special Series 30 & The Indiana University Folklore Monographs Series 25. Bloomington.
- 1979a: Conduit-Theorie. *Enzyklopädie des Märchens* 3. Berlin: Walter de Gruyter, 124–126.
- 1979b: Folklore of the Békevár Community. Robert Blumstock (ed.), *Working Papers of a Canadian Prairie Community*. Ottawa: The National Museum of Canada, 13–64.
- 1979c: Grimm's Household Tales and Its Place in the Household. The Social Relevance of a Controversial Classic. *Western Folklore* 38, 100–103.
- 1981a: The Peasant Element in the Hungarian and East European Magic Tale. *Cahiers de Litterature Orale* 9, 45–78.
- 1981b: The Magic Tale and its Magic. *International Folklore Review* 1, 71–76.
- 1982a: Erzählen, Erzähler. *Enzyklopädie des Märchens* 4. Berlin: Walter de Gruyter, 332–334.
- 1982b: The Jokes of an Irishman. See Brednich & Dittmar 1982, 90–108.
- 1983: Zur Rezeption der Grimmschen Märchen in den USA. See Doderer 1983, 116–128.
- 1985a: The Theory of Personal Experience Narrative. See Kvideland & Sellberg 1985, 233–242.
- 1985b: "When I Was Six We Moved West": The Theory of Personal Experience Narrative. *New York Folklore* XI/1–4, 99–108.
- 1985c: Frauenmärchen. *Enzyklopädie des Märchens* 5. Berlin: Walter de Gruyter, 211–220.
- 1988: What Did the Grimm Brothers Give to and Take from the Folk? See McGlathery 1988, 66–90.
- 1990: How Storytellers Interpret the Snakeprince Tale? See Nøjgaard 1990, 47–62.
- 1992a: What Kind of People Tell Legends? See Kvideland 1992, 104–113.
- 1992b: The Legend Conduit. See Bronner 1992, 105–126.

Dégh, Linda, Henry Glassie & Felix J. Oinas (eds.) 1976: *Folklore Today. A Festschrift for Richard M. Dorson*. Bloomington: Indiana University Press.

Dégh, Linda & Jaromír Jech 1957: Příspevek k studii interethnických vlivů v lidovém vypravování. *Slovensky Národopis* 5, 567–608.

Dégh, Linda & Andrew Vázsonyi 1971: Legend and Belief. *Genre* 4/3, 281–304.

- 1973: The Dialectics of the Legend. *Folklore Preprint Series* 6. Bloomington, 8–11.
- 1974: The Memorate and the Proto-Memorate. *Journal of American Folklore* 87, 225–239.
- 1975: The Hypothesis of Multi-Conduit Transmission in Folklore. See Ben-Amos & Goldstein 1975, 207–254.
- 1976: Legend and Belief. (Reprint of 1971.) See Ben-Amos 1976d, 93–123.
- 1978: The Crack on the Red Goblet, or Truth and Modern Legend. See Dorson 1978, 253–272.
- 1979: Magic for Sale. Märchen and Legend in TV Advertising. *Fabula* 20, 64–66.
- 1981: La parola "cane" morde? Dall'azione alla leggenda, dalla leggenda all'azione. See Bianco & Del Ninno 1981, 58–71.
- 1983: Does the Word "Dog" Bite? Ostensive Action: A Means of Legend-Telling. *Journal of Folklore Research* 20, 5–34.

Delargy, James H. 1945: *The Gaelic Story-Teller, with Some Notes on Gaelic Folktales*. London: Rhys Memorial Lecture.

Dobos, Ilona S. 1962: *Egy somogyi parasztcsalád meséi* [Tales of a peasant family of Somogy]. Uj Magyar Népköltési Gyüjtemény 10. Budapest: Akadémiai Kiadó.

– 1964: Az 'igaz'történetek müfajának kérdéséröl. *Ethnographia* 75, 198–215.

– 1978: True Stories. See Dégh 1978b, 167–206.

– 1981: *Áldozatok*. Budapest: Kozmosz.

Doderer, Klaus (ed.) 1983: *Über Märchen für Kinder von heute*. Veinheim und Basel: Beltz.

Dolby, Sandra 1977: The Oral Personal Narrative in Its Generic Context. *Fabula* 18, 18–39.

– 1985: A Literary Folkloristic Methodology for the Study of Meaning in Personal Narrative. *Journal of Folklore Research* 22, 45–69.

– 1989: *Literary Folkloristics and the Personal Narrative*. Bloomington: Indiana University Press.

Dolby-Stahl, Sandra. See Dolby, Sandra.

Dömötör, Tekla 1965: Zur Frage der sogenannten Kausalfiktionen. Georgios A . Megas (ed.), International Congress for Folk-Narrative Research in Athens. *Laographia* 22.

Donaldson, Scott 1969: *The Suburban Myth*. New York: Columbia University Press.

Dorson, Richard M. 1945: Print and American Folklore. *California Folklore Quarterly* 4, 207.

– 1948: Dialect Stories of the Upper Peninsula: A New Form of American Folklore. *Journal of American Folklore* 61, 113–150.

– 1956: *Negro Folktales in Michigan*. Cambridge: Harvard University Press.

– 1959a: *American Folklore*. Chicago: University of Chicago Press.

– 1959b: A Theory of American Folklore. *Journal of American Folklore* 72, 197–215.

– 1960: Oral Styles of American Folk Narrators. Thomas A. Sebeok (ed.), *Style in Language*. Cambridge, MA: MIT Press.

– 1968: *The British Folklorists. A History*. Chicago: University of Chicago Press.

– 1968–1969: The Ethnic Research Survey of Northwest Indiana. *Kontakte und Grenzen: Probleme der Volks-, Kultur-, und Sozialforschung. Festschrift für Gerhard Heilfurth zum 60. Geburtstag*. Göttingen: Schwartz, 65–69.

– 1970: Is There a Folk in the City? *Journal of American Folklore* 83, 185–222.

– (ed.) 1972: *Folklore and Folklife. An Introduction*. Chicago: University of Chicago Press.

– 1973: *America in Legend. Folklore from the Colonial Period to the Present*. New York: Pantheon Books.

– (ed.) 1978: *Folklore in the Modern World*. The Hague: Mouton.

– 1981: *Land of the Millrats*. Cambridge: Harvard University Press.

Dowling, Colette 1981: *The Cinderella Complex. Women's Hidden Fear of Independence*. New York: Simon and Schuster.

Dubois, William Edward Lee 1990: *Occult Crime Control. The Law Enforcement Manual of Investigation, Analysis and Prevention*.

Dundes, Alan 1961: Brown County Superstition. *Midwest Folklore* 9, 25–33.

– 1964: *The Morphology of North American Indian Folktales*. FF Communications 195. Helsinki: Academia Scientiarum Fennica.

– (ed.) 1965: *The Study of Folklore*. Englewood Cliffs, NJ: Prentice-Hall.

– 1966: Metafolklore, or Oral Literary Criticism. *The Monist* 50, 505–516.

– 1969a: The Devolutionary Premise in Folklore Theory. *Journal of the Folklore Institute* 6, 5–19.

– 1969b: Comment to Heda Jason: A Multidimensional Approach to Oral Literature. *Current Anthropology* 10:4, 421–422.

– 1971a: Folk Ideas as Units of Worldview. *Journal of American Folklore* 84: 93–103.

– 1971b: A Study of Ethnic Slurs: The Jew and the Polack in the United States. *Journal of American Folklore* 84, 186–203.

– (ed.) 1973: *Mother Wit from the Laughing Barrel*. Englewood Cliffs, NJ: Prentice-Hall.

– 1980: *Interpreting Folklore*. Bloomington: Indiana University Press.

- 1986: The Anthropologists and the Comparative Method in Folklore. *Journal of Folklore Research* 23, 125–146.
Dundes, Alan & E. O. Arewa 1964: Proverbs and the ethnography of speaking. J. J. Gumperz & Dell Hymes (eds.), The ethnography of communication. *American Anthropology* 66, part 2, 70–85.
Dundes, Alan & Carl Pagter 1975: *Urban Folklore from the Paperwork Empire*. Austin: Texas University Press.
Eastman, Mary Huse 1926: *Index to Fairy Tales and Legends*. Boston: F. W. Faxon Co.
Eco, Umberto 1975: Paramètres de la Sémiologie Theatrale. André Helbo (ed.), *Sémiologie de la Représentation. Theatre, Télévision, Bande Dessinée*. Editions Complexe.
- 1979: *A Theory of Semiotics*. Bloomington: Indiana University Press.
Ehlich, Konrad 1980: *Erzählen im Alltag*. Frankfurt: Suhrkamp.
Eliade, Mircea 1976: *Occultism, Witchcraft, and Cultural Fashions. Essays in Comparative Religion*. Chicago: University of Chicago Press.
Ellis, Bill 1989a: When Is a Legend? An Essay in Legend Morphology: The Questing Beast. *Perspectives on Contemporary Legend* 4, 31–54.
- 1989b: Death by Folklore: Ostension, Contemporary Legend, and Murder. *Western Folklore* 48, 201–220.
Ellis, John M. 1983: *One Fairy Story Too Many. The Brothers Grimm and Their Tales*. Chicago: University of Chicago Press.
El-Shamy, Hasan M. 1967: Folkloric Behavior. A Theory for the Study of Dynamics of Traditional Culture. Ph.D. dissertation. Indiana University, Bloomington.
- 1979: *Brother and Sister, Type 872*. A Cognitive Behavioristic Analysis of a Middle Eastern Oikotype*. Folklore Monograph Series 8. Bloomington: Folklore Publications Group, Indiana University.
- 1984: Vom Fisch geboren. *Enzyklopädie des Märchens* 4. Berlin: Walter de Gruyter.
Erdész, Sándor 1968: *Ámi Lajos meséi* [Tales of Lajos Ámi]. Vols. 1–3. Uj Magyar Népköltési Gyüjtemény 13–15. Budapest: Akadémiai Kiadó.
Evans, Charles 1991: *Teens and Devil-Worship. What Everyone Should Know*. Lafayette: Huntington House.
Evansville Courier 1991, February 14.
Fabré, Daniel & Jacques Lacroix 1974: *La Tradition Orale du Conte Occitan: Les Pyrénées Audoises*. Vols. 1–2. Paris: Presses Universitaires de France.
Fabula. Zeitschrift für Erzählforschung 1967: Special Issue, Conference of the International Society for Folk Narrative Research, Liblice, September 1–4, 1966.
Falassi, Alessandro 1980: *Folklore by the Fireside*. Austin: University of Texas Press.
Faragó, József 1969: *Kurcsi Minya havasi mesemondó* [Alpine storyteller Minya Kurcsi]. Bucharest: Irodalmi Könyvkiadó.
- 1971: Storytellers with Rich Repertoires. *Acta Ethnographica* 20, 439–443.
- 1978: Alpine Storyteller Minya Kurcsi. See Dégh 1978b, 559–668.
Fetscher, Iring 1974: *Wer hat Dornröschen wachgeküsst? Das Märchen-Verwirrbuch*. Hamburg & Düsseldorf: Claassen.
Fine, Gary Alan 1985: The Goliath Effect: Corporate Dominance and Mercantile Legends. *Journal of American Folklore* 98, 63–84.
Fine, Gary Alan & Janet S. Severance 1987: Gerücht. *Enzyklopädie des Märchens* 5. Berlin: Walter de Gruyter, 1102–1109.
Finnegan, Ruth 1967: *Limba Stories and Story-Telling*. Oxford: Clarendon Press.
Fischer, David M. 1970: *Historian's Fallacies. Toward a Logic of Historical Thought*. New York, Evanston & London.
Fischer, John L. 1965: The Sociopsychological Analysis of Folktales. *Current Anthropology* 4, 235–296.
Fishman, Joshua A. 1966: *Hungarian Language Maintenance in the United States*. Bloomington: Indiana University Press.
Fraiberg, Selma H. 1959: *The Magic Years*. New York: Scribner.

Franz, Marie-Louise von 1970: *An Introduction to the Psychology of Fairy Tales.* New York: Spring Publications.
 – 1972: *Problems of the Feminine in Fairytales.* Zürich: Spring Publications.
Gaál, Karoly 1965: *Angaben zu den abergläubischen Erzählungen aus den südlichen Burgenland.* Eisenstadt: Burgenländische Landesmuseum.
 – 1972: *Die Volksmärchen der Magyaren im südlichen Burgenland.* Berlin: Walter de Gruyter.
George, Philip Brandt 1972: The Ghost of Cline Avenue: "La Llorona" in the Calumet Region. *Indiana Folklore* 5, 56–91.
Georges, Robert A. 1969: Toward an Understanding of Storytelling Events. *Journal of American Folklore* 82, 313–328.
 – 1971: The General Concept of Legend. Some Assumptions to Be Re-examined and Reassessed. See Hand 1971, 1–19.
 – 1972: Process and Structure in Traditional Storytelling in the Balkans: Some Preliminary Remarks. H. Birnbaum & S. Vryonis (eds.), *Aspects of the Balkans. Continuity and Change.* The Hague, 319–337.
 – 1979: Feedback and Response in Storytelling. *Western Folklore* 38, 104–110.
 – 1981: Do Narrators Really Disgress? A Reconsideration of Audience Asides in Narrating. *Western Folklore* 40, 245–252.
 – 1986: The Pervasiveness in Contemporary Folklore Studies of Assumptions, Concepts and Constructs Usually Associated with the Historic-Geographic Method. *Journal of Folklore Research* 23, 87–104.
 – 1991: Earning, Appropriating, Concealing, and Denying the Identity of Folklorist. *Western Folklore* 50, 3–12.
Georges, Robert A. & Michael O. Jones 1980: *People Studying People. The Human Element in Fieldwork.* Berkeley: University of California Press.
Gide, Andre 1949: *Oscar Wilde: In memorium (reminiscences) de profundis.* (Translated from the French by Bernard Frechtman.) New York: Philosophical Library.
Girardot, N. J. 1977: Initiation and Meaning in the Tale of Snow White and the Seven Dwarfs. *Journal of American Folklore* 90, 279–280.
Glade, Dieter 1966: Zum Anderson'schen Gesetz der Selbstberichtigung. *Fabula* 8, 235–256.
Glassie, Henry n.d.: Take That Night Train to Selma. An Excursion to the Outskirts of Scholarship. Henry Glassie, Edward D. Ives & John F. Szwed (eds.), *Folksongs and Their Makers.* Bowling Green: Bowling Green University Popular Press.
 – 1975: *All Silver and No Brass. An Irish Christmas Mumming.* Bloomington.
 – 1983: The Moral Lore of Folklore. *Folklore Forum* 16, 123–152.
Goffman, Erving 1959: *The Presentation of Self in Everyday Life.* New York: Anchor Books.
 – 1974: *Frame Analysis.* New York: Harper & Row.
Goldberg, Christine 1986: The Construction of Folktales. *Journal of Folklore Research* 23, 163–176.
Goldstein, Kenneth S. 1964: *A Guide for Field Workers in Folklore.* Hatboro, PA: Folklore Associates.
 – 1967a: Experimental Folklore: Laboratory vs. Field. D. K. Wilgus (ed.), *Folklore International. Essays in Traditional Literature, Belief and Custom in Honor of Wayland Debs Hand.* Hatboro, PA: Folklore Associates, 72–84.
 – 1967b: The Induced Natural Context. An Ethnographic Folklore Field Technique. June Helm (ed.), *Essays on the Verbal and Visual Arts.* Seattle: University of Washington Press, 1–6.
Gordon, Milton M. 1964: *Assimilation in American Life.* New York: Oxford University Press.
Görög, Veronika, Platiel, Suzanne, Rey-Hulman, Diana & Christiane Seydon 1980: *Histoires d'enfants terribles.* Preface by Geneviève Griaule. Paris: G. P. Maisonneuve et Larose.

Görög-Karady, Veronika & Bruno de la Salle 1979: Qui conte en France? L'apparition de quelques nouveaux types de conteurs. Lecture at the Seventh Congress of the International Society for Folk Narrative Research, Edinburgh, Scotland.

Greenberg, Andrea 1973: Drugged and Seduced. A Contemporary Legend. *New York Folklore Quarterly* 29, 131–158.

Greverus, Ina-Maria 1978: *Kultur und Alltagswelt.* München: Beck.

Grider, Sylvia Ann 1973: Dormitory Legend Telling in Progress: Fall 1971 – Winter 1973. *Indiana Folklore* 6, 1–32.

– 1976: The Supernatural Narrative of Children. Unpublished Ph.D. dissertation. Indiana University, Bloomington.

– 1980: The Hatchet Man. Linda Dégh (ed.), *Indiana Folklore Reader.* Bloomington: Indiana University Press, 147–178.

Grimm, die Brüder 1857: *Deutsche Sagen.* München: Wilhelm Goldmann.

Grimm, Jacob & Wilhelm 1812–1815: *Kinder- und Hausmärchen,* I–II. Berlin.

Grimm, Wilhelm 1881–1887: *Kleinere Schriften,* I–IV. Berlin.

Gutowski, John 1992: The Beast of Busco: An American Tradition. Unpublished manuscript.

Gwyndaf, Robin 1976: The Prose Narrative Repertoire of a Passive Tradition Bearer in a Welsh Rural Community. Genre Analysis and Formation. See Pentikäinen & Juurikka 1976, 283–293.

Haiding, Karl 1953: Träger der Volkserzählungen in unseren Tagen. *Österreichisches Zeitschrift für Volkskunde* 17, 24–36.

Hall, Edward T. 1968: Proxemics. *Current Anthropology* 9, 83–108.

Halloween. The New Encyclopaedia Britannica in 30 volumes. Micropaedia vol. IV (1974), 862. Chicago & London.

Hampp, Irmgard 1961: *Beschwörung, Segen, Gebet: Untersuchungen zum Zauberspruch aus dem Bereich der Volksheilkunde.* Stuttgart.

Hand, Wayland D. 1961: Abergläubische Grundelemente in der amerikanischen Volkserzählung. See Ranke 1961b, 105–112.

– 1963a: Ein Katalog der amerikanischen Sagen. See Peeters 1963b, 43–48.

– 1963b: Die Märchen der Brüder Grimm in den Vereinigten Staaten. *Hessische Blätter* 54, 525–544.

– (ed.) 1971: *American Folk Legend. A Symposium.* Los Angeles: University of California Press.

Handlin, Oscar 1951: *The Uprooted.* New York: Little, Brown and Co.

– 1959: *Immigration as a Factor in American History.* Englewood Cliffs, NJ: Prentice-Hall.

Hansen, Marcus Lee 1960: *The Atlantic Migration 1607–1860.* Cambridge: Harvard University Press.

Harkort, Fritz 1968: Volkserzählungsforschung und Parapsychologie. F. Harkort, K. C. Peeters & R. Wildhaber (eds.), *Volksüberlieferung. Festschrift für Kurt Ranke zur Vollendung des 60. Lebensjahres.* Göttingen: Otto Schwartz, 89–105.

Hartland, Edwin Sidney 1891: *The Science of Fairy Tales.* London: W. Scott.

Hazelwood, Kim 1992: The Agony of Martensville. *Western Report,* June 22.

Heilfurth, Gerhard 1967: *Bergbau und Bergmann in der deutschsprachigen Sangenüberlieferung Mitteleuropas.* Marburg: N. G. Elwert.

Heim und Welt 1985, January 15.

Heine, Heinrich n.d.: *Sämtliche Werke,* Vol. 1. (Edited by Ernst Elster.) Leipzig und Vienna: Bibliographisches Institut.

Henssen, Gottfried 1939: Stand und Aufgaben der deutschen Erzählforschung. *Festschrift für Richard Wossilde.* Neumünster, 133–137.

– 1951: *Überlieferung und Persönlichkeit. Die Erzählungen und Lieder des Egbert Gerrits.* Münster: Aschendorff.

Hicks, Robert D. 1990: Police Pursuit of Satanic Crime. *Skeptical Inquirer* 14:I, 276–286; 14:II, 378–389.

- 1991: The Police Model of Satanism Crime. See Richardson, Best & Bromley 1991, 175–190.
Holbek, Bengt 1965: On the Classification of Folktales. *Laographia* 22, 158–161.
Holzer, Hans 1973: *The Witchcraft Report*. New York: Ace Books.
- 1974: *Ghost Hunter*. New York: Ace Books.
Honko, Lauri 1962: *Geisterglaube in Ingermanland*. FF Communications 185. Helsinki: Academia Scientiarum Fennica.
- 1965: Memorates and the Study of Folk-Beliefs. *Journal of the Folklore Institute* 1, 5–19.
- 1976: Genre Theory Revisited. See Pentikäinen & Juurikka 1976, 20–25.
- 1979/1980: Methods in Folk-Narrative Research: Their Status and Future. *Ethnologia Europea* 11.
- 1983: Research Traditions in Tradition Research. *Studia Fennica* 27, 13–22.
- 1984: Empty Texts, Full Meanings. On Transformal Meaning in Folklore. Papers I. The 8th Congress for the International Society for Folk Narrative Research, Bergen, Norway, 273–282.
- 1985: What Kind of Instruments for Folklore Protection? *NIF Newsletter* 13, 1–2, 3–11.
- 1986: Types of Comparison and Forms of Variation. *Journal of Folklore Research* 23, 105–124.
- 1989: Folkloristic Theories of Genre. Anna-Leena Siikala (ed.), Studies in Oral Narrative. *Studia Fennica* 33, 13–28.
- 1992: Folklorists Meet in Innsbruck. *FF Network* 5, 1–2.
Honti, János 1928: *Verzeichnis der publizierten ungarischen Volksmärchen*. FF Communications 81. Helsinki: Academia Scientiarum Fennica.
- 1937/1975: The Tale – Its World. *Studies in Oral Epic Tradition*. Budapest: Akadémiai Kiadó, 9–82.
- 1942: Dégh Linda: Pandur Péter meséi I–II. Kötet. [Book review of Tales of Péter Pandur by Linda Dégh.] *Ethnographia* 53, 238–240.
Honzl, Jindrich 1976: Dynamics of the Sign in the Theatre. Ladislav Matejka & Irwin R. Titunik (eds.), *Semiotics of Art*. Cambridge, MA: MIT Press.
Hoppál, Mihály 1969: Adalékok a lidérc hiedelemmondakör szemantikai modelljéhez. *Ethnographia* 80, 402–417.
Horn, Katalin 1983: Märchenmotive und gezeichneter Witz: Einige Möglichkeiten der Adaptation. *Österreichische Zeitschrift für Volkskunde* 37, 209–237.
Hough, Emerson 1920: Round our Town. *Saturday Evening Post*. February 14, 18–19.
Hufford, David J. 1982: *The Terror That Comes in the Night. An Experience-Centered Study of Supernatural Assault Tradition*. Philadelphia: University of Pennsylvania Press.
Hultkrantz, Åke 1968: "Miscellaneous Beliefs." Some Points of View concerning the Informal Religious Sayings. *Temenos* 3, 67–82.
Hunter, Ian M. L. 1964: *Memory*. Baltimore: Penguin Books.
Huntington, Ellsworth 1915: *Civilization and Climate*. New Haven: Yale University Press.
Ilf, Ilia Arnold & Jevgeni Petrov 1961: *The Twelve Chairs*. New York: Vintage Books.
Indianapolis Star 1972, May 6.
Ireland, Norma Olin 1973: *Index to Fairy Tales, 1941–1972*. Westwood, MA: F. W. Faxon Co.
Isler, Gotthilf 1971: Die Sennenpuppe. Eine Untersuchung über die religiöse Funktion einiger Alpensagen. *Schriften der Schweizerischen Gesellschaft für Volkskunde* 52. Basel: Verlag G. Krebs.
Jackson, Kenneth Hurlstone 1961: *The International Popular Tale and Early Welsh Tradition*. Cardiff: University of Wales Press.
Jacobs, Melville 1959: *The Content and Style of an Oral Literature. Clackamas Chinook Myths and Tales*. Chicago: University of Chicago Press.
- 1966a: A Look Ahead in Oral Literature Research. *Journal of American Folklore* 79, 413–427.
- (ed.) 1966b: The Anthropologist Looks at Myth. (First published in Journal of Ameri-

can Folklore 79.) *Publications of American Folklore Society, Bibliographical and Special Series* 17. Austin: University of Texas Press.

Jacobson, David J. 1948: *The Affairs of Dame Rumor*. New York: Rinehart.

Jahn, Ulrich 1891: *Volksmärchen aus Pommern und Rügen*. Leipzig: Norden.

Janning, Jürgen 1983: Märchenerzählen: Lässt er sich lernen – Kann man es lernen? See Wehse 1983, 126–140.

Jansen, William Hugh 1957: Classifying Performance in the Study of Verbal Folklore. See Richmond 1957, 110–118.

– 1959: The Esoteric-Exoteric Factor in Folklore. *Fabula* 2, 205–211.

– 1977: A Foreword. Ruth Ann Musick, *Coffin Hollow and Other Ghost Tales*. Lexington: University of Kentucky Press.

Jason, Heda 1969: A Multidimensional Approach to Oral Literature. *Current Anthropology* 10, 413–420.

– 1970: The Russian Criticism of the "Finnish School" in Folktale Scholarship. *Norveg* 14, 285–294.

Jech, Jaromir 1959: *Lidova vypravení z Kladska*. Prague.

Jeggle, Utz 1978: Alltag. Hermann Bausinger, Utz Jeggle, Gottfried Korff & Martin Scharfe (eds.), *Grundzüge der Volkskunde*. Darmstadt: Wissenschaftliche Buchgesellschaft, 81–126.

Jolles, André 1930: *Einfache Formen*. Tübingen: Max Niemeyer.

Jones, Steven Swann 1983: The Structure of Snow White. *Fabula* 24, 56–71.

– 1986: Structural and Thematic Application of the Comparative Method. *Journal of Folklore Research* 23, 147–162.

Jordan, Rosan A. & Susan Kalčík 1985: *Women's Folklore, Women's Culture*. Philadelphia: University of Pennsylvania Press.

Kalčík, Susan 1975: ". . . like Ann's gynecologist or the time I was almost raped." Personal Narratives in Women's Rap Groups. *Journal of American Folklore* 88, 3–11.

Kálmány, Lajos 1914: *Hagyományok* [Traditions]. Vols. I–II. Vác: A Néphagyományokat Gyüjtő Társaság.

Kamenetzky, Christa 1977: Folktale and Ideology in the Third Reich. *Journal of American Folklore* 90, 168–178.

Karlinger, Felix 1973a: 'Schneeweisschen und Rosenrot' in Sardinien: Zur Übernahme eines Buchmärchens in die volkstümliche Erzähltradition. *Hessische Blätter* 54, 585–593.

– (ed.) 1973b: *Wege der Märchenforschung*. Darmstadt.

Karpeles, Maud 1967: *Cecil Sharp. His Life and Works*. London: Routledge & Kegan Paul.

Katona, Imre 1980: Mannesfolklore – Weibesfolklore. Analyses der verschiedenen Gattungen. *Congressus Quintus Internationalis Fenno-Ugristarum*. Turku.

Katona, Lajos 1912: *Irodalmi Tanulmányai* [Literary essays]. Vols. I–II. Budapest: Franklin.

Kaufmann, Gerhard (ed.) 1975: *Stadt- und Land-Beziehungen. Verhandlungen des 19. deutschen Volkskunde-Kongresses in Hamburg vom 1. bis 7. Oktober 1973*. Göttingen: Otto Schwartz.

Keil, Charles 1979: The Concept of "the Folk." *Journal of the Folklore Institute* 16, 209–210.

Kirshenblatt-Gimblett, Barbara 1972: Traditional Storytelling in the Toronto Jewish Community. A Study in Performance and Creativity in an Immigrant Culture. Ph.D. dissertation. Indiana University, Bloomington.

Kiss, Gabriella 1959: AT 301-es mesetipus magyar redakciói (Csonka tehén fia) [Hungarian redactions of AT 301: Son of the cow with broken horn]. *Ethnographia* 70, 253–268.

Klapp, O. E. 1949: The Folk Hero. *Journal of American Folklore* 62, 17–25.

Kligman, Gail 1981: *Calus: Symbolic Transformation in Romanian Ritual*. Chicago: University of Chicago Press.

Klineberg, Otto 1958: *Social Psychology*. Revised edition. New York: Henry Holt & Co.

Kling, Samuel G. (ed.) 1966: *Legal encyclopedia for home and business*. New York: Benco editions.

Klintberg, Bengt af 1979: Modern Migratory Legends in Oral Tradition and Daily Papers. Papers of the Seventh Congress of the International Society for Folk Narrative Research, Edinburgh, Scotland. Abstracts of Papers, 61.

– 1990: *Die Ratte in der Pizza und andere moderne Sagen und Grosstadtmythen.* Kiel: Wolfgang Butt.

Klymasz, Robert 1973: A Canadian View of Process and Transition. *Journal of the Folklore Institute* 10, 131–140.

Kohli, Martin 1978: *Soziologie des Lebenslaufs.* Darmstadt: Luchterhand.

Köngäs-Maranda, Elli 1976: Individual and Tradition. See Pentikäinen & Juurikka 1976, 252–261.

König, Otto 1929: *Das Volk erzählt.* Vienna.

Korompay, Bertalan 1941: Népköltési kiadványainkról [Folklore publications]. *Ethnographia* 52, 169–179.

Kovács, Agnes 1944:*Kalotaszegi népmesék* [Folktales from Kalotaszeg]. Uj Magyar Népköltési Gyüjtemény 5–6. Budapest: Franklin.

– 1958: Die ungarische Märchenforschung der letzten Jahrzehnte. *Deutsches Jahrbuch für Volkskunde* 7, 453–466.

– 1961: Benedek Elek és a magyar néprajzkutatás [Elek Benedek and Hungarian folklore research]. *Ethnographia* 72, 430–444.

– 1980: A Bukovina Szekler Storyteller Today. See Burlakoff & Lindahl 1980, 372–381.

– 1984: Az égigérő fa meséjének redakciói és samanisztikus motivumai [The redactions of the sky-high tree and its shamanistic motifs]. *Folklór, folklorisztika és etnológia* 100, 16–29.

– (ed.) 1987–1990: *Catalogue of Hungarian Folktales* (in Hungarian with Summary in English). Vols. 1–9. Budapest: Ethnographical Institute.

Kovács, Agnes & L. Maróti 1966: *A rátótiádák tipusmutatója. A magyar falucsúfolók tipusai (AaTh 1200–1349)* [Index of Hungarian numskull tales (AaTh 1200–1349)]. Mimeographed. Nézprajzi Muzeum – MTA néprajzi Kutatócsoport. Budapest.

Kozocsa, Sándor 1963: Grimmsche Märchen in Ungarn: Eine Bibliographie. *Hessische Blätter* 9, 559–574.

Krohn, Kaarle 1926/1971: *Folklore Methodology. Formulated by Julius Krohn and Expanded by Nordic Researchers.* (Translated by Roger L. Welsch.) Austin: University of Texas Press.

Kvideland, Reimund (ed.) 1992: Folklore Processed, in Honour of Lauri Honko on his 60th Birthday 6th March 1992. *Studia Fennica Folkloristica* 1. Helsinki: Suomalaisen Kirjallisuuden Seura.

– 1993: The Study of Folktale Repertoires. Michael Chesnutt (ed.), *Telling Reality. Folklore Studies in Memory of Bengt Holbek.* NIF Publications 26. Copenhagen & Turku, 105–114.

Kvideland, Reimund & Torunn Sellberg (eds.) 1985: *Papers III. The 8th Congress for the International Society for Folk Narrative Research.* Bergen.

La Fave, Lawrence & Roger Mannell 1976: Does Ethnic Humor Serve Prejudice? *Journal of Communication* 26, 116–125.

Langlois, Janet 1985: *Belle Gunness: The Lady Bluebeard.* Bloomington: Indiana University Press.

Langness, L. L. 1965: *The Life History in Anthropological Science.* New York: Holt, Rinehart & Winston.

Lanham, Betty B. & Masao Shimura 1967: Folktales Commonly Told by American and Japanese Children. Ethical Themes of Omission and Commission. *Journal of American Folklore* 80, 33–48.

Larrabee, Eric & David Riesman 1964: Autos in America. See Riesman 1964, 255–292.

Leach, Maria (ed.) 1949: *Funk & Wagnalls Standard Dictionary of Folklore, Mythology, and Legend.* New York: Funk & Wagnalls.

Leary, James P. 1973: The Boondocks Monster of Camp Wapahani. *Indiana Folklore* 6, 174–190.

– 1976: Fists and Foul Mouths. Fights and Fight Stories in Contemporary Rural American Bars. *Journal of American Folklore* 89, 27–39.
Legman, G. 1968: *No Laughing Matter. An Analysis of Sexual Humor.* Vol. I. Bloomington: Indiana University Press.
– 1975: *No Laughing Matter. An Analysis of Sexual Humor.* Vol. II. Bloomington: Indiana University Press.
Lehmann, Albrecht 1983: *Erzählstruktur und Lebenslauf: Autobiographische Untersuchungen.* Frankfurt: Campus.
Lehtipuro, Outi 1979: The Untalented Storytellers. Papers of the Seventh Congress of the International Society for Folk Narrative Research, Edinburgh, Scotland. Abstracts of Papers, 72–74.
Lengyel, Emil 1948: *Americans from Hungary.* Philadelphia & New York: Lippincott.
LeVay, Anton Szandor 1969: *The Satanic Bible.* New York: Avon.
Levine, Lawrence W. 1977: *Black Culture and Black Consciousness.* New York: Oxford University Press.
Levy, Robert I. 1989: The Quest for Mind in Different Times and Different Places. Andrew E. Barnes & Peter N. Stearns (eds.), *Social History and Issues in Human Consciousness. Some Interdisciplinary Connections.* New York: New York University Press, 3–40.
Leyen, Friedrich von der 1911: *Das Märchen. Ein Versuch.* Leipzig.
Leyen, Friedrich von der & Kurt Schier 1958: *Das Märchen. Ein Versuch.* 4th revised edition. Heidelberg: Quelle & Meyer.
Littleton, Scott C. 1965: A two-dimensional scheme for the classification of narratives. *Journal of American Folklore* 78, 21–27.
Loftus, Elizabeth F. 1979: *Eyewitness Testimony.* Cambridge, MA: Harvard University Press.
Lord, Albert B. 1960: *Singer of Tales.* New York: Atheneum.
Lörincze, Lajos 1948: A tolna-baranyai (volt bukovinai) székelyek névadási szokásaihoz. *Ethnographia* 59, 36–47.
The Louisville Courier-Journal 1968, March 17, 2.
Loukatos, Demetrios 1974: Conteurs populaires transmettant leurs récits par écrit. Le cas d'un berger mi-illittré an Gréce. Paper delivered at the Folk-Narrative Congress, Helsinki.
Lüthi, Max 1974: *Das europäische Volksmärchen: Form und Wesen.* 4th edition. München: Francke.
– 1958: Hedvig von Beit: Symbolik des Märchen. A book review. *Fabula* 2, 182–189.
– 1959: Die Herkunft des Grimmschen Rapunzelmärchens. *Fabula* 3, 95–118.
– 1961/1966: *Volksmärchen und Volkssage. Zwei Grungformen erzählender Dichtung.* Bern & München: Francke.
– 1962/1979: *Märchen.* 7th revised edition. Stuttgart: Metzler.
– 1970/1976: *Once Upon a Time. On the Nature of Fairy Tales.* (Translated by Lee Chadeayne and Paul Gottwald. Introduction and notes by Francis Lee Utley.) Bloomington: Indiana University Press.
MacDougall, Curtis D. 1983: *Superstition and the Press.* Buffalo: Prometheus Books.
Mandelsberg, Rose S. 1991: *Cult Killers.* New York: Windsor.
Marót, Károly 1940: *Idios et koinoi. Gondolatok Fedics Mihály meséiröl* [Thoughts about the tales of Mihály Fedics]. Budapest: Egyetemes Philologiai Közlöny Budapest.
– 1956: *A görög irodalom kezdetei* [The beginnings of Greek literature]. Budapest: Akadémiai Kiadó.
Martin, Daniel & Gary Alan Fine 1991: Satanic Cults, Satanic Play: Is 'Dungeons & Dragons' a Breeding Ground for the Devil? See Richardson, Best & Bromley 1991, 107–123.
McCarl, Robert S. Jr. 1976: Smokejumper Initiation. Ritualized Communication in a Modern Occupation. *Journal of American Folklore* 89, 49–66.

McDowell, John 1982: Beyond Iconicity: The Texture of Kamsá Mythic Narrative. *Journal of the Folklore Institute* 19, 119–140.

McGlathery, James M. & al. 1988: *The Brothers Grimm and Folktale.* Urbana & Chicago: University of Illinois Press.

McNeil, William K. 1971: Mrs. F. – Little Joe. A Multiple Personality Experience and the Folklorist. *Indiana Folklore 4, 216–245.*

Megas, Georgios A. 1971: *Das Märchen von Amor und Psyche in der griechischen Volksüber-lieferung.* Athens: Athens Academy.

– 1975: Amor und Psyche. *Enzyklopädie des Märchens* 1. Berlin: Walter de Gruyter, 464–472.

Messinger, Sheldon L., Harold Sampson & Robert D. Towne 1968: Life as Theatre: Some Notes on the Dramaturgic Approach to Social Reality. See Truzzi 1968, 9–14.

Meyer zu Capellen, Renate 1980: Das Schöne Mädchen. Psychoanalytische Betrach-tungen zur 'Formwendung der Seele' des Mädchens. Helmut Brackert (ed.), *Und wenn sie nicht gestroben sind: Perspektiven auf das Märchen.* Frankfurt am Main: Suhr-kamp, 89–119.

Mieder, Wolfgang 1979: *Grimms Märchen – modern: Prosa, Gedichte, Karikaturen.* Stuttgart: Reclam.

Moldován, Domokos 1982: *A halottlátó. Filmek, dokumentumok.* Budapest: Gondolat.

Mook, Maurice A. 1968: Halloween in Central Pennsylvania. *Keystone Quarterly* 14, 124–129.

Moore, Powell A. 1959: *The Calumet Region.* Indianapolis: Indiana Historical Bureau.

Moser-Rath, Elfriede 1964: *Predigtmärlein der Barockzeit. Exempel, Sage, Schwank und Fabel in geistlichen Quellen der oberdeutsche Raumes.* Berlin: Walter de Gruyter.

Mulhern, Sherrill 1991: Satanism and Psychotherapy. A Rumor in Search of an Inquisi-tion. See Richardson, Best & Bromley 1991, 145–174.

Mullen, Patrick B. 1970: Department Store Snakes. *Indiana Folklore 3, 214–228.*

– 1978: The Folk Idea of Unlimited Good in American Buried Treasure Legends. *Journal of the Folklore Institute* 15, 209–220.

Müller, Ingeborg & Lutz Röhrich 1967: Deutscher Sagenkatalog. *Deutsches Jahrbuch für Volkskunde* 13, 353.

Myers, Robert J. 1948: *Celebrations. The Complete Book of American Holidays.* New York: Wilson Co.

Nadel, S. F. 1937–1938: A Field Experiment in Racial Psychology. *British Journal of Psychology* 28, 195–211.

Nagy, Géza 1985: *Karcsai mesék* [Folktales from Karcsa]. Vols. 1–2. (Collected, introduced, selected, and annotated by Sándor Erdész.) Budapest: Akadémiai Kiadó.

Nagy, Olga 1978: Personality and Community as Mirrored in the Formation of Klára Györi's Repertoire. See Dégh 1978b, 473–558.

Nathan, Debbie 1991: Satanism and Child Molestation. Constructing the Ritual Abuse and Scare. See Richardson, Best & Bromley 1991, 75–94.

Neumann, Siegfried 1964: *Des mecklenburgischer Volksschwank. Sein sozialer Gehalt und seine soziale Funktion.* Berlin: Akademie-Verlag.

– 1967a: Arbeitserinnerungen als Erzählungsinhalt. Gerhard Heilfurt (ed.), *Arbeit und Volksleben.* Göttingen, 274–284.

– 1967b: Volksprosa mit comischem Inhalt. *Fabula* 9, 137–148.

– 1970: *Ein mecklenburgischer Volkerzähler. Die Geschichten des August Rust.* Berlin: Akademie-Verlag.

New York Post 1982, December 21.

Nicolaisen, W. F. H. 1990: Variability and Creativity in Folk-Narrative. Veronika Görög-Karady (ed.), *D'un conte . . . à l'autre: La variabilité dans la littérature orale.* Paris: Editions du Centre National de la Recherche Scientifique, 39–46.

Nøjgaard, Morten (ed.) 1990: *The Telling of Stories. Approaches to a Traditional Craft. A Symposium.* Odense: Odense University Press.

Noy, Dov 1963: *Jefet Schwili erzählt*. Berlin.

Oberfeld, Charlotte 1970: *Märchen des Waldecker Landes*. Marburg.

Olrik, Axel 1909: Epische Gesetze der Volksdichtung. *Zeitschrift für Deutsches Altertum* 51, 1–12.

Oring, Elliott 1976: Three Functions of Folklore. Traditional Functionalism as Explanation in Folkloristics. *Journal of American Folklore* 89, 67–80.

Ortutay, Gyula 1940: *Fedics Mihály meséi* [Tales of Mihály Fedics]. Uj Magyar Népköltési Gyüjtemény 1. Budapest: Az Egyetemi Magyarságtudományi Intézet kiadása.

– 1955: The Science of Folklore in Hungary between the Two World Wars and the Period Subsequent to Liberation. *Acta Ethnographica* 4, 5–89.

– 1959: Principles of Oral Transmission in Folk Culture (Variations, 'Affinity'). *Acta Ethnographica* 8, 175–221.

– 1963a: Jacob Grimm und die ungarische Folkloristik. *Deutsches Jahrbuch für Volkskunde* 9, 169–189.

– 1963b: A magyar népmesekutatás eredményei és feladatai (Results and tasks of Hungarian folktale research). *A MTA Nyelv- és Irodalomtudományi Osztályának Közleményei* 1–4, 85–95, 109–112.

– 1965: A szájhagyományozás törvényszerüségei [Regularities in oral transmission]. *Ethnographia* 76, 3–9.

– 1972a: *Hungarian Folklore: Essays*. (Translated by István Butykai.) Budapest: Akadémiai Kiadó.

– 1972b: Mihály Fedics Relates Tales. See Ortutay 1972a, 225–285.

– 1972c: Principles of Oral Transmission in Folk Culture. See Ortutay 1972a, 132–174.

– 1973: A magam gyüjtéséröl [About my fieldwork]. *Tiszatáj* 8, 3–13.

– 1974a: A szimpozion célja [Goal of the symposium]. See Voigt 1974, 18–19.

– 1974b: Comments on Oral Tradition. See Voigt 1974, 79–81, 100–104.

Ortutay, Gyula, Linda Dégh & Agnes Kovács (eds.) 1960: *Magyar Népmesék* [Hungarian folktales]. Vols. 1–3. Budapest: Szépirodalmi Könyvkiadó.

Osolsobe, Ivo 1971: The Role of Models and Originals in Human Communication. The Theory of Signs and the Theory of Models. *Language Sciences* 14, 35.

– 1979: On Ostensive Communication. *Studia Semiotyczne* 9, 63–66.

Otto, Rudolf 1958: *The idea of the holy: And inquiry into the non-rational factor in the idea of the divine and its relation to the rational*. Oxford: Oxford University Press.

Oxendine, Jill (ed.) 1984–: *The National Storytelling Journal*.

Parade Magazine 1991, October 1991.

Park, Robert E. 1950: *Race and Culture*. Glencoe, IL: Free Press.

Peacock, James L. 1969: Society as Narrative. Robert S. Spencer (ed.), *Proceedings of the 1968 Annual Spring Meeting of the American Ethnological Society*. Seattle: University of Washington Press.

Peeters, K. C. 1963a: Theorie et pratique. See Peeters 1963b, 13–27.

– (ed.) 1963b: *Tagung der International Society for Folk-Narrative Research, Antwerpen, September 6–8, 1962*. Antwerpen: Centrum voor Studie en Documentatie.

Peirce, Charles Sanders 1960–1966: *Collected Papers*. (Edited by Charles Hartshorne and Paul Weiss.) Cambridge, MA: Belkamp.

Pentikäinen, Juha 1970a. See Pentikäinen, Juha 1971.

Pentikäinen, Juha 1970b: Perinne- ja uskontoantropologisen syvätutkimuksen menetelmästä [On the method of tradition- and religio-anthropological depth research]. *Sananjalka* 12. Turku.

– 1970c: Quellenanalytische Probleme der religiösen Überlieferung. *Temenos* 6, 89–118.

– 1971: *Marina Takalon uskonto*. Suomalaisen Kirjallisuuden Seuran Toimituksia 299. Helsinki: Suomalaisen Kirjallisuuden Seura.

– 1972: Depth Research. *Acta Ethnographica* 21, 127–131.

– 1978: *Oral Repertoire and World View. An Anthropological Study of Marina Takalo's Life History*. FF Communications 219. Helsinki: Academia Scientiarum Fennica.

Pentikäinen, Juha & Tuula Juurikka (eds.) 1976: Folk Narrative Research. Some Papers Presented at the VI Congress of the International Society for Folk Narrative Research, Helsinki. *Studia Fennica* 20. Helsinki: Suomalaisen Kirjallisuuden Seura.

Petsch, Robert 1900: *Formelhafte Schlüsse im Volksmärchen.* Berlin.

Peuckert, Will-Erich 1938: *Deutsche Volkstum in Märchen und Sage, Schwank und Rätsel.* Berlin: Walter de Gruyter.

– 1959: *Hochwies, Sagen, Schwänke und Märchen mit Beitragen von Alfred Karasek.* Göttingen.

– 1965: *Sagen: Geburt und Antwort der mythischen Welt.* Berlin: Erich Schmidt.

Phillips, Phil & Joan Hake Robie 1987: *Halloween and Satanism.* Lancaster, PA: Starburst Publishers.

Piaget, Jean 1929: *The Child's Conception of the World.* Totowa, NJ: Littlefield, Adams & Co.

– 1976: *Der Aufbau der Wirklichkeit beim Kind.* Gesammelte Werke II. Stuttgart: Suhrkamp.

Pitcher, Evelyn Goodenough & Ernst Prelinger 1969: *Children Tell Stories. An Analysis of Fantasy.* New York: International Universities Press.

Pop, Mihai 1958: Citeva Observatii Privind Cercetarea Folclorului Contemporan. *Revista de Folclor* 4, 57–66.

Potter, Jack M., May N. Diaz & George M. Foster (eds.) 1967: *Peasant Society. A Reader.* Boston: Little, Brown & Co.

Propp, Vladimir 1963: Märchen der Brüder Grimm im russischen Norden. *Deutsches Jahrbuch für Volkskunde* 9, 104–112.

Ranke, Friedrich 1935: *Volkssageforschung.* Breslau: Maruschke & Berendt.

– 1938: Kunstmärchen im Volksmund. *Zeitschrift für Volkskunde* 47, 129–130.

– 1969: Grundfragen der Volkssagenforschung. Leander Petzoldt (ed.), *Vergleichende Sagenforschung.* Darmstadt: Wissenschaftliche Buchgesellschaft, 1–20.

Ranke, Kurt 1955: Der Einfluss der Grimmschen Kinder- und Hausmärchen. *Papers of the International Congress of European and Western Ethnology.* Stockholm: International Commission of Folk Arts and Folklore, 126–135.

– 1958: Betrachtungen zum Wesen und zur Funktion des Märchens. *Studium Generale* 11, 647–664.

– 1961a: Einfache Formen. See Ranke 1961b, 1–11.

– (ed.) 1961b: *Internationaler Kongress der Volkserzählungsforscher in Kiel und Kopenhagen. Vorträge und Referate.* Berlin: Walter de Gruyter.

– 1965: Grenzsituationen des volkstümlichen Erzählgutes. Gyula Ortutay & Tibor Bodrogi (eds.), *Europa et Hungaria. Congressus Ethnographicus in Hungaria.* Budapest: Akadémiai Kiadó, 291–330.

– 1967a: Einfache Formen. *Journal of the Folklore Institute* 4, 17–31.

– 1967b: Kategorienprobleme der Volksprosa. *Fabula* 9, 4–12.

– 1969: Orale und Literale Kontinuität. See Bausinger & Brückner 1969, 102–116.

– 1978: *Die Welt der einfachen Formen.* Berlin: Walter de Gruyter.

Redfield, Robert 1960: *The Little Community. Peasant Society and Culture.* Chicago: the University of Chicago Press.

Rennick, Robert M. 1970: The Folklore of Place-Naming in Indiana. *Indiana Folklore* 3, 35–94.

Richardson, James T., Joel Best & David G. Bromley (eds.) 1991: *The Satanism Scare.* New York: Aldine, de Gruyter.

Richmond, Winthorp Edson (ed.) 1957: *Studies in Folklore.* Bloomington: Indiana University Press.

Riesman, David (ed.) 1964: *Abundance for What? And Other Essays.* New York: Doubleday.

Roberts, Leonard 1969: *Old Greasybeard. Tales from the Cumberland Gap.* Detroit: Folklore Associates.

– 1974: *Sang Branch Settlers. Folksongs and Tales of a Kentucky Mountain Family.* Austin: American Folklore Society.

Robinson, John A. 1981: Personal Narratives Reconsidered. *Journal of American Folklore* 94, 58–85.

Roemer, Danielle 1971: Scary Story Legends. *Folklore Annual of the University Folklore Association, Austin, Texas* 3, 1–16.

Rogge, Jan Uwe 1983: Märchen in den Medien: Über Möglichkeiten und Grenzen medialer Märchen-Adaption. See Doderer 1983, 129–154.

Röhrich, Lutz 1958: Die deutsche Volkssage. *Studium Generale* 11, 664–691.

– 1969: Das Kontinuitätsproblem bei der Erforschung der Volksprosa. See Bausinger & Brückner 1969, 117–133.

– 1974: *Märchen und Wirklichkeit*. 4th edition. Wiesbaden: Franz Steiner.

– 1976a: Argumente für und gegen das Märchen. See Röhrich 1976c.

– 1976b: Autobiographie. *Enzyklopädie des Märchens* 1. Berlin: Walter de Gruyter, 1080–1085.

– 1976c: *Sage und Märchen. Erzählsforschung heute.* Freiburg: Herder.

– 1977: *Der Witz. Seine Formen und Funktionen.* München: Deutsche Taschenbuch Verlag.

– 1979: Der Froschkönig und seine Wandlungen. *Fabula* 20, 170–192.

– 1983: Metamorphosen des Märchens heute. See Doderer 1983, 97–115.

Röhrich, Lutz & Sabine Wienker-Piepho 1990: *Storytelling in Contemporary Societies.* Tübingen: Gunter Narr.

Rölleke, Heinz 1984: John M. Ellis: One Fairy Story Too Many. *Fabula* 25, 330–332.

– 1985: *Die Märchen der Brüder Grimm.* München: Artemis.

Rooth, Anna Birgitta 1951: *The Cinderella Cycle.* Lund: Gleerup.

– 1976: *The Importance of Storytelling. A Study Based on Field Work in Northern Alaska.* Uppsala: Almquist & Wiksell International.

Rumpf, Marianne 1955: *Ursprung und Entstehung von Warn- und Schreckmärchen.* FF Communications 160. Helsinki: Academia Scientiarum Fennica.

Satke, Antonin 1958: *Hlučinsky pohádkár Josef Smolka.* Ostrava: Krajske nakl.

Schenda, Rudolf 1970: Einheitlich – Urtümlich – noch heute. Probleme der volkstümlichen Befragung. Klaus Geiger, Utz Jeggle & Gottfried Korff (eds.), *Abschied vom Volksleben.* Tübingen: Tübinger Vereinigung für Volkskunde, 124–154.

– 1981a: Autobiographen erzählen Geschichten. *Zeitschrift für Volkskunde* 77, 67–87.

– 1981b: Folkloristik und Sozialgeschichte. Rolf Kleopfer & Gisela Janetzke-Dillner (eds.), *Erzählung und Erzählforschung im 20. Jahrhundert.* Stuttgart: Kohlhammer, 489–530.

– 1983: Märchen erzählen – Märchen verbreiten: Wandel in den Mitteilungsformen einer populären Gattung. See Doderer 1983, 25–43.

– 1992: Folklore und Massenkultur. Reimund Kvideland (ed.), *Tradition and Modernisation. Plenary Papers Read at the 4th International Congress of the Societé Internationale d'Ethnologie et de Folklore.* Turku: Nordic Institute of Folklore, 2–40.

Schenda, Rudolf & Ruth Böckli (eds.) 1982: *Lebenszeiten. Autobiographien der Pro Senectute-Aktion.* Zürich: Unionsverlag.

Schier, Kurt 1955: Praktische Untersuchungen zur mündlichen Weitergabe von Volkererzählungen. Ph.D. dissertation. München.

Schmitz, Karoline 1930: Über das anschauliche Denken und die Frage einer Korrelation zwischen eidetischer Anlage und Intelligenz. *Zeitschrift für Psychologie.*

Schütz, Alfred & Thomas Luckmann 1984: *Struktur der Lebenswelt.* Vols. 1–2. Frankfurt: Suhrkamp.

Schwartzmann, Helen B. 1978: *Transformations. The Anthropology of Children's Play.* New York: Plenum Press.

Schwietering, Julius 1935: Volksmärchen und Volksglaube, Dichtung und Volkstum. Neue Folge des Euphorion. *Zeitschrift für Literaturgeschichte* 35, 73–78.

Sebeok, Thomas A. 1957: Towards a Statistical Contingency Method in Folklore Research. See Richmond 1957, 130–140.

Sebestyén, Ádám 1979–1986: *Bukovinai Székely népmesék* [Székely folktales from the Bukovina]. Vols. 1–4. (Annotated by Ágnes Kovács.) Szekszárd: Tolnamegyei Tanács V. B. Könyvtára.

See, Carolyn 1979: The Beast, the Mermaid, the Happy Ending. Paper presented at the 1979 Modern Language Association, San Francisco, California, December 29.

Segal, Dmitri 1976: Folklore Text and Social Context. Review of Dan Ben-Amos and Kenneth S. Goldstein (eds.), Folklore: Performance and Communication. *PTL: A Journal for Descriptive Poetics and Theory of Literature* 1, 367–382.

Shannon, David A. 1960: *The Great Depression*. Englewood Cliffs, NJ: Prentice-Hall.

Sharp, Cecil J. 1907: *English Folk-Song: Some Conclusions*. London: Wessex Press.

Shibutani, Tamotsu 1966: *Improvised News. A Sociological Study of Rumor*. Indianapolis: Bobbs-Merrill Co.

Siegel, Barry 1992: The Devil & Rupert, Idaho. *Los Angeles Times Magazine*, May 12.

Siikala, Anna-Leena 1990: *Interpreting Oral Narrative*. FF Communications 245. Helsinki: Academia Scientiarum Fennica.

Sirovátka, Oldrich 1969: Zur Morphologie der Sage. Leander Petzoldt (ed.), *Vergleichende Sagenforschung*. Darmstadt: Wissenschaftliche Buchgesellschaft, 330–331.

– 1975: Die Alltagserzählung als Gattung de heutigen Volksüberlieferung. W. van Nespen (ed.), *Miscellanea. Festschrift für Prof. em. K. C. Peeters*. Antwerp: Drukkerijen C. Govaerts, 662–669.

Smart, James 1970: We Pop the Elephant Myth. *Small World*, Fall edition [magazine for Volkswagen owners in the United States].

Smith, Henry Nash 1970: *Virgin Land: The American West as Symbol and Myth*. Cambridge: Harvard University Press.

Smith, Moira 1982: Cars on Rooftops and Tipping over Outhouses. Symbolic Inversion in Halloween and Legend. Unpublished Manuscript, December 18..

Snow, Loudell F. 1979: Mail Order Magic: The Commercial Exploitation of Folk Belief. *Journal of Folklore Institute* 16, 44–74.

Sokolov, Iuri 1938/1966: *Russian Folklore*. (Translated by Catherine Ruth Smith.) Hatboro, PA: Folklore Associates.

Stahl, Sandra Dolby. See Dolby, Sandra.

Stein, Helga 1979: Einige Bemerkungen über die Märchengarten. Paper presented at the Congress of the International Society for Folk Narrative Research, Edinburgh, Scotland.

Sterba, Richard 1948: On Hallowe'en. *American Imago* 5, 217.

Stern, William 1903–1906: *Beiträge zur Psychologie der Aussage*. Leipzig.

Stewart, George R. 1956: *Names on the Land*. Boston: Houghton-Miffin.

Stone, Kay 1975a: Things Walt Disney Never Told Us. *Journal of American Folklore* 88, 42–50.

– 1975b: Romantic Heroines in Anglo-American Folk and Popular Literature. Ph.D. dissertation. Indiana University, Bloomington.

– 1978: Fairy Tales for Adults. Unpublished manuscript.

– 1983: Misbrauchte Verzauberung: Aschenputtel als Weiblichkeitsideal in Nordamerika. See Doderer 1983, 78–96.

Sutton-Smith, Brian 1972: *The Folkgames of Children*. Austin: American Folklore Society.

Swahn, Jan Öjvind 1955: *The Tale of Cupid and Psyche (AT 425–428)*. Lund: C. W. K. Gleerup.

Sydow, Carl Wilhelm von 1934: Kategorien der Prosa-Volksdichtung. *Volkskundliche Gaben John Meier zum siebzigsten Geburtstag dargebracht*. Berlin & Leipzig: Walter de Gruyter, 253–268.

– 1948: *Selected Papers on Folklore*. Copenhagen: Rosenkilde & Bagge.

Swenson, Greta E. 1989: *Festival of Sharing. Family Reunions in America*. New York: AMS Press.

Swift, Jonathan 1977: *Gulliver's Travels*. New York: Oxford University Press.

Szondi, Lipót 1947: *Experimentelle Triebdiagnostik*. Bern: Verlag Hans Huber.

Szondi, Lipót, Ulrich Moser & Marvin W. Webb 1959: *The Szondi Test: In Diagnosis, Prognosis and Treatment*. Philadelphia: J. B. Limmincott Co.

Tegethoff, Ernst 1922: *Studien zum Märchentypus von Amor und Psyche*. Bonn & Leipzig: K. Schroeder.

Thigpen, Kenneth A. 1971: *Adolescent Legends in Brown County*. Indiana Folklore 4, 141–215.

Thompson, Stith 1946: *The Folktale*. New York: Knopf.

–   1953: *Four Symposia on Folklore. Papers given at the Mid-Century International Folklore Conference*. Bloomington: Indiana University Press.

–   1955: Myths and Folktales. *Journal of American Folklore* 68, 482–488.

–   1960: Fifty Years of Folktale Indexing. Wayland D. Hand (ed.), *Humaniora Essays in Literature, Folklore, Bibliography Honoring Archer Taylor on His Seventieth Birthday*. New York: Augustin, 49–57.

Thorne, Tanis 1976: Legends of the Surfer Subculture. *Western Folklore* 35, 209–217.

Tillhagen, Carl-Herman 1948: *Taikon erzählt*. Zürich.

–   1964: Was ist eine Sage? Eine Definition und ein Vorschlag für ein europäisches Sagensystem. *Acta Ethnographica* 13, 9–17.

Time Magazine 1972: Ghost at the point. December 4, 6.

Time Magazine 1988, May 5.

Tolksdorf, Ulrich 1980: *Eine ostpreussische Volkserzählerin: Geschichten – Geschichte – Lebensgeschichte*. Marburg: Elwert Verlag.

Truzzi, Marzello (ed.) 1968: *Sociology and Everyday Life*. Englewood Cliffs, NJ: Prentice-Hall.

Tucker, Elizabeth 1977: Tradition and Creativity in the Storytelling of Pre-Adolescent Girls. Ph.D. dissertation. Indiana University, Bloomington.

Turner, Victor W. 1969: *The Ritual Process: Structure and Anti-Structure*. Chicago: Aldine.

–   1976: *The Forest of Symbols. Aspects of Ndemba Ritual*. Ithaca: Cornell University Press.

Uffer, Leza 1945: *Rätoromanische Märchen und ihre Erzähler*. Schriften der Schweizerischen Gesellschaft für Volkskunde. Band 29. Basel: Schweizerische Gesellschaft für Volkskunde.

Vikár, Béla 1892: Somogyi tanulmányutamról [My fieldtrip in Somogy county]. *Ethnographia* 2, 120.

Virtanen, Leea 1976: Paranormale Spontanerlebnisse in der modernen Erzähltradition. See Pentikäinen & Juurikka 1976, 338–347.

–   1990: *"That Must Have Been ESP!"* (Translated by John Atkinson and Thomas DuBois.) Bloomington: Indiana University Press.

Viski, Károly (ed.) n.d.: *A Magyarság néprajza* [Hungarian ethnography]. Vol. 3, Szellemi néprajz: Népköltészet, stilus és nyelv [Spiritual folklore: folk poetry, style, and language]. Budapest: Egyetemi nyomda.

Vlach, John M. 1971: One black eye and other horrors. A case for the humourous anti-legend. *Indiana Folklore* 4, 95–125.

Voigt, Vilmos 1972: *A folklór alkotások elemzése* [Analysis of folklore products]. Budapest: Akadémia.

–   (ed.) 1974: *A szájhagyományozás törvényszerűségei. Nemzetközi szimpozion Budapesten* [Laws of oral tradition. International symposium in Budapest]. Budapest: Akadémiai Kiadó.

–   1976: Towards a Theory of Theory of Genres in Folklore. See Dégh, Glassie & Oinas 1976, 485–496.

–   1986: A néprajztudomány mai kérdései [Current questions of the science of folklore]. *Kritika*, July.

Vries, Jan de 1954: *Betrachtungen zum Märchen besonders in seinem Verhältnis zu Heldensage und Mythos*. FF Communications 150. Helsinki: Academia Scientiarum Fennica.

Wachs, Eleanor 1988: *Crime-Victim Stories within New York City's Urban Folklore*. Bloomington: Indiana University Press.

Wallis, Mieczyslaw 1975: *Arts and Signs*. Indiana University Publications. Bloomington: Indiana University Press.

Ward, Donald 1976: American and European Narratives as Socio-Psychological Indicators. See Pentikäinen & Juurikka 1976, 348–353.

Warner, W. Lloyd 1963: *Yankee City*. One vol. abridged ed. New Haven: Yale University Press.

Weber-Kellermann, Ingeborg 1955: Berliner Sagenbildung 1952. *Zeitschrift für Volkskunde* 52, 482–488.

Wehse, Rainer (ed.) 1983: *Märchenerzähler – Erzählgemeinschaft*. Kassel: Röth.

Weinstein, Deena & Michael A. Weinstein 1974: *Living Sociology*. New York: David McKay Inc.

Weiss, Richard 1946: *Volkskunde der Schweiz*. Erlenbach & Zürich: Eugen Rentsch.

Wesselski, Albert 1931: *Versuch einer Theorie des Märchens*. Reichenberg: Sudetendeutscher Verlag Franz Kraus.

–   1934: Die Formen des Volkskundlichen Erzählguts. Adolf Spamer (ed.), *Die deutsche Volkskunde*. Vol. 1. Leipzig: Bibliographisches Institut, 216–248.

Wheeler, Ladd 1966: Toward a Theory of Behavioral Contagion. *Psychological Review* 73, 172–192.

Willems, Emilio 1955: On the Concept of Assimilation. *American Anthropologist* 57, 225–226.

Wisser, Wilhelm 1926: *Auf der Märchensuche: Die Entstehung meiner Märchensammlung*. Hamburg: Hanseatische Verlagsanstalt.

Wolf, Eric R. 1964: *Anthropology*. Englewood Cliffs, NJ: Prentice-Hall.

–   1966: *Peasants*. Englewood Cliffs, NJ: Prentice-Hall.

Wolff, Werner 1943: *The Expression of Personality: Experimental Depth Psychology*. New York: Harper & Row.

Wood, Robert C. 1958: *Suburbia. Its People and Their Politics*. Boston: Houghton Miffin.

Wrigglesworth, Hazel 1975: Folk Rhetoric in the Narration of Ilianan Monobo Folktales. Ph.D. dissertation. Indiana University, Bloomington.

Zender, Matthias 1937: Quellen und Träger der deutschen Volkserzählung. *Rheinische Vierteljahrsblätter* 7, 25–46.

Zipes, Jack 1979–1980: Who's Afraid of the Brothers Grimm? Socialization and Politicization Through Fairy Tales. *The Lion and the Unicorn* 3:2, 4–56.

–   1982: *Rotkäppchens Lust und Leid: Biographie eines Europäischen Märchens. Beschrieben und dokumentiert*. Köln: Diederichs Verlag.

–   1983: Klassische Märchen im Zivilizationsprozess: Die Schattenseite von 'La Belle et la Béte.' See Doderer 1983, 57–77.

Zyl, John van 1979: Towards a Socio-Semiotic of Performance. *Semiotic Scene* 3, 103.